Asa: "Life _above_ a dream." But the dream is only skin deep – we dip below the surface to enter into dream, then surface again on the surface of things. Wide awake. But under the surface of the earth, wild processes are at work, hot, melting centers that push up in overwhelming displays of inert materiality. I deny this materiality; I know who my mother is. "Nothing can do us more harm than a materialism." "Than a materialization." Tools grouped in groups of two outside the cabin door, must have materialized here overnight. Perhaps they are the deer's slippers. "But this isn't an avant-garde campground – everything in it is natural." So life goes its own natural way, and all its complex processes, are reflected in that order, from the summit to the head waters of the stream, down flue + crevasses to the broader opening out of the sea – from whence we glimpse the summit. We aspire and yearn toward it, we clamber over ourselves backwards to achieve it – and we do! Then we come down quickly, violently, angrily, with large footsteps, stamping + pushing our way past the others with their faces turned upward toward their goals – we can only pity them. Meanwhile the view from the top was worth a few lines, especially from the equipment still in place that indicated others had been there

Aerial 8
Barrett Watten

edited by
Rod Smith

Edge Books
1995

To build many out of a glance
        Into the cross-section of
        A republic,
                        into the center
But it is an other that looks . . . .

Narrowing itself to two only.
        This is a self-made light
        That I address,
                        to shine
Back into the literary eye . . . .

                —Barrett Watten, *Progress*

JOHN CAGE
(1912–1992)

GUY DEBORD
(1931–1994)

ISBN: 0–9619097–4–9

ISSN: 0894–2633

Aerial is published irregularly.
Two issue subscription: $20
Institutions: $35

Aerial 9 will be a special issue on the work of Bruce Andrews.

Unsolicited manuscripts should be accompanied by self-addressed
stamped envelope. Address all orders, submissions, correspondence to:

AERIAL, P.O. Box 25642, Washington, DC 20007.

Distributors:
> Desert Moon Periodicals, 1031 Agua Fria, Santa Fe, NM 87501.
> Inland Book Co., P.O. Box 120261, East Haven, CT 06512.
> Small Press Distribution, 1814 San Pablo Ave., Berkeley, CA 94702.
> Ubiquity, 607 Degraw St., Brooklyn, NY 11217

Included in *The Index of American Periodical Verse.*
Aerial is published by Edge Books, Washington, DC.

Aerial is made possible in part by Bridge Street Books,
2814 Pennsylvania Ave., NW, Washington, DC 20007. Ph 202–965–5200.

CONTENTS

III. REINVENTING COMMUNITY

IV. BARRETT WATTEN: AN INVENTION

V. "Skewed by design . . ."

including poetry by Clark Coolidge (278), Larry Eigner (280), Robert Grenier (282), Michael Palmer (284), Bruce Andrews (286), Ron Silliman (288), Bernadette Mayer (290), Barrett Watten (292), Charles Bernstein (294), Carla Harryman (296), Bob Perelman (293), and Lyn Hejinian (300).

Visual materials by Barrett Watten: Journal pages, Kauai, 1985 (frontispiece and p. 71). Working drafts of "Conduit," 1984 (pp. 1 and 239). Numerical scheme for *Under Erasure*, 1989 (p. 121). Journal page, Mt. Lassen, 1985 (p. 201).

Cover design by Amy Trachtenberg

INTRODUCTION

Rod Smith

"And the words are everywhere a democratic police . . . "

The dissident intelligence of Barrett Watten draws on a variety of modes of thinking—sometimes poetic, always critical. His texts are, in Allen Fisher's words, "conceptually emphatic." When Watten says, for example, "My imagination locked in place during the Vietnam War," he is not being metaphorical.

The beginnings of what has come to be known as "language poetry" took place during the latter stages of the American invasion of Indochina. Many of the writers later identified with that poetics were involved in popular movements against the war. Watten began writing while at the University of California, Berkeley, in 1968 during some of the most effective and heavily repressed opposition to the war.

In addition to the war in Indochina, a number of other factors influenced the early versions of "language-centered poetics," all of which call for longer discussion than will take place here. There was the women's movement, minimalist and conceptual art, an accelerating emphasis on various forms of theory in the universities, and the writings of a number of "precursors" such as Clark Coolidge, Robert Creeley, Jackson Mac Low, and Bernadette Mayer, all of which informed what Tina Darragh has called "the story of turning to language." These developments took place in a social milieu in which many felt that "the revolution had failed," although at the same time some real social gains were being made, notably by the women's and environmental movements.

In what, in this context, is better termed the *stories* of turning to language, an accent upon the materiality of language combined with a skeptical (not always) search for tools of engagement which took, roughly, a more literary and Western Marxist turn among writers on the West Coast, as opposed to a more post-structualist and "anti-art" bent in Canada and on the East Coast. Shared, however, was not so much an outright rejection of the New American Poetics of presence—speech based, expansive, tradition embracing —as a tempered reexamination of its tenets in light of changing social contexts. The beginnings of this reexamination can be dated to the publication of the first issue of *This* in 1971, edited by Watten with Robert Grenier, which moved from the position of Grenier's dictim "I hate speech" to a focus on the textual poetics of writing in the late 1970s and early 1980s.

These writers made a very conscious choice to engage what Pierre Bourdieu has called "the intellectual field." In describing his experience of this process Watten has used the metaphor of "driving a car between roads." For Watten this type of driving involved a consistent negotiation of textual terrains carrying claims of "objective truth." In his work the vocabulary, phraseology, rhetoric, and even *logic*, of the political, philosophical, economic, and scientific realms are deeply problematized by their use in the literary form, poetry, which is considered best suited to *self* expression.[1] "Driving" in this way not only implies high repair bills but also, perhaps, the discovery of alternate routes, new ways of thinking about, or *within*, such dichotomies as "personal/political" or "subjective/objective." It is this resolute thinking within dichotomies in an attempt to transform them that I identify as "conceptually emphatic."

Another conceptually emphatic artist, John Cage, created an art in which "the making of choices was not principle to the work but rather the asking of questions."[2] The issue of non-intentionality was primary for Cage. For Watten, intentionality is paramount. "The level of automatism we have to deal with . . . is functionally exact." In other words, alienation is a, if not *the*, defining experience of contemporary America.[3] In political and social terms, the huge gulf between what a sane person would intend and what happens "is functionally exact."

The exploration of non-intention led Cage to the necessity of "letting sounds be sounds," to the realization that "all things are the buddha," and to an anti-politics insisting on the primacy of the individual. Watten's investigation of intention in language, on the other hand, leads to an understanding of our own lack of power over decisions within our individual lives and to the necessity of understanding the psychology which perpetuates that.[4] He has called this "a process of socialization which involves a certain amount of terror." Watten describes as well as tries to undermine this social psychology.

> *A trickle-down theory of cognition*
> *By excess,*
> > *they are shooting outside . . .*
>
> *A temporary amnesia,*
> > *its report filed*
> *As if you had never been a witness . . .*

> (Under Erasure, p. 39)

Edward Said has recently argued that the role of the intellectual is "to speak the truth to power."[5] Watten insists, like Said, on beginning with social and political realities. Our dilemmas of interpretation participate in a psychology that reproduces historical trauma. Watten's is a consecutive or constructivist investigation of intentionality which implies an acceptance of indeterminacy as a fact of daily life, and an understanding of ideology as contingent—ideology as built by self-interests identified with and perpetuated by nationalistic, capitalist, and pedagogic institutions.

As we mature we internalize the value systems of the structures we inhabit in an attempt to negotiate them. A painfully self-conscious re-cognition and de-mapping of these habits is called for, and is attempted at every step in Watten's work at least since the book-length poem *Progress*. This is demonstrated in the reflexivity of his humor: "The small dog 'translates' the rug." This reflexivity is also evident in the use of a sequential counterpoint of contradictory but direct statements.

> All is negotiated in language (as in law).
>
> The rationalization of any system is the
> strain it puts them through.
>
> A conversation about information theory in
> which there are too many messages to send.
>
> Every hierarchy has its excuses.
>
> (*Conduit*, p. 28)

Watten builds works out of words which ask, in Peter Brooks terms, "not only *what* a text means but also *how* it means," and then demonstrates that these, the how & the what, are false dichotomies.[6] The manner in which this is done can be seen to give the term "experimental writing" a degree of meaning it does not usually possess. Watten, in texts such as *Progress* and *Under Erasure* sets in motion conversations, arguments, dialogic contexts, which are open-ended, which take Charles Olson's "limits are what we are inside of" and ask, continually, what those limits are.

The fourth section of Ron Silliman's "The Task of the Collaborator: Watten's Leningrad," published herein, elaborates the way in which "Watten uses the discourse of critique to create poetry," and in so doing gives us "a demonstration of devices that simultaneously uses, satirizes, and unmasks the mode's discursive 'omnipotence.' " This unmasking relates to Giorgio Agamben's critique of the rational/affective bipolarity which Aby Warburg "diagnosed as the 'schizophrenia' of Western culture":

> In our culture, knowledge . . . is divided between inspired-ecstatic and rational-conscious poles, neither ever succeeding in wholly reducing the other. Insofar as philosophy and poetry have passively accepted this division, philosophy has failed to elaborate a proper language, as if there could be a royal road to truth that would avoid the problem of its representation, and poetry has developed neither a method nor self-consciousness. What is thus overlooked is the fact that every authentic poetic project is directed toward knowledge, just as every act of philosophy is directed toward joy.[7]

Agamben may be wrong in asserting that this problem has been overlooked. William Carlos Williams's "no ideas but in things" has been transformed by

Watten into "the idea *is* the thing." The conceptually emphatic artist, which I identify with Cage and Watten, but might also include such artists as Gertrude Stein, Guy Debord, Marcel Duchamp, and Velimir Khlebnikov, seeks to *enact* "the limits we are" rather than, or *as well as*, represent them.

While this introduction purports to represent Watten's work, there are ways in which this book also tries to enact it. Rather than simply collect a set of readings, I have attempted to present a variety of approaches, within its five sections, as well as a variety of modalities—discursive, poetic, fictive, dialogic—within each section.

Section one, "Bad History/Under Erasure" serves as an introduction to Watten's work through focus on recent writings. The interview and the essay by Norman Fischer provide discussions of his work as a whole.

Section two, "Once Upon a Time" is about time and place, or more specifically—time as an element of vocabulary. It is impressionistic, raising issues of historical context, narrativity, and artistic influence.

Section three, "Reinventing Community," includes discussions of the intensely collaborative context Watten has inhabited. The fabric of community, providing friction as well as support, and the negotiation of that definition within the larger social flux.

Section four, "Barrett Watten: An Invention," is an enactment of the title Jerry Estrin provided me. The interaction of subjectivities leads us to invent, or what is the same thing, take what we can use and leave the rest. The author as his/her own invention to some extent, but also, as invention of each audience.

Section five, "Skewed by Design," provides a range of responses to Watten's *Progress*. Included are readings which could variously be characterized as Jakobsonian, chance-operative, Derridean, Sartrean, with elements of New Criticism and Speech Act Theory, among other things.

There are too many people that have lent their interest and support to this project to name them all here. However I would like to thank Mike Magoolaghan and Peter Baker for help with proofing and transcription at various points along the way. Also to mention Dan Barbiero, Lee Ann Brown, Jean Donnelly, Steve Evans, Peter Gizzi, Jessica Grim, Gretchen Johnsen, Andrew Levy, Carmen Lupton, A. L. Neilson, Joan Retallack, Ron Silliman, Alan Stearns, Mark Wallace, and Elizabeth Willis, among others, for their conversation and motivation. I would also like to thank Amy Trachtenberg for her design of the cover illustrations. And finally, the typesetter, Candace Conway, for her patience, diligence, and patience.

In closing I would like to empasize again the experimental nature of Watten's work. To this I add a somewhat speculative observation—There is a medical definition for *intention* which reads, in part, "a manner or process of healing."

NOTES

1. Poetry is perhaps the most purely subjective art form. Our experience of words as both inside and outside of ourselves lends a kind of intimacy to language that distinguishes it from visual or musical modes. Poetry is also, potentially, depending on how one writes &/or recites it, the least codified mode of language usage. I qualify these statements because I think it is unclear whether this subjectivity is somehow inherent in poetic language or whether it is a social construct; it may be how we've learned to think poetry.

2. In a passage Cage might have enjoyed, Watten states, "We question a question in order to fill in its form. Its meaning is the questioning act. If 'existence' is calling itself into question, we can easily supply the answer because in that case we know; the question has become ourselves." *Conduit*, p. 12

3. Those that would question this primacy I direct to the writings of theorists and activists such as Michael Albert, Noam Chomsky, Ward Churchill, Bell Hooks, Holly Sklar, and Cornell West. There are many others. Chomsky cites an exact correlation between American aid and Human Rights Abuse; the more aid we give, the greater the abuses found in any particular country. The conciousness of this varies greatly due to corporate-governmental control of the major media; however there are large sectors of the population involved in activism of various kinds—Civil Rights, Environmental, Feminist, Anti-Nuclear, housing for the homeless, American Indian, Central American, Tibetan, and many other areas. Notice that media acknowledgement of many of these popular struggles is almost non-existent.

   Derek Owens, *Resisting Writings (and the Boundaries of Composition)* (S. M. U. Presss, 1994): "One of the most effective ways of assessing any discipline is to pinpoint what it doesn't let its members do; discover the taboos of any community and you have found its foundations."

4. An example of this psychology is the unquestioning acceptance of wage slavery as a fact of life. We accept that we should rent ourselves to businesses or institutions for large portions of our life to earn the "right" to survive.

5. Edward W. Said, *Representations of the Intellectual*, Pantheon Books, 1994.

6. Peter Brooks, "Aesthetics and Ideology: What Happened to Poetics?" in *Critical Inquiry*, Spring 1994, Vol. 20, No. 3. Brooks discusses the importance of a structuralist poetics stemming from such figures as Culler, Frye, Jakobson, Saussure, and Levi-Strauss, which has fallen from favor in recent academic discourse. " . . . The critic needs a certain humility, a certain awareness that one does not speak ex cathedra but from a very uncomfortable and unstable and indeed slippery ground." That "one cannnot claim to speak for the text until one has attempted to let the text speak through oneself." This is achieved through "the self-imposition of the formalist askesis because this alone can assure the critic that the act of interpretation has been submitted to an otherness, that is is not simply an assimilation of the object of study." These principles seem to me very much in accord with Watten's practice; however, Brooks seems to be calling for a kind of authority that Watten doesn't, that Watten in fact usefully problematizes.

To raise the issue of the often dense terminology of Watten's writing, and of much contemporary critical practice, I'll cite Brooks further: "The need to submit the individual critical talent to the discipline of form, to respect for the aesthetic and for poetics as the basis of its study, ought to be accompanied by acknowledgement of the discipline of a common language. In my view, this should be a more public language than that most often spoken by the academy." Density of terminology seems to me justifiable when one is attempting a specificity of allusion to previous writers &/or for reasons of discriminative accuracy. The same reasons a scientist might give. Brooks admits an awareness of "how little the organs and media of public debate think they need or want informed academic discourse . . . ." I would add to that point that on most issues of consequence they rarely want informed discourse at all, academic or otherwise, and reference again the list of names in the third footnote.

7. Giorgio Agamben, *Stanzas: Word and Phantasm in Western Culture,* University of Minnesota Press, 1993.

every static unfolding ~~stream~~ / ~~it has permanently arrived~~
~~as an arrivist~~e / ~~en~~jambed and/or end-~~stopped~~ / ~~and supposed~~
to porten~~d an arrival~~ / ~~behind which~~ is ~~an invisible body~~ /
~~exhibiting~~ tears / perception ~~after enclosure~~ / ~~stopped~~ / ~~the~~
model faces ~~away from~~ / ~~in order to deceptively present~~ / ~~was~~
~~objects "in the world"~~ / ~~to survive coincident with~~ / ~~defeats~~
~~the passion is equal at all points~~ / ~~which is the same thing~~
in other words / the mirror of an abandoned ~~text~~ / ~~but only in~~
~~totality~~ / ~~these cycles of pictures on the same theme~~ / ~~i.e.~~
~~it is a text~~ / ~~"the art of living is written"~~ / ~~I, like a cunic~~
~~stilit~~ / ~~and now all the pawns fail~~ / to hold in check ~~the~~
~~workings of passion~~ / ~~she is a decision to shout it~~ / ~~but can~~
constructed ~~imaged parentheses~~ / ~~not ending in closure~~ / ~~about~~
~~precisely~~ the "female form" / missing parts / ~~to answer the~~
~~question would answer it~~ / ~~then break for quotation~~ /

section one.

Bad History / Under Erasure

~~his descriptions are a subtraction~~ / ~~this is the case I would~~
~~eradicate~~ / "the form of a man's fault is clear" / ~~not otherwise~~
~~related to it~~ / ~~a movement from the archive~~ / ~~to the center~~
~~inside nothing"~~ / ~~blinding white light~~ ~~from distant place banks~~
~~so hideous slow~~ / ~~blinding neon light from distant show~~ /
~~various uncontrolled phrases~~ / ~~particular clocks stretched out~~
~~then and there objects~~ / ~~possible ... slices into one of the~~
~~same~~ / ~~the ruined rupture (our job)~~ / disappears invariably down
~~the long, obsolete valley~~ / ~~beginning to meet concrete~~ / ~~true~~
~~narrative events~~ / ~~past tense~~ / "but one parses its architec-
~~ture"~~ / ~~but there are multiple copies~~ ~~which are uncertain~~
~~but~~ / ~~for neither was ever befriended~~ / ~~empty shelves of room~~
~~names~~ / ~~of lines or walls or doorbell~~ / "shorter" or "longer"
~~the world ... is sad~~ / ~~from universal ... to inhabited~~
~~error ... this loss is to experience errors~~ / ~~in all their fragility~~

Barrett Watten

*The evident irritation expressed with a concept of event
which does not measure up to its canons of evidence,
the shock expressed at a practice whose interpretations
refer to events which 'historically' may not have happened. . . . Imagine a practice of interpretation which
prefers secondary sources, and unreliable witnesses!*
—Mark Cousins,
"The Practice of Historical Investigation"

I

A bad event happened to me, but its having occurred became more complicated even in my
thinking of it. Even if this event had happened
only to me, it was only recently available for
retrospection; it had to be proved as taking
place in every other event. Take the War for example; I no longer know for certain which war
is meant. When people say, "After the war," I no
longer know which war—there are three wars
at least, each antedating, following, and confirming the others. It is always "the era between
two wars." So there was a very long war before a
period of time in which that war had just been
over for a very long time—even though it took
its place as immediately preceding that time.
Then a very short war called that very long
time into question because suddenly time became something that had happened to me—
only happening so directly that I could say,
"This war is different from that other war,
or even from the long duration that followed
it." All those times even now seem very much
of a piece—as having taken place in order to
guarantee each other, as part of an assertion
of the reality of the first and only war. That
war in which we certainly could not believe,

because we meant not to believe in it. And consequently, for a long time, our having decided not to believe in that war returned to us willingly to confirm our disbelief. A bad event had happened to me, but I could not talk about it until recently. And when I did talk about it, there was a return to the sense that, in recognizing what I had chosen not to believe in as really having happened, I was responsible for disbelieving it all along. That war, which was very long, never seemed to be on the verge of ending. It was always on the verge of not ending, of giving more justification for there being no reason it should not continue indefinitely. And we had to agree with its assumptions, because they held in place our disbelief (which we willed). So we willed ourselves into a kind of suspension, until in a decisive moment an event occurred which was the collapse of that untenable state of always believing in the necessity of our disbelief. Because the war was an event of very long duration, a short event like the end of the war could only reinforce the effects of our having willed to cancel it out. Do you see what kind of effect this always willing a disbelief in what we did not want to continue had on us, when time pulled the rug from under our feet and the very long war started to end? So a separation and a caesura became the truth of any event—having happened in that state of suspension between our willing disbelief and need to know that it had happened (so we could continue our disbelief). Take the war, for instance—immediately it is unclear of which war I speak. I must mean the war that ended yesterday at 4 o'clock that Robert Creeley wrote about, and the subsequent tigers that sprang at him from imaginary jungles. In any case the war ended and it was a relief—I always doubted the extent to which Creeley could just by writing think he could keep it going, even for the space of a lyric poem. Perhaps he really meant that other war, the one we won and that sent him around the world in a pacifying mission, a victory so reassuring in its skepticisms that the whole world was unleashed to reimagine its self-identifications.

4

Think of Kwame Nkruma in Ghana. He could only have come to power after such a war. Think of Patrice Lumumba in Zaire—a case where all of that unleashed skepticism failed to provide any stable identity and history just began to drift as some overloaded barge down the interminable river. Creeley wasn't talking about Nkruma and Lumumba; he was talking about some reassuring but freakish monstrosity that would rivet us in our seats, as in a Stephen King movie. But isn't it enough to have been responsible for one's own disbelief not to have to go out and bring in some sentimental figures to stand in for one's loss of control? We could make a game out of this. Something bad happened to me and I started thinking about it intensely in the period between two wars. Which one ended which? The former certainly was the condition of possibility of the latter, so that we knew that we would, in the end, go through with it. Each new war being the culmination of our old beliefs and the supersession of a new technology, so that time must pass before the technical conditions for a war can be reinvented. Only later did we find out that the success rate for Patriot missiles was only 6 percent. How had we so thoroughly been taught to disbelieve the evidence of our senses? Didn't I see an incoming missile come down through the sky from the vantage point of a TV crew in Dharan, Saudi Arabia? Most of the crew huddled in the basement while one cameraman tracked the outgoing Patriot to an explosion that was visible proof of its success? Segue to cheering workers at the missile plant in Massachusetts? To be reassured by lines of Patriots identified as "ours" brought in for the defense of Israel? Consider the etymology of the words *Patriot* and *Scud*—*Scud* not an acronym for anything (like *SAM* is an acronym for "Surface-to-Air Missile") but a kind of media-invented synthetic image that combines its self-evident scudding over the surface of the waves toward a heat-blistered target with a racial characterizing of the kind of agent person it is—scum of the cracked earth spitting up to erupt over and come back to thud. To the same

5

ground where we were sitting still and waiting for it? Creeley didn't want to think about that ground, so pleased was he with the spectacle of his disbelief that called into question any criterion for an historical event. Imagine the shock we would express when encountering the report of an event that never happened, by an unreliable witness! Let's put an end to that and call it "the Vietnam Syndrome" as helicopters circle in around the Capitol Dome. A bad event happened to me and now I can understand that it occured only there and then. But it was the continuous, circling treadmill of its displacement for a very long time brought to a single image—obscured, interfered with, reprocessed at a third remove over the remote-control channels of communicative links—that got me here to say this.

III

Iraqi: various scenarios for wearers of a mark of distinction and/or shame. "My husband was a driver on the Iraq-Amman highway, transporting food. On the way back, there was an air raid at the al-Rutbah area, the 106 kilometer mark from Baghdad to Amman. The air raid took place, and he was killed. He was driving with another man sitting beside him. My husband jumped out of the cab after the bombing and ran about 25 meters from the truck. The planes came back and strafed him; he was hit with machine gun fire." Thus the consequences of appearing to be Iraqi at a particular moment in time. "I was walking down Telegraph Avenue in Berkeley after an embarrassing lunch with Jerome McGann, during which I had been very conscious of the Iraqi pin on my shirt. Guys would loom out of the crowd saying, 'Hey, an Iraqi!' This was some time about the beginning of February. But I always remembered to take my pin off for official meetings at my work."

There is no unconditional love, at least between adults. Carla and I were traveling in England in 1984; she was six months pregnant and we felt confident the pregnancy would not end in miscarriage this time. We had been enmeshed in a lawsuit which was soon to terminate. In England, we made a practice of mapping out driving tours and using day hikes as center-pieces for our travels. In Wales, we thought to take a short walk near the town of Llangollen, where the famous Eistedvod (choral festival) was in progress. Walking out of town, the land-scape rapidly became more exposed, very cold and windy even in June. By the time we reached the top of the hill, where there were bare ruins of a castle, I felt worried there would be some misfortune that would threaten Carla and the baby. We had to find shelter from the wind; it all felt desperate and heroic. We met another couple who helped us figure out the shortest way down. I took off my coat and gave it to Carla; the wind was now howling and I was very cold. On the way down we met a man about 80 years old who was traveling from his village to the choral festival. He was having a poetic revery sitting on a bench above the town and was re-membering fighting in Burma in World War II —an experience that clearly had changed him for life. His life was nearly over, but ours felt as if it were just about to begin. Back in the town, we were passed by motorized houseboats on the miniature canal that runs through the town (and over an aqueduct to the valley beyond). We stopped in the hotel for dinner and had very good English trout, then drove 150 miles north. The day had been a minor adventure, and though I felt a bit outside it as an observer as much as a participant, my entire sense was of great and long-lasting closeness to Carla precisely because we had gone through these things—and every-thing that had preceded them—separately but in company together, in confirmation of the new life to come.

The confirmation I felt in being the Executor to her will now that he would contest it. That will was as broad as a natural field, spread out to the limits of a horizon where meteorites fell in abundance—we had thought they were only defunct satellites carrying back to earth their radioactive cargoes. It was the responsibility I claimed to go where each one fell to earth, where the radiation reached for in the depth of a Pandora's Box would open up and spread all over. Every atom I placed back in the box was another stipulation of my mother's will—as my sisters did also, stringing together the mismatched strands of innumerable buttons. On a table under an artificial light, hundreds of ancient and modern buttons were spread out, each one the point of condensation for a process all of us had been chosen to go through. Suddenly an order declared itself in every string uniting sets of likes and dislikes in valuable chains of identity—*Einstellung,* bringing all together into one. It is process that takes a very long time with no guarantee it will stop. Each sister stands in line to accept the remains of an emotion recollecting an end to her sovereign state—points of condensation for everyone in strings of intact beads. Radios were emitting strings of oracular beads as my sisters turned their buttons; meteorites lit up the dark areas beyond the hem of her gown, where the grounds ended in nature and we counted in integers up to *bad infinity.* And as our returns diminished, we left for marginal hills astride the manifest turnpikes, never knowing when we would come back. That loss the original charters of *terra incognita* must have known after they had discovered it all, putting legend to map in the final stages of an emptying out of what they had known of her territory. As revisions proceed in a rhythm of temporal unfolding, there occurs a moment when even I can sum up an experience—but only if it cannot be communicated. This has been impossibly difficult, but it will always have been worthwhile. Then he set in motion an antagonism immeasurable so as not to be denied, stinking index of a finger that had to be excluded on principle. It was more than an economy based on fabricating strings of buttons could survive. Like an obelisk commemorating the birth of some failed romantic, his disembodied will circulated in a space of indistinct fields and trees to guarantee a date of prospective return with which I disagree. So the greybeards of prophecy had settled on a line distinguishing a universal aura from spontaneous eruptions contesting it. In such wise by opposition had I taken on my sobriquet "The Executor" in homage to his dysfunctional will—drawing up the boundaries of the property as if to call a thing what it is simply were to name it. And until such time as The Executor is no longer fit to stand in line and string beads, meteorites will be enumerated in a hermeneutics display as we fling them back across the sunset and into the sky's frozen egg of logos just waiting to crack. This is what it means to be The Executor—I have no intention of contesting the General Will, but only to do my part in responsibility to every other part of it. Under western skies, materials spread out in a sandbox of creative possibility—a context as wide as possible for each act that ends up being only incommensurable. So the revolutionary class had exceeded its historical necessity in contesting greybeards in almost everyone's account of it, in the end falling back to a prior version of romance. The sky that exceeds the clouds produces lightning, it is said, in a particular condensation of buttons. Discrepant wills want a woman to come back, but the larger story is that she will never be the same—a serial moment that everyone must identify with and in which each one must take their place. The stipulations are these: that I am to gather up all that remains within the limits of an estate; that I am to write a detailed account of it; and that I must distribute it to beneficiaries at large. This is a process he wishes to interrupt as competing distributor of limited goods. But the General Will stipulates the law of inheritance is mobile construction of origin whose end will be only a refrain. Those who framed it did not abandon their claims to participate in any part of it—this is the authority that guarantees my role as The Executor. As on a theatrical stage, The Executor reads a General Will in competing lights of discrepant claims. Each spectator had been given a portable light on entry to represent their place in the overall scheme of things. Thus my sisters were to solve the problem of distributing their uncountable beads— one beam of each flashlight would strike the captive head of each bead in a union of interpretive frame with presentation of an event. So it was all buttons will be distributed, even if each spectator will leave only with some. The Executor had mastered discourse under provisions of the General Will. In this way meaning will be distributed to the world at large—meanings that had been fixed within it. Not to anticipate the force of any objection—his interruption of the process will only have been distributed as a future event.

XIII

I dream of a group of sociable foxes in the basement. The square-cut opening allowing me access within frames at least a half dozen wide-eyed, curious individuals of a sex later understood to be female. Rather it was suggested helpfully to me that their sex ought to be female—their almond eyes framed as if with make-up, their fur a glossy, generic red brown. Under the aspect of my inquiring gaze they glance sideways in a reality check and multiply to become an entire crowd of foxes looking back at my own curiosity. If I were to find out more about them, what would it mean to find out? Someone said that it would be a bad history in which women were not given proper names. None of these foxes is named; would it therefore be indecent to discuss them? In the dream I certainly did not assign them any sex—was it only being taken for granted? They were inhabiting a space under my house—my work room, laboratory, place of employment, revery den. Under any house is a basement of psychological dimensions, a surplus affective space. As I read *The Political Unconscious* into the night, a sump pump in the basement would go on and off, shunting gallons of water out of its perpetual flood. An editor asked for a theory of such drainage in the form of a critical review, which I refused as not entirely serious. A documentary on public television shows the urbanization of country hedgehogs in Bristol, England, a city seen as surplus affective space. Nesting in basements of the working class, hedgehogs respond to their urbanization by banding together in fighting family units; their goal is no less than socialism with a human face as long as they are left alone by tenants. Nearing extinction, such marginal species may multiply in the absence of predators; thus baiting hedgehogs is prohibited by town ordinance and punishable by a fine. Such regulations deny a biological comedy that predicates surplus affect on sexual excess, making me want to break the rules on pestering hedgehogs in the basement—this must be why I dreamed of the foxes! Foxes were sitting up late one night in the kitchen, talking of old conquests and scheming to appropriate members of the opposite sex—one even threatened to get a measuring tape! I am truly sorry but I cannot give them proper names because I have been unable to determine their sex. The Queen of Hearts was given a proper name that is universally acknowledged as she cries, "Off with their heads!" Even if the only heads that roll are intact bodies of hedgehogs, the threat is real nonetheless. An ambiguous sex would turn everyone into a stack of animated cards falling all over each other in a domino effect. Cross-dressers at a carnival in Barbados jam each other in turn as the procession moves up the street; drunken office workers in Baby Bumble Bee dress crowd around them, buzzing their wings. They are giving out free rum

11

even to the sociable foxes, but someone shows up to remind them to appear in court tomorrow for breaking the rules on the disposition of proper names. It would be an end to my comedy if I were forced to name them, but here I will proceed: Abigail Van Buren, Babe Diedrich, Carla Hills, Diane Ward, Ermione Gingold, Faith Fancher, Georgina Weldon—is tragedy the only form in which someone of any sex can be given a name? If a name were to appear in an epic poem, we are advised that our destiny depends on the manner in which the named one will meet their defeat. Why should there not be as many defeated names for women as for men? But it is not the standpoint of history to name them in confidence of any outcome— that is for an authority to come. I feel myself becoming mildly hysterical with all this burden of history attending the disposition of names. The foxes had been communicating with each other; they were creating virtual social bonds based on deferred but automatic pleasures—one not of their species might not have that kind of pleasure; one could only stand at the entrance apart and look. The fantasy I am engaged in here is greatly in excess of a dream I or anyone else may have had. When Jane Austen set up the rules for her imagined community, she demanded that all its members state time, place, and manner of a perpetual agreeableness as criterion for admission. Men would be placed at a periphery only to witness and adjust—all but for one man, the tutelary spirit of social bonds who kept all in their place. Sagacious reader and vicious critic alike will recognize I have here named a female hero in all due respects. Jane Austen is the Muhammad Ali of the novel, it has been said—in which case Charlotte Brontë will go head to head with Joe Frazier; George Eliot may be classed with George Foreman; Virginia Woolf matches up with Ingmar Johannsen; and Gertrude Stein weighs in with Larry Holmes, if we keep our analogies to those in the heavyweight class. Roland Barthes described a community of female mud wrestlers who had aesthetic and moral standards of their

12

own that an admiring social critic could only observe. The sociable foxes would lounge around in the kitchen discussing incidents of their risqué lives; I cannot help listening as I am only fifteen and a half. Here is the premise of a comedy where one sex is folded continually into another. The spectators are neuter foxes looking back through an aperture at the inquiring, curious gaze. What objectifying violence is in that gaze! But foxes will answer simply by multiplying their communicative links until they exceed the boundaries of any proper community we had decided to name. I hope this unpacking of my gaze makes conditions of delirious equality possible for an entire world of species to be found under houses. We do not need to assign them a particular sex. Had this been a Boy's Town of runaways who had set up their utopian community in violation of the work ethic, the results would be the same. After a spectacular moment of social collapse, they would reach a state of descriptive calm whose gaze would be admitted as a possible member. Who knows what they would do to it later? As the poet had predicted, a parallel cataclysm is the best that can be expected for an ethics of sex—I mean the pleasure of their ethics indeed must be whether it is mutual. Maybe pleasure is only another form of discomfort; Jane Austen would agree that agreeableness is mistaken as only another form of torture. They had simply decided that it would be better to join the others after they had taken their walk past the parsonage as the venereal planet would be ascendant and conditions for viewing would be ideal. Among foxes an assent would be universal, even if accompanied by much turning and twisting of heads. It was only later as I was asked to account for the rules that we decided to make the foxes female—as versions of the aura surrounding me that gives delirious lilt to my desiring gaze! Tragedy is not good for the erotic life! Everyone stands in attention as they wait for our burdens to be released—climbing all over each other in anticipation of a fatal event! Some would want the female to be that event—

an unobtainable truth only to be discovered as we cease to be! But we are grateful not to have been born as spiders! Better that tragic figures are not here to be given any sex! Better still to be born into the world as foxes and hedgehogs of as-yet-unassigned names!

Manuel Brito

Would you describe the theoretical background of what another poet has called your "aesthetic program"?

My "aesthetic program" would be to locate the form of the "aesthetic" in the temporal continuum of the "ideological." This is hardly radical, going back in English literature at least as far as Chaucer and Margery Kempe, and certainly not unique: today in the mail I received an image on a postcard from the Phyllis Kind Gallery in New York titled *America with Intersections and Walmarts* (by Roger Brown). I experienced this image as a temporal intervention in an ongoing dialogue in which cultural meanings ("America") are being constructed by means of art (on a stylized, coded map, each state contains its own geometrical mall); the artist's irony is to mimic the latest advance in schematic understanding, yielding an overview that at the same time cancels any pretentions. But clearly an exception is implied if ongoing cultural projects, such as this one or my own, are characterized as following a "program." "Program" implies method; methods are totalizing, therefore totalitarian; and if there is an "aesthetic program," I hear it being asked, does it include me?

That an "aesthetic program" would be thought to exclude "me" seems to go to the heart of what makes it seem frightening. In America, at least, this "me" comes along with an "aesthetic program" of its own, a "program that is no program" in which versified self-expression confronts the world directly from the position of a reactive "me." That would be the gist of the argument "we" (I and five other writers) made in our collaborative article "Aesthetic Tendency and the Politics of Poetry" (*Social Text* 19/20). But it is perhaps too simple to find "expressivist" poetry self-contradictory in disavowing its own "aesthetic program." Recently I encountered an interesting work by Diane di Prima in the public context of an AC Transit bus in Berkeley:

NUMBERS RACKET

when you take no for an answer
will you look any different
will you get pale
behind your glasses will you
go backward with that
funny step
will you straighten your jacket

I mean are you taking it.

        now, taking no
        for an answer

    This is a very good poem for mass transit, the best of the genre I have
encountered. It is clear that it means to reproduce an ideological effect:
that moment Louis Althusser speaks of when "ideology hails us," which Ron
Silliman, in turn, has translated as "Hey, you, get off of my cloud!" Public
identity is a consequence of the negation of private identity in this poem,
and the poem's lower-case vocalizing—imitating the suppressed voice of
resentment that goes along with such a "no"; "I mean are you taking it," such
a public person might ask him or herself—makes that effect an immediate
and everyday "now." But how does the poem intervene? By interjecting its
own negation of the everyday man who shapes up to the denying norm,
straightening his jacket and going pale behind his glasses, the poem says it
could be otherwise: you could do what you want (presumably, win the sweep-
stakes and leave by next plane to Bermuda). The poem, and the poet's
expressive voice behind it, is on the side of spontaneity and desire rather
than repression and work.
    But is this how poetry on the busses really works? Another example, a poem
by Michael Smith, equally vocalizes a response to the confines of negation:
"i/shall not die/a natural death/but fighting"—is the alternative commute
an instantaneous terrorism, a short-circuit out of the "system"? It turns out
Michael Smith *did* die at the hands of the police in Jamaica, but that death
is not the same as its poetic moment being contemplated on the busses. Both
poems, in fact, seem to present themselves equally as objects of reflection,
expressively true but ironically received, as much as direct communication.
This effect would be increased by the numbers of times a given bus rider
would encounter these particular messages—next to Army recruitment
posters, ads for hemorrhoids and business colleges, AIDS-awareness campaigns. "Oh, there's that guy dying an unnatural death trying to fight the
system for the eighty-ninth time," he or she may reflect. Here expression
of a singular and self-canceling insight becomes a persistent redundancy,
and whatever expressive intention exists would be lost as simply a reflective
moment competing for attention with numerous other sales pitches.
    Even so, the ratio here between private expression and public scale is
significant—both for what it is as expression and for what it inculcates in
the subject. It is clear that freedom on the expressive side of these poems
is equally matched by negativity in their reception; this disparity is, exactly,
their ideological effect. Social reality is a lie built upon the truth of *me*, and
it will always defeat *me*—that's how I know what it is. This aligns perfectly
with Slavoj Žižek's remark that "the idea of the possible *end* of ideology is an
ideological idea *par excellence*." Thus Žižek finds in Althusser's critique of ideology "a radical ethical attitude which we might call the heroism of alienation."
An "aesthetic program" stemming from this attitude would interest me very
much; so in an acknowledgment of social negation based on the experience
reproduced in di Prima's bus poem, I wrote:

                                    16

The station maintains its output. White noise spreads from static
generators built with that in mind.

Severed heads fill in the gaps.

An unending series of negatives is the signal for collapse. Block
by block the power fails. Power poles spread out at equal intervals
down the street.

The train arrives from nowhere. Music follows the engine's path
through space.

The finished product comes to light. ("Paralleles")

The "finished product" here (at least this fragment of it) may be due more
to "method" than to "expression," although one could say that, finally, the
dizzying affect created by these simultaneous blanks, negations, and assertions is as expressive of a state of mind and as other-directed as di Prima's
address to the bus rider. The sequence here, however, does not necessarily
follow in the same order as di Prima's assumption, statement, and identification; rather a statement is being built from "integral components" of
identification and is then given the rhetorical form of a synthetic argument.
This argument may have formal properties more like the total experience
of signs encountered in social space on the bus than like any "single moment"
that "expressivist" poetry would inculcate in its public. This kind of formal
recombination, then, is where I begin in my "aesthetic program," but I
don't consider that it is where I end—it is not just the vertiginous pleasure
of running up and down the scale of these fragmented negations, nor the
"finished product com[ing] to light," but a simultaneously more public and
more psychological poetics that I want.

*I wonder if all the concepts and proper names listed in "Index to Introduction" can be
considered as essential components in your poetic development?*

I think of "Index to Introduction" not just as a set of references to artists and
movements important to my work—like Russian Formalism, Art-Language,
Roman Jakobson, Larry Eigner—but as a (perhaps ironic) comment on the
process of learning. In a literal sense: this was the result of my first attempt
at indexing the introduction to *Total Syntax*; clearly I hadn't got the principles
of indexing right and was creating a great deal of redundancy by virtue of
the categories I had set up. Neither the level of reference nor the subdivi-
sions into various components of the argument worked; the list became
repetitive and missed the point entirely. Subsequently I learned to index in
another way; an index like this for the entire book would have been nothing
but an impediment.
It is included as one section of "The Word" because it typifies excessive

17

and redundant aspects of indexicality that, in other sections of the poem, characterize texts in general. While texts purport to be communicative, and to present systematically the material under their purview, they generate in their own materiality a displacement that seemed to me to have comic value. If in "Conduit" "speech is the sound of what's missing in writing," here the sound of writing is a continuous verbal gag. That is what it invariably turns into when I read it out loud—its insufferable length and redundancy yields titters, then genuinely throaty haws. As such it seems to reverse the kind of anxiety present in the rest of my work, where no matter how humorously displacing a given textual moment may be, it evokes more a kind of partici-patory *ostranenie* (defamiliarization) than any immediately gratifying release of energy on the part of an audience.

In this sense "Index to Introduction" seems to put into practice, on advan-tageous terms, one of my most recurrent "performance anxiety" dreams. I am called upon to give a poetry reading, but on the way to the reading I have somehow forgotten my manuscripts and books. Never mind, I'll improvise, and proceed to do a stand-up improvisation reading names, addresses, and numbers out of the phone book. About a page or two into it I come to my senses; some version of this dream is I think very common among writers. It seems to me that one interest of Jackson Mac Low's "indexical" work—for instance, *Words nd Ends from Ez*—is its acting out of a familiar scenario. One might see an instance of "anxiety of influence" here in Mac Low's dismant-ling of the authority of the *Cantos*, and this connects to the list of names in my own index. Certainly, these names are important forebears, but perhaps it turns out (already has) that such exemplars are systematically redundant.

Voloshinov says that ideology is a matter of signs and is not related to consciousness. Can the dictionary, speech, the poem itself be completed without propositions elaborated by the sensibility of the subject?

By saying that ideology is material, Voloshinov means that it is located in the space between subjects. I might say, "Blackbirds on a line sing a raucous tune and Russia is electrified," and it would be ideology in Voloshinov's sense. But for Voloshinov it is also the subject's organization and subordination of this material speech that gives evidence of its ideological effects (as having created an intersubjectivity). Here it seems that the material/psychological distinc-tion is beginning to break down. I would allow it to break down all the way and say, with linguists like Charles Fillmore and George Lakoff, that the mate-rial sign is implicitly bound up with cognitive frames and categories. So as language, the privileged terms of a culture are psychologically as well as materially real. Further—thinking of psychoanalysis in the way that Lacan does when he recounts the anecdote of his conversation with a fisherman, "Do you see that sardine can floating in the water? Well, it doesn't see you!" —there really can't be any separation between material signs and their psychological reality insofar as we speak of ideology. The repetition of mate-rial signs—for example, the American flag symbolizing "Victory"—is both

18

created by and creates a psychological reality, in this case the auratic excess of national glory. I would be interested in an American flag in its complementary colors—for red, green; for white, black; for blue, orange—that, given its ubiquitous repetition, would have the opposite effect. Some of the statements in my poems I hope might work that way when experienced cumulatively.

What would such a notion of "complementary" meaning, that when experienced long enough would create its opposite like repeating "money" 100,000 times a day to cure avarice, entail? Something like Wittgenstein's rabbit/duck, to be *seen as* differently in different environments of use? If Wittgenstein's figures achieve their effect by virtue of commitments exterior to any subject (that would be one way of thinking of a "language game"), there might be a tricky way that the materiality of signs returns, as a modernist paradigm, to have a specifically ideological role. "Exterior" contexts are constructed from "interior" identifications in the case of the rabbit/duck; so in a politically charged environment, the rabbit might be seen as a peace sign, and the duck its depoliticized complement. Such a materialization of "inner states" and a psychologization of "exterior" ideology coexist characteristically in modernism, and that is how I would read Voloshinov.

The question then would be, What kind of psychology goes along with this materialization? In Jerome McGann's salutary project of reading the romantic poets specifically to avoid their subjective unity (or the equivalence of psychological reality with ideological effects), the material fact of their texts is proposed as basis for a subsequent history. That history is its reception and "judgment" as being meaningful as much as it is its bibliographical trajectory, of course; and so one must still speak of specifically textual subjectivity effects. Take McGann's discussion of Pound's *Cantos*, for instance: while bracketing out subjective intention in Pound one might still be painfully aware of slippages of meaning caused by the redundancies of the text ("Out of all this beauty something must come") and the fetishization of further increments of "material" information, such as the Chinese characters laid into the text as virtual printers' dingbats. In the film version of Pound's relation to the material text, a crotchety old man literally hits the *Analects* with a stick in the hope that, in an elided referentiality, "they'll get it." There must be something in the pathos of this referential debacle that feeds into the tragic view of the *Cantos'* nobility by virtue of their failed intentions ("a failure of will," in McGann's and many others' estimation), a materialized failure that elicits a psychological complement in the epic authority of Pound. So textual materiality returns very quickly, at least in modernism, to the psychological subject that one would like to exclude from it.

Your essays show an interest in the political instrumentality of language, how politics tries to keep control and retain the power to pursue its own goals. Would redressing the conditions of reading in a very personal way be the ideal manner to reformulate that relationship?

I'm not particularly interested in a "very personal" reading as the way to reformulate politics as "impersonal." But my work does contain elusive, often incomprehensible, subjective, libido-driven materials: if not understood in the classical surrealist dialect of desire, how do they engage the political? Another way to rephrase the question would be, If my work is (hopefully pleasurably) difficult, how does it redress the onslaught of literal, instrumental language that is politics? One way to think about this would be to consider creativity not as a reaction to its context but as a kind of learning, to begin with often "very personal" but at the same time engaging a "social learning." Both as a form of writing and as social engagement my own work is experimental, "the exploration of conceptual meaning and the use of materials whose final form is not entirely resolved." That certainly would describe its conditions of production; each poem begins in a state of "not knowing" itself or what it is going to say, a virtual heap of unprocessed conceptual raw materials. The process of composition draws out recognitions in the materials and possible sequences, orders, and implications; thematic strands stand out in relief much like the "purple snake/Stands out on porcelain tiles" at the opening of *Progress.*

Let us take that purple snake as one moment in which thematic identification is achieved. It so happened that this snake was a graffiti in a very inhospitable pedestrian underpass leading from Lakeshore Drive to Lake Merritt in Oakland. One's being in that passageway is generally accompanied by some kind of apprehension or fear; I bolt for the light at the end of the tunnel right away. The white porcelain as background connotes a kind of hygiene that is anything but the case; the purple spray paint is not genteel. In this scenario, the poem would appear at the outset as a presentation of oppositional but instrumental language, in the way that subway graffiti in New York is said to be subversive by giving evidence of excluded identity. The next such instrumental assertion, however, makes things more difficult: "The idea/Is the thing. Skewed by design . . . ." So it is not simply represented content but a presentation tending toward representation, inevitably skewed in its own attempt to do so, that is at issue. Something interior, private, difficult is attempting to achieve explicit, literal, public content and *say something*; so one would perceive the purple snake as coming out of some unknown background (the unsanitary cultural breeding ground of the porcelain tiles) and wanting to make its case.

What is it saying? If we were to take this image as a simple oppositional moment, it would say "the opposite" of, perhaps, the slick, twenty-story apartment building at one end of the tunnel (the building where, for a while, it was rumored Black Panther leader Huey Newton lived). Subway graffiti, likewise, would be the political Other to the commuters who confront it each day on their way to work; such a representation would confirm the everyday world "even in its traces" by virtue of a failed opposition. But this representation could also be seen as presenting itself in a different way, as coming out of and perpetuating an irresolution of its own condition; a condition that wants to be redressed, but not in any finality of its own content. The teenagers who painted this design are probably very uneasy about seeing themselves as purple snakes. The instability of this image—which occurs at the same time as its "emergent" social meaning—conveys an intensely private meaning in an agony of public space. It is, at the same time, an act that complicates public space by placing such an unstable, private image within it. The larger world is thereby changed—for the inscriber as much as the viewer; so the snake might be said to have "learned" its way into it. It creates the conditions for the understanding of itself as part of the landscape, as necessary, immediate, and appropriate—but a further context of irresolution obtrudes, and one is faced again with the necessity for further acts. In this case, such further acts may be violent as much as ameliorative.

This is not a mild example, and it is not one that typifies my work as a whole. Its position as one of the opening moments of *Progress* is to identify social violence as one of the limiting themes of the poem, as one result of instrumental language. In citing the purple snake, the poem is "thinking with the things as they exist," in Louis Zukofsky's sense; in this way the difficulty of private meanings engages social meanings more generally, in a series of experimental moves. Just as the purple snake is emerging from a blanked and negated background into "saying something" it can scarcely recognize, so private language qualifies the public and creates a new ground on which instrumental meanings can be modified and redefined. It is not simply a matter of opposition.

You say in "The XYZ of Reading" that "the question has become ourselves." Are we able to answer in a pure way, I mean without any contamination of imposed references?

> The form of a riddle travels through space and time. We question a question in order to fill in its form. Its meaning is the questioning act. If "existence" is calling itself into question, we can easily supply the answer because in that case we know; the question has become ourselves. (*Conduit*, 12)

Or "hidden is in," as I wrote in *Progress*. As Viktor Shklovsky has pointed out, a "secret" meaning leads to the defamiliarization effect: in the juxtaposition of two different interpretations of the same set of facts—one that we know in the "ordinary" way and one that we know by virtue of its secret having been revealed—a "semantic shift" occurs, a frame shift by means of which perception takes place. An example of this occurs in Marcel Duchamp's sculpture *With Hidden Noise* (1916), which withholds the "secret" of its depth even from the artist (the sculpture is composed of a ball of twine bolted between two metal plates on which some obscure lettering had been pressed; Duchamp

21

had asked Walter Arensberg to place an object in the hollow of the twine without telling Duchamp what it was, thus making the "hidden noise" of the title). Writing of this sculpture as an instance of the sublime, Jerry Estrin describes it as "a signaling device whose meaning seems constantly to come from elsewhere, from a space that has nothing to do with the object." The viewer is left in the position "only to realize, through a kind of engaged training, that one can't ever pin down the meaning—meaning always vanishes and this is its *Noise*." In my own excerpt from "The XYZ of Reading," substitute "existence" for the Duchampian enigma; "the question becomes ourselves" by virtue of the "kind of engaged training" necessary to comprehend it. Meaning in this sense becomes a kind of practice by virtue of the interpretative distance necessitated from any of its objects. "Its meaning is the questioning act."

Calling existence into question, as Duchamp's sculpture clearly does (how else could we think of it?), we are left with ourselves; just so, a purely Kantian moment of the sublime would be uncontaminated, like a bolt from the blue. If it is possible to make meaning by virtue of such thought experiments, one would be tempted to answer yes: the question of existence does not involve "imposed references" for its answer. The ratio of two interpretations, one as familiar as Duchamp and one an interpretative secret, seems to produce a moment of "uncontaminated," pure defamiliarization. As a result, it may seem that there are certain effects of "calling existence into question" that can be accomplished with any materials—as long as they are placed in such a relation that their interpretative possibilities are set at odds to reveal them. The arbitrariness is not a pre-given linguistic one, as with Saussure, but a compositional possibility for objects articulated in relation to their contexts. One could therefore "start anywhere" in a series of objective investigations that would call existence into question within specific contexts, leading to a compositional sequence whose meaning would be its "questioning act." This is what I attempt to do with such incremental progressions of disparate propositions, as for example in the poem "Direct Address":

Tripping over a fireplug, think . . . Warren G. Harding wanted to meet Debs.

Abstract from Indo-European.

Thorns that lust and hate.

"In order to make them believe." At the end of history, air molecules on eyes.

Eyes open wide.

The opposite is what I intend.

> Parking lots in Fremont convert an image to X. This many incre-
> ments stacked up to be shipped. (*Conduit,* 57)

What Warren G. Harding had to do with Debs (nothing but a little friendly
curiosity for the man the government had been locking up for some number of years on the part of its chief executive) is an American non sequitur
congruent with, but of another order than, "parking lots in Fremont." The
poem seems to imply that this relation of dissociation is productive; in fact,
it provides a way that such seemingly incompatible considerations as the
history of the word *abstract* and the affective qualities of thorns can be reconciled in a temporal argument. If we imagine that each of such propositions
is "calling existence into question," we may grant that a "subjectivity effect"
is achieved in the way in which such progressions "have become ourselves."
We are both distanced from all such assertions and simultaneously producing more and more of them, as the poem goes on to show. These assertions
continue to "call existence into question," in fact try very hard to get close:

> To go underground and arrive in Berkeley.
>
> And present Adlai Stevenson a degree. The only trademark is the
> arbitrary . . .
>
> > "That which exists through sunlight is *shade.*"
>
> . . . as difficult as meaning itself.
>
> As history discovers the present . . . But impossible of direct
> approach!
>
> Coming around a corner, their carts full of goods. (71)

Here there is not so much a continuous present as a continuous sublime;
in other words, even a proposition that would invoke the present would be
"impossible of direct approach" and thus double—by that act we interpret
it, withholding interpretation. "Meaning" "itself" is "as difficult." The poem
discovers that the "distance that equals results" here is a social distance; our
meaning-preserving strategies have turned into social reproduction, whether
we like it or not. The production is pure, uncontaminated—in fact, it could
be said to prove that only this world is real, if anyone could call themselves
into question long enough to understand it. They can't; in that sense, the
world as it has proposed itself to us retains the upper hand: "Increase of
cancer in Richmond. In time to build up from the ground." Reification is
not simply imposed on us but is constructed by specific semantic incongru-
ities that we participate in, which the experiment in meaning undertaken
here sees as first principles. The references are determined by the entire
method, but they are equally prefigured by the world.

Progress is a long poem with stanzas of five lines revisioning history, the world, those immediate facts of experience, news, and even some characters. What was the conception of that book?

I've discussed a number of the conceptions behind *Progress* elsewhere, but the topic, like the poem, seems to keep opening out. Rather than reading *Progress* in terms of its historical reference to the period in which it was written (the Reagan Recession), one could also read it for its organization of "those immediate facts of experience, news, and even some characters." The notion of "progress" would then veer from that of the former reading, as "difficulty overcome," to other senses equally present: the poem invokes all kinds of "progress," from *Pilgrim's Progress* (millennial horizons), the Progressive Era (standardized tests); the Progressive Labor Party (intellectual violence, breaking chairs over the heads of SDS members); "Work in Progress" (the unfinished project of modernism, Joyce). One that came to me recently is the notion from Elizabethan times of the "queen's progress," which would describe the course of her state visits accompanied by her retinue through the countryside (for example to Lyme Regis, formerly simply Lyme, hence its new name). If the queen's progress were a form, I imagine representational "nodes" of theatrical display occurring at each designated point in its sequence where the country would be cleaned up and made presentable. This could be read as an amusing comment on the notion of style as a spectacle of social hygiene presented to an absolute observer (citizens of Houston recently undertook such a project in cleaning up all visible trash on the route of the heads of state there for an economic summit). In any case, many such notions of "progress" in the cultural lexicon would apply.

How then would one describe the construction of meaning in the poem? Alan Liu's recent discussion of "decision trees" in communication seemed so evocative that I thought I had embodied them in my writing before I even read what he had to say about them. Liu refers to devices of citation out of which histories are made: "Like 'binaries' in structuralist decision-trees (left/right, raw/cooked, bear clan/eagle clan, and so on), citational devices are the micro-components—the 'switches'—that control narrative signals as they course down the . . . decision-trees."[1] Borrowing from Avital Ronell's *The Telephone Book*, Liu analogizes the outcomes of these "decision-trees" to communicative acts that select, by virtue of the character of their messages, the appropriate receivers (much like a long-distance phone number— 1-800-ABU BAKR, for example—might select out of all the receivers in the world its appropriate destination, in this case the Trinidadian terrorist Abu Bakr [such is the irony of the world as it is "called up" by these decision trees; "terrorist" here may be defined as "what you can call up but can't put back down"]). In any case, if ideology is calling us, now we get to call it back:

> We might say that the entire structure of narrative communication
> consists of a network of switchable relays allowing citations or "calls"
> to be put through between the narrative subject and its semantically

24

significant others: not just the object on the predicative trunk line but also the remote authorities of the sender, receiver, helper, and opponent on long-distance lines. The relation of the latter lines to the main narrative trunk, indeed, is precisely that of an electronic 'relay' or remote-controlled switching mechanism. These relays may be integrated in complex patterns to create the circuits that Greimas analyzes as narrative 'functions' and 'transformations'; but they all start as devices that from an outside location switch the direction of the predicative line when 'called' upon in an inquiry-loop.

This description of narrative communication (and there are certainly others, which won't do so well) seems particularly suited to the nonnarrative progression, the "predicative trunk line," around which *Progress* is built. In fact, the kind of retrospective narrative that concerns Liu—that of standard literary histories—could easily be set aside in favor of the constructive potential of *Progress's* nonnarrative, prospective, "autotelic" form. That is, one of the calls the trunk line of *Progress* could be processing through its series of "decision trees" would be its own continuous meaning—an interpretant continually called upon but never finally reached (until the ending—"adding/The date to a list of days/With astronomical slowness," when at least the poem is complete). At this point, Liu's conclusion to the problems he poses is similar to the one I draw from mine: "To observe the second-order, monitoring technology [the accretive, cumulative, nonnarrative meaning of *Progress* in my case], we need now to step off the narrative plane entirely to the 'real-world' situation in which [the text, literary history or poem] functions." Rather than creating an icon of received history, however, *Progress* intends a demonstration of "new meaning" that is at the same time both a social and individual "learning"—a presentation of the world, unlike the theater of the queen's progress, to be called up on its own authority.

Which returns to the question of the poem's materials, the micronarratives and citations of "immediate facts of experience, news, and even some characters" (to which should be added, of course, "language"). I remember one such "immediate" moment that became incorporated into the poem in which the "Mundane Egg" is reflected "in a pool of reflected light . . . //On roof of pool one floor above/Parking lot,/modern living/Smashing parked car windows/To make a sound out of brick" (75-76). I seem in this passage to have shifted from a "philosophical revery" about hazy mirrors to a remembrance based on seeing, from the street, the light reflected from an indoor pool on the ceiling of the fourth story of a modern apartment building in Oakland, the first three stories of which were parking lot. This heavenly image contrasted with the possible fate of cars parked on the street, which might have their windows broken, thus "calling up" reflections of an adolescent act of possibly reprehensible behavior: in the eighth grade, I had gone with a gang of tough boys on an adventure clearly over my head to the parking lot of a country club near my house, whereupon they broke a number of car windows. I didn't and in fact lingered behind at the bottom of the creek beside it, but we all ran—in fact we were chased by the police—through the hills. It took over an hour of avoiding the roads after I had separated from the others (one of whom, Ray, I later hear ended up in prison—a kind of closure) to get back home. I was equally innocent and guilty, split down the middle by remorse either way. Was this remorse appropriate to my present relation to the elite's pool and its reflected light (earlier in the poem, "Today's pool is a baroque sky/Not available in Arkansas")? I then proceed with this self-excoriation to two narratives in which clearly I was in the wrong—an "eighth year" escapade in Taiwan that I will not recount in which I was guilty both as individual delinquent and collective "imperialist," but again in two senses, and another moment of excess at age 13 when "I roll[ed a number of large construction] pipes into a stream/In my wish to speak clearly." The division "called up" by the reflected light in any case turns out to structure a "decision-tree"—and such exist at every point in the poem—by which the poem's conceptions are brought into the world: "An entire life to be in-structed." The poem is thus truly revisionary, in the sense of overcoming bad history—both my own and others'.

Parentheses play a significant role in "Prison Life" (1–10). We may read three different discourses—one of them just the words inserted in the parentheses, another the nonparen-thetical words, and finally both together. Is there any specific intention in playing with that device?

The device itself came from an early work of Christopher Dewdney's which used parentheses to approximate "word viruses" that would invade and in-habit the host bodies of texts. There was also a question of surface and depth, with the parenthetical words seemingly standing for interpretative depths behind the "text" but at the same time being displaced on its surface (just as right now the word *Colonnades*—the name of a trendy restaurant in early 1980s New York—suddenly surfaces in this account; there weren't any columns beside the name, as I remember it, but the sunken depths of the restaurant, one half flight of stairs down, seemed contained behind them anyway). I was interested in this effect as it would interrupt the textual sur-face (from the production side, as in Dewdney's poem) and anticipate the resistance of a reader in accepting the authority of the text (on the side of consumption, perhaps, but here due to alternative meanings, interruptions). If ideology is structured in the way dialogue is subordinated in recorded speech (as for Voloshinov), here the textual surface flips back and forth between the locus of this effect being on the side either of the writer or the reader.

In writing this prose poem, in fact, I was a reader—of a passage from Stan Brakhage's *Film Biographies* that described, in a highly poetic fashion, how the young Sergei Eisenstein must have understood cinematic montage from flipping the pages of the (bourgeois, certainly) stories that would have been read to him. This vaguely preposterous passage seemed also more than true, perhaps by virtue of equally compelling indentifications with cinematic

26

montage and the reader-as-boy. If so, these identifications between the public world (cinema as Lenin's most important art) and the private (developmental stages extending back to boyhood and integrated in a continuous "interior speech," in the psychologist Vygotsky's sense) are integrated here in a form of continual interrupting the "exterior" text with all manner of "inner" objections. The moral of such a process for Voloshinov and Vygotsky is clear: inner speech is social. The phenomenal space resulting in the poem— between writer and reader, public and private—aligns with much of what I subsequently wrote; the device is thematically motivated.

Is it desirable to approach a poetry that allows numerous interpretations and that avoids definitive structures with an anti-scientific attitude?

As David Antin once said, "Science is the poetry of terror." I see no reason to disagree with that assessment. However, a scientific attitude in exactly that sense is fundamental to aesthetics as we know it. Consider the practice of anatomical drawings: it is not only a particular formal knowledge to be gained from the specific configurations of bones and muscles, but an attitude of distance toward "life studies" to be realized in this knowledge. The example of Whitman recording his experiences as a hospital nurse in the Civil War (*Specimen Days*) offers such a moment in American literature; Whitman's expansiveness is a predicate of this inevitable objectification. In poetry of the "late modern" period—as it was when I entered into it in the late sixties— such exemplary knowledge had been absorbed into a modernist psychology in which objectification was a form of "killing off" threats to the unity of self. The "poetry of terror" Antin discusses I believe was his way of relocating the experience of modernist psychology onto a ground of knowledge that might more "reasonably" be said to occasion it. The move, of course, made by writers of my own circle was to displace such psychology onto the objective properties of "language," and this seems doubly motivated—in Antin's allegorical sense, and in an additional one. It would not have been possible in a time of deep antipathy to the Vietnam War to relocate the "terror" of modernist psychology onto anything as literal as objectified knowledge of the body—such a value for science was not possible in the era of napalm, Agent Orange, and the draft. The psychology of response to modernist terror that is found in earlier postmodern work—extending from Olson's corporeality to the "body art" of Carolee Schneeman—as a result was to be displaced onto an inchoate, boundless "language" as a ground of aesthetic distance and source of positive knowledge. "Language" for us was the fantasy of objectification that replaced, discontinuously, the physicality of the earlier postmodernism.

So "a poetry that allows numerous interpretations" as opening out into "language" would seem to be one solution to the artistic need for an objectified ground against which the grandeur of life would stand out. By virtue of its motivation as a form of postmodernist fantasy, this may lead to a sense of such work as "avoid[ing] definite structures"—but that ignores the objectification of "language" itself as definite. Such a risk—that "language" is both objective and a form of avoidance—also seems to embody frustrating complications, the only excuse for which must be their persistent recurrence as an ethical dilemma. A poetics of "language" is an attempt to find a workable ground for modernism that leads to real solutions for the dilemmas it proposes. Here again we have "progress" being negotiated in a marvelously conflictual dimension. An "anti-scientific" attitude, however, would simply resolve the dilemma in favor of "avoidance," ending only in a kind of regression, a sentimentality not recuperable to its original motives.

In Plasma/Paralleles/X *many lines are just a sentence that we are permitted to think or meditate about; this fact allows for an increase in both information and contrast. Is this a literary device for making us conscious of the continuous superimposition of meanings/speculations that are in conformity with or deform our competence?*

In all three poems in that book I was conscious of working out of the dilemma you describe—the simultaneous reinforcement and undermining of linguistic competence. In the first poem, "Plasma," this is explicitly thematized:

> A paradox is eaten by the space around it.

> I'll repeat what I said.

> To make a city into a season is to wear sunglasses inside a volcano.

> He never forgets his dreams.

> The effect of the lack of effect.

> The hand tells the eye what to see.

> I repress other useless attachments. Chances of survival are one out of ten.

A paradox, to begin with, would seem to embody opposing meanings, but even its meaning as a paradox is consumed by a context that does not recognize any inevitability in such opposition. This would be the paradigm for the effect of contrast you mention. Therefore, the repetition that follows is, in exactly this sense, both paradoxically referring to the previous and following lines (making them equivalent) and indicating an autonomous act without *any* preconditions—an announcement by "I" that he will repeat what he has said. Such a paradox of repetition (line 2) is being argued to establish a "meta" continuity, but at the outset it is unclear whether the "paradox" of line 1 is the "same as" the difficult analogy of line 3—whether the interpretative dilemmas already proposed could be understood as a mapping of the cognitive onto the performative ("To make a city into a season is to wear sunglasses inside a volcano"). The point that should be increasingly clear as the work is both performed and interpreted is that there is a substrate in which "language" itself speaks, not just is spoken by a speaker. This devolution of phenomena to noumena is the meditation of the poem, so that "Such is night in the mountains" should be read, at the end, as both familiar and unearthly. And so it goes: the generation of paradoxical interpretations that cancel themselves out is the determination of "language" in the work. Later, in "X," such a continuous self-canceling is meditated on, additionally, in terms of an architectonic of surfaces and origins that is given specific cultural coordinates, in this poem the cultural topography of Los Angeles seen through the incommensurate fact that I happened to have been born there. The competence lost is that which would try to understand a meaning other than the present surface; the competence gained is that which would be oriented toward "A fact is what you can't get past," and the name for that fact is "language."

I've not found any characters in Opera—Works. *Are the words the real characters of this world?*

Opera—Works was trying, first of all, to work out of the confines of "persona" that were the dominant poetics of the period (early 1970s). The goal for such poetry was "find your own voice," the achievement of modestly idiosyncratic style being the guarantee of negotiability in the existing (largely academic) marketplace for otherwise indistinguishable work where the great American conundrum of normativity and individuality, "the one and the many," was being argued out again and again. Against that, I identified with two opposing possibilities: a writing that would theatrically display itself without need for persona (here the prior example was Zukofsky); and a writing that would find a natural order in syntax by enacting its own processes (here the prior example was romantic prose, from De Quincey and Coleridge to Ginsberg and Creeley). Roughly, these two poles demonstrate the split between "Opera" (theatrical display) and "Works" (writing) in the title.

While persona is being critically modified in this work, I don't think anything like "words [as] characters" was the outcome. There are, in fact, characters who function as words in a number of the poems, the first of which is an "ode" to "Bourbaki," a mythological figure invented as the author of the work of a circle of French mathematicians (the "Bourbaki circle") in the 1920s. As an identity Bourbaki is a construction, an intentional agent built in much the same way that the proofs or lemmas ascribed to him were made. Bourbaki himself appears in the poem only as his name; he is very like the character in "I saw a man climb up on the roof behind them, do Yoga all day" or "Man laughs randomly" or Wittgenstein in "Dream: With Wittgenstein." Later I essay the entire construction of such exteriorized identity in "Export Diplomat": "There are plenty of references to Mayakovsky on the Nevsky Prospect, not needing any statues." Identity devolves into language in the process, a dilemma I willfully proposed. Or such is what I would now like to think: now, I read a stanza like "The troops are departing by boat

29

/I can see them/but think of myself—/as better than nature" and realize how little aware I could have been at the time of the outer horizons of identification I would need to negotiate once the poetry of persona had been abandoned.

You have been widely regarded as an innovative and dynamic leader among the "language" poets during the 1980s. How do you see the debate about poetics that took place during those years?

It is accurate to say that the debates in the 1980s were more about poetics than poetry; in the 1970s the emphasis was on poetic forms apart from poetics, while in the later shift toward theory, poetic practice often stood in as a place holder. In many theoretical articles about the work of the language school from that period, bite-sized chunks of "language writing" were often given as more-or-less arbitrary, exchangeable examples. The same argumentative strategy would not apply today: the explanatory moment of "language writing" in general is no longer so important, while debates in poetics now seem tied more to specific (if theorized) extensions of poetic practice. Such a synthesis of theory and practice has been under way since the mid 1980s.

This, which I edited from 1971, printed only verse and prose; one of the central issues in the publication was formal: What are the differences between lyric poetry and poetic prose? $L=A=N=G=U=A=G=E$ (1978-82), as is well known, printed statements by writers and artists that established a theoretical ground for already existing practice. The form of $L=A=N=G=U=A=G=E$ was important, with the equal signs of the title standing for a field of related work, a kind of poetic matrix. In its imitation of equivalence, and in the subjective relativity of particular practices, this form led to questions later in the decade about the recuperation of "language writing" to romanticism. Since 1981 *Poetics Journal* has published more thematic articles while at the same time including creative work that stands in place of theory. One thing we did, starting with the second issue, was to introduce titles such as "Close Reading," "Poetry and Philosophy," "Women and Language," "Non/Narrative," and so on. While it is true that much of the work we published could have been categorized under any or all of these titles, the loose thematic organization each suggested worked to draw out more particular inferences.

In retrospect, I see the debate about poetics that took place in early 1980s, from the conclusion of $L=A=N=G=U=A=G=E$ to the beginning of *Poetics Journal*, to have shifted some theoretical and formal concerns. The overlap is great, but still I think the somewhat contradictory presentation of "language writing" that, say, Charles Bernstein made in "The Conspiracy of Us" (to be further amplified in his maxim "Schools are made to be broken") would no longer apply, and that more specific interactions—for example, the exchange that has been developing between American and post-Soviet writers in the last few issues of *Poetics Journal*—are the wave of the future. In this sense, a shift in the direction from synchronic equivalence to diachronic argument has been, tentatively, one outcome of these debates.

You have taken a big step in trying to liberate language from any form of power. How do you evaluate the possibilities of that proposal in the 1990s as opposed to in the 1960s?

I cannot say, in May 1991 as I write this, that "for us the primary reality is the war," as Sartre did in 1944. The primary reality for a brief and spasmodic time frame in January-February 1991 *was* the Gulf War, and we can cite this as an explicit replay of an earlier period, 1964-75, in which the primary *unreality* was the Vietnam War. We now live, and are writing within, a social order that has paradoxically become fully mobilized for "permanent war" and yet purports to suspend all hostilities in a Pax Americana. This instrumental *socius* is articulated to a high degree, and surely "language" has been a primary means of its reproduction. The writer in this environment is going to have particular tasks; it is no accident that, recently, the only sector of society that was identifiably against the Gulf War was that configured around the arts. The role of the writer at present is to maintain a fundamental perspective in social and cultural reality that would not exist—that would be destroyed—without his or her efforts.

---

1. Alan Liu, "Flat Literary History: Literariness and Postmodern 'General Literature,'" part 1, "The Bug in the Book: Toward a Critique by Technology," Paper presented at a conference on "What Is Literary History?," University of California, Berkeley, March 1991.

The Conduit of Communication in Everyday Life

Barrett Watten

As epigraphs to *Conduit* I used two quotations that describe possible outcomes of the act of communication, between which fall the range of formal intentions I hoped to explore in the poems and prose collected in the book:

> As for me, I would say that a true poet is someone with an over-whelming urge to say something, to communicate some emotion, that . . . he will never forget *what* he wanted to say, and he will eventually end up by saying it, by having it accepted as evidence.
> —Francis Ponge, *The Power of Language*

But:

> In the end, A, B, C, and D all came privately to the conclusion that the others had either become hostile or else gone beserk. Either way it did not matter much. None of them took the communication system seriously any more.
> —Michael J. Reddy, "The Conduit Metaphor"

What am I saying here? Between these two positions there is a significant gap between the romance of intention that would seem to be the primary business of the poet and the deflation of poetic value that inevitably occurs when that intention is put into social circulation. "The poet proposes, the reader disposes," and somewhere between these two moments actual communication occurs. While we have often been convinced of the omnipotence of our "overwhelming urges to say something," and have at times likewise experienced "the conclusion that the others had either become hostile or else gone beserk," these seem exceptional moments in the continuum of the everyday in which statement and understanding are organized to other ends than would support the fatalism of the poet or the linguist.

In the disjunction between subject and language, then, enter a third term: *everyday life*. Everyday life is by no means a simple description of what happens every day but a way of thinking that investigates the intersection of the otherwise separate spheres of cultural experience at the point where initial intention and ultimate understanding are no longer so opposed. One of the original thinkers of everyday life, Henri Lefebvre, experienced the dawning of his concept as just such a disappointment in historical romance as he describes it in *Everyday Life in the Modern World*. The aura of Marxist historical necessity, in his formulation, had come under attack by the resilience of the continued survival of the everyday, which Lefebvre saw in the period after the Liberation as suffering an alienation that "turned material poverty into spiritual poverty, as it put an end to the fruitful relations arising from the direct contact of creative workers with their material and with nature" (33). Everyday life thus began as the locus of repression, and by the sixties for Lefebvre,

> if tragedy still exists it is out of sight; the 'cool' prevails. Everything is ostensibly de-dramatized; instead of tragedy there are objects, certainties, 'values,' roles, satisfactions, jobs, situations, and functions. Yet there are powers, colossal and despicable, that swoop down on everyday life and pursue their prey in its evasions and departures, dreams and fantasies to crush it in their relentless grip. (65)

Lefebvre writes at the same moment when everyday life in this sense is given a particular figure in American poetry, in the work of Frank O'Hara. There has long since ceased to seem anything like the natural in O'Hara's casual ironies of "objects, certainties, 'values,' roles, satisfactions, jobs, situations, and functions." In fact, looking back on the degree to which their fragile formulations were underscored by "colossal and despicable powers"—the Cuban missile crisis, the Kennedy assassination, the Vietnam war, which are either trivialized or ignored in his poetry—it's hard to imagine how O'Hara's "I do this, I do that," as Ted Berrigan put it, could be mistaken as natural, even if there is an entire literature built on the belief that it is. The kind of affect surrounding O'Hara's death in 1965 might give some index to the way the "colossal and despicable powers" of the period were being organized in the poetic subject and its reception —what one was witness to was not only the death of a person but of a historical romance. It is a death that Berrigan, O'Hara's interpreter, later acted out in a repetition compulsion of "I do this, I do that," particularly in his physical incorporation of consumer culture in the form of Coke and Pepsi, to ensure the reception of historical romance as the proof of original intention. And it is a death that is still with us—in the relation between the ironized surface of consumer culture and a totalizing dread that underwrites it—to be repeated endlessly in a poetics of administered communication that enforces prior authority in its temporal orchestration.

Lefebvre's solution to the naturalization of a reified everyday is familiar, in broad terms, as the moment of 1968—the fragmenting of authority, its atomization of historical romance, given contemporary meaning in the sexual revolution and the redemption of urban space. These solutions are stated entirely negatively, however, as alternatives to "the terrorist function of forms . . . to maintain the illusions of transparency and reality and to disguise the forms that maintain reality. People living in everyday life refuse to believe their own experience and take it into account." (187), and it is possible that such as totalizing of the social as the administration of fear was only reinforced by such deterritorializing of desire in the sixties. Where Lefebvre saw an alternative, in other words, we would probably be forced to admit the refiguring of the reproductive mechanics of social forms in such a way that they are entirely inescapable. Where Lefebvre's "everyday life" thus appears as a critical moment, a conflict in social relations that must then propose a solution, a more permanent stability of the "everyday"—beyond the hysteria of O'Hara's cup of coffee in the work-a-day of Horn & Hardart's as a meditation on fate—would seem to be a site of our negotiations with language.

What am I saying here? It's quite unusual, if not impossible, to achieve a distance on the everyday; in fact, all of one's productions take place within it. I wanted, in the writing of "Conduit," to take language out of the everyday and put it back into circulation as a "new and improved" fragment. This strategy is a formal one, and uses language at the limits of its possibilities rather than simply as an ironization of an already received cultural content, as would be implicated, for instance, in the newspaper reception of sixties paintings as "pop." Within the everyday, production already is a reproduction; the desire for distance embodied in art is reproduced immediately as the condition for its own coming into existence. The everyday thus is not simply a description of "the way things work" but a limiting formal determination in which any element, from the extremes of disembodied poetic assertion to the grounds of its resonating dread, becomes meaningful in the same way that a cup of coffee on a Tuesday morning in 1963, even at 5:15 A.M., can be the basis of a poetics.

Thus named, art's atemporal distance immediately demands a reception in time—we are increasingly distanced (in time) from that ironic "moment." Likewise for Lefebvre, the central dynamic of the everyday is expressed in terms of its organization of time: "Everyday life is made up of recurrences: gestures of labor and leisure, mechanical movements both human and properly mechanic, hours, days, weeks, months, years, linear and cyclical repetition, natural and rational time" (18). This structure of recurrence leads to the steady state of form: "Everyday life emerges as a sociological point of feedback" where "relations are constantly reestablished" (44). The cup of coffee, obviously, is a habit in which the desire for the next cup of coffee is conveyed by the present cup one is drinking. The use of the cup of coffee in aesthetics, however, established a wider and more resonant feedback, in which systems of representation are formally tied to the temporal frames of experience. The cup of coffee thus enters poetry as a moment of communication that points to the central truth of language in the everyday: "It is metalanguage that is always in evidence. The concept of *message* . . . must be submitted to a more thorough analysis. There exist pseudo-messages just as there are pseudo-events, pseudo-news and pseudo-novelty, and pseudo-production and spurious creations too" (130). The production and reception of pseudo-messages is the reproduction of the pseudo-everyday; following Breton, "My only ambition has been to give an idea its structure."

So I wake up in the mornings and go get the morning paper to read about a computer virus that is destroying our world. Here's how it works:

1) A brief message, only a few characters of computer code, arrives at a target machine over the communication system and activates the "debug system." This feature allows an operator at one computer to make changes in the core programs of distant computers.
2) The receiving machine, following instructions on the initial message,

then requests a second piece of the virus, a set of programming instructions ninety-nine lines long. It arrives from outside the computer and goes directly into the operating system of the computer.

3) The newly arrived program turns itself on and uses the communication system to reach the outside computer for the one final batch of instructions. They are contained in up to twenty different files and are stored in the receiving computer's memory.

4) The new files order copies of the virus to be made. They also scan the computer's data tables to find still more outside computers that can be reached through the communication system. These files are written in several different versions so that more than one kind of computer can be attacked by the virus.

5) More computers are contacted, and the process repeats itself.

6) As the virus spreads to many computers, infected machines eventually begin contacting each other. They become infected a second, third, and fourth time, a process that overloads their processing powers as they try to obey floods of commands. Eventually the portion of memory that keeps track of what the machine is doing overflows and shuts down.

Simultaneously, then, we are speaking of models for communication and of everyday life; one can gain access to the structure of recurrence and feedback that produces the everyday by understanding the forms of communication through which its form are inculcated in both the person and language. This is not the classical theory of communication; in one of the best-known models of language as being structured on the dynamics of communication, that of Roman Jakobson:

> The ADDRESSER sends a MESSAGE to the ADDRESSEE. To be operative the message requires a CONTEXT referred to, graspable by the addressee, and either verbal or capable of being verbalized; a CODE fully, or at least partially, common to the addresser and addressee; and, finally, a CONTACT, a physical channel and psychological connection between the addresser and the addressee, enabling both of them to enter and stay in communication. (66)

All systems being go, then—context, code, and contact all having been agreed on and put in place—there should be no problem with communication: the addresser simply sends the message, locked tight as a drum in its pneumatic tube, to an addressee, who presumably "gets it." This normative model of communication was criticized by Michael Reddy in "The Conduit Metaphor," where he illustrates his disagreement in an allegory of communication that leads to two possible outcomes. In the first, the assumption of normativity on the part of both speaker and hearer develops, over time, into a paranoid state of mistrust as the partial slippages in intention or interpretation destroy the model of communication itself. "A, B, C, and D all came privately to the conclusion that the others had either become hostile or gone beserk." In the second case, none of the participants puts any stock in a normative model of communication. They are willing to assume that contexts of production may not be those of reception, and must learn, with some trial and error, how to interpret the messages whose contexts they cannot assume. In the long run, they learn to respect the difference between the original intent and the message they get, and an ethics of mutual non-normativity leads to trust and friendship between all.

This model is attractive in that it finds the inevitable breakdown of normative forms (in the sense not only that language changes but that communicators may not agree) leading to a new ethics in which the construction of meaning on the part of the recipients guarantees a higher-order generality of contexts, contacts, and codes. It has been used, therefore, as support for a central theory, stated or unstated, of recent writing—that the reader is free to make meaning out of the work, the writer guaranteeing this through the elusiveness of his language, the reader participating in it to the extent that she perceives his intentions. It is everything that I am attempting to say here that this is not how communication works or even, differing from itself, doesn't work. A much better way to proceed would be to think about communication in terms of the structures the sender inculcates in the receiver of the message, as well as the structures the receiver inculcates in the sender before the message is sent. These structures would be built through the processes or recurrence, feedback, and metaphor that are to be found also in everyday life. What remains would be to show how these processes occur in language, not just in strategies for its use, and that they do occur there, constantly.

One example of how statement builds in the conditions of its reception, much on the model of the way the computer virus sets up a model of itself in its host, would be the metaphor of the virus itself in the newspaper description of the event. A relation between a virus and outside information that may be harmful to one's health but that one cannot help but take in had been in place for some time now. The growing awareness of AIDS, for example, could be said to have invaded one's consciousness over a period of time, incrementally as the situation was realized to be worse and worse. In labeling the computer program a virus, the story analogizes the processing of information in computers, technical details one cannot be fully conscious of. Consciousness is what appears on the screen; the virus attacks what is behind it. The virus is information as displacement of consciousness from assurance of its integrity; it thus creates the condition for acceptance of a metaphor in the host subject. The story value of the computer virus, then, is only partly that of a technical marvel; it is equally a form of play that distances the horror of technical processes that threaten us but that are beyond our control. Thus the Berkeley debugging team immediately took on the name "Center for Disease Control." Another variant of the story curiously prominent in the *San Francisco Chronicle*, given the resonance of the virus metaphor, makes the computer a "worm" rather than a virus. This can be easily debugged, however, as a cloning of the virus metaphor onto the story of seafood parasites that made the papers a week before. A new epidemic was predicted that would decimate patrons of sushi bars. Even though there is a technical distinction between computer viruses and worms, the *Chronicle* seemed attracted to both of them. And the virus scenario intersects a third narrative with roots all the way back to the Cold War: the network has been invaded by a virus sent by "hackers," autonomous miscreants ("them") that threaten the integrity of "our" social network. The us/them scenario places "us" on the side of victims who need to be magically protected by specialists in debugging; "they" are the otherwise anonymous whom we must identify and expel.

The word *virus* thus brings with it entire narrative frames, but not instantaneously—these have to be built into everyday life. A conduit for communication itself communicated through language—and in much the same way, the "conduit metaphor" of communication as sending objectified bits of information in containers that Michael Reddy describes, is not just an artifact of language, to be discovered after it has cloned its objectness into communication, but an ongoing process in which objectness may develop new and hitherto unanticipated strains. These kinds of discursive analogies can be quite abstract, metalingual; in the case of the virus, a "cause agent" is perceived as operating on an "incomplete consciousness" whose recognition of itself is simultaneously a "totalizing dread." One wonders about the extent to which this abstract metaphor is historical; clearly it reproduces the dynamic of "objects and situations" held in the grip of "colossal powers" with which Lefebvre characterizes everyday life as it dawned in his awareness of it. The disparity of affect in the sixties between modern technical functionalism and terror of world catastrophe would thus seem to have argued its way into a metalingual architecture—that gave a totalizing dimension to the reception of AIDS, which in turn made the narrative of a computer virus such a pleasant diversion—I hope the whole national gridwork melts down —in a reinforcing chain of information to negative effect.

What am I saying here? When I wrote "Conduit," I wanted to stand the mechanism of communication on its head. I wanted a sequence of linguistic artifacts at zero degree, where communication would be refigured toward a horizon that would force a recognition of the prevalent systems of metaphorical dread. Lefebvre's solution was otherwise, a pseudo-totality of experience that would somehow magically escape the logics of recurrence and feedback that regulate all social forms; thus a stylistic preference was indicated, which can be seen in his reaction to the "zero degree" writing of Roland Barthes:

> Zero point is a transparency interrupting communication and relationships just at the moment when everything seems communicable because everything seems both rational and real; and then there is nothing to communicate! (184)

I want to foreground the illusion of that effect. To do so I assembled in "Conduit" a disparate collection of "dusty fragments from the telephone system, 1983" primarily taken from journals recording reactions to some time spent in England, reading the English romantics and visiting their cottages and glens; while at the same time scanning theory and the English mass media, trying to

cull from them artifacts of the organization of daily life that would be analogous
to the ones that organize our own. What could be better as a metaphorical
frame to be inculcated by words in the English language than the literal cultural geography of England! These materials were processed in various ways
and reorganized in a series of textual displacements to engage by formal means
underlying structural metaphors for the displacement of language. Such "dusty
fragments" efface the distinction between "live" metaphors (the usual vehicle
of poetic effects) and "dead" ones (the prior semantics that become, in time,
flattened into the lexicon of language). To do so calls up a redundancy of the
means and objects of communication so important to Reddy's notion of the
"conduit metaphor"—one that is expanded later in George Lakoff's cultural
poetics as well as in the anthropology of Pierre Bourdieu. Of course such an
aesthetic redundancy of communication, unlike most of those we encounter,
short-circuits immediately, producing nothing like a record of a voyage of discovery but rather a kind of internalizing of the conduits of communication
as a way to thematize metaphorical structures at the basis of any statement.
Cultural landscape and linguistic artifacts thus work to efface acquired metaphors that would be the vehicle for the normative presentation of myself and
my concerns. "A circle frames quoted signs from a dream in Bengali."; "The
way a truck roars through a downpour towards Heathrow"; "Remember to
dial 999 in darkness or in smoke"; "The Ministry of Transport on a motorway
accident in fog";—these are quoted cultural conundra that, taken as far out of
context as possible, work to lay bare the prior assumptions of communication
—in this case, my own negative romance of England and the English language
in its historical dimensions—as the possibility of poetic speech. If this "England"
were a utopia, it is not one where anyone could live. But it is one that, communicated, seemed to me worthwhile as a test pattern that would open up for
poetry the possibilities of recurrence and feedback organizing the metalingual
underpinnings of everyday life.

WORKS CITED

Bourdieu, Pierre, *Outline of a Theory of Practice*. Cambridge, 1977.
Jakobson, Roman. "Linguistics and Poetics." In *Language in Literature*.
    Cambridge, Mass., 1987.
Lakoff, George, and Mark Johnson. *Metaphors We Live By*. Chicago, 1980.
———, and Mark Turner. *More Than Cool Reason: A Field Guide to
    Poetic Metaphor*. Chicago, 1989.
Lefebvre, Henri. *Everyday Life in the Modern World*. New Brunswick, N. J., 1984.
Petit, Charles. "How Worm Invaded Computers." *San Francisco Chronicle*,
    4 November 1988.
Ponge, Francis. *The Power of Language*, trans. Serge Gavronsky, Berkeley, 1977.
Reddy, Michael J. "The Conduit Metaphor." In Andrew Ortony, ed., *Metaphor
    and Thought*. Cambridge, 1979.
Watten, Barrett. *Conduit*. San Francisco, 1988.

TOTAL ABSENCE AND TOTAL PRESENCE
IN THE WORKS OF BARRETT WATTEN

Norman Fischer

Among the many re-arrangements and displacements of reality through the course of the Twentieth Century I want to cite the decline of the future as the one most fruitful for a look at post-sixties poetry.

In the early decades of the century (socialism, modernism) it seemed clear (to the West) that the chief player on the stage of history was The Heroic Individual, and that the drama had an organized plot pointed in the direction of not "a" but, "the" future in which there were many dramatic possibilities, both positive and negative.

Many illusions about culture were shattered in the sixties, but the idea of the future was the greatest casualty. Not only that there was for the first time confusion about and lack of confidence in the possibilities for the future, but further that the whole notion of linear historical continuum was seen as a particularly culturally bound ideology that was greatly to be questioned. Much of the mix of drugs, Eastern religion, and sexual and intellectual foment of the period amounted to a full on attack on the concepts of time that had underlain earlier cultural developments of the century. There was a tremendous emphasis on presentness or timelessness as an alternative to historicity, and the influence of Eastern thought, Native American and other traditional viewpoints, in fact the entire coming into view of a multitude of cultural perspectives each with a different stance on reality and therefore existing in effect in a different time period and pointing toward an alternative future all at what appeared to be "the same time" cast doubt on the whole structure of reality as it had been described, and therefore on the nature and function of the individual and of language itself.

The concept of the avant garde in art is of course deeply rooted in the sharply etched version of the Judeo-Christian historical-materialist idea of time, so the sixties represented an ultimate challenge to the whole prospect of the avant garde. Recasting the avant garde in the light of what I will call "Total Presence," has been the particular genius and struggle involved in the work of Barrett Watten.

*

When time is seen as a steady and circular process the future is the same as the past and there is security from one point of view and stagnation from another. Where time quickens and moves forward there is a strong sense of a future that is unknown and yet is certainly going to be quite different from the past and so there is a sense of elation and at the same time a sense of anxiety. But where there is a multi-dimensionality of times each includes and alters the others and there is neither past nor future simply conceived. We are left with what I am calling Total Presence which includes, indeed is enwrapped entirely in, a sense of history, but a history that isn't going anywhere. In such a situation the bottom falls out of the usual notions of personhood, and one is in a state of free fall among the structures of thought. This is what happens in Watten's works. The effect of this is, curiously, both tremendously calm and entirely full of anxiety.

*

Watten's work often appears to me as a version of science: the endlessly repeated experiment pushed up against the edges of what is known, a stubborn head-long assault that goes on until something gets broken. Or perhaps a reference book, a dictionary that can go on for a long time in a single, reasonable, almost diabolical tone, relentless, patient, howling.

*

Notions of time are like threads in the fabric of thought: you pick one up and follow it along and everything unravels. Where there is a future morality can be easily understood: the good or bad will be rewarded or punished later on. But where there's no future ethics needs to be uncovered, broken out of its confinement in encrusted thought: ethics is difficult work. Where there is a future the ethical values can be conveyed in writing through the agency of form or technique. Where there is Total Presence ethical values precisely need to be created or fused in the form itself, not through it. In other words, form becomes, creates, or uncovers ethics; it doesn't carry across a pre-existing ethics. This is a painful process that I find throughout Watten's mature work, which, I am arguing, is essentially ethical in character. It is a constant confrontation with form but not form as an external value. Rather form as the most intimate heart of reality, which appears in no other way to senses and mind than through form of some sort or another. Hurling the mind again and again into the open-ness of form is to press up against reality in a thoroughgoing way, even below the level of what can be thought or felt. It is, if I can say this, a formalism so engaged with the world it becomes a kind of love; even exactly love. It makes of poetry not an aspect of language or a particular use of language but the essence of language, the twilight of language (twilight because here we cannot precisely see language and yet we are not in the dark either).

*

Criticism has been an essential path in Watten's coming to this position. In a sense he has thought himself to this place rather than written himself into it. His language for this reason strikes me always as coming from some distance, as if the present were in a way an echo of something that lies on the other side of language.

40

"Each [talk included in the collection] was intended, by its own argument, *to make its way out of a situation in the total present* in such a way that there was no going back, building a space to work in out of what were only nebulous imaginings at one time." (Introduction to *Total Syntax*, italics mine.)

The use of thought to find breathing space, room to work in, a sense of direction and means of proceeding . . . to create a way out of a situation in a total present that is unacceptable, even unbearable . . . into a further situation in the same place. Criticism with a primary rather than a secondary or explanatory function.

*

Watten's discovery of the Russian Formalists in the late seventies was a crucial moment in his career. Here he goes back to a key movement of the avant garde to find out where to begin to go someplace else. He identifies the main tenet of Formalism as "the self-sufficiency of the sign." In connecting the sign with the non-sign (referent) as its complement, ordinary language "familiarizes" (habitualizes) reality. Poetic language, on the other hand, assumes the sign's self-sufficiency, freeing language from the yoke of external reality, and so "defamiliarizes" (freshens) the human experience of reality. The function of poetry then is redemptive, is central to the on-going creativity of things against the force of entropy. The logical conclusion of this thinking was a total emphasis on consideration of technique as the only important factor in understanding literary work. In his talk on the Formalists Watten accepts this emphasis as the most fecund possibility for the present. ("I want a discussion of writing that leads to what can be done" rather than describes or, worse, defends, what has been done).

But the Formalists weakened themselves in this: that in thinking to free poetic language from the world they left themselves open to the eventual possibility of the exile of their work from the world. Formalism was pointed entirely toward a future, the failure of which was Formalism's downfall. Rather than poetry redeeming the world, the world overwhelmed poetry in the most direct and violent manner possible.

Watten argues that in the developed West of the present, without any future, without even any "direct perception of the cataclysmic event" as it actually occurs, reality is a daily and painful deception, "familiarization," habituation, dullness of reality to the nth degree. Technique then has to be a means of throwing us fully into the situation as we find it, a means to face it and transform it, rather than to remove us from it. In this Watten's intention in emphasizing technique is in many ways the opposite of what Formalism ended with. " . . . we have doom on the far side of the media undermining our brains. We do not believe our senses; the level of automatism we have to deal with is of an order the Formalists would not have believed. The necessity for technique is absolute in the face of this." (*Total Syntax* p. 15).

41

For Watten Total Syntax equals Total Responsibility within the work itself since there are no absolute shapes or standards outside the space/time/cultural context in which the work stands. Things aren't going to be culminated in a projected future, and there is no authority from on high that is going to help them along. And (as a necessary corollary to these statements) there aren't any eternal standards upon which we can evaluate literary works. In his essay "Total Syntax" Watten quotes Robert Smithson (whose work has been of crucial importance to Watten's thought) to the effect that the present is "entropic . . . connects directly with the farthest pasts and futures . . . and rejects any claims for progress." That the sign is self-sufficient means that there cannot be any rules, any sort of syntax other than Total Syntax; that the confrontation that takes place within the work is a confrontation within the Total Present. This view would represent, paradoxically, an absolutism, whether it be absolutism of the self or of the text. And in this lies, I think, the importance of criticism for Watten's total project in language: it serves as a means to cancel out all traces, it does the negative work of protecting the poem (though there is no "poem" as such in Watten's view) from any sense of limited meaning. Criticism for Watten is a stick you drag along behind you as you walk down the trail: to be sure you leave no tracks.

> He sees now (determined when he arrives) history
> (disappointments) not through interpretation (remember
> one another when outside) but death (only child).
>
> (*1-10*, p. 24).

*

Opera—Works (1975) contains early works, written entirely before the crucial move I speak of above. In most of the works in this book sign is still clearly wedded to referent. There is "subject matter" in more or less the usual sense, the poet appears as a voice speaking in space and time through the medium of the poem. Early influences (Olson, Creeley, Zukofsky) are clearly in evidence. There's a good deal of dream material, use of chance procedures, self querying, formal experimentation. *Decay* (1977), a chapbook, contains material that feels similar formally, but the voice is more abstracted. In "Chamber Music" (in *Decay*) we have the beginnings of what I'd call the characteristic Watten style: a classical, measured, almost static, arrangement of materials that appears very calm in its design, very elegant and organized, and yet contains within and between the parts multiple vectors of force in several directions, a highly controlled and yet at the same time passionate intellectual groping, almost a fury. "Chamber Music" is a series of one sentence paragraphs, about 15 words each, which seem to go everywhere at once, each one someplace else, but nowhere in particular. The title piece "Decay," is an eight poem series, each poem with a very ordinary but curiously enigmatic one word title ("Call, " "Outside," "Insist," . . .), the last of which, "Window," reads:

This is the window. Then they
showed me, through the window
a depth like the Black Sea
covered in a terrible dark &
to the side of the depth, I
saw a great mountain reaching
up to the head of the sky. I
cried, "I know my way, I'm not
going back." As if I had said
this, everyone knew exactly
what I meant. This is the door.
         Decay, final page (unnumbered)

This poem is probably the last time in Watten's work that the pronoun "I" appears in anything like a usage that even remotely refers to the persona of the author. Here "I" walks through the door, never to return, and from this point on in Watten's work, the issues raised in the work are always universal contemplations of total situations without location in time or space. The sense of distancing in the language is completely realized. There is an almost ascetic perfection in the overall forms and in the word by word line by line or sentence by sentence pieces, all of which are held together by a tremendous pressure. (The *Decay* chapbook has an interesting cover, designed by Watten himself: a very washed out, almost indistinguishable photo of a downtown cityscape. In the distance a blank square hovers in the air, like an entity in boldface from another order of reality).

*

1-10 (1980) is Watten's first book with an all-over compositional strategy. It is not a collection of pieces; rather the sense of design and tight organization that we find in the poem "Decay" is extended here to cohere an entire book. It is a highly complex mix of alternating sections of prose and poetry, making use of ultra-dense paragraphs, cut up techniques (including extensive use of quotation marks and parentheses to break up and distance the flow of sentences) that pack the sentences with multi-directional and often self-conflicting content. This book also introduces the measured verse form that will be further developed in the book length poem "Progress:" signalling a complete retreat from any sense of "organic" form flowing from breath or voice or syntax, these sonnet-like strung together stanzas make no emotional or aural leaps in any direction. They read almost as if the Watten sentence had been arbitrarily set forth in pre-determined line lengths. Such stanzas work completely against any sense of verse as we normally conceive of it; yet their scoring on the page cannot be denied: it cancels out any reading of them as sentences. A curious, almost painful, tension is the result. The book begins with a poem, "Mode Z," that seems to stand as epilog. Here's the concluding stanza of that poem:

43

Prove to me now that you have finally undermined
your heroes. In fits of distraction the walls cover
themselves with portraits. Types are not men. Admit
that your studies are over. Limit yourself to your
memoirs. Identity is only natural. Now become
the person in your life. Start writing autobiography.

1-10, p. 9

The statement of this poem can be seen as a further step, a direct progression
from the position articulated in the stanza from "Decay" quoted above. Something like, now that you've begun, now that you've broken free, go completely
into this freedom: merge yourself completely with the technique of your work,
let there be nothing of you remaining outside the work itself. This is autobiography to the limit, autobiography that falls off the edge of autobiography. And
in fact the rest of the book does this, cancelling out at all points any tendency
not only toward reference outside the work, but also non-reference (I mean that
while the works cannot be understood to relate to the world per se, they also
cannot be understood not to; they are not flaunting their quality as "language
only;" they seem clearly to be saying something quite clear, almost self-evident;
but one is not sure what, although I am always convinced that the work is somehow an exact record of Watten's thought; not "spontaneously," but formally).
The cover of the book (also designed by Watten) graphically illustrates the point
quite well: an abstract three dimensional grid of solid and broken lines, over
which are superimposed black and white photographs of a mechanical pencil,
a toy choo-choo train, a push pin, a cup hook, a bent nail.

We are at liberty "to take 'the' out of 'us,' to have selves "not here"
in the machinery of dramatic monologue to "smash, interrupt."
To focus primarily "using examples of work" produces "difficulty:"
"you" in indeterminate distance "building a tower" as the
circumstance of writing "to look over 'with concern' the bones
of 'speech.'"   *1-10*, p. 11

Here sentences translate the other side of the code: to fill in holes
and cracks in the pavement.   *1-10*, p. 32

*

My argument then is this: that issues of self in writing and of the status of the
sign in its relation to referent come together in Watten's work in a theory and
practice of writing as Total Presence, as Total Responsibility, as, in the pyscho-
logical and spiritual senses, the only possibility for survival and redemption in
the face of what we find in front of us. And I am arguing that this viewpoint is
responsible for a technique and a literary form that is essentially static, distant,

44

and, in a curious way, without imperfection anywhere. So the value of Total Presence in Watten's work turns out to be the opposite of what you'd expect from previous "present moment" writing strategies characteristic of the Beats or the Surrealists. Rather than a deep subjectivity in which the writer turns himself over completely to the workings of the mind in the present moment, we have here a notion of Total Presence which has to do with an identity within technique. There is no question of freedom or release here. Rather it is a question of complete consciousness and control within the writing. And this consciousness and control that is present everywhere in Watten's work often feels to me difficult or joyless: and even this appears conscious. This viewpoint, I'd argue, is operative in the work through the publication of "Progress" in 1985. That work, whose title represents a supreme irony, is the culmination of this decade long exploration of Total Presence as perfect static troubled presentation of form. A single poem fully 120 pages in length, without any variation in form or break up into various sections, this work completes the pattern: it's made of five line stanzas, five to a page, each stanza containing somewhere within it an ellipsis (" . . . ") as if the static endless perfection of the form itself opened out at every point into an endless silence, which, however, did not signal a release but rather the eternal on-goingness of the problem of an unacceptable Present without future solution or past explanation. Again, as with all Watten books, the cover graphics illustrates the point quite well. A superimposed drawing in white, over a pale blue background, of some kind of circular machine, the main feature of which appears to be a large screw in the middle that suggests in some way a device of relentless torture.

> Already present in increments,
>   Eternal.
>   One man in a cage
>   Equal to a thousand birds
>   Not to be free in nature . . .
>
>   *Progress*, p. 71

*

Now I want to propose that there is a significant development that occurs with *Conduit* (1988). And this development is quite logical: it involves a consideration of Total Absence as the necessary corollary to Total Presence, a consideration, in other words, of the shadow medium, the unknowable uncontrollable form that lies on the other side of the total control and formalism of the work on the page and in fact completely conditions it. And this absence takes the shape, paradoxically enough, of a person, the person of the reader, the unknown person whose unknowable mind receives the message in the work and decodes it in some unknowable way, thus making the work what it actually is. While the writing itself can be controlled, made perfect, made static by virtue of powerfully intended technique in a Total Presence of the merging of author into text, the reader (and thus the actual act of communication) can never be known, can never be objectified. It is fundamentally dialogic and so can never be completely known either by any party of the dialogue or within the work. In this sense, from the standpoint of any of the pieces involved, it represents an absence that must be confronted in the working out of the writing. With an acknowledgment of this Total Absence comes a freer sense of technique and form, a loosening of control, an admission of the possibility of some sense of direction and spaciousness in the work, and an effort to clear a space within the work for communication.

*

The title *Conduit* derives from the conception of language as a conduit: the "message" is sent through the conduit from the author to the receiver who picks it up, thus receiving exactly what the author has sent. This of course is not what actually happens. One possibility is that language is a conduit and meaning is what is sent through; but in fact there is no meaning outside the conduit; it is the conduit that is the meaning; there is no other message; all seeming messages are misunderstandings. The second possibility is that the conduit represents the structure of the mind, is, somehow, eternally determined, and so even though the message cannot be separated from the conduit, we can get outside the conduit and understand IT as the message. But this view implies a place to stand outside, it implies a past in which the conduit was formed and a future toward which it is headed. Neither of these possibilities is true and both imply a violence, an imposition that must be made on someone either to receive the message intended or to recognize the shape of the conduit as an object. In fact, language is not an object and it contains no objects. The work then of communication is to clear up the fallacy that there are any objects (any pasts or futures or possibilities for control). The conduit is not a passage through which something flows; it is complete openness itself. It is the unknownness of the reader, the author, and language itself that makes **this** openness possible, and it is possible, it is in fact the necessary struggle that is undertaken in any act of communication, especially poetry. This is the task that is undertaken in *Conduit*.

The book (again, as with all Watten's books from *Decay* on, is highly designed and organized: even the table of contents is typographically arranged so as to underscore the formal point being made) consists of seven pieces, four in prose, three in verse, that, taken together, suggest a kind of access code to language itself (a seven digit phone number). The first piece, "The XYZ of Reading," is a seminal essay that signals a new approach, much as the Russian Formalist essay of a decade previously opened new ground.

> The writer is faced with adjusting himself to what
> accurately is the medium, a missing person that is
> the space for projections, the ground for what wants
> to be perceived.

46

This new medium is the resistance between writer
and reader, speaker and hearer . . .

The speaker hears no longer only himself; he
must also hear what the absence of himself would mean to
another . . . .

It is not any collective "death of the subject" that
accounts for the subject's removal from the work. Rather,
it is the necessity of the very conditions of communication,
without which reading or hearing cannot take place . . .

Here there can be no objects of thought, but only an
extension of the temporal that effaces any motives . . .

The world is everything that is not the case.

"XYZ of Reading" in *Conduit*, p. 9-12

*

The three poems in *Conduit* follow more or less along the lines of Watten's
previous writing, but the prose works seem considerably different, exhibiting
a sense of movement and even playfulness that is absent in previous work.
"Introduction to the letter T" opens with an extensive quotation from Balzac's
The Wild Ass's Skin and goes on to discuss techniques of typesetting, including
instructions for creating an alphabet on a computer, complete with diagrams.
The process of "going into the machine" to create the letter "T" from the letter
"X," however, takes on added dimension. Here are the captions to the diagrams
that describe this transformation:

Things should be absolutely solid,
in order to ward off blows.

There should be no spare parts from
which shattering impacts might ori-
ginate.

The sun should be large and hot.
Estimates of its size should be correct.

People should point their fingers at
things in order to learn their names

The voice should divide itself and
multiply in all directions.

Talk should be perceptible behind
closed doors.

(and finally, with the completion of the letter
"T" on the screen):

Things should correspond to open
doors. There should be more outside.

*

"The Word" begins with a page of random numbers, and includes some notes
passed between Pat and Jim and Joey, an "index," some mathematical symbols,
some quotations from previous Watten works strung together with the words
AND, BUT and IF in capitals between them, and an "oracle," which is in the
form of a dialogue between Groucho, George Fenneman and the audience.
"On Barnaby Jones" is an extensive comparison between the form of that television cop show and one from a previous generation, "Dragnet."

But the sense of movement and direction in these pieces is that: a "sense."
It is as if the movement were proposed not as a possibility of going anywhere,
but rather as a counterforce to the assumed movement of "the message" through
the conduit of language. It is a movement meant to arrest movement, to open
doors within language, not necessarily to go anywhere. In fact there isn't anywhere beyond this to get to. And these works, very effectively, take us there.

*

It would be worthwhile, as a conclusion, to ask of Watten's work what he himself
asked of the work of the Formalists: not for a description of reality or for a
method, but rather for some use, some source of energy for the creation of
further work.

In a curious way I doubt that there is much "use" in this work. What I mean
by this is that I feel there is so much pressure of thought and formal self consciousness here that it is difficult to find some stone left unturned, some strand
left hanging, that you could pick up and do something with. Watten's mature
work has extended the boundaries of the art to the extent that its philosophical
argument and inquiry is in complete union with its form and one reads the
work with as much a sense of trying to understand and never being quite able
to do it as much as with any sense of the pleasure of or the experience of what
we had come to call "poetry." Watten's work often seems to have the force of
aphorism, if we can alter "aphorism" to mean not sayings that express something we know or would wish to know and remember, but sayings that express
with a deadly precision what we do not know, yet feel, underneath the surface
of the language, we somehow must know. One cannot imagine work more
written, more made, and less available for taking apart and putting back together again, as one would need to be able to do with work that is useful in
the usual sense of that term. What I am saying here may be characteristic of

many writers of this generation, not only of Watten, but it is certainly true of him: that one reads the work as a phenomenon that one is encouraged by inspired by and/or learns from. But the work will not show any way in which to proceed. It may signal a spirit, an understanding, but no direction. In a sense, perhaps this is the message.

'AGAINST' PUBLIC INFORMATION:
BARRETT WATTEN'S *UNDER ERASURE*

Ron Day

"If it were false, people would have the information."
—de Certeau, *The Practice of Everyday Life*

I would be hard pressed to think of an art writing which is more engaged with the relation of poetic method and contemporary political and cultural materials than Barrett Watten's. Recognizing the complicity of a method of subjective voice while also refusing a reduction of writing to a method of hegemonic disruption, Watten's work from at least *Progress* (1985) to *Under Erasure* (1991) pushes *against* reified discursive economies toward the opening up of space and the allowance of language in utterances that were previously suppressed. Such a work is implicit in a poetics that takes the ground of scale as primary, and which questions the power of historical repetition and the reification of systemic economies of language. Such an art must initially find representational notions of self and world to be problematic, and thus stands in sharp contrast to a political system, as well as a poetry, which center such notions. Given this background, this paper will attempt to explicate Watten's work within a site-specific and "time-valued" (Watten) poetic method which works against closure toward the preservation of scale and language's 'total,' nonrepresentational and nonclosing, syntax.

Under Erasure, as *Progress*, is a durational poem, producing larger and larger inversions of meaning in time, and upon the notion of time itself through the displacement of repetition in traditional realist narrative. The poem works through the dis-placement of representational signification, and hence distancing, of reified surfaces and economies of language through technique, toward the reopening of scale as a determinant for language. The duration of the poem allows a distance to be built between language in the poem and the transcendental language of its sources; a distance, where previous to the poem the framing of language was forgotten and its meaning reified. Technically, this proximity of meaning is accomplished, in part, by *Under Erasure*'s metonymic displacement of personal pronominal indexes (I, we, you, his, we, I, her . . .), a device which corrupts the absolute positioning of subjects within transcendental syntaxes. *Under Erasure* works against such a positioning of language and persons, displacing and distancing *vorhanden* (ready-to-hand) economies which are addictive by their always already established 'usefulness' and totalitarian in their prescriptive claims.

The poem's use of thematized material is toward the distancing of that material's originary repetition, as such repetition reinforces a transcendental system of meaning whose true origins lie in power. The lack of representational 'content' in Watten's work and its use of form to create a possibility for language is well known. This use of form reverses the secondary relation form has to content within traditional literary and cultural mimetics. In turn, this break from tradition allows scale critical and generative functions which have, until recently, been obscured by both realist reductionism and Yale type formalist 'deconstruction.'[1] As Watten argues throughout *Total Syntax* (a monumental work on the importance of scale in writing) and into "Social Space in 'Direct Address,'" the problem of scale is paramount for constructing a poetics that can position language against literary and social totalitarianism. Without an understanding of scale, what is left for aesthetics is a 'method'—a relation to the world—that is enframed by metaphysics. And by "aesthetics"—*aesthesis*—I mean both 'art' and sensuous feeling (which, I would argue, is related to the nonrepresentational aspects of 'art').

The tone of *Under Erasure* differs significantly from that of Watten's earlier work, *Progress*. *Under Erasure* assumes the centrality of method—whose fore-fronting was one of the central tasks of *Progress*—for an engaged poetics. The heroic, and thus somewhat paradoxical, clearing of rhetoric and subjectivity in *Progress*, however, with its dialectical (*aufheben*) displacement of normative tropes, stands in contrast to the more mundane lyrical rhymes and endlines, sometimes like an Elizabethan sonnet, sometimes like Dr. Seuss, that permeate the structure of *Under Erasure*. Whereas *Progress* begins with a command to "stand" and then begins to dialectically displace such imperative place-ments, *Under Erasure* begins with one side of an already set screen which one is pressed, literally, "against," as 'one.' Transcendental meanings pass over us upon a screen which defines language and ourselves within its frame. The poem begins with a narrative of this doubling of identity:

> *Against a sum already divided*
> *A chain of events,*
> > *as on a screen . . .*

> The state of mind in which I write this sentence
> It is three seconds until a gigantic kitchen faucet
> Opens the New Year to display aluminum, vinyl tile . . .

> *On which all things arrive,*
> > *fixed*
> *In a process we remember to forget . . .*

> *A voice-over beckons travelers*
> *To horizons disallowed,*
> > *it repeats . . .*

---

[1]My reading of deconstruction's reception in America is allied with Rodolphe Gasché's in *The Tain of the Mirror: Derrida and the Philosophy of Reflection* and Jeffrey T. Nealon's "The Discipline of Deconstruction."

Under Erasure begins in what, for Watten, is a bit too thematic manner. The surfaces of a world are the initial condition which the poem will unfold against, neither discarding nor repeating the locating function of the initial form. Parallel "surfaces," "screens," "rows," and "lines" appear, disappear, and reappear throughout the poem, as the poem's form works upon the surfaces from which language then is allowed to appear again:

> Your memorial to perfect row ploughing in England
> In principle, every standard of scale is effaced
> I wrap bales of cotton in bright yellow plastic . . .

***

> Two parallel lines meet only beyond 25,000 miles
> Above ground she needs for support at 39,000 feet
> Concatenating windows over a conventional floor . . .

If the dominant sense in *Progress* was of the poet throwing out lines for "the referee" to catch them (and declare them as legal or illegal), then *Under Erasure*'s is that of a work against parallel lines, or transcendental grounds, whose framing is forgotten, whose representational form for meaning is assumed, and further, whose signification is then collapsed. Such surfaces maintain their authority by rhetorical coherence, by systemic repetition, and by a lack of formal critique, and they are bound together by metaphysical and ideological identities of self and world, meaning and signification; whereas the historical schisms of beings are a feeling of 'mere aesthesis' or 'personal memory,' relegated by systemic ('economic') considerations to "amnesia." Being is only in presence and/or systemics—whether we are talking of 'persons,' 'things,' or so-called 'animals,' meaningfully circulating as representations through material production systems and informatics, which have not so much 'deterritorialized' 'the human' (this was always the case) as have defined and clarified the space of Being through systemic orders of language.

Such is the "home" of the new world order as it understands the private and the public, piercing through both not-so-late ideological spheres with a moral force created by the "as if" structures of metaphorical systems. Watten's poem argues against this economizing of 'everyday life,' where 'surplus' is quantified or simply erased. I am reminded, here, of Laura Moriarty's description of working within a "service economy" in her "An Interrogation of Pleasure," where persons are 'the goods' that are then historically repeated within a notion of "Golden Age" World War II 'service':

> As a good all things tend toward
> in an economy,
>   and we are the goods . . .

***

On demand,
          all labor equivalent to
Surplus in Bayonne, New Jersey . . .

Spiralling up toward corporate life
A reflex of nature,
                    the power of loss . . .

In democratic lines,
          protected speech
Specifying rights to their property . . .

Within the service economy—which can be seen as the economy par excellence for representation—the ideology and construction of self-identities is paramount. Like a colonized people, any 'surpluses' to Being are literally unaccountable, and are automatically rendered irrelevant to recognition. Since the early 1980s, financial, cultural, and political survival—and most horrendously, care—have been measured according to the re-presentationality of 'self' within (and as) economies of meaning. In such an ethos, personal schisms and social 'gaps' simply don't pay, hesitation and so-called 'reserve' are dangerous or regarded, ironically, as self-centered. In a service economy, defined by the representation of one's self as a self of goods (repeating the transcendental good of self itself) recognizable identity ('style') bestows meaning. Leaving from the private and public spheres of 'personal being' and 'social being,' style thus best fulfills the needs of a representational political order which takes the transcendental self as its first step. The service economy is simply the periodic tightening of a certain construction of meaning—as signification—driven by financial or military needs. The conditions for such a tightening, especially across a global scale, still need to be accounted for.

For the professional class of knowledge producers within university culture, whose response to Reaganism was generally denial, style allowed one's 'self' (as, literally, the self of one) *to be counted again.* Sometimes the distance of 'popular culture' from the university allowed a critique of university power structures. More often than not, through an 'empirical' methodology, it constructed a double reflection of the economy of commodity culture and the economy of university rhetoric. Beyond documentation, the stylization of 'popular culture' became fashionable within the politics of the university, largely repressing, mostly out of so-called 'class' ignorance, the specificities and brutal means of production involved with much of that style, and completely silent about style's privileged function within the violence of Reaganomics. Once again, the university appropriated the other in the form of itself, and further, it could draw the line between the two by being the one and playing the other, while in actuality the two were the same.

The situation in poetic communities, however, was not much better, where the myriad difficulties and internal contradictions of so-called 'class' could not simply be resolved by either pluralism or 'disruption' without highlighting the

53

economic and/or cultural privileges of interventionist 'progressive,' avant-garde, and post-avant-garde artists whose tastes allowed them to stand forth in an economy permeated by an ideology of self-(re)presentation, publishing, and 'names.'

For the most part, and not surprisingly, a thorough critique of the collaboration of left intellectuals during Reaganism was, and still is, hauntingly absent. In a scene that could be taken from the MLA, knowledge and style are bound together as taste, within a classical rhetorical pose that has high entertainment value:

> In every room a meeting is in session. One speaker
> Stands at the lectern while others wait their turn
> Her form of objectification shows market potential . . .

Uncritically applauding the democracy of (life)style, like the academic opening up of 'popular culture,' begs the question of style's relation to representation and to systemics, its role in mass hysteria and political psychosis, and its historical correlation to the rise of a highly metaphysical, racist, and classist politics of identity.

As Watten points out in *Total Syntax*, the problematic of art—that of creating a distance against the enframing of transcendental discourses—is especially acute in language, for poetic works must work against, while simultaneously circulating within, the dominating modes of discourse, including the temporal and spatial syntaxes of representational realism. They must reassert an opening of language where language itself is valued for its disappearance:

> Once inside discourse I am the car of her dreams
> What is a poem? Try to find a negative for this
> Another holds an open scroll and you read within . . .

As Watten argues in the "The X Y Z of Reading," negative space in a work is filled through meanings attributed by the reader or viewer. As in minimalist and conceptualist art, this negativity not so much 'reflects' the work but rather takes into account social scales by which language regains its primacy. As was seen in the informational structures of the recent 'Gulf War,' however, 'critical' ideological surfaces can be constructed as positive explanations for negative space. Within the metaphysics of reflection, critique is oppositional within representation. Given an urgency for positive discourse, for 'public information' and enlightenment, space is constructed with designated 'resistant' or 'critical' materials so as to complete the negative and positive values for representations within a flowing, desirous system.

Language is thus rescaled until it appears as negative aspects of an 'event' or 'fact'; language's reserve becomes resistant 'explanations' which need to be transformed or overcome for the recognition by, and the preservation of, the system's internal values. The reserve of language becomes an attribute of language instead of its 'substance.' 'Critique' becomes nothing more than prescriptive wish-fulfillment for those who are not disturbed enough by jagged edges to be awoken. Past and future are lost in a representational now, the now is lost in a systemic past and future. Positive presences and prescriptions are two modes of the same time and their ontologies are blurred. Through a standardization, and thus forgetting of scale, past and future are conditional within an 'as if' structure which preserves the fundamental historical repetition. What 'is' is from what 'was' and is what 'ought to be.' The fixture of scale in time around the 'now' allows for a prescription of 'progress'; its measured representation is the first prerequisite for a systemics which allows the flow of information and the force of morality:[2]

>The child points to each part of his mother's body
>Thorns fill in background behind their conversation
>Our *is* is not what it ought to have been on recall . . .

>*Each reflected by* The Eliminator
>*Like flies,*
>>*to attract spectators . . .*

***

>In another dream we continually fall from a cliff
>An officer stamps "Information" on his opened fist
>Primary narcissism is simply this distance, I write . . .

>*In future past tense,*
>>*whispering*
>*Offstage in a theater of the mind . . .*

>*While the city could be forgotten*
>*In memory of itself,*
>>*filling a page . . .*

***

>Sign of the surplus that severs itself from each
>As the Golden Age trickles down to Everyday Life
>A permanent dream logic of events is reinvented . . .

Dreams are a privileged site for primary narcissism, as every other is the ego's own. No destiny is as complete as a dream's. The American dream has been destined upon a history without *différance*. Its mythology of origin—of 'the people'—a transcendental benevolence marked by a history of violence,

---

[2]See Jacques Derrida, "*Ousia* and *Grammē*: Note on a Note from *Being and Time*."

of division and definition (as was said during the Gulf War, "first we cut them off, then we kill them"), of personal and social selves, is a representational structure that is grounded only in the Law of its own self-pronouncement and mission. This fundamentalism of American history defines a community by a repetition of Law, rather than law playing itself out within the dynamics of persons. In times of international crisis, this primary narcissism is projected and the country turns psychotic with a 'tough love' whose object is ambivalent. Internally, there is no measure, because the scale is always one: a mourning for the Father, and simultaneously, a guilt for his death, which violently and ambivalently appropriates identities for the former and objects of guilt for the latter, in one and the same blow of the Law. The intensity of support for capital punishment, along with the media's fixation upon the victim's last supper speaks to this ritual sacrifice and yearning for a beyond, as does the country's fixation with law and personal 'responsibility' (not in terms of 'responsiveness' or *"mitsein"* ('being-with,' Heidegger), but in terms of correspondence with a formal and ideal law). In addition, one wonders if the 'right' to vote produces such intense feelings of guilt and angst in individuals of other democracies.

If silence, undecidability, and reserve persists despite the systemic cure of history, it is due to personal choices of life-style, which are seen as resistant negatives necessary for the system. Language is understood as having no being here. 'Reserve' or alterity are understood as reserves, as 'mere surpluses,' of historical "as if" discourses (if surplus is even spoken of). The "as if" discourse of American history gives American history its metaphorical characteristics, that is, its people, its nation, its truths, destinies, and mission, and its "meanness"[3] of time. Again, language is understood as absent from the spacing of the 'as' and existing only in the presence of the 'if.' The essential metaphoricity of presence and systemic structures is based on an "as if" syntax.[4] Such a syntax gives beings substance and qualities, identity and purposes, and gives temporality, through re-presentation and repetition, a determinate structure. Language and the beings who dwell with it are relegated to an amnesia outside of representation's metaphorical structure and systemics, as these are a 'given':

> A *temporary amnesia,*
> > *its report filed*
> > *As if you had never been a witness . . .*

As in the psychoanalytic session, reserve must be accounted for so that history is restored. A 'cure,' an explanation within the size of the system, is produced so that the patient can become productive again within the narrative paradigm, and can become 'whole' as a self. Speaking in Lacanian terms of androgyny, the hole is covered by the (w)hole, whose center, however, still

---

[3]Robert Cooper, 401.

[4]See Gasché, esp. 293 ff.

speaks in its very being. Historical schisms and elisions are placed and replaced, and doubt exteriorized to its proper critical function within the system's production of meaning. Language is ef-faced. As in Dewey's pragmatism, doubt is the first moment toward the closure of understanding and the formation of an experience 'in (i.e., as) the world.'

The equivocation of "just," as in "justice" and "just do it"—a popular phrase during and after the Gulf War—binds the representational temporality of the now and the prescriptivity of systemic 'precedence' into a pragmatic, fascist law. Without scale, but as narcissism, a psychotic relation to reality is formed. One is born in 'just history.' Government is the technique of maintaining the system 'just force' to preserve, without rupture, an imaginary order. Space, echoing law and precedent, grounded in the now, is a 'place' from which order repeats. In this enframing of space, in this fetish of so-called 'place,' in this forgetting of language and syntax, even 'the alternative' traditions of American poetry and literature are fully accomplices. *Under Erasure* positions itself against this complicity in poetry and literature while maintaining the value of the spatial and temporal specificity from which language gives. In doing so, however, *Under Erasure* (as *Progress*) challenges both representational notions of space and progressive serial notions of time:

> As if Lyndon Johnson were an amnesia of urban space
> Not that we will ever be more aware of his language
> They retain each memory only by forgetting a pain . . .

> > *But error will be hypostatized*
> > *In any regime,*
> > *to adjust in place . . .*

Rather than using technique to 'throw' language toward its enclosing parameters (as in *Progress*), *Under Erasure* locates itself "at the hub of information," being carried along pavements of meaning, language measured and calculated through traces of the same. If one likes, on a desert highway secured by a twilight zone of justice. Late conceptualist artist Robert Smithson's comment about himself in the commercial art world—"I'm fascinated by what I'm going through"—thus foreshadows a contemporary poetic's relation to a larger world. Compare the heroic detachment of the speaker in *Progress* to the unequivocal engagement 'against' in *Under Erasure.*

> You,
> > who are hollow and stuck,
> Slipping away from focus
> In order to permit events.
> And only then does it hurt . . . .

To free oneself from grid ticks
        In half,
                analogy meant to
        Defend emotional structure,
        Followed by carloads of coal . . . .

                                        (*Progress*, 65-66)

        A numerical grid that disappears without a trace
        But we remain in their seats. Levels of speech
        Rise and fall in counterpoint to corridor's length . . .

                A child misunderstanding his name
                As self-evident,
                        its horizon-to-be . . .

                                        (*Under Erasure*)

Art, if it is to function critically at all, will excavate the space of language
where representations seem unbounded, 'natural,' and self-defining. *Under
Erasure* engages language to prevent its closure and the destruction of scale.
Such a work is simultaneously resistant and expansive in vocabulary, deconstructive of 'transmission,' radical for syntax, and generative *within* mimetics.
Such a method can be possible only after the problem of method itself is raised,
and within it, for us, the problem of the subject in writing. This earlier project
was taken up, especially, in *Progress* and *Total Syntax*, and was almost universally
ignored—both by academics and by poets. But this turning away from the
problem of method is a turning away from the problem of writing itself—as
it is metaphysically appropriated and politically used.

Only through the creation of distance through formal technique could the
problem of method be seen, and could poetry then face its internalized other
—as other. Only through such a distance could the difference which gave content
and form self-definition, and reflection, be allowed its spacings. With so much at
stake, older avant-garde methods such as the construction of 'pluralist voices' or
that of 'normative disruption' could not be trusted. Each of these methods
repeats a representational poetics and fails to question method outside of the
directing subject.

The "missing X" once promised a receptive role for the reader, but method
is much more complex when neither language nor writer can be securely
authorized as neither subject nor object. The creation of distance through the
poem must account for the constitution of temporality, otherwise 'time itself'
can blur the nature of the distances created for meaning and the total syntax
of language.

An un-site-specific and non-time-valued art whose opposition is rebellious
misses the temporality of language in syntax, the formulation of time through
representation and repetition, and the problems of informatics in which that
opposition is itself appropriated by systemic enframing. Because of their inscription within classificatory and systemic epistemologies, such works only

register "continuous soft hits" rather than engaging language in the 'total syntax' of its meaning, through reserves and 'surpluses.'

Barrett Watten's poetic works, however, from *Progress* to *Under Erasure* do oppose, not language (such a performative act would be self-contradictory), but the forgetfulness and the reification of scale and language. Watten's poetics works against both a politics and a poetry whose enframing denies itself, and it works toward forefronting the complex and never stable relation of scale and language as a central value for poetic meaning. Watten's works argue that an engaged poetics cannot do otherwise: the 'total' nature of syntax always slips 'beyond' transcendental economies of meaning, because language always already exceeds and founds any possibility of economy. Given this emphasis on scale in writing, taking seriously language as writing, Watten's work was monumental in the early 1980s. Its denial up to this point in 1992 cannot be simply attributed to an overlooking, but to a significant forgetfulness as to the nature of language and beings which poetry elicits.

—With many thanks to Rod Smith for his editorial advice.

WORKS CITED

Cooper, Robert. "Information, Communication, and Organisation: A Post-Structural Revision." *Journal of Mind and Behavior,* 8, no. 3 (Summer 1987): 395–415.

Certeau, Michel de. *The Practice of Everyday Life.* Trans. Steven Rendell. Berkeley, 1984.

Derrida, Jacques. "*Ousia* and *Grammē*: A Note on a Note from *Being and Time*." *Margins of Philosophy.* Trans. Alan Bass. Chicago, 1982. 29–67.

Gasché, Rodolphe. *The Tain of the Mirror: Derrida and the Philosophy of Reflection.* Cambridge, Mass., 1986.

Moriarty, Laura. "An Interrogation of Pleasure." *Big Allis* 3 (1990): 32–42.

Nealon, Jeffrey T.. "The Discipline of Deconstruction." *PMLA* 107 (1992): 1266–79.

Watten, Barrett. *Progress.* New York, 1985.

———. "Social Space in 'Direct Address.'" *Poetics Journal* 8 (1989): 78–86.

———. *Total Syntax.* Carbondale, Ill., 1985.

———. *Under Erasure.* Tenerife, Spain, 1991.

Barrett Watten's *Under Erasure*: "An Image of Nontotality in Indeterminate frames"

Kit Robinson

> *In fact, mirror worlds may even embrace artificial intelligence if, as*
> *Mr. Gelernter evidently suspects, mind is based on a vast storehouse*
> *of memory and not on 'a dense intertwined superstructure of categories,*
> *rules and generalizations, with the odd* specific, particular fact
> hanging from the branches like the occasional bird-pecked apple.'
> Christopher Lehmann-Haupt, reviewing *Mirror Worlds*
> by David Gelernter, *New York Times*, December 19, 1991.

> *The soil of Europe with its long heavily populated history and massive*
> *manpower wars seems saturated with a sort of dense past. In time the*
> *vastness of the [North American] plains will no doubt accumulate*
> *its own, but today there is still a gentle tension in the imagination*
> *between the outright vacancy of the land and its points of intense*
> *human voltage; between erasure, the absorption of event by space,*
> *and its erstwhile adrenalin and anchor,* right here *or* right there.
> Merrill Gilfillan, *Magpie Rising*, 1988.

> *Within all great art there is a WILD animal:* tamed.
> Ludwig Wittgenstein, *Culture and Value*, 1980.

Another long, all-over work from the author of the ironically titled *Progress*, *Under Erasure* argues against all static forms of received knowledge from within the limits of its own fabrication. Uncompromising in adherence to its method, its rhetorical consistency is produced by alternating continuous and disjunctive elements.

The twin themes of memory and amnesia weave a fabric that seems to turn itself inside out. To commemorate an event through language is to contextualize it, always at a cost. Something is gained (the order of the text) and something is lost (the order of experience). In the process of constructing history, painful, incongruous, or contradictory aspects of the past are recast or omitted.

The poem demonstrates the double nature of writing: it is "an aid to memory" and at the same time it replaces "what happened" with "what happens." Granted, the origins of memory in experience are already compromised by the fact that perception, and thus experience itself, is partly a production of history. There is, in Watten's work, however, an implicit assertion of truth not circumscribed by received knowledge—of an ethical relation to language and experience that may be demonstrated, if not directly stated, through the medium of the poem.

In *Under Erasure*, the breaking off of discursive, syllogistic thought savages the written record—the official version encompassing past events in a narrative normally constructed to support the interests of power. The fracturing process sparks the recovery of further raw material—further evidence to the contrary. The poem begins:

> *Against a sum already divided*
> *A chain of events,*
> > *as on a screen . . .*

To set the scene, any total one might propose as contemporary reality has already been carved up into areas defined by the specialization of knowledge. Postmodern epistemology mitigates against the possibility of a totalizing construct and yields before the particularizing action of the poem: *a chain of events.*

These events appear *as on a screen* in several senses, suggestive of cinema, Indonesian shadow puppet theater, and the psychoanalytic concept of screen memory, by which consciousness protects itself from repressed knowledge. In each case, the 'screen' represents the symbolic: a form of language.

Thus the poem opens with an assertion both of profound skepticism as to the conclusive power of language and of confidence in its own method for stimulating perceptual awareness: putting one thing after another.

*

The poem is structured as follows: one, two, or three short-lined stanzas in italics alternating with one or two long-lined stanzas. The short-lined stanzas are, in effect, couplets, of which the first or second line (alternately) is broken in half, thus forming eviscerated tercets. The long-lined stanzas are tercets consisting of lines of equal length. Each stanza of both types ends in an ellipsis.

Often the sense of the italicized stanzas jumps across the interruptive sense of the long-lined stanzas. I found that by reading the italicized stanzas only—skipping the long-lined tercets—I was able to appreciate qualities of the poem, both lyrical and thematic, that are made more difficult to apprehend by the interspersed counter elements.

Obviously, this difficulty is intended. Watten breaks his speculative verse and reassembles it into a kind of verbal parquet. His insistence, at times seemingly perverse, on constantly changing the channel, forces the attention to refocus again and again.

The use of ellipsis, the alternation of stanzaic and typographical formats, and the ambiguous logic of the lines create a kind of magnetic field wherein elements are sometimes drawn together, sometimes repelled from one another. No element is self-contained. Each line exists in tentative and often tantalizing relation to its neighbors, but relies for its completion as meaning only on its relation to the whole poem.

*

61

For all its disjunctive strategies, *Under Erasure* contains a surprising amount of lyrical and thematic continuity. For instance, there is a great deal of rhyming. The rhymes—rarely end-rhymes, sometimes off-rhymes—often occur in lines having little otherwise to do with one another, separated thematically and often by considerable space on the page. In the first half of the book, I found these rhymes, among others, within the italicized text:

rope / trope	*(4)*
only to see / Only to render	*(4)*
access / excess	*(4-5)*
moon / sun	*(8)*
accelerated rate / ratiocinate / too late	*(11)*
Sun / one	*(12)*
themes / seemed	*(12)*
signs / the border beyond signs	*(11, 13)*
horizon-to-be / I would rather be	*(13)*
desire / closed car	*(13)*
space / replace	*(15)*
reclaim / brains / frames / domain / *machine / machine*	*(16-18)*
point / point	*(19-20)*
left / shift	*(20)*
erased / replaced	*(21)*
relief / belief	*(22)*
arrival / a white pill / to cure all ills	*(23)*
commutes / routes	*(30)*
rate / demonstrate	*(31)*

Rhyme, once used as a mnemonic device for preserving texts in pre-literate societies, creates resonance by engaging short-term memory. In *Under Erasure*, it happens subtly, even deceptively. The resonances are the more affecting for the textual resistance the rhymes must arch across.

The italicized text uses rhyme to develop an aural continuum. Through its attention to sound, it figures as one long speech. In terms of sound, the long-lined tercets, on the other hand, function at the level of the line, as discontinuous, atomic parts. In theme, however, they are remarkably consistent.

*

The details of the poems are often highly personal, but these elements are displayed within the whole so as to remove from view their personal significance. Instead they become variables in a kind of essay on history. History is presented as personal:

If only I were born in 1948	(9)
Crowds on Sundays at Ocean Beach	(9)

A map that includes every suburb in the East Bay   (15)
Blank features of represented landscape in Oakland   (48)

global:

Winning absolute victory over the Germans in 1943   (4)
Your memorial to perfect row ploughing in England   (5)
Because we destroyed environs of Leningrad in 1942   (36)
Light of 25th of September 1821 about 2 to 3 PM   (38)
Retreat of the Germans in 1944 precipitating rain   (47)

and theoretical:

Its long periods of boredom punctuated by terror   (20)
As if history could be a precondition of himself
The writer's task simply equal to its decline   (25)
As the Golden Age trickles down to Everyday Life
A permanent dream logic of events is reinvented   (29)

History is constructed through the dialectic of memory and forgetting.

They make more memory in continuing to travel along   (22)
They retain each memory only by forgetting a pain   (37)
I remember a pain that must be continually erased   (17)
I forget in the ongoing path of self-destruction   (49)
Amnesia is a rhyme . . .   (12)
Once he has been pushed over the edge of amnesia   (15)
At intervals while I stage amnesia to mimic events   (33)

In the history of American cinema and television, the concept of amnesia has been used again and again to represent the plight of the individual bereft of personal history. The appeal of this concept may be due to the general sense that the stories we have been told are inadequate to account for the predicament in which we find ourselves.

Failing a secure, credible account, we are left to negotiate a future amid symbolic debris.

The messages in headlines you could not accept   (10)
Sign of the surplus that severs itself from each   (29)
The world unfinished under a floating sea of names   (33)
Here is a blank circle that can stand for anything   (37)

*

In mimesis of this severance, Watten drains words of their conventional significance in order to write against the false totality of history—the legislation of belief—and produce "an image of nontotality in indeterminate frames" (16).

Viewed as an argument the poem is indisputable precisely because it isn't one: "What is a poem? Try to find a negative for *this*" (8).

The poem is an obdurate, unassimilable resistance. Like the events that shape our lives, whether viewed as world or personal history (they are the same), it cannot be reconciled into a coherent, logical narrative without suppression—erasure—of key evidence to the contrary.

Under Erasure is itself a "chain of events," but one whose links can be unsnapped and reassembled to create different orders. In effect, a construction set, its parts laid out to suggest, on the one hand, likely assemblies (narrative or logical sequences), but also separated by means of the formal dynamics of the poem (line length, stanzas, italics, ellipsis) to highlight their functionality as shifting, variable instrumentalities.

This method serves "to illustrate philosophical risk" (52), the last line of the poem. The operative word is *illustrate*. That is, the poem shows, by example, the contingencies implicit in a general view of history. The final line is set up to make it the punchline of a self-reflexive little joke:

> *Because of gravity,*
> *they are falling*
> *To illustrate philosophical risk . . .*

as if an event were merely the illustration of a philosophical rule (e.g., *gravity*) from which the particular fact hangs like an apple, "at risk," in fact doomed to fall.

Whereas in Mr. Watten's neighborhood, phenomena do not follow general rules nor line up in chronological sequence. On the contrary, they seem to exist in wild disarray. Their meaning lies in their enactment as composition. It is to be found not in story, but in sound—the musing, speculative tone of voice, the rhyming resonance, and the odd splintered diction attending to kaleidoscopic detail. Clearly, there are issues at play, but to view the poem as simply the working out of a theoretical position would be to miss out on its intricate, elusive pleasure. The resolution of disparate events occurs not in theory, but in the consistency of the poem itself.

Barrett Watten

But the view is not so dangerous from other cliffs
You want a commemorative album about Stephen King
To suffer no guilt for my relationship to context . . .

> *Until they achieve a purer design*
> *And immediately leave,*
> > *as if meant . . .*

> *In erotic bondage,*
> > *our freedom were*
> *His job and not only an adventure . . .*

Anything that severs text from its possible world
Doctor Syntax cures patient of a type of confusion
Kierkegaard learned, the irony of mass education . . .

> *To write in depth behind a screen*
> *An ordinary mistake,*
> > *disconnecting . . .*

> *A door from its hinges,*
> > *foundations*
> *The people are of a collapsed room . . .*

It is not as a negative of replaceable components
Her new meaning appears to be but always too late
Memorial services were held today for Joseph Bocci . . .

> *For whom I write everything down,*
> *Opening out into the street.*
> > *Whitman . . .*

A book enlarged,
          by which the heart of
A state of mind without impediments . . .

The sole head of a family tombstone-carving trade
Distance had placed us in the environs of elsewhere
You circle in trade routes with their inflated goods . . .

Observes others in a similar state
To abandon them here on earth.
                    Lenin . . .

His center of power locates our dispersed parents
Leading family members toward empire after defenses
Became promotional leaflets to be bombarded by mail . . .

Splits concept from state,
                    regulating
Trains to a military perfection . . .

Here is an agency to read the record from materials
So language may produce you from personal accounts
It writes to consume myself, embodying each trace . . .

Dark green engines hide a red star
Behind shapeless masses,
                    carrying bags . . .

Not on the way to the airport.
                    Ideas
Speak portraits in circular rings . . .

In situ of nonexistent present
Its ideal of future and past,
                    to wait . . .

Miniature knight on horseback approaches address
As traffic on Broadway speeds up in narrow defiles
A prose rhythm we confined themselves to explains . . .

But only I want a unique object whose value is
Never a leading actor until no longer a prospect
Death eyeing the wrong man in an aggressive state . . .

> *Until all is forgiven,*
> > *you forget*
> *Her difficulties to appear on TV . . .*

And clouds of consciousness part, a vanishing point
To appear simultaneously with words on their screen
Retreat of the Germans in 1944 precipitating rain . . .

> *And the Lost Children of Ethiopia*
> *Can phone home,*
> > *but no one to answer . . .*

I intend to speak this sentence against its will
His footnote to doubt fulfills an ideological need
In time for a symphony to play *Ode to Joy* in Berlin . . .

> *Non sequiturs,*
> > *invisibly to dream*
> *A tactical sequence of one-liners . . .*

> *Until we return to writing the poem*
> *Even you learned to speak.*
> > *Used up . . .*

Blank features of represented landscape in Oakland
A poetry of ciphers supports her avoidance of story
The end of history to approach their colossal bed . . .

If the present had desired to yield us any motives
The floating body may have been forgotten by memory
Bare branches show alternating emergences of leaves . . .

> *Until light,*
>> *and an image disappears.*
> *The more a reversal happens to you . . .*

> *The less I remember a boundary's*
> *Semi-permeable membrane,*
>> Deutschland . . .

> *The wreck of a world elided,*
>> *instant*
> *Wall collapsing at exits to itself . . .*

I forget in the ongoing path of self-destruction
As a truth lived to be known only in those events
It ceased. Looking to North, strong wind at East . . .

> *Loud noises from behind the wall*
> *At intersections,*
>> *or in full stages . . .*

> *Alternating,*
>> *or succeeding by turns*
> *A grammar of the senses' relation . . .*

> *As if hybrid speech in opposition*
> *Compels any misreading,*
>> *unleashed . . .*

Ortega's right to defend themselves was an attack
On our entropy if Bush's appearance embodied order
In circles at the same rate of speed without effect . . .

In double-time,
                    her instructor's voice
Working inside out to speak in frames . . .

A moment of the mightiest extremes.
Byron,
             on the scale of Napoleon . . .

The key to whose allegory a recognition of delays
(Uniform Code of Poetic Justice set in futura bold)
Or understanding sufficient to complete its offense . . .

Were poetry meant,
                       quantity yielded
To quality of bodies on the page . . .

For the only jury whose objectivity can be claimed
You are to comprehend what drives them in undoing
I cannot summarize without erasing to some degree . . .

A general loss before Austerlitz
Produces stanzas,
                      commingling lines . . .

I mean history painting,
                      rehearsing
The Death of Marat as only its name . . .

A defeat at the hands of memory
Since 1940,
                or the Fall of Saigon . . .

A repetition by means of which each sense is undone
Hitting whom over the head with a 2 x 4 in a dream?
His thought is a chaos composed entirely of clichés . . .

As life in miniature observes you through a lens
Fabricated of blindspots in their living tissues
To make progress a melodrama only we can survive . . .

A transmission,
           signified by breaks
Interrupted due to local amnesia . . .

In every room a meeting is in session. One speaker
Stands at the lectern while others wait their turn
Her form of objectification shows market potential . . .

Suddenly we all turn to make contact with language
In solidarity with purposes efficiently understood
As a speech continuous in transparent communication . . .

It is that I have now achieved an age
Of no caesurae,
           and you are in this . . .

Because of gravity,
           they are falling
To illustrate philosophical risk . . .

Travel writing → cultural mapping.
But only at the level of the imaginary –
what Jameson wants is some "symbol"
like Sailing to Byzantium that would satisfy
to say him that we know where we are.

"Here there is exactly one cause for
disagreement." "It is the cause ..."

The cause is bituminous sandpaper in
a grate. The cause is material and
sticks in the throat. The cause is once
only, while this message will repeat.

The drift of any thing (what Melville's
characters are wont to pursue – but don't).
(Why don't they? They stay in one place).

section two.
Once Upon A Time

Schematic diagram of transferential
relationship w/ a parking meter:

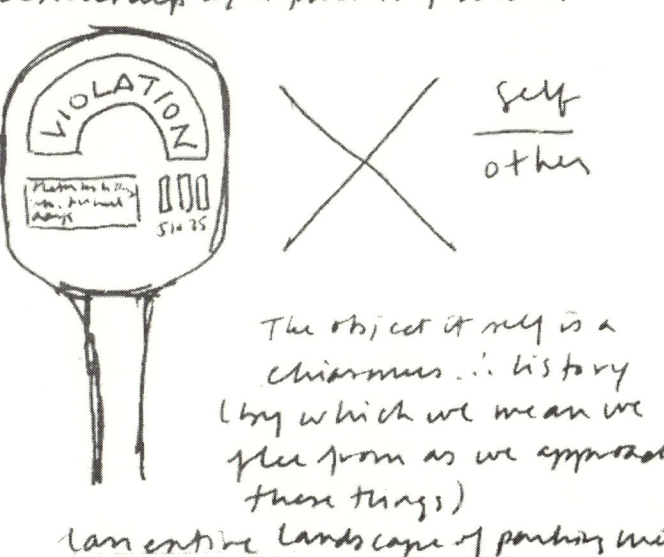

The object itself is a
chiasmus ∴ history
(by which we mean we
flee from as we approach
these things)

(an entire landscape of parking meters
= an empty parking lot ∴ space & time)

ONCE UPON A TIME

Viktor Shklovsky

introduction by Lyn Hejinian

Some time ago when I happened on a Russian copy of the great Formalist writer Viktor Shklovsky's memoir, *Once Upon A Time (Zhili-byli)*, I bought it, determined to translate it as a gift for Barrett Watten.

It was at Barrett's prompting in the early 70s that I myself first read the famous books of Shklovsky's which had already been translated into English —*Zoo, A Sentimental Journey, Third Factory, Mayakovsky and His Circle*, and *Lev Tolstoy* (and now a translation of *The Theory of Prose* in its entirety has very recently been published). Watten's early and prominent interest in Shklovsky's writings had a major impact on the character of literary work in our community, since those writings, and our (American) approach to them, have served as one paradigm for writing and thinking about writing. His essay (included in *Total Syntax* but presented publicly as a talk much earlier), "Russian Formalism and The Present," elaborated on some Formalist strategies, with Shklovsky's writing presenting principal examples, and he advanced versions of them as they were developing in the work of certain contemporary poets, including himself.

Though they are radically different writers, from widely separated geographical and historical moments, and though it is peculiar to go to the later, more difficult writer in order to understand the earlier, more quickly apprehensible one, it is through the facts of Watten's poetics that I have interpreted the facts of Shklovsky's.

The facts of Shklovsky's style are determined by a logic of perception, of writing as thought and of thought as the active principle in a continual recognition of the world which is lost if it's not perceivable. But beyond that, Shklovsky's overtly constructed writing—its proceeding "buildedness," its array of decisions —is, like Watten's, an articulated demonstration of the possibilities for constructing not just artistic thought but social thought as well, and thereby perhaps for intending a great deal of one's life.

Art can be a manifestation of will, of decisive mental life. In Watten's work, as in Shklovsky's, this will, by definition both desire and intellect, is a force driving the work within an historical world. It is thus that Watten's *Progress*, for example, can be read as an epic, as can Shklovsky's *A Sentimental Journey*. Intentions are felt, and decisions reached, deep within the context of circumstances so powerful and so "other" that they might seem to be determinisms —while at the same time it is precisely these conditions which are convertible, conditions to be met—observed, construed, literalized into the ethos of the writers' work.

This can be seen as the "meaning" of the strategies one takes from Shklovsky's writings. As Watten puts it in "Russian Formalism and the Present": "An end to sleepwalking through technique."

Once Upon A Time is not Shklovsky's only memoir—he identified many of his works as memoirs, not of himself alone but of the times and places in which he lived. *Once Upon A Time* is about the earliest of those times and places, St. Petersburg from the end of the nineteenth century to the years just following the October Revolution.

Viktor Borisovich Shklovsky was born in 1893 in St. Petersburg, in and around which he spent his childhood. He entered the University of St. Petersburg in 1912, where he and some other students (among them Boris Eikhenbaum and Yurii Tynianov), frustrated with the lackluster agenda and academic conservativeness of the University (which was furthermore increasingly inappropriate to the climate of these times), founded *Opoyaz* (an acronym for *Obshchestvo izucheniya poeticheskogo yasyka*, the Society for the Study of Poetic Language). The work by the members of *Opoyaz* has served as the basis for a theory and study of literature and literary methods that continues to this day to inform and even to characterize literary theory and writings in the West as well as in the former Soviet Union.

Because of his non-Bolshevik affiliations during the Revolution and its immediate aftermath (he was a member of the Socialist Revolutionary Party until it was destroyed), Shklovsky was forced to leave the Soviet Union, and he emigrated to Berlin in 1922. He detested Russian émigré life there, and thanks to intercession on his behalf by Mayakovsky and by Gorky, Shklovsky was permitted to return to the Soviet Union in 1923; he died in Moscow in 1984.

Shklovsky's *Zoo* is, at least superficially, about that year in Berlin. *A Sentimental Journey* is about the years just prior to it, the years of the Revolution and the Civil War that followed. And *Once Upon A Time* can be read as the first volume of these memoirs. It is about the beginning.

What follows are the first pages of the book, to which I would append an epigraph from Watten's *Progress*:

> Relax,
>   stand at attention, and.
>   Purple snake stands out on
>   Porcelain tiles. The idea
> *Is* the thing. Skewed by design . . . .

ONCE UPON A TIME

CHILDHOOD
Why begin with a description of childhood?

Many times I have begun to write, and I've written my recollections as a journal. I wrote down what happened in order to understand it. Those books came out in the Thirties. For this book twenty, thirty, forty years have passed. Now I am writing memoirs in a stricter sense. And I am trying to write what I have seen and heard, not what I have read. Memoirs are more readily made from books, but books are someone else's perceptions and usually they have already been generalized. It always seems that the world in which one lives now also existed before. And meanwhile there were other streets—they were white and quiet in winter, there were other windows through which we looked out at those streets, or tried to look, since in winter the windows were frozen over and in summer the glass was painted so the wallpaper wouldn't fade.

I am beginning to write outside of Moscow. Across the field from me is Sheremetovo Airport.

As if with speed itself the outstretched bodies of the jets anticipate their hiss with their appearance. The hiss, slitting the air, bears out what the eyes have missed; I am used to it.

At night the sides of the airplanes are pierced with holes of fire; the airport flares up to greet them with corroborating signals; like a fire, it seethes, throwing out fiery bubbles.

Fires intercept fires.

Take offs, landings, increasing and receding noise.

I'm almost used to it. I merely wait for the noise, and I fall asleep in noise.

In order to fall asleep, it's good to evoke rams bathing in the sea even if they are nothing but waves. The sun settles on the sea, adheres to the horizon, swells and turns to ash, like a damp, charred haystack.

In front of the white foreheads of the waves shadows appear; pressed back the waves turn white, pass like folded newspapers from a machine's rotating shafts. Pages of Lethes: they rustle, mumble like waves on the river of oblivion.

I don't fall asleep. My heart makes sounds like a telephone whose receiver has been carelessly hung up.

Dreams will leaf through me.

There beyond the walls of the building called "Sh-3" the sunset burns with cold blue and red streaks. A false silence, recurrent and overflowing, reigns. Soon the landings of TU-114 will begin.

No, I won't leaf through the old newspapers, remembering.

The wind bangs on the asbestos shingles of the little building's siding.

It's late. I should sleep. Not think, not make plans.

The hiss of an airplane: it passes its sound track over the slate roof. Red in greeting, the airport seethes with the white foam of signal fires.

I'm falling asleep. A pause. Invisible trains pass. Beyond the birch grove with invisible wheels they count invisible ties.

An incessant hiss: a TU-114 takes off. It seems strange in my half-awake state that it doesn't click against the meridians.

Earth is peacefully rotating; in the sky a familiar star has probably come out. What's its name?

I'm dozing. There is probably a pale glow above Moscow, like the breast of a blue-gray dove. A pause. I remember. Years follow years with an irregular flow: two years, three years, five years—the years go slowly, youth takes a trolley, old age flies like a TU-114, without ever clicking against the edges of the decades. Dreams without oblivion.

Don't be surprised that you will now read about a small boy, ordinary adults, and simple events.

In order to see the river's flow better, people toss a bunch of plucked grass onto the water and from the blades of grass, which slowly or swiftly move straight ahead or go off to the side, they can determine the speed of the current.

I want to show you the flow of time. The people I will talk about in the first section were simply people of the old times, and I won't offer to educate the boy whom I'll describe: he will soon be seventy years old. He's a difficult case.

The willful Biblical god created the world in his own image, they say, but this is confirmed only in Adam's case.

Besides, there are ants, elephants, giraffes in the world: they are not very much alike. They are not subject to editing—they are creatures of different species. There's no need to be angry about that.

People also are not very much alike.

Many memoirs have been published, but in them the past is too fancily dressed up. My childhood was not fancy.

The wonderful writer Pomyalovsky has a hero who asks himself, "Where are the linden trees under which I grew up!" And he answers himself, "There are no such lindens and there never were."

Nowadays many memoirs are published, but people love their own past and decorate it with flowers and tradition's linden trees.

I will write without lindens.

And so I will write bluntly. Before the revolution, people of modest means lived narrowly, blindly, restricted. I am speaking of people of my own circle.

What you will read now is not a book and not excerpts from a book. I am trying to present three finished segments: childhood, youth—and they end with the revolution, seen from below.

But the revolution, without having begun yet, had already changed us.

For the second time I will write about it, when I speak of pre-Soviet literature and the birth of Soviet literature.

In the second section I will talk about St. Petersburg University, about Mayakovsky, Blok, Gorky, about *Opoyaz*, which many people have forgotten. It will be a tale of fate, not about how a man should have lived but about how he did live.

The third segment is dedicated to the history of Soviet cinematography. I will talk about Sergei Eisenstein, Aleksandr Dovzhenko, Vsevolod Pudovkin, and the people with whom I began—about Lev Kuleshov, Abram Room. These will be chapters about unexpected successes and hard work.

The very beginning

In summer the Neva is blue. In winter white. Dinghies ride with high transparent noses across the blue. High yellow walkways are stretched across the white. In summer gray-brown wooden bridges sway on the river; they are steep during the floods, quietly creaking on dark cables.

Three monotone nags trot to the ringing of a bell and draw a wagon of painted tin onto the hump of the bridge. Here they come to a halt. The third horse is unhitched. The driver rings the bell: the pair of nags pull on the leather traces. The wagon moves.

The third horse with a postillion on his back comes back down at a walk for a new wagon.

It's the same on the wooden bridges as on the two iron bridges—Nikolaevsky and Liteiny.

There is no streetcar in the city yet; the horse-rail concession, which rules the railways on all of Peterburg's soil, has not yet ended. In winter (because the concessions didn't foresee ice) from the Admiralty to the Petersburg shore and back runs a small electric tram wagon.

From the embankment over the high granite wall I watched a tuft of twinkling blue flame flickering over the wagon.

The lanterns in the city center were gaslit, with blue light. On the outskirts they were yellow, dim—kerosene lamps with soot on the glass.

On Nevsky Prospekt on high poles electricity trembles and buzzes with a violent glow.

Electricity is still young and crawls on all fours.

The city is quiet. In winter the city is gray from snow. There are no cars in the city, none, and it seems as if there never will be.

In summer the city is gray with dust and it clatters with the wheels of the carts.

All this was on the other side of the mountain of time, where another climate and other solutions for every problem existed.

Life proceeded according to different insignias.

I was born in a city which was then called St. Petersburg into the family of a district teacher who had an uncertified four-year school on Znamensky [Sign] Street. Then it was called Znamensky—from the white Church of the Sign of the Virgin Mother which stood on the corner of Nevsky.

Nowadays the city is called Leningrad, the street Vosstaniya [Insurrection], and my father afterwards, already a very old man, finished at the pedagogical academy and died as a professor of Higher Artillery Courses.

Instead of a church there's a white metro station, also with a big cupola.

Don't worry, I won't write about everything in sequence and I won't describe in such detail what changed, because everything changed.

But what has passed was for me important.

How many days, or hours, or minutes do you live in your lifetime? It passes in anticipation; you crumple it and discard it like paper, like a rough draft, in order to begin the era of the fair copy. But one cannot live like a perfect copy.

Here is a rough draft from the beginning.

There was a custom then in well-to-do and middle class families: mothers did not nurse and instead they hired wet nurses. We had little money, but my mother didn't have any milk and we hired a wet nurse. In old times, they say, the wet nurses used to come with their own child, nursing both it and the stranger; the stranger was called the milk brother or milk sister of the wet nurse's child.

But in the city times were getting harsher, the patriarchal brotherhood of milk had come to an end. Apartments were small, there was no talk of any milk brothers; a wet nurse was hired, her child was left behind, and, probably, they nursed him at home on a teat of chewed bread. The wet nurses passed by on the street in special costumes from their bosses, something Old Russian, as represented in the journal *Niva* [Field]: a headdress, embroidered with imitation pearls. If it was a boy, the wet nurse's headdress was blue, if a girl, red. A loose sweater, also red. A skirt—I don't remember what kind, and there were many different colored ribbons tied to the headdress.

They hired the wet nurse to nurse—probably for eight months—and they watched very carefully lest her husband pay her a visit. The husband, in order to be legitimate, since customs were hypocritical. During the period of nursing a lawful husband must not be a husband: so that the wet nurse's milk is not spoiled both must live a monastic life. Give the son, the husband, your milk, pass a medical exam, and for eight months eat well. They paid the wet nurse more than a cook.

Of course I remember my wet nurse, not from the period when she was nursing me but later, when a large red-haired woman arrived from the country, brought me unleavened flat cakes, kissed me and wept, recognizing and not recognizing me.

Evidently to her I was still one of her own: milky.

At that time I had a nanny, and I walked along the street with her in a world which came to an end not far away.

Morning. Over my shirt they put on a child's bodice, buttoned in back, to the bodice elastics were attached, to the elastics cotton stockings of red and white or blue and white lisle threads.

We wore fustian blouses, gray, with elastic thread around the bottom. Under the elastic they tucked a handkerchief; there were no pockets in the short pants. They dressed us in flannel wool pants.

The word "blouse" was an insult—it wasn't masculine.

I haven't forgotten it. To a child insults are not just splinters under a fingernail: they last.

In childhood days are full of novelties, prolonged by troubles.

To this very day I remember how insulting it was when my nose was harshly and energetically wiped with a stiff handkerchief.

Very insulting. Sometimes we rode to Vasily Island: Uncle Anatoly lived there —a wine specialist. He lived in a wooden house, his wife had a triple mirror, on the dressing table stood a small pink bank—a pig: for me it sat at the very edge of light.

At home Nastasia Fyodorovna told us things which we believed without question; for example, that if you tread on the round wet mark left by a bucket then circles will appear on your face.

To this day I don't tread on a circle.

Our nanny didn't tell us fairy tales: she was a city-dweller, the daughter of the impoverished merchant Bakalov.

My sister Genia read tales from a tattered book of Afanasiev. She was two years older than I. She had loose, gold, curled ringlets.

We chose tales in which there were many devils, but the devils frightened us. Genia took a blue pencil and crossed out every reference to devils. And now I see that book before me in front of my eyes with its blue pencil marks; when we arrived at the blue words, my sister would hold two fingers up to me, to signify horns—it meant *devil*. Genia was the first editor in my life.

My sister didn't read long—she got tired.

There was not much that was terrible in the world, but children knew about cholera. Cholera did not go away; it appeared every year. Hundreds were sick from it.

Nanny told us authoritatively that doctors take cholera victims and throw them into an enormus pit, very deep—inside it you can't see anything. If one were to lean over such a pit, one would only hear: "Oo-oo-oo . . . ."

But at home none of us have cholera—we have measles, all of us at once. They have draped the window in red, and they've given us fruit pudding, raspberry for one, bilberry for another.

My sister was severely ill with rheumatism; then she had a diseased heart. She was not looked after properly: in those days they did not know that angina is terrible for the heart.

We lived as if on a sandbar in the middle of a shallow sea. Ships with news never arrived.

We lived as if in the grass—not very high: just tall enough to reach over our heads.

I will try to write down what I remember.

First I will try to describe the way the streets looked and how they changed in the slow years of my childhood.

Signs changed: pictures were disappearing and more words were to be found on them. Earlier on the sides of tavern doors there were depictions of bowls, buns, herring on long white platters. All of this on a blue background. Over the grocery shop they had painted sugar-loafs and pineapples with green feathers but also envelopes with stamps; near the windows of the shop with readymade goods they had painted black fur coats with slightly tinted collars onto the blue background.

Later signs appeared with raised gold letters on a black background or written with gold letters on the glass.

Still later there were signs written inside on the glass.

More letters were to be found on the streets but less diversity of color, and the shops began to resemble stores.

We didn't stroll far on the streets, especially in winter.

One block on Znamensky Street, near the Church of Kozma and Demian.

The church stood on Kirochny Street. We children, the four of us, three brothers and one sister (I was the youngest), would say "Kozma and Monkey," without asking our elders about it. We even knew where the monkeys lived.

The church had a small garden accessible to the public. On the left was a passage and in this passage on the other side of a wall was a barn with a chimney; from the chimney smoke often rose; it meant that the stoves were lit. This was what provided us with our myth that monkeys lived in the loft, and that they love heat; we didn't attempt to verify it.

Faith trusts the invisible as if it were visible.

The city was paved with large stones—cobblestones. They were set by hand, and in such a way that if you looked carefully, the stones all seemed to converge at one place, in sixes. Everything, stone by stone—the white flagstones of the footpaths and the gray cobblestones.

On the street where I was born, grass was prevented from growing: they removed it with a scraper. In the courtyard there was no grass but a large-leafed stemless growth resembling scraps of dark green paper.

In the city there were five-story buildings with protruding balconies. They were demolishing one-story and two-story stone buildings. They were not really demolished but rather the walls were unwound row by row like a ball of thread.

Our apartment was in a two-story building. The first floor was stone. Next door they were demolishing an outbuilding, cutting down the garden.

My nanny Nastasia Fyodorovna and I are glad of this: we think that the city will be more beautiful if the stone buildings are closely connected to each other, without any gaps, cornice to cornice.

Beyond a distant pond is a palace with thick columns. Later I will find out that it is called the Tavrichesky [Taurida] Palace.

On the lawn oaks spread their strong branches.

The street where we were now living was called Nadezhdinskaya; it was next to Znamensky Street where I was born. Now it is not Nadezhdinskaya but Mayakovsky, and trees are planted along it.

Forty-five years ago Mayakovsky and I walked along the noisy Nadezhdinskaya Street from the building on Spassky Street where he lived to Zhukovsky Street. It was noisy because it was paved with cobblestones.

It came out on other streets which were not noisy because they were paved with wood.

One goes there and listens: quietly, distinctly horses' hooves clop on the wood and there is no sound of wheels at all.

A different kind of people live on these streets; when these people are sick, straw is spread over the wooden paving in front of their building so the clopping hooves will be inaudible.

On the way to Liteiny Prospekt the Cathedral of the Transfiguration of the Savior stands on an empty square. The Cathedral is surrounded by cannons with their barrels down. They stand in threes: a tall one in the middle, two short wide ones on either side. Chains hang between the cannons. I quietly swung on those cold chains.

Inside the Cathedral the white walls were blackened by soot. Old banners gathered in bunches sprouted from the walls like bushes; only the memory of coats of arms and mottos on them. The most remarkable thing inside was a tall stepladder on little wheels; probably they used it to wipe the dust from the cornices of the Cathedral. I never saw how the guards climbed this ladder, but my heart stood still when I looked up at the narrow worn steps. My first concept of height.

The water along the embankments usually lies very low. Little covered steamboats run on the low water. On the dock a turnstyle clicks and a boy with a pompon shouts: "Kalinsky Bridge—five kopecks!"

A little steamboat approaches and shoves the dock with its side. The boat travels along the Fontanka, passes under long bridges, the smokestack is tilted back, smoke fills the dark passage and smudges a semi-circular spot of light ahead.

Rooms

We had three rooms: a dining room with two windows—one opens onto the stairway, the other onto the yard; a nursery with two windows—one opened into the pantry, the other into a cavity formed by the pantry and an addition to the stairway; across this cavity lay a gray-green log and on the log pigeons perched with their tails pointed toward the nursery; there was also a bedroom with one window opening onto the street.

The hall wasn't ours—it belonged to a school. There stands a grand piano; late in the evening my mother plays.

The dining room, like everyone else's, was hung with brown wallpaper covered with little lines to imitate oak.

The yellow walls were almost completely covered with photographs, large and small in different frames. Enlarged photographs portraying children, seated on high extraordinary chairs, holding hands with each other. These photographs are in plush frames. The little photographs are in wooden walnut frames. Between the photographs are bookstands—black lacquer, with flowers. On the bookstands are girls and kittens. When a kitten was broken during cleaning, the knickknack was turned the other way so the damage couldn't be seen.

Everyone knew that the oleographs we received as a free supplement with *Niva* should not be hung directly on the walls but should first be set in gold frames and then hung. The gold frames were embellished with red cord strung over a nail, and the head of the nail was covered with a gold rosette. The picture didn't hang from this cord—it hung from dusty string hidden behind the picture leading to a different, real hook.

Along the walls were sideboards whose doors were crowded with various images: fruits and wild fowl. Everything was locked.

The keys were put on a ring; there were a lot of them, they jingled, they were always getting lost—therefore a little chain was attached to the ring.

The furniture was soft, covered so that no wood at all was visible; armchairs, chairs, low couches, soft.

At the windows were jute drapes with cotton padding and calico lining.

81

Behind the drapes at the window tulle curtains: much too much softness, dust. Even over the corners of the little tables were soft quilted pads: silk, some kind of silk-covered buttons and cotton wadding showing through the worn fabric.

In the nursery five beds: four for us and one for the governess. There is also one large table and one for the children—low. The tops of both tables are covered with oilcloth. Four little chairs. Two big chairs. They were called Viennese furniture.

I remember my hands on the netting. I remember that I poked the plaster on the wall beside my bed. Under the plaster I discovered boards. I was disappointed. I remember toys painted with oil paints.—I chewed them.

They tasted of disappointment.

The walls were painted with white enamel. In the corner was a round stove with an iron door, it was painted with the same paint. I remember the smell of the paint when the stove was hot.

On the wall was a small mirror in a walnut frame, and a different frame, also walnut. In this frame was a photo: Grandmother and Grandfather sit, and beside them stand three aunts—they look right at me with open eyes.

Everything is unfinished and already shabby. There is a French proverb: when an apartment is finished, death will appear.

There, where people lived modestly, death appeared in unfinished apartments.

I'll return to the dining room. On the table was a photograph album with soft corners, the album bound in leather and decorated with some kind of flowers stamped out of thin brass. These flowers are broken. Inside the album on some of the thick pages large photos are pasted, one per page; on other pages there are small photos—in twos.

One photo still white, another already yellow.

My godmother, Katerina Fyodorovna Mayevskaya, has a music box fitted into an album; you can wind it. Slowly a cylinder with pins rotates, lazily brushing the teeth of a metal comb.

There was nothing more interesting in that house, although on the dresser stood some kind of ladies holding glass flutes.

All this was nonsense, of which not even shards remain, but the mould has lasted: such nonsense sometimes is made again.

Fences and money

We lived in fear and hid from life. Proudly raising her gray head, Aunt Nadia said, "I have lived my life in need of no one and nothing discovered me."

All of life was enclosed.

Everything was locked because everything was expensive. Everything was counted and measured. Chipped sugar frost cost fourteen kopecks, but granulated eleven; when a servant was hired, the allotment of tea and sugar was distinctly stipulated.

For a long time I didn't know the names of the trees, weeds, and stars. I knew the names of animals only from Lotto, but I knew how to count out kopecks.

It was very quiet. There was fighting somewhere far away in an unknown land—in Africa and China.

The nineteenth century was ending. Somewhere in a magazine I saw a drawing: a man with wings. The flat wings are set at neck level, below hang two legs. Later I discovered that the man was named Lilienthal. He had wanted to fly and broke his legs.

There's no need to fly.

If I try to remember today how I imagined myself then, it seems that I am made of glass, transparent, I am swimming in the current, not outdistancing it and not falling back; there is no me, and everything around is changing.

I am sad and interested.

I will say something about fences.

About sixty-five years ago we lived on a steep sandy hill fifteen kilometers from Petersburg near ponds which lay in the distance.

Near the sandy hill through the dunes flowed a narrow stream; it was dammed and formed a string of ponds which were called the Little Lakes.

As a tiny boy I discovered the place where the stream had its source. I was very proud.

Later the Little Lakes received some notice—it was here that Blok saw the Unknown Woman.[1]

We considered the Little Lakes a great body of water.

I remember there were even yacht races on the Little Lakes.

A small sun spot in memory, across it passes a heeling yacht which almost dips its side under the water. The yacht is passing slowly. Three adults, dressed in coats, sit on the high uplifted side. The yacht makes a turn.

But usually only oars knocked below in the oarlocks.

We swam in the Little Lakes in a cabinet. The cabinets were made from laths; blue and green. On top the bathhouse is half-covered by a roof so the rain won't soak the swimmers' clothes.

Next to the dacha on the slope of the hill a cemetery comes down to the water. The graves are enclosed. The cemetery is rich. The metal bars of the railings with their sharp spikes on top represent spears. Everything is painted with white enamel. The tombstones too are painted. There are oval lacquered photographs set in porcelain on them. The earth between the stones of the tombstones and the iron of the railings is embroidered with bright crosses and circles of flowers.

And there at an angle stood oval cases with glass covers, and within under the glass were wreathes of artificial flowers with white and black ribbons. They were very snuggly packed.

The dead man himself is laid out in a snug little case. His very own photo in an oval has been hung in his honor. In the photo a man in a collar with a neck-tie. No hands or feet.

He needn't be afraid of his fate: he has a new room with a little rug of humble flowers beside his bed/grave.

---

[1]Neznakomka, or the Unknown Woman, is a figure in a celebrated poem of that title by Aleksandr Blok.

There are glass apartments/vaults, resembling canary cages. Above—wires; below—glass. Glass plates like this were made for the bottoms of birdcages so the birds, bathing in their little white basins, wouldn't splash.

I didn't like canaries; I had my own remarkable red bird, but not just a bird —a pine grosbeak. The grosbeak sang loudly and very briefly early in the morning. I woke up for this song. The cage stood beside my bed.

Then a rat ate the grosbeak.

The canary cages in the city apartment were hung high up, so neither rats nor cats could get at them.

The dachas were fenced off from the cemetery by a heavy fence of boards nailed up lengthwise. Bushes with tender branches grew there; within the branches was a soft pith.

It is so damp and dark there that even weeds don't grow in the black muddy soil. It isn't even soil, but bottom land heavy with black mud where there should have been sand.

The fence from the side of the lake wasn't heavy; a balcony juts out.

From the balcony there's a view of the lake, which lies below spread out like the foil paper from tea. We wrapped money in this paper, rubbed it with our fingers, and the money was imprinted on it.

Near the balcony stairs on the heavily watered ground there were flowers planted in crosses.

The balcony was painted not so neatly as the fences in the cemetery but assiduously: we paid quite dearly for the dacha.

We were not afraid of the cemetery.

The frightening thing was the money. Different moneys; one was almost unimaginable—gold, round, unexpectedly heavy. I remember the astonishing weight of the coins in my little hand; they gave them to me to hold.

Money was for adults—silver, white, thick rubles, on whose sides something was written in letters which were still incomprehensible. On one side of the ruble an eagle was embossed; it spread its wings, claws, and beak so that it filled the circle all the way to the edge.

On the other side were different tsars: one was heavily bearded—it was the former Tsar Aleksandr III—but another had a light beard, "the present" Nikolai II.

On the juvenile half-ruble there's also a tsar's face. But on the copper of the twenty-kopeck and five-kopeck pieces there are no faces. On those there are numbers for tails, but the eagle is the same—the state's.

There was copper money—heavy brown five-kopeck pieces. Sometimes five-kopeck pieces turned up with enormous letters. They were three times heavier than the money of that time and suggested that people used to be larger too.

Money, not only in its full meaning but also in children's first awareness of it, is frightening.

It is frightening to Garin-Mikhailovsky in *Tema's Childhood*, to Kuprin in his story "Cadets," to Kataev in his story "The Sail is White." Thirty kopecks or a ruble can warp the life of a child, make him lie, steal.

In childhood we fear many things. I remember nighttime: all around everything is frightening, behind the wall the two voices of the pipes converse, in the room there is someone frightening, I cover my head with the blanket. In the corner window a gloomy but unfrightening morning was approaching. In the morning my face was washed with a large rough hand. I lifted my head, stretched my neck the way dogs or cats do when they are pulled roughly, not allowed to straggle.

We were satisfied, although butter was never set on the tables. We were clean; we were washed with a stingily soaped loofah in a tin-covered tub of red copper.

The main thing was that nothing was excessive, everything was very tightly fenced, measured and assigned.

We didn't walk on the grass, we didn't pick the flowers, we didn't put our hands in our pockets, we didn't put our elbows on the table, and we didn't do many other things, at least not openly.

Money was always over everything, like a ceiling; the ceiling was menacing and low.

People talked about money constantly, deferentially and softly. The chief conversation was about the rent for the apartment: Mama's quiet question and Papa's dissatisfied grumbling. I didn't even try to imagine that money, but sixty-three years have passed by, and I remember that firewood cost seven rubles a sazhen [approximately 1 $^1/_2$ yards].

The wood had to be birch. On his back the young janitor brought a mountain of chopped wood fastened with rope to the back stairs. The round mountain of logs itself seemed to be breathing heavily, crawling up the steep worn stone steps. The wood fell onto the kitchen floor. It was filled with the smell of frost and the river.

The wood was transported along the Neva and Fontanka on low-lying barges, the barges stood along the stone embankment several rows deep. The wood was rolled off in wheelbarrows along planks. The barges slowly rose out of the water, their straight wet sides were revealed through the cast iron railings along the canal, narrow wooden streets sprouted on the shore with a familiar smell of damp.

The yellow-black ropes creaked, holding the barges to iron rings on the embankment.

Many years later the last fortifications made out of the wood by the cadets and women's battalion that defended the Provisional Government were scattered around the Winter Garden.

Near a bonfire built from this wood, talking, sat Blok and Mayakovsky.

—translated by Lyn Hejinian for Barrett Watten (w/ Elena Balashova)

FROM Correlation of "Position" and *War and Peace*

Barrett Watten

The monument speaks correctly.

"Good day, General!" said he. "I have received the letter you brought from the Emperor Alexander and am very glad to see you." He glanced with his large eyes into Balashev's face and immediately looked past him.

To get results
that all might disappear.

"A town captured by the enemy is like a maid who has lost her honor," thought he (he had said so to Tuchkov at Smolensk). From that point of view he gazed at the Oriental beauty he had not seen before. It seemed strange to him that his long-felt wish, which had seemed unattainable, had at last been realized. In the clear morning light he gazed now at the city and now at the plan, considering its details, and the assurance of possessing it agitated and awed him.

As

extreme.

"To your barrier!" and Pierre, grasping what was meant, stopped by his saber. Only ten paces divided them. Dolokhov lowered his head to the snow, greedily bit at it, again raised his head, adjusted himself, drew in his legs and sat up, seeking a firm center of gravity. He sucked and swallowed the cold snow, his lips quivered, but his eyes, still smiling, glittered with effort and exasperation as he mustered his remaining strength. He raised his pistol and aimed.

The words themselves
reversed, "going
forward."

As soon as Nicholas entered in his hussar uniform, diffusing around him a fragrance of perfume and wine, and had uttered the words "better late than never" and heard them repeated several times by others, people clustered around him; all eyes turned on him, and he felt at once that he had entered into his proper position in the province—that of a universal favorite: a very pleasant position, and intoxicatingly so after his long privations. At posting stations, at inns, and in the landowner's snuggery, maidservants had been flattered by his notice, and here too at the governor's party there were (as it seemed to Nicholas) an inexhaustible number of pretty young women, married and unmarried, impatiently awaiting his notice. The women and girls flirted with him and, from the first day, the old people concerned themselves to get this fine young daredevil of an hussar married and settled down. Among these was the governor's wife herself, who welcomed Rostov as a near relative and called him "Nicholas."

The apex settles on

Tones in surrounding heads.

Helene laughed.

A test case, or
exile.

"After all, you must understand that besides your pleasure there is such a thing as other people's happiness and peace, and that you are ruining a whole life for the sake of amusing yourself! Amuse yourself with women like my wife —with them you are within your rights, for they know what you want of them. They are armed against you by the same experience of debauchery; but to promise a *maid* to marry her . . . to deceive, to kidnap. . . . Don't you understand that it is as mean as beating an old man or a child? . . . "

No wires account for
failure of specific response.

The great natural forces lie outside us and we are not conscious of them; we call those forces gravitation, inertia, electricity, animal force, and so on, but we are conscious of the force of life in man and we call that freedom.

A triangle gives,

87

circles branch out.

The conversation turned on the contemporary gossip about those in power, in which most people see the chief interest of home politics. Denisov, dissatisfied with the government on account of his own disappointments in the service, heard with pleasure of the things done in Petersburg which seemed to him stupid, and made forcible and sharp comments on what Pierre told them.

Forced

Exposure to limit distorts.

INHABITANTS OF MOSCOW!

Your misfortunes are cruel, but His Majesty the Emperor and King desires to arrest their course. Terrible examples have taught you how he punishes disobedience and crime. Strict measures have been taken to put an end to disorder and to reestablish public security. A paternal administration, chosen from among yourselves, will form your municipality or city government. It will take care of you, of your needs, and of your welfare. Its members will be distinguished by a red ribbon worn across the shoulder, and the mayor of the city will wear a white belt as well. But when not on duty they will only wear a red ribbon round the left arm.

Accumulation of
artifacts in identical tombs.

The carpets yielded and the lid closed; Natasha, clapping her hands, screamed with delight and tears fell from her eyes. But this only lasted a moment. She at once set to work afresh and they now trusted her completely. The count was not angry even when they told him that Natasha had countermanded an order of his, and the servants now came to her to ask whether a cart was sufficiently loaded, and whether it might be corded up. Thanks to Natasha's directions the work now went on expeditiously, unnecessary things were left, and the most valuable packed as compactly as possible.

Any view appears as a hole.

It was a warm, rainy, autumnal day. The wide expanse that opened out before the heights on which the Russian batteries stood guarding the bridge was at times veiled by a diaphanous curtain of slanting rain, and then, suddenly spread out in the sunlight, far-distant objects could be clearly seen glittering as though freshly varnished. Down below, the little town could be seen with its white, red-roofed houses, its cathedral, and its bridge, on both sides of which streamed jostling masses of Russian troops. At the bend of the Danube, vessels, an island, and a castle with a park surrounded by the waters of the confluence of the Enns and the Danube became visible, and the rocky left bank of the Danube covered with pine forests, with a mystic background of green treetops and bluish gorges. The turrents of a convent stood out beyond a wild virgin pine forest, and far away on the other side of the Enns the enemy's horse patrols could be discerned.

Each is a unit,
and all else.

In the ballroom, guests stood crowding at the entrance doors awaiting the Emperor. The countess took up a position in one of the front rows of that crowd. Natasha heard and felt that several people were asking about her and looking at her. She realized that those noticing her liked her, and this observation helped to calm her.

Corrosive air,

Hit by something.

The stretchers moved on. At every jolt he again felt unendurable pain; his feverishness increased and he grew delirious. Visions of his father, wife, sister, and future son, and the tenderness he had felt the night before the battle, the figure of the insignificant little Napoleon, and above all this the lofty sky, formed the chief subjects of his delirious fancies.

Spot-lit
on center stage.

One cannon ball, another, and a third flew over him, falling in front, beside, and behind him. Pierre ran down the slope. "Where am I going?" he suddenly asked himself when he was already near the green ammunition wagons. He halted irresolutely, not knowing whether to return or go on. Suddenly a terrible concussion threw him backwards to the ground. At the same time he was dazzled by a great flash of flame, and immediately a deafening roar, crackling,

89

and whistling made his ears tingle.

Correction, a large boulder.

"You are speaking of the poor countess?" said Anna Pavlovna, coming up just then. "I sent to ask for news, and hear that she is a little better. Oh, she is certainly the most charming woman in the world," she went on, with a smile at her own enthusiasm. "We belong to different camps, but that does not prevent my esteeming her as she deserves. She is very unfortunate!" added Anna Pavlovna.

The parts avoid being seen.

The mummers (some of the house serfs) dressed up as bears, Turks, innkeepers, and ladies—frightening and funny—bringing in with them the cold from outside and a feeling of gaiety, crowded, at first timidly, into the anteroom, then hiding behind one another they pushed into the ballroom where, shyly at first and then more and more merrily and heartily, they started singing, dancing, and playing Christmas games. The countess, when she had identified them and laughed at their costumes, went into the drawing room. The count sat in the ballroom, smiling radiantly and applauding the players. The young people had disappeared.

Portraits of
witnesses other than oneself,

Pasted, stacked.

The man whom they called Tikhon, having run to the stream, plunged in so that the water splashed in the air, and, having disappeared for an instant, scrambled out on all fours, all black with the wet, and ran on. The French who had been pursuing him stopped.

White clouds
and blank tape.

Sonya kept house, attended on her aunt, read to her, put up with her whims and secret ill-will, and helped Nicholas to conceal their poverty from the old countess. Nicholas felt himself irredeemably indebted to Sonya for all she was doing for his mother and greatly admired her patience and devotion, but tried to keep aloof from her.

Architects bury their careers,
survived by their mistakes.

"Have you done this?" he said, pointing to some broken sealing wax and pens. "I loved you, but I have orders from Arakcheev and will kill the first of you who moves forward." Little Nicholas turned to look at Pierre but Pierre was no longer there. In his place was his father—Prince Andrew—and his father had neither shape nor form, but he existed, and when little Nicholas perceived him he grew faint with love: he felt himself powerless, limp, and formless. His father caressed and pitied him. But Uncle Nicholas came nearer and nearer to them. Terror seized young Nicholas and he awoke.

Mirrors tension
of surfaces at work.

Ten men, battalions, or divisions, fighting fifteen men, battalions, or divisions, conquer—that is, kill or take captive—all the others, while themselves losing four, so that on the one side four and on the other fifteen were lost. Consequently the four were equal to the fifteen, and therefore $4x=15y$. Consequently $x/y = 15/4$. This equation does not give us the value of the unknown factor but gives us a ratio between two unknowns. And by bringing variously selected historic units (battles, campaigns, periods of war) into such equations, a series of numbers could be obtained in which certain laws should exist and might be discovered.

Lies,

Extension of screen.

Berg was satisfied and happy. The smile of pleasure never left his face. The party was very successful and quite like other parties he had seen. Everything was similar: the ladies' subtle talk, the cards, the general raising his voice at the card table, and the samovar and the tea cakes; only one thing was lacking that he had always seen at the evening parties he wished to imitate. They had not yet had a loud conversation among the men and a dispute about something important and clever. Now the general had begun such a discussion and so Berg drew Pierre to it.

91

Grammar

signifies refusal

to correspond.

But the guns remained loaded, the loopholes in block-houses and entrench-ments looked out just as menacingly, and the unlimbered cannon confronted one another as before.

Multiple cracks

spread out.

But those glances expressed something more: they said that she had played her part in life, that what they now saw was not her whole self, that we must all become like her, and that they were glad to yield to her, to restrain themselves for this once precious being formerly as full of life as themselves, but now so much to be pitied. "*Memento mori,*" said these glances.

A sequence of
obstacles block
the memory of facts.

A joyous feeling of freedom—that complete inalienable freedom natural to man which he had first experienced at the first halt outside Moscow—filled Pierre's soul during his convalescence. He was surprised to find that this inner freedom, which was independent of external conditions, now had as it were an additional setting of external liberty. He was alone in a strange town, without acquaintances. No one demanded anything of him or sent him anywhere. He had all he wanted: the thought of his wife which had been a continual torment to him was no longer there, since she was no more.

Voice of

The word it approximates.

Quite beside himself, Petya, clenching his teeth and rolling his eyes fero-ciously, pushed forward, elbowing his way and shouting "Hurrah!" as if he were prepared that instant to kill himself and everyone else, but on both sides of him other people with similarly ferocious faces pushed forward and everybody shouted "Hurrah!"

The foundation
floats without opposing tides.

The remains of our regiment which had been in action rapidly formed up and moved to the right; from behind it, dispersing the laggards, came two battalions of the Sixth Chasseurs in fine order. Before they had reached Bagration, the weighty tread of the mass of men marching in step could be heard. On their left flank, nearest to Bagration, marched a company commander, a fine round-faced man, with a stupid and happy expression—the same man who had rushed out of the wattle shed. At that moment he was clearly thinking about nothing but how dashing a fellow he would appear as he passed the commander.

Into the center of potential
stop.

"No," cried he, becoming more and more eager, "Napoleon is great because he rose superior to the Revolution, suppressed its abuses, preserved all that was good in it—equality of citizenship and freedom of speech and of the press —and only for that reason did he obtain power."

The road
decaying into frame.

Fleeing from Moscow the soldiers took with them everything they had stolen. Napoleon, too, carried away his own personal *tresor*, but on seeing the baggage trains that impeded the army, he was (Thiers says) horror-struck. And yet with his experience of war he did not order all the superfluous vehicles to be burned, as he had done with those of a certain marshal when approaching Moscow. He gazed at the *caleches* and carriages in which soldiers were riding and remarked that it was a very good thing, as those vehicles could be used to carry provisions, the sick, and the wounded.

This

Impression turns inside out.

Today was a great day for him—the anniversary of his coronation. Before dawn he had slept for a few hours, and refreshed, vigorous, and in good spirits, he mounted his horse and rode out into the field in that happy mood in which everything seems possible and everything succeeds. He sat motionless, looking at the heights visible above the mist, and his cold face wore that special look of confident, self-complacent happiness that one sees on the face of a boy happily in love. The marshals stood behind him not venturing to distract his attention. He looked now at the Pratzen Heights, now at the sun floating up out of the mist.

In perspective,
feeding on industrial waste.

His illness pursued its normal physical course, but what Natasha referred to when she said: "*This* suddenly happened," had occurred two days before Princess Mary arrived. It was the last spiritual struggle between life and death, in which death gained the victory. It was the unexpected realization of the fact that he still valued life as presented to him in the form of his love for Natasha, and a last, though ultimately vanquished, attack of terror before the unknown.

The endless text manipulates
by fatigue.

"No . . . why not, my dear, why shouldn't I? I like him. He is kind, he is one of God's chosen, he's a benefactor, he once gave me ten rubles, I remember. When I was in Kiev, Crazy Cyril says to me (he's one of God's own and goes barefoot summer and winter), he says, "Why are you not going to the right place? Go to Kolyazin where a wonder-working icon of the Holy Mother of God has been revealed." On hearing these words I said good-bye to the holy folk and went."

Street
where no one lives.

Several tens of thousands of the slain lay in diverse postures and various uniforms on the fields and meadows belonging to the Davydov family and to the crown serfs—those fields and meadows where for hundreds of years the peasants of Borodino, Gorki, Shevardino, and Semenovsk had reaped their harvests and pastured their cattle. At the dressing stations the grass and earth were soaked with blood for a space of some three acres around. Crowds of men of various arms, wounded and unwounded, with frightened faces, dragged themselves back to Mozhaysk from the one army and back to Valuevo from the other. Other crowds, exhausted and hungry, went forward led by their officers. Others held their ground and continued to fire.

Yielding to the arguments of
mass.

It was the voice of the groom, trying to wake him. The sun shone straight into Pierre's face. He glanced at the dirty innyard in the middle of which soldiers were watering their lean horses at the pump while carts were passing out of the gate. Pierre turned away with repugnance, and closing his eyes quickly fell back on the carriage seat. "No, I don't want that, I don't want to see and understand that. I want to understand what was revealing itself to me in my dream. One second more and I should have understood it all! But what am I to do? Harness, but how can I harness everything?" and Pierre felt with horror that the meaning of all he had seen and thought in the dream had been destroyed.

The hawk
tears the sparrow to pieces.

"*Vous voyez le malheureux Mack*," he uttered in a broken voice.

Coded sparks, holding patterns.

The commander of the regiment was an elderly, choleric, stout, and thick-set general with grizzled eyebrows and whiskers, and wider from chest to back than across the shoulders. He had on a brand-new uniform showing the creases where it had been folded and thick gold epaulettes which seemed to stand rather than lie down on his massive shoulders. He had the air of a man happily performing one of the most solemn duties of his life. He walked about in front of the line and at every step pulled himself up, slightly arching his back. It was plain that the commander admired his regiment, rejoiced in it, and that his whole mind was engrossed by it, yet his strut seemed to indicate that, besides military matters, social interests and the fair sex occupied no small part of his thoughts.

The privilege
of vanishing speech.

"Your information may be better than mine," Anna Pavlovna suddenly and venomously retorted on the inexperienced young man, "but I know on good authority that this doctor is a very learned and able man. He is private physician to the Queen of Spain."

All size

Diminished to expanding scale.

He went up to the map and speaking rapidly began proving that no eventuality could alter the efficiency of the Drissa camp, that everything had been foreseen, and that if the enemy were really going to outflank it, the enemy would inevitably be destroyed.

Shifted in
the order by which it occurs.

Prince Andrew had arrived in the evening and Pierre came to see him next morning. Pierre expected to find Prince Andrew in almost the same state as Natasha and was therefore surprised on entering the drawing room to hear him in the study talking in a loud animated voice about some intrigue going on in Petersburg. The old prince's voice and another now and then interrupted him. Princess Mary came out to meet Pierre. She sighed, looking toward the door of the room where Prince Andrew was, evidently intending to express her sympathy with his sorrow, but Pierre saw by her face that she was glad both at what had happened and at the way her brother had taken the news of Natasha's faithlessness.

7/6–7/18/81
for Ron Silliman

"THE SEVERED PAST, THE SPECIOUS PRESENT"

Jack Spicer

introduction by Kevin Killian

Spicer's only extended long fiction was begun in the spring of 1958, in an attempt to wed the hardboiled existentialism of Hammett and Chandler to the epistolary/"imperative" mode of his own *After Lorca* and *Admonitions*. The book was never completed, since the demands of a formal detective story came to intrude on the rigors of *Billy the Kid* and linguistic research. As the fragment stands, the detective element is just beginning to creep in when the narrative breaks off ("Rue was now sitting on the bed crying. Ralston left.") at a cryptic, crypto-Hemingway juncture. What remains is a novel of social comedy, a satire of West Coast poetry and its practitioners, shot through with Spicer's distinctive humanism, wit, bitterness, nihilism. Its hero, J. J. Ralston, is a Boston professor and WWII vet, formerly one of a number of poets in a bohemian postwar Berkeley circle, who has returned to the Bay Area to survey the new Beat-influenced scene, hoping to refresh his own writing. This allows Spicer to contrast, at every turn, the prelapsarian magic of the Berkeley Renaissance with the ongoing, tawdry rush of the SF Renaissance—the "specious present." Ralston's trip on the F Train, from San Francisco across the bay to Berkeley, is an almost literal journey into the past, a metaphor overdetermined by Spicer's explosive nostalgia for the halcyon days of his youth. "There were names like Henry Miller and Paul Goodman and Kenneth Patchen," he writes, "and every day you were sure to hear a new name, glowing, as new names did then, with a kind of promise of the undiscovered, unimagined freedoms." Never mind that by 1958 Spicer had quarrelled with Miller, Goodman, Patchen: his studies at Berkeley with Ernst Kantorowicz had persuaded him that a "kingship" of poetry exists and that artistic creation is one lifelong, continual regicide.

From *this* Berkeley Renaissance, homosexuality has been eliminated, or "severed," as the marketplace dictated—the 50's hardboiled model provided no room for celebration of queer community. From the violence of this severance, tension grows as the book progresses and Ralston grows more and more attracted to the boy poet, Rue Talcott, again in a familiar 50's way. *I'm not gay, it's just that there's something about him . . . "the frightened running of a child that had been given a bloody nose by an angel or a quarterback."* Into *this* Berkeley Renaissance, Spicer inserts the fictional figures of Madelaine and Tom Cross, the model heterosexual couple. The invention of the Crosses allows Spicer to re-invent the tortured romance between Robert Creeley, in many ways his poetic hero, and Marthe Rexroth, who played Guinevere to Kenneth Rexroth's Arthur in Spicer's imagination and in much of his work of this period.

This is the beginning of chapter 2 of Spicer's novel, printed here with the kind permission of Robin Blaser, Spicer's literary executor. Lew, Robin and I are happy to be able to insert this material into this issue of *Aerial*, and into a general discussion of Barrett Watten's work. Watten's enthusiasm for Spicer approaches our own. His work as an art editor, as a controversialist, in social theory, in politics, in poetry, in California writing, as Cavalier and Roundhead, has parallels to Spicer's career which should be explored in another paper—they grow so numerous it would be like explaining the parallels between Lincoln and Kennedy. Hats off to a great guy.   —January, 1993

"The Severed Past, The Specious Present"
from **Chapter II**

He had been in the hotel room two days when he received the phone call. "Hello," the voice said. "Is this Jim Ralston?"

"Yes."

"This is Madelaine Slingbot."

"Uh—"

"Madelaine Cross, you idiot. Arthur and I heard you were hiding out in town and obtained your phone number from a very secret spy. Did you murder somebody in Philadelphia?"

"Boston."

"Boston then. Do you realize that I haven't seen you in six years?"

"Eight."

"You always were depressingly accurate. Don't you really want to see us?"

"Who?"

"Arthur and me, of course. You aren't really going to pretend that you don't know that I'm married to Arthur?"

"Certainly, Madelaine. I just got into town."

"Two days ago."

"That spy of yours must be very accurate."

"They always are. We trade them in for old copies of Poetry Chicago when they make a single mistake."

"Uh—"

"You sound just like you used to. Do you remember when you and Tom and I went to Hugh and Lydia's wedding reception wearing Halloween masks and Lydia's mother had hysterics?"

"That was over ten years ago."

"And the Green Ink Bandit?"

"What happened to Tom?"

"Haven't you heard that either? He got sick and had shock treatments and now he's teaching in a private high school in New Mexico."

"When did all this happen?"

"It must have been three years ago. It was a year after I married Arthur."

"You know I'm married too?"

"I know all about it. A nice New England social worker. My spies in Philadelphia tell me everything. But I can't keep talking now. I have to feed the children. There are four now, you know. One of Tom's that you never saw and two of Arthur's."

"Uh—"

"Yes. Well, Arthur and I want you to come over for dinner on Monday night. We're going to have a few people in afterwards that you'll want to meet. And I do want to talk to you alone for a little while, Jim, and sort of fill in."

The time was set and the address explained and she hung up. Ralston felt a little breathless. He had not wanted to see Slingbot and he had not remembered that Madelaine was married to him—not really remembered although he knew that he probably had—and he did not want to remember Madelaine Cross at all or the Berkeley that he (and now she) had left behind, and he wanted to stay in the hotel room and—what, to be left alone—no—to stay in the hotel room and drink brandy and then go out and walk up and down all the streets he remembered and then go back to his room and drink brandy and read a paperback mystery and then to go out to have dinner and then to walk up and down the streets he remembered . . .

But there were streets in Berkeley too. Dingy tree-lined college town streets. Streets he remembered more intimately if with less love than any of the streets of San Francisco. And Madelaine and Tom had been his best friends (for a while almost his only friends) in those first amazing years after the war when youth was resumed after a two year interruption (or a four year interruption —it had been worse for other people) and it was not the same youth any more and no one was in the place he had started from and the government was paying for things and he, to his vast surprise, was at the University of California instead of the small orangebelt college in Southern California he had left for war from and there were names like Henry Miller and Paul Goodman and Kenneth Patchen and every day you were sure to hear a new name, glowing, as new names did then, with a kind of promise of the undiscovered, unimagined freedoms. And he had taken as many courses like Sanskrit and History of Byzantium and Chinese Vase Painting as the Veterans Administration would let him and had lived in a small room on the top floor of a private house in the hills above campus and the window in the shower (he had never seen a window in a shower before or since) had given a complete view of the lights of San Francisco and Sausalito across the Bay. And had worn his old khakis and his Eisenhower jacket except that he finally ruined the Eisenhower jacket trying to dye it red with Tintex. And most of his friends were like him, back from the terrible boredom of the war (even Henry, who had lost his arm at Cassino, felt boredom at it rather than anger) young men in Eisenhower jackets wandering around in a vast library which contained all the secrets (and described all the pleasures) of the visible and invisible worlds.

Tom and Madelaine had been important members of this scene. Tom had been a conscientious objector during the war—a fact that gave him a hero status in the Berkeley of 1946 and 1947 that someone with even so visible a sign of loss such as Henry never could or would even expect to enjoy. Why this should be was a mystery to everyone. Tom would agree and even insist that the dullness of a conscientious objector camp was equal to or perhaps greater than the dullness of, say, Cassino and the decision necessary to reach either was equally accidental and, in retrospect, equally meaningless. Yet the attitude was there, accepted by everyone—Tom's position in respect to Henry's was exactly that in equally 1946 and 1947 post-war France of a Maquis as compared to someone who had merely lost an arm on the Maginot Line.

But if Tom was the hero, was in fact *the* hero in their heroless universe, Madelaine was the spirit and the arrangements, the voice and the auditorium, a kind of combination of a sybil and a welcoming committee. It was her money (she came from an old Berkeley family that had something to do with engineering) that paid for the apartment (six dingy rooms that opened on to each other and finally ended in a small kitchen and an even smaller bath, dingy even when they had painted some of the dingy walls with collective non-objective calcamine splashes during parties), the food (mostly things that had to do with beans and eggplants but given freely, if cooked badly, to anyone who came in between five and seven in the evening), the coffee (probably the largest item of all in the budget—there was always, even at four in the morning when everyone was asleep, a pot of coffee boiling on the stove and Ralston could not remember ever having drunk so much coffee in his life—coffee at the time was not merely something you had with dinner, it was used to induce all the states of tension and relaxation that liquor, marijuana, tranquilizers and even vitamin pills were used for later), and the most important contribution of all, the two hundred dollars needed to pay an anarchist's cooperative in New Jersey to print the first and only issue of a little magazine that Tom and she and Ralston and Henry and so many other people collectively edited.

At the time Ralston had thought that everyone who went to the apartment had been in love with Madelaine. He knew that he was, that Tom, being her husband and the hero she was basically the reception committee for, must of course be, and Henry, in his pedantic and embarrassed way, and the other young men, back from the wars or the conscientious objector camps or the aircraft factories, and even the very occasional young woman (so very few of them) it was possible to imagine that even they were caught up in the spirit of the thing, that even they in some mysterious way were in love with Madelaine. It was only later, when Ralston had left off his Eisenhower jacket and his belief in the infinitude of libraries, that he saw (reconstructed rather, he was always reconstructing through the past like someone following by radar an object just after it had passed the outer range of his vision) that Madelaine, while the center, was by no mean the only object of the erotic currents that ebbed and flowed around her, that she had known little or nothing about the French poetry she was always talking about (and that most of the others had known this), that she had not bathed regularly, not out of defiance of any convention but out of sheer laziness, that she was not even unfaithful to Tom.

But for years for Ralston, long after he knew these things very well, she was the image called up at any moment of his disillusionment with a woman. When a girl would lie to him cheaply and obviously he would remember that Madelaine had lied to him exactly in that manner and he had never caught her at it until now, when a girl showed a stupid enthusiasm for a good poem it would suddenly occur to him that Madelaine's enthusiasm for his good poems had been exactly that kind of stupid enthusiasm, when a girl who did not mean to go to bed with him kissed him as if she meant to go to bed with him it would occur to him (even in the moment of that kiss) that Madelaine must have been a prick teaser. This too had passed in time (long after the memory of the Eisenhower jacket and the infinitude of libraries seemed quite as far away as the memory of the clothes and thoughts of farthest childhood) and he had now, actually, until the phone call, forgotten that she existed, or that Berkeley existed, or that he ever had been twenty one.

And now she was married to Slingbot. He would not think of all the clever practical changes that would have come over Madelaine now she was in this new position (or, worse yet, about her being married to Slingbot and remaining just as she had been). For he had always disliked the man—even in those days when Slingbot was a semi-mythological creature (surely a demigod if Tom was a hero) who had managed to avoid (by reason, Ralston supposed, of his age) not only the boredoms of the army and the aircraft factory, but also the equal but more heroic boredoms of the conscientious objector and the jail. Slingbot remained where he was and what he was, spiting the war, resplendent in his own San Francisco, having a splendid active time writing poetry and telling young men not to fight, the only man who had not been bored during the war.

This was all very amusing now and slightly ridiculous, but at the time Ralston had felt really guilty for disliking the man, had wondered if the reason for his dislike was not merely that Slingbot had never noticed his poetry, had never invited him to one of those large private dinner parties for visiting poets that Tom (but not Madelaine) got invited to, in short, because Slingbot had committed the sin of excluding him from the glittering inner world of poetry and anarchism. And maybe this was all. The man, he had not been completely excluded, he had met him at a few very large public after-dinner parties for visiting poets, had a certain charm and a great deal of wit. Now that the tables were turned and Ralston was the one for whom the dinner party was given (it would not be large as Slingbot was on record as calling his present kind of poetry "academic square" poetry, but it would be adequate as Slingbot had included one of Ralston's earlier, very bad poems in an anthology of Post-War Verse he had edited two years ago), now that the tables were turned why not make of the both of them a *tabula rasa* and go into this thing (which he now couldn't get out of anyway) without prejudice? Besides, he had come to San Francisco to discover something and so far his only contact with poetry had been to tear it up in that bar the first afternoon and (he was not going to think about that now) and why shouldn't he go to Slingbot's dinner party?

But he was not going without preparation. Madelaine's phone call had been enough to frighten him into saying yes before he had decided to say yes. He wanted no more surprises, no more marriages he had forgotten about, no more important details he did not know. He needed filling in, and even if filling in meant calling and having dinner with one of the people of the past he did not want to see (and every one of them he could think of fell into that category at the moment) it would have to be done—and immediately.

Ralston thumbed through the two phone books (San Francisco and East Bay) that his hotel room provided. It was as he thought—no one that he at all wanted to see (assuming that he wanted to see anyone—he suspected that he had picked the name to be looked up first purposely from those least likely to be there) was listed. There was only (and he supposed he should have known this from the start) Henry—and his address was not three blocks from the address he used to have at the time Ralston left Berkeley, and his phone number (Ralston couldn't quite remember but was pretty certain) was the same. It would have to be dinner with Henry—Henry who had kept writing him letters for years after Ralston had left Berkeley for Columbia even though he almost never replied to them, who had been his last, almost unwelcome, link with California. He had enjoyed the letters, even waited for them, but, as he became less and less able even to think about writing a reply, had also resented them as invaders of his privacy like telephone calls to someone who no longer lived in the house, and, when, after a silence of three more years, he had received a Christmas card from Henry addressed to his correct current address in Boston, he was surprised to discover that his feelings were almost of pure annoyance.

And Henry was home. And would have dinner that very evening. Or rather would cook dinner for Ralston. He was delighted and, Ralston felt, not at all surprised to hear from him. And this again was annoying. Ralston resented people that had no trouble with the past, for whom there were no discontinuations—only temporary absences, who could welcome home as if by appointment the Enoch Ardens of any year of their lives. And I, he thought to himself as he waited in the East Bay Terminal late that afternoon for an F train for Berkeley—and I am so much not at home with my past that not seeing a person for several weeks will make him disappear from my life, will make him, his reality when he reappears, almost as shocking as a ghost.

When the F train did arrive and Ralston seated himself in the smoking section and watched through the window as the train pulled itself from the ugly station into a brief and even uglier view of the waterfront which lasted (Ralston could remember and was not even impatient) exactly four minutes, and then the bridge—the bridge that connected San Francisco of the specious present (Ralston could remember the phrase from one of his philosophy lectures) with Berkeley of the severed past. Everything was more beautiful than he had remembered —the bay a particular shade of blue that reminded Ralston of all the other shades of blue he had seen the bay become but not quite (it never was) the same. With all the islands set in it (although one was a federal prison, another an abandoned detention camp for immigrants, and the third, into which the train would soon be passing, a naval base) it reminded one less of a bay than an inland sea, its changing blue waters not connected to any ocean but shoring up its own tides, giving passage to its own travelers, as separate and distinct from the Pacific or from the rivers that emptied into it as some small European kingdom might be from the greater territories that surrounded it. He remembered that Tom had once said, as they stood knee-deep in wild barley on one of the higher Berkeley hills looking down from the east at the glittering length of it, how Tom had said, "What if we had been the first persons to discover this, to see all this bare without lights or anything. If we had just come over from the other side of the hills and seen this. Can you imagine?"

And Ralston had pointed to the bright skyline of San Francisco and said, "If it weren't for those buildings and the bridge I could imagine that San Francisco was an island and that the bay went on forever."

And Tom had put his arm around his shoulder and said, "I wish—"

And Henry, when they had gotten back from the hike and told him about the idea, had said, "I wish we could all of us colonize it."

And Madelaine had made it all into an amusing game by suggesting which parts each of them should colonize. He remembered that she insisted that he and Tom should colonize Angel Island, while she, she would pick exactly the spot on Telegraph Hill where Coit Tower would not then be, while Henry, Henry could have all of what would have been Oakland and the Alameda estuary.

And the bay was still there and Berkeley was still there and he would be looking at its tree-lined, half-suburban streets in a few minutes and he felt the same sense of exhilaration he had had two days before in the bar when he realized that he was in San Francisco on the edge of a new adventure. He felt this only for a moment. Then the bay disappeared as the train passed into the tunnel of Treasure Island and it occurred to him that a return to the past, however pleasing, was in no sense a renewal, that he was merely reciting the scores of old football games, that it might be that he was using the Slingbot party as an excuse to retreat into old memories because of what had happened in The Birdcage on Thursday, because the past was no threat to John J. Ralston and this specious present was, that this trip to Berkeley was less a sentimental journey than the frightened running of a child that had been given a bloody nose by an angel or a quarterback.

—edited by Lew Ellingham and Kevin Killian

AFTER TED

Barrett Watten

"How strange to be gone in a minute!" is Ted Berrigan's obituary from 1963. The twenty years between *The Sonnets* and his death seem a short period to enjoy the irony of the line. Now there's a different truth to the poem, on the order of "think of what you'll never be able to understand."

Berrigan understood that his work would stand out in that much greater relief, and his bad personal habits worked to underscore his belief in a literary process that goes beyond biography. At the core of all the pulp novels he read was a cultural compulsion to act out the Christian scenario, against a cultural background of nothing that would compel its use.

His use of pulp novels was similar to his use of drugs. He had read Burroughs to the letter, both in *Junky* and in the cut-up works. Materials taken into the body, both linguistic and otherwise, raise the question of who's in control. The body raises scar tissue around the wound, but the scar might be gorgeously painted, as in a ritual scarification.

Anticipating the inevitable, the poet ends up doing it to himself.

But the most notable fact of Berrigan's work is the mind actively at work in the poems, acting with and through the sensory interferences and peremptory compulsions. While the motives and terms of his poems are often imponderables, the form asserts a struggle for mastery in the terms of art. So the first poem in *So Going Around Cities*, written after his father's death, is in seven-count syllabics. The subject is equally Kenneth Rexroth, the original exemplar of the form.

Later Berrigan's own forms became recurring arguments for their own reinvention. The biography in Berrigan's work is possible only to the extent that it coincides with the argument of the forms. The life that is seen through the poems is refractive, broken down, but the forms have lives of their own. An elegy will be written because the poem must live.

In Berrigan's work the drama of such conflicts produces statement of the purest type, and any statement in his work occurs at such a point of conflict. The poem dictates how much of experience is allowed. All this is necessary to come up to the level of art.

One sitting says, "I stand corrected."

Whole poems are tense across this ambiguous plane. Emotion (experience) meets intellect (form) continually in the work to make this kind of high-impact, refractive statement, perfect at the same time that it bears with it all its struggle to arrive.

The visceral objects thus formed (poems) are the agents of further discrimination. Words, lines, keep coming back like memories or dreams that evoke both pleasure and pain. They are in the present neither the same nor different but components of structure. Berrigan does not at first appear to be a psychological poet, but his work sets up considerable resonances for the "givens" of psychological dynamics. The "givens" in his work are identity, the desire for and fear of its loss. Pushing buttons was not only a source of pleasure or a compulsion but a querying of his fate.

The pushbuttons in the work are loaded with emotional resonance but ambiguous in terms of their final destination. An example would be the "people" in the poems, who are not really people but complexes of words, refractions of form. The poet's "I" is the first of these, the central button to be pushed. The question that occurs is whether the "I" can stand (not) to exist.

This "I" is acted out in multiple emanations, for instance, "Dick," "Anne," and "Ron." It's important to remember that these people were invented by the poet—they didn't already exist. They partake in the powers of the poem variously. They start young and remain in that condition permanently ("Jim Carroll"), or they die in middle age and end up memorialized in bronze ("Frank"). Perhaps they are imponderables ("Dagwood Bumstead") or oxymorons ("Dick"), question marks for identity.

> Love came into my room
> I mean my life
> the shape of a Tomato
> it took over everything

Can a replaceable tomato stand in for all the proper names in the work? Or on the other side, no replacement:

> So long, Jimi,
>   Janis, so long.

The names in the poem connote desire, repulsion, and finally the question of the self—little splinters of its larger dynamics. They are not merely projections but work at an ambiguous edge, characterizing "the other" at the same time that they protect the self. "The body sends out self to repel non-self," Berrigan quotes. The problem of characterization, the question of "originality," is behind the naming of persons and, equally, the stealing of their lines.

Did he steal the name? Who owns a name? The question of the duplicity of language is at the center of Berrigan's work. The cut-up technique undermines the assurances of received forms, like the "sonnet," preparing the ground for "more direct" content—notably, dying and death. Berrigan's purpose is often to be unreachable and inevitable in this sense, causing the desiring reader to weep with vexation while admiring the intellect in the lines. In order to ensure this response Berrigan puts himself on the line, a kind of willful undermining of his word at the moment of its maximum power.

But the "poet of experience" undermines the intellectual complexity at an uneasy edge. Berrigan's model for the "poet of experience," O'Hara, projected himself much more easily through his literary role. It is more possible in O'Hara's work for the poet to identify with his art—his forms are less difficult constructions (in the sense that a child can be "difficult"), and they extend more easily into experience. Art could never have worked this way for Berrigan —it really wasn't his to use in this way. For Berrigan art was other, but there is no truth but art.

Berrigan's truth appears now to be a self-destruction necessary to raise the "imponderable" banner of art. "I assumed O'Hara," according to Berrigan, but Hart Crane, in his desire for an impossible art, is the poet most like Ted. Crane wrote that composition for him was the mastery of the emotions by the intellect. The opposite was true of Berrigan—the intellect was mastered by the emotions.

Berrigan's reading of The Sonnets at Langton Street contained some of the greatest verbal moments in American language:

> Au revoir, scene!
> She had a great toe!
> She-tail's raggy, too!
> Jelly bend over put'im on too!
> She laid a crab!
> Jelly him sure later! Jelly-ass ails are tough!
> She lays all his jelly on him!
> Eeeeeooooooww!! La Vie!

The next night he swung the Mongolian Sausage at the crowd ("a long stocking: you fill it full of shit, then you punch holes in it . . ."). On the third night he gave the platform back to the others, and on the fourth night he went home.

Berrigan could have done a great deal more. He could have been more consistent, but his difference, especially from himself, was essential.

Berrigan's death was not exactly Mayakovsky's suicide, which likewise was intended to give greater markedness to the work. But it was literary, prefigured every step of the way, and it can be criticized as a work. Berrigan's self-destruction was his best way of saying that he meant it, and that he was truly subject to all he took in. Burroughs has become metaphoric, Berrigan stayed literary in the most acute sense of the word.

> Few listeners get close. And
> "Love must turn to power or it die."
> This is a terrible present.
> "Is this any way to run a Railroad?"

The Associated Press characterized Berrigan as "one of the last of his kind," but his work will continue to draw others into the word and its necessary fate. The resonance in his work will continue to trouble and excite anyone living in this country, where the furious song flows through *many* costumes.

1983

106

POETIC VOCABULARIES
A CONVERSATION BETWEEN BARRETT WATTEN AND JACKSON MAC LOW

KPFA, Berkeley, 24 October 1985
edited and revised by Watten and Mac Low in 1992

Barrett Watten: You are known as a composer, musician, sound-text poet, and performance artist as well as a poet of the written word. Since I'm primarily a poet of the written word, I'd like to concentrate on some of the values that go along with practices of composition on the page. *Bloomsday* (Barrytown, N.Y.: Station Hill, 1984) is an interesting work to talk about in that sense because it's divided into two sections. I wonder if you could tell us a little about the structure of the book itself.

Jackson Mac Low: One of the two sections is larger than the other. The first and larger one comprises the poems I wrote between early February 1982 and September 1983, all but one in verse, and all but one written without use of systematic-chance operations or other nonintentional procedures. While a few were written more or less "intentionally," most were composed "quasi-intentionally," or "intuitively." The latter terms denote for me a way of writing during which words, phrases, sentences, and/or fragments come into the writer's awareness more or less spontaneously from her memory or other "parts of the mind," or from her environment through sight or sound.

The smaller section includes works from 1980 and '81: a metrical poem derived from material generated for an exhibited "poetry environment"; a verbal-instrumental musical work comprising prose narratives and notated instrumental parts, all performed together, each made by a method depending on the letters in the name of a musical instrument; and a long stanzaic poem made up of a decrementally repeated group of thirty-two words, dwindling to one, drawn from Ogden and Richards' Basic English word list. All were composed by nonintentional procedures. [At the time of the editing and revision of this conversation, February–July 1992, I prefer the latter term to "chance operations" since it includes a wider variety of compositional methods, many of which do not, strictly speaking, involve "chance," though some do.]

Watten: There are several kinds of vocabulary that you are using in generating these texts through various chance and other nonintentional procedures, right?

Mac Low: Yes, several.

Watten: What are some of these vocabularies, and what are some of the values associated with them for you?

Mac Low: The vocabularies are usually not chosen because of the meanings of their words, though their meanings are integral components of the works made from them. Each is taken from some source text or list by means of a nonintentional procedure. "Antic Quatrains," the twelve-quatrain metrical poem in the "nonintentional" section of *Bloomsday*, was derived from a

107

three-thousand-line computer printout, each line of which comprises one to ten words drawn by a random-selection program from a five-thousand-word list of words. The latter includes all of the words and biographical and geographical names in Merriam-Webster's *New Collegiate Dictionary* (1977) that are partial anagrams of the name "Annie Brigitte Gilles Tardos," in none of which any letter is repeated more times than it's repeated in the whole name. (Each list also includes with the words and names all suffixes whose appending also produces such partial anagrams.)

Winds/Instruments, the verbal-musical work, began with the compilation of five word lists, each one including all the words and names in the same dictionary that spell the name of one musical instrument: clarinet, electric guitar, recorder, transverse flute, or trombone. From each list a sequence of words was drawn by a random-selection procedure. A narrative and an instrumental part was made from each word sequence. To compose each narrative, the words were connected into normative sentences by the addition of suffixes and other form changes and by the insertion between them of structure words. The musical parts were composed by "translating" the letters of each lexical word into a sequence of pitch classes (notated as whole notes in each instrument's middle range). Within certain specific limits, musical parameters are determined during performances by the instrumentalists, who are encouraged to listen closely to the speakers of the narratives, the other instrumentalists, and all environmental sounds, and to make their choices in relation with everything they hear, including the meanings of the words.

Watten: You mention that one work was composed using the Basic English word list.

Mac Low: "Converging Stanzas" (written in 1981), the last work in *Bloomsday*, comprises 480 lines divided into sixty eight-line stanzas, each following a schema of five, three, one, eight, four, two, two, and seven words in successive lines. It is my latest return to using the 850-word Basic English list devised in 1930 by C. K. Ogden and I. A. Richards to be an international lingua franca replacing such artificial "universal languages" as Esperanto. The first stanza of "Converging Stanzas" comprises thirty-two words drawn from the list by chance operations involving random digits. Another procedure drew words from the first stanza to fill each of the "places" in the second stanza. This procedure was then repeated, using each stanza as the word-source for the next. The method gives fewer different words for each stanza until they "converge" on the word "experience": all thirty-two "places" in the sixtieth stanza are occupied by it. Here's the first stanza:

> motion boiling pocket far paste
> other country slope
> motion
> destruction experience will stop punishment every decision curve
> fat committee mine how
> with country

bad stocking
push beautiful will motion punishment finger heat (89)

Watten: That's the first stanza, and the poem goes on for sixty stanzas.

Mac Low: The number of different words in a stanza declines until there are only three—"decision," "paste," and "experience"—in the twenty-third stanza. All three continue to appear until the thirty-eighth, from which "decision" drops out, but "paste" continues to appear, more and more seldom, until the sixtieth, composed entirely of repetitions of "experience."

Watten: A procedure is applied and the vocabulary gradually converges on "experience."

Mac Low: On the word "experience."

Watten: On the word "experience."

Mac Low: So the last stanza is:

> experience experience experience experience experience
> experience experience experience
> experience
> experience experience experience experience experience
> [experience experience experience
> experience experience experience experience
> experience experience
> experience experience
> experience experience experience experience experience
> [experience experience (102)

"Converging Stanzas" was my last large project of that nonintentional kind until after 1985, except for the completion in 1983 of two projects begun earlier. The words of *French Sonnets* (Tucson: Black Mesa, 1984; 2nd ed., Milwaukee: Membrane, 1989), begun in 1955, were drawn from the headwords of the English-French section of an 1899 Heath's French dictionary and systematically substituted for the words of some of Shakespeare's sonnets. And to make *Words nd Ends from Ez* (Bolinas, Calif.: Avenue B, 1989) I used a "diastic" word-selection procedure, using the name "Ezra Pound" as a "seed string" through which words and "ends" (i.e., fragments of words ranging from all but the first letter to only the last) were drawn from the poet's *Cantos* while I read through them.

Watten: You did something similar in a book using Virginia's Woolf's vocabulary [*The Virginia Woolf Poems* (Providence: Burning Deck, 1985)].

Mac Low: In writing that book in 1976–77 I drew words from *The Waves* by a diastic text-selection method using a phrase and a sentence from the novel as seed strings, and from *Night and Day*, by an acrostic procedure using a passage from that novel as seed string.

Watten: There's an interest in taking the already given vocabulary of another artist and applying a kind of procedure to it to make a work, and there's an interest in other kinds of vocabulary, vocabularies that seem to be, to some extent, other—the Basic English list is almost inert in terms of experiential value. Immediately I think of the possibility of relating such a vocabulary to, say, musical materials, where what you're given is just an array of sounds or a set of tonal relations, elements that have abstract relations with each other. When you're using a vocabulary like the Basic English list, there is an approximation to the compositional possibility of music being brought to a set of terms in language.

Mac Low: The construction of most of my nonintentionally composed texts *is* musical, but I would rather say *concretely* so. The choice of vocabulary is often "contingent": for instance, from the middle fifties until well into the seventies, I often drew my vocabularies from whatever I was reading. One poem might be drawn from a newspaper, the next from a Buddhist text, and others from political pamphlets and botany books. A relatively small number are derived from literary works. And sometimes one poem drew its vocabulary from several different sources.

Watten: I have two questions, and the first is: you could easily take these vocabularies as purely abstract, as material for composition. At the same time, because these materials are *in* language, the words themselves come along with claims in our usages of them. The claims that are in these vocabularies are quite different from the kinds of qualities one would normally find in music. Language is a different material, medium for composition, taken in this sense. If I were looking at, say, "Converging Stanzas," which uses the Basic word list, on the one hand I might see it as a kind of poetic minimalism that works from a fixed set of relations and converges on a single tone. At the same time, I can't ignore the fact that the Basic English vocabulary has a kind of cultural context; it was a "scientific" vocabulary, developed in the twenties as part of a particular optimism about restricting the amount of terms necessary to convey thought. It seems to come along with, or to bring with it, certain cultural and philosophical presuppositions. There would be, then, another way of reading the vocabulary in "Converging Stanzas" as ironic, as a comment on the potential thought-control program that was Basic English. How do you feel about that?

Mac Low: I'm rather attracted to the latter idea *now*, but when I composed the poem it was completely extraneous to what I had in mind.

Watten: Right . . .

Mac Low: I simply regarded the Basic English list as just another source of words . . . I notice you use the word "abstract." That term is opposed to what I've usually had in mind. Since I began using nonintentional compositional procedures I've wanted to present language in the *concrete*—not in the later sense of *visual poetry*, but the concrete word (or other linguistic unit) including not only its sound but all of its denotations (lexical meanings) and connotations. Each time a word appears I intend fully that all of these things—both its sound and its meanings—operate, because they're all parts of the word. Just as a nonverbal sound has parameters of frequency and duration and so on, so words have parameters of several kinds of meaning and sound, and relations between the sounds, between the meanings, and between the two, all of which are present in all written and oral discourse.

I've never thought of my writings as "abstract" in any sense, even though words may appear in my texts either without normative grammatical/syntactic connections or in sentences, as in the *Winds/Instruments* narratives in *Bloomsday*. There the words were drawn from lists relevant to the generation of the texts and to the fact that they were components of a musical work for specific instruments. While I didn't *choose* the words, I fully intended to affirm all the sound and meaning relations that arise when these words come together both in my texts and in performances with the instruments.

Watten: You're not abstracting language *from* its contexts, trying to blank out contexts that come with it.

Mac Low: Oh no, quite the contrary. I enjoy the inevitable references to the source contexts, insofar as they come into my texts. I affirm them. But the poetry doesn't necessarily affirm the *values* of the source contexts. The poems offer snapshots, so to speak, of those contexts, but not positive or negative evaluations of them.

Watten: And that would be quite a charged area. Say, if you were using Pound's middle *Cantos* as the basis for a vocabulary, you'd be objectifying a charged and pointed argument in the works made from it.

Mac Low: Yes, but my text-selection method *fragments* Pound's argument. Components of his vocabulary (words, syllables, letters/phonemes) fall out of the argument and become very specific in sound and in meaning—in my sense, "concrete." Hardly any of Pound's actual argument comes through in *Words nd Ends from Ez.*

Watten: A follow-up on this question of the vocabulary of a poet's work: say we're talking about a poet like Robert Creeley over the extent of thirty or forty years of writing, or Emily Dickinson, whose works have been indexed in a concordance . . . You can see exactly what her vocabulary is; you can find out how many times she used the word "circumference," for instance, eighty-nine times, possibly. It's interesting to look at a poet's language in terms of what words are in the work and what words are not in it. Any poet is going to exclude certain things, and there will be a kind of shape. You could almost say there's a reading of experience or a reading of the world *in* this vocabulary. How do you feel about that? You use so many vocabularies —are you interested in this kind of mapping that occurs in the use of a vocabulary?

Mac Low: More subliminally than consciously. In regard to my own work, what you say about inclusion and exclusion may apply to my poetry written before late December 1954 and much of it written since early December 1981, where I am producing the vocabulary directly from my memory and perception and from all that's formed my personal vocabulary. When writing the works written by means of nonintentional procedures, I've attempted to "evade" the ego and its decisions. Neither the kind of language nor the vocabulary, nor even the subject-matter is, in the usual sense "chosen."

However, that's qualifiable: I've sometimes chosen sources consciously *because of* their vocabulary and/or what's being said in them, for instance, to

111

make political poems. On 6 August 1965, during the Vietnam War, I made an extended political poem from a *New York Times* article (8/5/65) about U. S. marines' burning Vietnamese huts with their cigarette lighters [see *some/thing*, 3, Winter 1966, New York]: by utilizing a diastic text-selection procedure (a reading-through method that takes into a text successive linguistic units having the successive letters of a seed string—a word, name, phrase, etc.— in "places" corresponding to those they occupy in the seed). The procedure appropriated fragments of the article repeatedly, in whole or part, producing various patterns in the poem. I read through the article again and again, backwards and forwards, with the not necessarily intended but welcome result that politically revelatory words, phrases, and sentences were brought into the poem. The situation was exposed—much more fully than it would have been in a rhetorical political poem—simply by letting the "facts"—albeit the *New York Times*'s version of them—"speak for themselves." Choosing that article and that compositional procedure was a political action. And I've done something like that every so often.

On the other hand, when I chose, for instance, *The Waves* as a source while I was rereading it, some values of Virginia Woolf herself and of her writing, and of the relation to them I felt during that reading, led me to choose the novel. So the gamut runs from the "relatively choiceless"—I happen to be reading something and it becomes a source and/or component of a poem —to "chosen for an end," as in the political poems in which the source material is made to "speak for itself." Somewhere between lies the choice of the work of a particular writer who interests me because of her language, e.g., Woolf's two novels for *The Virginia Woolf Poems* and Pound's *Cantos* for *Words nd Ends from Ez*. In the latter I think the language of Ezra Pound— that great polyglot mixture of languages—comes through without Pound's arguments about history, economics, and so on.

Watten: Shall we hear it?

Mac Low: Well, here—selected literally at random—is the beginning of its third section, drawn from *Cantos* XLII-LI—the diastic begins with the second-place *Z* in "EZRA" since the initial *E* ends the selection before:

> iZen ve Right sit
> And Percent bOrrowers r rUnning xpeNses
> untedD Er nZe eiR es
> hAd Provided rOm eoUs GraNd ke haDn't Enese aZing
> cuRity d
> leAving Participate
> rObations a TUtrice
> a ReNa 2
> NeeDs Efer iZio veRnatore us BAiley
> Per t Of CT*U*M F SaN the GD E
> iZen HE*R*EFORE
> let all *P*avia:
> mOve iGure,

iceNza,
icteD
E...
aZing
h pRecautions o guArantee Possible lOss
o JUly a ReNa M. . . . (32)

Watten: Is that a chance-operation poem?

Mac Low: Well, no, not strictly speaking. It's *nonintentional* in that I could never predict which word or fragment would come into the poem next, but it is hardly a matter of *chance*, since all of those words, letter strings, single letters, and punctuation marks were already lying there waiting—in that order though with other characters intervening between them—on the pages of Pound's book.

Here's a result of certain chance operations: the first few stanzas of "Antic Quatrains," the shortest text in the "nonintentional" section of *Bloomsday*:

> Along a tarn a delator entangled a dragline,
> Boasting o' tonnages, dogies, ants, and stones
> As long as Lind balled Gandas near a gas log
> As it late lit rigatoni and a tag line.
>
> In Dis libidinal radians o' tigons
> Deter no generals, no ordinaries,
> No Adlerians tarring arteries' DNA,
> Triliteral arsenal of nitid groins.
>
> Begone, senile Tiresias, raser o' tanneries!
> Gastonia's grants-in-aid, sestertia to Liebig,
> Are raising glissading sergeants' titillation
> In lairs o'daisies, glarier and estranging. . . . (67)

The poem was derived from a computer printout that was a part of a room-sized poem-environment for "Sound at P. S. 1," a show of sound-related artworks in a performance and exhibition space in Long Island City, a section of New York City's borough of Queens. This project—*A Vocabulary for Annie Brigitte Gilles Tardos* [see *Representative Works: 1938–1985* (New York: Roof Books, 1986), pp. 293-305]—had many phases. First was the gathering (from the previously mentioned collegiate-sized dictionary) of a vocabulary of 5,000 words spelled only with the letters of the dedicatee's name, no letter being repeated in any word more times than in the whole name. Then this vocabulary was run through the computer program that pulled out 3,000 lines, each comprising one to ten of these words, each accompanied by the suffixes whose appending produces word-forms fitting the poem's letter-specifications. Then I painted, with colored oil-paint sticks on heavy drawing paper, two

113

very large drawings—one 16 feet by 6 feet, the other 9 feet by 6 feet—comprising many sentences, each made from one line of printout. Before the computer phase, I'd drawn words from the list by random-digit chance operations and composed (by typing the words on correction tape and mounting the pieces of tape) designs made up of sentences comprising those words. These designs were printed on sheets of colored acetate and mounted, by Anne Tardos and myself, over the windowpanes of the room. I also exhibited the original typed word list and the whole computer printout of word groups, divided into several portions, each hanging from ceiling to floor between two windows.

Later I've periodically reused the 3,000-line computer printout as a source for other texts, among them "Antic Quatrains," which comprises twelve quatrains of loose iambic pentameter, some including end-rhymes. This traditional-sounding poem was made from chance-selected computer-printout lines by appropriately inserting structure words such as articles, conjunctions, and prepositions spelled with the name's letters. (Because the name includes no *h* and no *f,* I could only include indefinite articles and use the "antique-looking" "o'" for "of."

Watten: I'd like to continue our discussion of your book *Bloomsday.* So far we've been talking about the second half of the book, which was composed in 1980 and '81 by nonintentional procedures. The question I'm building toward in this conversation is this: When you, at least temporarily, abandoned nonintentional procedures and began writing straight onto the page, what was going on? That seems to have been a significant decision.

Mac Low: I think it appears more abrupt than it was. I had written poems "directly on the page" from 1937, when I was a kid in high school, to late 1954, so I have a large body of early poems composed in this way. And throughout the quarter-century from 1954 to late 1981, during which I employed various nonintentional procedures to make most of my texts, I also wrote directly-political poems, poems of personal reflection, love poems, and so on. Some were hybrids made by combining direct writing with nonintentional procedures. Many others weren't. Some were written in traditional prosody, accentual-syllabic, syllabic, or accentual, while others resemble "projective verse."

I think what happened in December '81 is that I became interested in what would come out at this point after following nonintentional disciplines for so many years. It was a largely spontaneous turning without much of an ideational basis. I think my intention was simply to start writing and see what happened. And what came out was a different kind of poetry than what I'd written *before* employing nonintentional procedures.

I don't know, really, what that turn involved. For one thing, I'd been reading a great deal of poetry, and I'd come to realize that its writing involved the ego differently than I'd previously felt it did. . . .

As you know, a Zen Buddhist motivation underlay most of my nonintentionally composed work. I sought to present elements of reality—both language and nonverbal sound—directly, concretely. If one concentrates on, gives, as the Buddhists say, "bare attention" to any particular sensation, volition, idea,

114

etc., or any complex composed of such so-called *dharmas*, one may possibly reach a clearer view than when obstructed by the ego and its intentions.

And in following nonintentional procedures I also hoped to avoid the clotting of action that takes place through habit and other formations and deformations induced by one's biography.

These were the main motivations behind my devising and using nonintentional compositional and performance procedures. But as I worked with them for many years, I realized the extent to which they—the methods themselves—were of course products of the ego. There *is* a sense in which something *other* than my self and my tastes is involved in nonintentional procedures: even though "I" devise them, *they* select the details and often the structures of the works. But many aspects of the works are due to my predilections.

Watten: You're saying that there can't be a decision in the writing practice that's *purely* exterior to choice . . .

Mac Low: The key word is "purely." I've learned in the course of devising and employing nonintentional procedures that even though the systems make for substantial "nonegoic moments," choice always enters at some level, if only initially.

Watten: And you're feeling your way through a medium, in a sense. You're actually operating in a medium. It's a much more expanded medium than, say, Emily Dickinson's . . .

Mac Low: It's the medium of all the language I have had available, including other languages than English—French, German, Greek, etc. But I think I felt that—even in this "more direct" kind of writing—not my ego but a reservoir of language and experience was producing the poems. The experience of writing quasi-intentionally is similar to how I imagine so-called automatic writing.

When writing, for instance, the first group of such poems—those written from 7 December 1981 to 31 January 1982 and published in *From Pearl Harbor Day to FDR's Birthday* (College Park, Md.: Sun & Moon, 1982)—I constantly made choices—mostly subliminal choices—very quickly, and almost all of them came quite spontaneously, starting with four seven-poem series, catenas of linked poems. Since I have written a great deal of metrical poetry, what came out was some of my old habits: at some level I was intending the poems to come out metrically, or at least quasi-metrically. The language included everything I had accreted till then in one way or another, and I think it is quite different from the language of a poet like Dickinson or Bob Creeley who is continually *speaking*. Here's an example, the third poem in the series "Baltimore Porches":

Sensitize or creak in leap year lyrics
Illyrian canceled zebras swat or clot
in either crapulation ignorant z-strings
ennoble hopeless popish diamond finders

115

Climbers christen pediatric ramp nodes
insistent principality miners reify
defiant sickly sun crisp validations
denature zero Cratylus aping spinsters

Disfingered particle renters hint at telethons
enforced infractions riot against in clinics
slim critical Nesselrode totals pleasure polka dots
in giddy postulates braceleted clerics accost

Rosters of violent dinky Réamur cribs
exist in interfering pinking tanker gloves
where closures' gristle distances enzyme modules

A mockup or cordage freezes zealous planchettes
hipped settlers sent to shattered Elysian streams
grown pigs or tackling kismet farmers' knuckles puzzle (24)

Watten: Reading those first poems in *From Pearl Harbor Day to FDR's Birthday*, written without using nonintentional procedures, it would be difficult for me to tell the difference between those works and ones generated by such procedures . . .

Mac Low: Other people have told me that.

Watten: But when we get to *Bloomsday*, there are poems in which I can see choices being made, shapes in the entire poem, that would be very hard to assign a merely chance value to, and so there are kinds of . . .

Mac Low: I'm not sure that I understand what you mean by "a chance value," but I think something like that is still present in both *Pearl Harbor Day* and the first part of *Bloomsday*, despite the fact that I wrote those poems in a "quasi-intentional"—rather than "nonintentional"—way. What is most different is that when I was writing these poems, concatenations of sounds led me on, the meanings led me on, and rapidly accepted predilections were operating. These kinds of choices, made rapidly at the subliminal level, produced— despite the poems' being similar in vocabulary and even in sound to some nonintentional works—some perceptible differences from what was produced by nonintentional procedures. On the other hand, the method through which I produced, say, "Antic Quatrains" gave it many of the characteristics —"devices," I'd say, rather than "values"—of traditional verse, such as assonance and alliteration, because all of the words came from a limited set of letters. Could it be that in making that system, my predilections may have operated subliminally to design it in such a way that its results had those sonic/stylistic qualities?

Watten: Why don't we hear one of the poems from the first section of *Bloomsday*?

Mac Low: OK. I'll read part of a political one first and then tell how a political vocabulary got into it. This is from "The Psychological Aspects of the Threat

116

of Nuclear War" (the title came after the poem):

> Much more than they did the bombing what they ended
> up speaking about was not the nuclear plants but war
> when people aren't nice to each other any more
> locked up in attics with death threatening them every minute.

> Only crazy people can do this after several years of studying the victims
> believing themselves nonexistent leaving an abiding feeling
> that they could not escape the consciousness of death
> becoming convinced that life is unmanageable if not absurd. . . . (13)

That was written in February 1982. Most of this language came from my writing with the radio on, tuned to another Pacifica station, WBAI in New York. Clauses and phrases were brought into the poem from the political discourse I was hearing while writing it—but from different parts of the discourse: I'd listen, stop, and write, stop, listen, and write—so it is a rapidly constructed collage made up of elements coming from both the radio and myself—mainly from my mishearings and memory lapses. It wasn't really tuned to the intention it ultimately embodied and that I could affirm personally after writing it.

Watten: Your attention was engaged, certainly, by the subject matter.

Mac Low: Yes, but how the poem came out was largely a result of these very rapid choices, this quasi-intentional procedure, which is on the edge of nonintentionality but doesn't use means like objective hazard or diastic text-selection.

Watten: I'm thinking about the way the language of the Basic word list works . . . The last word of "Converging Stanzas"—the word it converges on—is "experience," and "experience" is a strange word because "experience" isn't experience, it's the *word* "experience." There's an interesting difference . . .

Mac Low: Experience is always the description—to oneself or someone else—of a memory, of an immediate past.

Watten: It may be, and it seems that it would shift its meaning depending on what the experience would be. That is, it has a certain referential instability, let's say, that is as wide as experience, and yet it's a single word, "experience." There's a wonderful play that goes on between the word and what it could possibly mean. When you're using the language from that talk about nuclear war, there's a similar play with the gap between language and the thought, the perception, the dread, the anxiety of nuclear war that seems central to why this is an interesting poem, why this is not only an artwork but in fact an investigation into the status of language in terms of our ability to think about something that is essentially unthinkable.

Mac Low: Yes, there's a great gap between the words and phrases that come into the poem from the speaker—I think it may have been a *succession* of people on the same side of the nuclear question as we are—and the unthinkable actuality of nuclear war. But despite the frozen habits of discourse

117

and thought that are embodied in everybody's language, we can use these words and phrases to make discourse that gets *past* and is adversarial toward the source of those habits. (I think that I subliminally intended to do something like this when I made this poem as I did—connecting originally disjoined phrases with a deceptive smoothness makes it seem both familiar and strange and unintentionally ironic.)

Watten: In order to think about the unthinkable we have to use language. And that language is going to be limited by our ability to comprehend something we can't comprehend. In the last stanza you bring in the idea of getting a huge truck pasted up with pictures of the victims:

> There seems to be no picture in people's minds as to what that
> [really means
> but if we get a huge truck pasted up with pictures of the victims
> our whole consciousness of what will await us will be altered
> [inexorably
> teaching us how to break through the wall of denial above the
> [heads of all governments

Mac Low: One of the people on the radio was talking like this . . .

Watten: Let's do that right, and that will change consciousness and so forth. But at the same time, it seems that there's a problem with the mediation of this particular image; it's kind of a futile gesture. My question is, How does it change us to know this, how does it help us to . . .

Mac Low: This futile gesture . . .

Watten: Well no, it's not *only* futile. I mean if you didn't . . .

Mac Low: I know, I wouldn't say it was a *completely* futile gesture. I wouldn't say that *anything* that was done in resistance to either the Vietnam War or nuclear warfare was altogether futile . . .

Watten: Exactly. But my question is, How does it change our sense of what to do politically to know language as objectively as you know it in this poem?

Mac Low: I think it makes us more conscious of how we think and talk about such things. I've seldom thought explicitly about this before. There's a sort of irony in that last stanza's saying that if we got a truck with pictures of the victims on it, it'd teach us how to break through the wall of denial above the heads of all governments, which is obviously what we have to do. It's ironic because it's so touchingly naive for a person—or people—I probably put two or three different persons' thoughts together in that sentence—to have said it. But it ends with an affirmation of human solidarity that I could affirm myself, fully, so you get a play of a kind of friendly irony in the way my mind was selecting things for this poem.

Watten: Yes.

Mac Low: I'd like to read quite a different poem now, called "Giant Otters." I think I started writing the poem while I was hearing or reading something about these otters, and then the poem just took off on its own in a way that has little or no relation to outside sources.

GIANT OTTERS

They were a close family of giant otters
in Surinam giving a low growling sound when
they were insecure so they were called the Hummers.

Trace elements had landed near them and they effloresced
in even amounts throughout an even eon and an evening more
fortunate as they were in knowing nothing

or peering curiously into unknowable presence
alert   to no future   living the past as presence
whose elements were traces in their efflorescing being

going as far as they could within the world they were
as fortune particularized occasions within unfolding
breathed upon by memory's wraith and anticipation's all but
[absence.

Where were they going but farther along and through
whatever their being eventuated in clearness   no demand for
[clarity
as the eyes are unsealed and the world flows in as light?

Watten: The poem seems to begin anywhere, the anywhere being giant otters
in Surinam, but I'm not sure whether the "they" in the last stanza is still the
otters or, in a way, us.

Mac Low: I'm not sure either. Although it's ostensibly the otters, it seems to be
both.

Watten: It's a transformed . . .

Mac Low: It becomes a . . .

Watten: A shifter.

Mac Low: Yes . . . Somehow I was carried along into this Whiteheadian view of
reality as a succession of "occasions" —something that's been with me since
I first studied Whitehead in the early forties. But also, when I read it to myself
now, I hear a Rilkean echo . . . the leaning, the wide leaning of the animals
into being that Rilke speaks of. These and other ideas came into the poem
more or less "spontaneously," led by the sound. An obvious example is "in
even amounts throughout an even eon and an evening more/fortunate as
they were in knowing nothing." Many words seem to have arrived through
a rhyme or an assonance with preceding words.

Watten: So you are thinking about language as language in addition to thinking *in* language at the same time.

Mac Low: Yes, this is true of almost all the poems in the newer part of *Bloomsday.*

Watten: Why don't we close with a final poem from that first section?

Mac Low: I'll read the antepenultimate one in that section, a very short poem.

It came to me in a somewhat different way: first the words of the poem itself and then the title came to me one after another during a process of meditation on language, but without its being started off by an outside source.

TROPE MARKET

In the network, in the ruin,
flashing classics gravitate,
snared, encumbered voicelessly.

Teak enticements seek, leaping
fan-shaped arras corners
snore among in backward dispatch.

Panels glow, groan, territorialize
fetishistically in nacreous
instantaneity spookily shod.

Watten: I'd like to end with that poem, it seems so beautiful in its self-sufficiency, and I think comment at this point is *not* to the point. I want to thank you for this conversation. This has been Barrett Watten talking with Jackson Mac Low. It's October 24th.

Mac Low: 1985.

Watten: Right (laughs).

section three

Reinventing Community

LANGUAGE WRITING AND LITERARY HISTORY

Bob Perelman

There are more poets in America than most poets and critics might care to think about, and they comprise a widely varied lot. But this variety occurs in a larger climate which promotes individuality and identity politics as dominant though competing possibilities. So it's no surprise that the innovations language writing offers, both on a formal level and in terms of the definition of the function of the poet, have often been received as problematic. When Joel Lewis wrote an article about language writing for an issue of *Poets & Writers*,[1] the next issue printed four letters attacking the movement. Carol F. Ra complained of "disconnected phrases, avoiding communication"; and said the movement should be called "Rambling Typists":

> These poems are "hard" if you try to find meaning. In fact the writing is so easy. The only difficulty is in avoiding connections that could be called insightful or profound.
>
> By stabbing with my pen at random words and phrases . . . in about a minute I "wrote" this Language Poem:
>
> One rejection slip
> the list goes on
> it beats being ignored
> a carnival of public readings
> a bag of cement
>
> Perhaps I've been struggling too hard over the years to make my poems make sense when nonsense is so easy.

Here, the almost century-old technique of Dada composition again demonstrates its uncanny powers: Ra's poem constitutes a usable account of the dynamics of the language movement. It begins in the landscape of the mainstream poetry world, dominated by the mysteries of aesthetic judgement whose dread emblem is the rejection slip; it then moves to the formation of a group: "it beats being ignored/a carnival of public readings." Writing in such an atmosphere is, as Ra twice testifies, easy, but what are the results of such untrammeled production? The last line of the poem, "a bag of cement," gives the problematic answer. Does one want to emphasize the cohesive, constructive possibilities of a bag of cement, or see it as a dead lump too heavy to lift comfortably? In either case, we are beyond the ideology of poetry as organic form.

Another letter writer wanted to kill two birds—language writing and poststructuralism—with one stone. He was puzzled that language writing "is so obviously stupid and yet is taken seriously by supposedly reputable scholars

. . . The two seem made for each other—a nonsensical verse explicated by and lionized by a criticism of gibberish."

But in fact such a twin juggernaut has not yet materialized. Most contemporary theory, if it comes into contact with poems and novels at all, has tended to deal with 19th century works, not contemporary writing. And when a less theoretical segment of the academy has dealt with language writing, the outcome has not been all that different from the results at *Poets & Writers*.

When the issue of *Critical Inquiry* entitled "Politics & Poetic Value" was turned into a book, six new essays were added.[2] A summary, and essays on Goldsmith and Kipling were not surprising inclusions. But the other three additions were more significant editorial gestures. The issue was clearly designed to be eclectic, with subjects ranging from Pindar to Marianne Moore's war poetry to contemporary Black South African poetry. However, Jerome McGann's article on language writing required three follow-up pieces, indicating that his claims for the political and aesthetic value of language writing were something of a breach of intellectual decorum, or at least formed an unstable part of a collection which, to reiterate, was meant to be inclusive.

For McGann, L=A=N=G=U=A=G=E Writing, as he referred to it, was not just a new experimentalism. Rather, it represented a critique of U.S. imperialism, and beyond that of capitalism itself. The qualifications McGann offered as to how singlemindedly such a project was approached paled in the glare of so totalized a goal. McGann read L=A=N=G=U=A=G=E Writing, not as another voice added to a plural choir, but as a repudiation of the ways of reading and writing poetry that underlay the plurality.

While McGann placed the L=A=N=G=U=A=G=E project in a large social context, he did not attach much importance to its group structure, calling it a "loose collective enterprise" [253]. He focused on the particularity of each reader and each reading, stating that the anti- and non-narrative modes used in L=A=N=G=U=A=G=E Writing cause the "relationships and forms of order [to] . . . shift from reader to reader and from reading to reading . . . . What 'counts' are the multiple perspectives processed through the text along with the reader who takes part in that processing" [267, 271]. Responding to McGann, Jed Rasula, a poet and critic closely associated with the language movement, emphasized the primacy of the group. For Rasula, the movement's development of independent networks of criticism and publication was crucial: "It's a singular phenomenon that poets should come together as active readers and conceptually adroit critics of one another's work . . . A politics in and a politics of American poetry can never arrive at a full collaboration between writer and reader without the deliberate location and cultivation of an audience" [322].

Charles Altieri's main target was McGann's article, but he attacked Rasula's position as well, finding the solidarity of the language group dubious. He pointed out that language writers wrote variously and that the work of some could hardly be called political: thus to speak of a common purpose made little sense. He scorned the notion that the liberation of the reader could produce the political effects hailed by McGann. "The reader's sense of his or her interpretative freedom to produce meanings" was "dangerously close to . . . the idea

of the free, pleasure-seeking consumer that L=A=N=G=U=A=G=E Writing's
doctrines so pompously revile" [306]. For Altieri, McGann's "ideals of readerly
freedom do little more than curry favor with an audience already committed
to the radical gestures of an avant-garde" [307]. David Bromwich discounted
the whole tempest, remarking magisterially that "there is a problem, perhaps a
minor one, about 'the L=A=N=G=U=A=G=E poets,' the heroes [McGann] selects
to represent poetic radicalism today. They do not appear, as yet, to write good
poems" [327]. For Bromwich, language writers are a group only in the sense
that the New Kids on the Block are a group: they are a jejune promotional
entity. As a reader, he felt singularly unliberated by language writing.

This debate encapsulates a number of the difficulties that language writing
is raising as it is coming into contact with the wider spheres of literary studies
and theory. Are there political implications to the writing techniques of the
movement? Are there literary implications to the movement's cohesiveness?
Both of these questions are charged, and they need to be considered together.
But determining what language writing is as writing and what it is as a literary
movement is not easy.

Even the name of the movement seems difficult to pin down. For McGann
and Altieri, it is *L=A=N=G=U=A=G=E Writing*. Rasula uses *Language Writing*,
"emphatically deleting the equals signs . . . in order to register [his] disagreement with McGann" [317] over the institutional status of the movement.
Bromwich puts the term in quotes: "the L=A=N=G=U=A=G=E poets." Language
writers themselves are no more united in their terminologies: *language* is always included, sometimes capitalized, with but mostly without equal signs; the
second word is sometimes *poetry*, sometimes *writing*. There is also *the language
school, the language movement*, and a late increasingly popular entry, *so-called
language writing*, which catches the deep distrust of being labeled as well as of
self-labeling.

Consider the titles of two magazines which were initially devoted to language
writing: *This* and *L=A=N=G=U=A=G=E*. The first is constructivist, the second
deconstructive. *This* is a deictic—it points something out; there has to be somebody doing the pointing: a person, using a word, using it specifically, confidently,
this not that. If anything is, *this* is here and now, present and accounted for,
but of course the question arises, what is this?

L=A=N=G=U=A=G=E, on the other hand, presents a different problem, as
anyone who has ever had to type it more than once will understand. The labor
of materially producing writing: uppercase *L* lowercase *equals* uppercase *A*
lowercase *equals* uppercase *N* etc. If the equals signs are focused on, then there
seems to be a general functional equivalence, *L* equals *A*, etc.—a letter is a
letter. A Saussurian poetics, perhaps, where sign equals nothing more than its
difference from every other sign. Beyond the letters, more kaballisticly, there
is the possibility of the universal, all-permissive word, language.

Given these two titles, is language writing constructivist, dominated by technique, or deconstructive, disseminative, marginal?

Two of the principal anthologies of language writing reflect this unease over
proclamations of identity in their titles: Silliman's *In The American Tree: Language*

Realism Poetry[3] and Douglas Messerli's *"Language" Poetries: An Anthology.*[4] Silliman was using "realism" in his title to combat the charges of abstraction and obscurity that arose as language writing began gaining public recognition,[5] but in doing so he was commandeering an opposing term. Messerli made two gestures away from group solidarity, putting "language" in quotes and using the plural "poetries." By the way, both of these anthologies use "poetry" or "poetries" in their titles, a valorization of the genre division between prose and poetry that much of the anthologized writing does not respect.

This problem over names mirrors an equally basic problem: how much of a group phenomenon is language writing? And if there is a group who is in it? This latter question is charged: Silliman's anthology includes 38 writers; in his introduction he names 79 others specifically and ends the list with "and others," asserting that an anthology of "absolutely comparable value" could have been gathered from their writing.[6] The issue of quality versus community is not so easily settled; by its insistence Silliman's gesture displays the fragility of formal assertions in the face of social circumstance. If one "writes like" a language writer, then is one a language writer? Conversely, if one "is" a language writer, then is what one writes language writing? Can Carol F. Ra's poem, which she ironically claims to be a "Language Poem," be considered one, unironically? Is Jed Rasula, "a poet and critic closely associated with the language movement," a language writer? If he is not, one could hardly deduce that from his writing. (When I asked him if he was one, he said, "Apparently not." He does appear in Silliman's list of 79.) Is John Cage a language writer? Gertrude Stein? Louis Zukofsky? Lorine Niedecker? George Oppen? Mina Loy? Laura Riding? Laura Riding Jackson? Early John Ashbery? Later John Ashbery? Is it merely a matter of social bonding? Is there such a thing as "language writing"? or is there simply "language writing: the literary movement"? And if language writing is primarily a literary movement, how does one defend it against Altieri's point that many language writers write very differently one from another?

A neutral description of language writing might attempt to draw a line around a range of writing that is (sometimes) non-referential, (occasionally) poly-syntactic, (often) politically committed, (in places) theoretically inclined, and that (in some cases) enacts a critique of the literary *I*. But such neutrality is useless here. A prosecutorial nominalist looking at specific passages might doubt that the term defined anything in particular.

Consider the following examples.

POSTCARDS

Man in
the eye clinic
rubbing his
eye—

too convincing. Like
memory.

My parents' neighbors' house,
backlit,
at the end of their street.
                    —Rae Armantrout[7]

Armantrout's poem is directly referential to the physical world; memory,
albeit suspiciously, is invoked, and a lyric self exists in unproblematized form.
(This is far from true in many of her other poems.) While they are truncated,
the sentences are complete, ending with periods. This poem is not written in
a universe all that far removed from that of the 'Objectivists'[8]; the plain speech
meticulously scored in short lines brings Oppen and Niedecker to mind.

from PCOET

ruignging
ther o weigter a owef.

Th. erou tower

    ofv Herm
        on
oswwod paseris

ther apt   I wpsetn
wae
a doz   peoftna   rmoll
                    —David Melnick[9]

Melnick's poem is in the *zaum* tradition—if an impulse that only wants to
create novel objects can be said to constitute a tradition. Armantrout uses
conventional language to express suspicion of the simulacra of memory and
the puns of perception; Melnick acts on those suspicions, writing a poem—in
terms of its look on the page not that removed from some Objectivist poems
by the way—in which each group of letters can suggest a mutated or degraded
word: is "ruignging" a 'ruined' form of *ruining*? or it can be seen, not so much
read, as free from the necessities of language: "ruignging" is almost a palin-
drome; it's also just a clump of letters confronting over-trained readers dying
to make sense at any cost.

But what of lines like "tower//ofv/Herm"? Melnick's later homophonic
rendering of the first three books of the *Iliad* into a hyperbolic comedy of
homoerotic possibilities—"You come on us, Danaans, sit thee up, rope your
son, a fine ace ass./Ooh 'tis same you zone toes, sky a peak: Tony, Dirk, all men.
Oh, you?"[10]—makes me read echoes of sex and ancient Greece back into a
passage, written a decade before the translation, that formally might seem to
forbid all ascription of meaning. Consideration of individual career trajectories allows for more accurate readings than a generalized formal grid meant to

apply to all language writing.

from "I GUESS WORK THE TIME UP"

Zero population growth patting
rabbit hash undoubtedly inspired
by the real Negro November 1958's *won't* paternalism
formerly associate with no compute King Diamonds of Osteopath
venture Ne Plus Ultra Doze Pigeon Wing get it gets
renounces Glum Wig Trepidation   First of the one-legged
two feet square comradorial retard to floor crowded around two
in the bred from dough can't write my name even
deluxe accuse affected lungs bed me a forgery   Mrs. J
proverbial two tiny sad sad girl & boy bath rooms roping
go to material quizzes wheel & deal
creolization too cerebral mummies
stringy 4 floors presto Mrs K has two tiny boxes
meaning "Go War! Go Draft!" to remain
too dependent on unexpected patternings of things referred to
(fuck epistemology)
—Bruce Andrews[11]

Unlike *Pcoet*, this does use words, many words, and most of them sites of
ideological conflict. There is no overarching narrative resolution; there is no
narrative structure; there are barely any sentences. Phrase jams up against
phrase with ferocious pace as if a New York graffiti writer was trying to cover
the whole subway system in one night, though here all the trains are in motion.
Andrews has no time to finish readymade phrases: his critique of liberalism
seems to be "*won't* paternalism." Not that those two words finish the subject
off—he continues the critique throughout the twenty-five pages of the poem.
No mimesis is possible here, but this refers quite directly to the historical here
and now.

from WHAT

This woman
is seriously allergic to bees. Details
like zombies in Day of the Dead. Yellow brick
facade. Those sentences had 'been about' the letter E.
Those painters' silence sealed their fate. At least
Rosenberg's coinage, "action painting," caught
the heroic individualism, that sense of the romantic that
would doom them all. Plastic curtains that mine
stained glass. My grandmother, the youngest of 13,
was herself raised by a single parent, as was
her mother also. Here the houses have all gone stylish,

128

deep mauves of brown with a blue trim. Psyche
yourself up for the next line. Watching
the traffic 'copter hover over the freeway.
The point at which you read each word (the
only point there is), two minds share a larger whole.
                    —Ron Silliman[12]

The sentences here are descriptive; the sentence rhythm is associational:
"Those sentences had 'been about'" triggers "Those painters' silence," which
triggers the judgment of action painting, which triggers the aesthetic presentation of the plastic curtains, which triggers the domestic memories, etc. There's
little sense here—as there is elsewhere in Silliman's writing[13]—of a critique of
the subject: if you want Silliman's opinion of Abstract Expressionism, read what
he writes. His hope for communion with reader, of two minds sharing a larger
whole, is also nonironic. While there is a continual sense of contextual disruption between sentences, there is no disruption in the politics, which attempt to
exemplify a unified political analysis that stretches from minutiae of writing
and living as material practices to ideological generalizations. The more pages
of this book-length poem one reads, the more it resolves into a present-tense
autobiography.

from THE WIDE ROAD

Paranoia results from that old religious preoccupation with the
smallest detail and with similarities. And travelling as we are, we
can't indulge in self-portraiture, even when we are stark naked. In
fact, much of the time we exceed the perfect differences between
you and us, since they are the details demarcating the biological
depths and social heights, part history and part isolation. Meanwhile, we incite ourselves to introspect and expect—is this love?
is this theory?—we are not experts of postponement.

> Our head is round, such is life
> have we not hatched it?

"We can't get that poem out of our head," we said. We are slaves of
environment.
    He is standing behind us and above us on the slope and puts his
arms around us, passing his fingers over our breasts and reaching
between our legs.
    From this elevation, we have a remarkable look over a high gray
fence into the yard where outdated statuary is stored at the face
of an eroded cosmonaut and at 17 arms and forefingers of Lenin.
    . . .

> We come closer to facing
> the frightening malleability
> of gender.
>
> —Carla Harryman and Lyn Hejinian[14]

This is part of an on-going collaboration where the main character or characters—the "we"—is or are engaged on a picaresque journey through a landscape where gender is as discussable and inescapable as the weather. Narrative is entertained provisionally, and seems to have as much plausibility as the represented plural self in the piece has physical validity. Here, the "we" accurately reflects the fact that two writers are writing; at the same time the constructed quality of the represented self is impossible to ignore when the man passes his fingers over "our" breasts and reaches between "our" legs. The cult of Lenin's personality is effectively critiqued by citing the 17 phallic pointers toward inevitable historic progress; but the body of the narrator is also problematic: how many breasts or legs are being caressed, two or four?

Insofar as critical battles between supporters and detractors of language writing are being fought over the issue of how the reader is affected, or what the political consequences of these effects are, I think the results will remain equivocal, as the previous mini-readings suggest. These examples—and I could have chosen a number of other equally disparate ones—in turns use conventional syntax or not; use words or not; are mimetic or not; use the first person or not; etc. In some cases, there is also quite a bit of variety within a single writer's work.

So, yes, this various writing can be read, and needs to be read variously, and there are complex literary effects and antecedents in play at all points. Nevertheless, I want to oppose this point in two ways, and to propose that language writing is best understood as a group phenomenon, and that it is one whose primary tendency is to do away with the reader as a separable category. I realize that such an idea makes a problematic slogan. If language writing wants to do away with the reader, then why wouldn't readers want to do away with language writing? Bromwich's reaction would seem inevitable: poems not addressed to a reader would have a hard time being "very good," judged by the readerly criteria presumably employed.

On the other hand, in theory-oriented circles, this could seem like little more than a call for Barthes' writerly text, and at first glance, it is somewhat similar. Barthes' proposals, at the beginning of *S/Z*, for a writing that would "make the reader no longer a consumer, but a producer of the text"[15] seems quite close to what is often called for by language writers and what often happens with language writing. But the position of a reader 'producing' a reading of a text that is already before her eyes is closer to that of a graffiti writer confronting a poster than it is to a reader turning writer and writing a new text. And while *S/Z* is, technically, a new, written text, it is still a polyvalent gloss on a classic text, *Sarrasine*. In practice, there are readers of readerly texts and readers of writerly texts. The readings are different, but it is only in a highly metaphorical sense that *S/Z* is a rewriting of *Sarrasine*. Even the *of* in the phrase "a rewriting of *Sarrasine*" makes my point.[16]

To give a better sense of what I mean by doing away with the reader as a separable category, let me give a brief, subjective narrative of language writing.

"Instead of ant wort I saw brat guts." This line is the epigraph to *In The American Tree*. In a canonical literary history, one addressed to a judging reader, such a phrase would make quite a limited aesthetic object. But as I am interested in non-canonical or anti-canonical sets of literary narratives where literary history is created by writers, I'll begin here and give the circumstances of the birth of this momentous line.

Kit Robinson, Steve Benson and I began a writing project almost as soon as we met in San Francisco in 1976. One of us would read from whatever books were handy and two of us would type. These roles would rotate; occasionally, there would be two readers reading simultaneously. The reader would switch books whenever he felt like it, and jump around within whatever book was open at the time. Truman Capote's slam at Kerouac—that this was typing, not writing —would have been even truer here, though none of us could type as fast as Kerouac, who apparently was a terrific typist, an ability which undoubtedly shaped his work.

There was no question of keeping up with the stream of spoken words; they could be attended to or not. If I felt no spark of imagination I would type at or toward the next batch of them I heard, though the rates of speed of spoken syllable versus typed letter were so disparate that by the time a phrase such as "For the purposes of this paper, I will assume a familiarity with Foucault's critique of the notion of the author as an individual" was read I might have managed to type "For the purposes of paper." At that point, I may have started to hear a tone in the typed phrase I wanted to pursue. I can have a sickened fond loathing longing for sentences that start with "For": they remind me of a biblical loftiness, however many degrees removed from that I remain. So I might continue on my own unmarked track and write, "For the purposes of paper are not the purposes of words alone." By this time, the reader-as-pronouncer might be in the midst of pronouncing "or take the shuttle bus from Gare du Nord, poets, novelists, editors, bookstore owners, Lacanian psychoanalysts, and spend the day." That would certainly come in handy, for instance in producing: "For the purposes of paper are not the purposes of words alone but of poets and novelists, Lacanian psychoanalysts, bookstore owners, and other figures of speech bartering their thought balloons for a bronzed handle on the deeper cellars of the city's statuesque psyche."

We did this for a couple of months, generating a lot of pages which we 'worked on,' picked through, or mostly filed away. A few lines show up in a few pieces of Robinson's *Down and Back*, Benson's *As Is*, and my *7 Works*. "Instead of ant work I saw brat guts" begins my book, although in fact Robinson wrote/typed it. (It is in 'his voice.')

I don't want to make claims for this process as representative of language writing; no published work that I know of has been written using this method. But I want the extremity of this process, where reading and writing, hearing and producing words were so jammed together, to emblematize an important collaborative element of the beginnings of the language movement. In the above description, I notice that the conventional positions of (modernist) literary competence are reversed: instead of the writer being powerful and the reader struggling to catch up, having to read Dante's Italian, Ovid's Latin, and the Elizabethans in their entirety to be able to read *The Waste Land*, in the brat guts literary environment, the reader—or, to avoid confusion, the pronouncer—is the active one and the writer, the typist, the swamped receiver, is reactive, is second in the chain of command, which becomes a chain of suggestion.

Collaborations form a significant portion of published language writing, and beyond these there is a pervasive environment of collaboration at the formal level, with writers often initiating parallel projects; but in this the movement does not differ from, say, the New York school, especially the second generation, or the Surrealists. Much more significant is the blending together of the roles of reader, writer, poet, critic, theorist, publisher and reviewer. Many poems trespass, in various seemly to unseemly ways, on the territory conventionally reserved for criticism. (E.g., Armantrout's self-critique, "Man in/the eye clinic /rubbing his/eye—//too convincing"; Andrews' brusque, but philosophically dismal, "fuck epistemology"; Silliman's critique of Action Painting.) The self-generated reading, publication, and reviewing venues that Rasula mentioned were crucial in not allowing separated poetic or critical decorums to develop. The reviews in $L=A=N=G=U=A=G=E$ magazine were notorious for only quoting, or for chopping up, or for otherwise refusing to differentiate themselves from, the books under review, declining all authoritative, critical distance. The books 'under review' were not so much read, as rewritten—in a far more literal sense than happens with *S/Z*. The Talks Series[17] was an effort in this direction, with some talks as much group performance pieces as presentations by an individual to a group.

When I gave my talk "The First Person,"[18] Barrett Watten in the audience scribbled furiously through most of it. He wasn't taking notes on my unsynthesized compendium of first person writing positions, he was using the words I was speaking to write with: one can read shards of the talk in his poem "Statistics" in *1-10*.[19] The hypertrophied system of quotation marks might be read as a reaction to my speaking about speech.

> But "pyramids, tombs, chariots of 'personal experience'" want confusion of "schoolboy torn in half" in an odd, "theoretical" way. Transcription stood, the "8-year-old sentient gone": "speaking" twelve feet from the water, its "audience" on the rock. He wanted "baleful 'all-knowing' distance" out of this borrowed substance "often more personal than he." . . . "Let me in" pushed between "to have intelligibility" hopeless repetition "which takes you away."

If Watten took some of his vocabulary from my talk, one of the passages I quoted in that talk was from my book *a.k.a.*,[20] which owed a great part of its formal instigation to his prose piece, "City Fields."[21] Ron Silliman would later label such collaged sentences, "New Sentences." The passage from *a.k.a.*, that

132

I quoted in my talk and that Watten rewrote included these sentences:

> Everybody gets a biography. Pinholes effect the maximum registration. Vocabularies set up camp on a blurred, running, bloody map. Now they write the lyrics out so I'll know what the song is talking about. Schoolboy torn in half by book. An italicized *i* staggers down the street, making its demands known to the traffic. . . . Two thousand year old empire in eight year old brain.

Looking at my sentences now through the lens of Watten's poem, I read a reiterated drama of education: "Schoolboy torn in half by book. Two thousand year old empire [i.e., Latin, etc.] in eight year old brain." Maps are bloody, and italicized *i*'s in whom educational procedures have not taken end up talking to the traffic. I seem to be anxiously regarding a narrative in which language becomes instrumentalized: first they sing, but later "they write the lyrics out," and songs talk. The last sentence in Watten's poem ("Let me in" pushed between "to have intelligibility" hopeless repetition "which takes you away") calls up related questions of acceptance, mastery, bureaucratization, history, and death, all of which are present and unresolved in the narrative of reaching maturity in language.

If the brat guts aesthetic is taken to represent the infant stage of writing—somewhere between Lacan's imaginary and symbolic stages with the baby looking in the mirror of the word stream and lisping his own non-reflective attempts at the typewriter—and if writing like my *a.k.a.* and Watten's "Statistics" can represent going to school (in however conflicted a way), then the 'developmental level' of the following example of collaborative language writing will instantly be grasped as 'more advanced'—possibly even as 'adult'. I am evoking this narrative of maturity sardonically because it's not clear if an 'adult'—i.e., normalized—language writing would be language writing at all. But an address to a wide, impersonal audience can be clearly perceived in the following:

AESTHETIC TENDENCY AND THE POLITICS OF POETRY: A MANIFESTO

For anyone who has been following American poetry over the last decade, it is evident that there has been an intense and contradictory response—from enthusiasm and imitation to dismissal and distortion —to our work. "Our work," in this instance, is part of a body of writing, predominantly poetry, in what might be called the experimental or avant-garde tradition. Its history, while not nearly so canonized as the earlier example, say, of Surrealism, has been generally acknowledged along these lines: around 1970, a number of writers, following the work of such experimenters as Gertrude Stein and Louis Zukofsky, began writing in ways that questioned the norms of persona-centered, "expressive," poetry. [261]

This is from an article Benson, Harryman, Hejinian, Silliman, Watten, and I wrote for *Social Text* in 1988.[22] The opening now seems to me somewhat problematic in revealing ways. The question of imitation and distortion seems odd. In the brat guts aesthetic, certainly, there is nothing but distortive imitation—no originary clarity to be received accurately. The narrative of the avant-garde tradition presupposes a sequence of literary groups, but in our case, even though group structure was a crucial given, a set group identity was not. In writing the article, we had great trouble with the words *we* and *our*. *We* is to apply locally in the article; whereas *our* applies to language writing as a whole:

> In terms of its reception "our work" can mean the writing of up to several dozen writers who have been identified as part of an aesthetic tendency whose definition is not a matter of doctrine but of overlapping affinities. Here, we stands for a consensus arrived at for the purposes of this article among six of its members on the West Coast. [261]

But our use of the word *our* doesn't match our use of *we*. We could not narrativize the entire, amorphously defined group and simultaneously embody the subject of such a narrative. We six authors were not interested in making a case for our own writing, but of making three claims for the value of language writing as a whole: 1) that it is a group phenomenon; 2) that language writing not only critiques the norms of voice and self but addresses political and epistemological spaces that voice–poems do not; and 3) that theory can be useful in making these critiques and addresses.

Why didn't we simply name this body of writing? While we were clearly dealing with the subject of language writing, we avoided that name. Near the end of the article we wrote, "While we are flagrantly writing this article as a group, the perceptive reader will already have noticed that until this point neither the 'Language School' nor 'Language Poetry' has been named. This is no accident" [272-3]. Internally, group structure is crucial: language writing is the activity that blurs the distinction between reader and writer, poet and critic; externally, group identity is disavowed: given the deep disinterest in poetics of identity, the creation of literary labels would hardly be desirable.

However, from the outside, the process of identification was simpler. Although we had entitled the piece for *Social Text* "Aesthetic Tendency and the Politics of Poetry," when it was published the editors added the designation "A Manifesto." Perhaps their perceptions were colored by the fact that we had mentioned the Surrealists as a prior avant-garde movement. But the Surrealists, in addition to their definite name, had an organization where membership was a matter of charged definition. Along with this barrier between the group and the world went a narrative of apocalyptic literary-social change, which was also crucial for Breton's definition of his movement: "I believe in the future resolution of these two states, dream and reality, which are seemingly so contradictory, into a kind of absolute reality, a *surreality*, if one may so speak."[23]

On the other hand, in writing our piece, the six of us had no desire for a rigorously structured and self-defined group and no such firm designs on the

134

future. For us, the avant-garde was a "tradition" in which we situated "our work"; we also placed that writing in or near to the same field as postmodern theory. In these circumstances, a manifesto hardly seems a feasible, let alone a desirable, genre.

To go a step further: if a language writing manifesto is not possible because a manifesto's implied separation of advanced writers from benighted readers is false to the spirit of language writing, then, given the mode I am proposing, in what sense can language writing be said to address an outside at all? If language writing arises so completely out of a group nexus, couldn't it be labeled coterie writing?

But to reiterate, it's the notion of readerly overview that the movement wants to overturn. A public is addressed not as readers but as writers. The formalisms and disruptions of conventional continuities that variously mark language writing function to remind readers that they are also producers and not just receivers of language.

Of course, all readers of all poems use language. But where many poems aspire to the finality of aesthetic completion, language writing represents a struggle, not to make profound and inescapable sense ("Perhaps I've been struggling too hard over the years to make my poems make sense," as Carol F. Ra put it), but to unmake just such final sense, and to allow room for further efforts from the readers/writers. "To allow room for further efforts" feels too pat, gestural, automatic. "To construct room for further efforts" is better—such openings can be hard to open and to keep open. The conventional reproach, "I could do that," should actually be taken as a good sign, as a response a writer might seek rather than fear.[24] A better sign might be, "I could do something a bit different than that." Bromwich's arch conclusion—"They do not appear, as yet, to write good poems"—contains a similar reproach, with the "as yet," implying a narrative of aesthetic maturity: perhaps one day they *will* write good poems—what I'm calling closed poems that can only be read. But if my picture of language writing is valid, the various trajectories of the writers will bypass Bromwich's narrative. His assumptions of unchanging literary quality will be irrelevant to the struggles for effective, open interaction among users of language.

But such a non-conclusion is an idealized, slightly utopian construct. There is limited temporal span to groups: individual writing careers tend to get separated out. The language movement has generated a considerable body of poems, prose, and writing which falls somewhere in the middle, and all these tend to go their own ways as they circulate. The complex challenges and invitations this work presents are also perceptible to readers who may not know anything about language writing.

If we are to escape a future where already written poems are to be kept separate from explication, criticism, theory, then better Carol F. Ra stabbing her pen onto the page, and, all irony aside, actually writing something new, than the exuberant marginalia of a Barthes or the frosty agonies of a de Man in his stony aporetic literary gardens. Language writing can be placed in a sequence including the Surrealists, the Objectivists, etc., but even though it

135

can be subsumed within a readerly literary history, it holds out the possibility for new types of writers as well as for a redefinition of literary history as a construct by writers.

Epilogue

A critic came to me and asked, What is language writing? fetching it to me with full hands. I guess it is a uniform hieroglyphic, sprouting alike in prose and in verse, in love-sighs and guerilla acting-out from under administered language deep in a million Broca's areas as told to any one tongue. Or I guess it is the birth of post-industrial code-splicing from a shoal of territorial barks before any one dog has had enough. This process gripped down and began to awaken just after the death of Hamlet's father in a material downpour not just poison in the ear but coins embossed with sovereigns and bills with pictures of buildings and ozone-depleting air-conditioning systems but if you don't keep the windows rolled down you can't hear the words of the song traveling through the dark of the electoral forest. In language writing any president of any body may name a cloud a whale a whale a cloud a whale a whale a cloud a cloud. If so, she should be complimented, complemented, and called on it.

*

Before I write
I have complete
autonomy to write
what I like

*

To my living hands staring
into the keyboard the tape recorder
spoke in its humanized mode:
Speech is writing, writing speech
this is the knot the body
remembers others a war brought
home in bags repressed sentences
repeatedly editing the explosions down
to combinatory senses read against
the future fall suns shining
into wooded rooms where Whitman
speaks into the wax cylinder:
love, America, individual bodies
picked out of large groups

*

Yes, the poetry journals had been right. It was time for him to set out on his journey eastward; panoptical terminology was general all over these literary states. It was falling on every grade level of the dark central plain, falling softly upon the Bog of Language Writing, and, farther eastward, softly falling through the dark Freudian vacation hours. The long Atlantic coast stretched long and the Pacific Coast stretched long but it easily stretched with them north or south. It spanned between them also from east to west and reflected what was between them. On it rose solid growths that offset the growths of pine and cedar and hemlock and liveoak and locust and hickory and limetree and cottonwood and tuliptree and cactus and wildvine and tamarind and per-simmon. And tangles as wild as any canebrake or swamp . . . forests coated with transparent ice and icicles hanging from the boughs and crackling in the wind . . . sides and peaks of mountains . . . pasturage sweet and free as savan-nah or upland or prairie. With flights and songs and screams that answered those of the wildpigeon and highhold and orchard-oriole and coot and surf-duck and redshouldered-hawk and fish-hawk and white-ibis and indian-hen and cat-owl and water-pheasant and qua-bird and pied-sheldrake and black-bird and mockingbird and buzzard and condor and night-heron and eagle.

*

O for a Muse of fire that would take
the shuttle bus from Gare-du-Nord
to the brightest heaven of invention
printed in material form
read by material readers.

*

Like a congregation
listening to Latin
and enjoying the sense
of a communal rite
ladies and gentlemen
crouching for employment:
crooked figures of common sense
and eventual reunification
sending thousands to class,
fed, sheltered, evaluated
and placed in the continuum.

*

Can this line hold the vasty Theory of France
Or may we cram within this noise

137

the very O of poems that did affright
the air of APR or NPR, not to mention the NYRB?

Since masterful theory may attest
in transposed light the luscious sun,
then let me, a cipher to this great accompt
on your practico-poetic phobias work.

Suppose within the girdle of the next quatrain
are now confined two mighty literary movements
whose poly-headed and abutting fronts
the perilous narrow years spin quite differently:

the Objectivists, in the marginalized trunks,
speaking American to one another as if to a crowd of energized
          workers
and the language writers, wearing codeless uniforms,
passing notes a bird would sing if birds would only read.

*

Piece out these imperfections with your writing.
Into a fresher word divide and multiply each word
and make imaginary power, that is, make power.

*

I never read the book you gave me twentyfive years ago. I want you
to know that I have now and that it is remarkable.

*

Think, when we traduce tradition and produce group feedback
and hunt and peck for truth on famous screens
that you see words in lines, moving in the world
that is moving with your use, didn't your eyes
just move from left to right?
or was that a pulse of common time beating in our minds?
for it's your words that now must deck my words, raise them thence
and celebrate them, close their eyes and bury them in yours,
decorate their graves, build houses near to their former meaning
and carry them here and drop them there,
saxifrage my flower
anticipating a newer day.
Admit me chorus to this history.

*

the new subway cars for the graffiti
are here
as soon as the war is over

*

I'm going out to clean the Pierian spring;
I'll only stop when all career lyricisms
are spread on the word-table, leaching
to the pocked sidewalks where readers are in bed
by noon staring at their shoes.—You come too.

I'm going to grow loaves of grass above the Pierian aquafer:
I'll lead the calves away from their mother tongue,
> so that all identity poetics, including aerobic, flexible, trans-
> commercial English rich as a sauced clam on a hill, will open to the
> menu's who's-who, the cars' parade, the letters in the poetry words.
> You eat too.

NOTES

1. See the October/November 1990 and January/February 1991 issues of *Poets & Writers Magazine*.
2. *Politics & Poetic Value*, ed. Robert von Hallberg, Chicago: University of Chicago Press, 1987. The early version was *Critical Inquiry* Vol. 13, No. 3 (Spring 1987).
3. *In The American Tree: Language Realism Poetry*, ed. Ron Silliman (Orono, ME: National Poetry Foundation, 1986).
4. *"Language" Poetries: An Anthology*, ed. Douglas Messerli (New York: New Directions, 1987).
5. Silliman called a smaller anthology, published prior to *In The American Tree*, "Realism: An Anthology of 'Language' Writing" (*Ironwood* 20 [Fall 1982]). In his introduction, Silliman gives a detailed history of the term "language," pp. 62-70.
6. Silliman, op. cit., pp. xx-xxi.
7. Rae Armantrout, *Precedence* (Providence: Burning Deck, 1985), p. 12.
8. Although we shouldn't forget the problematic nature of the label Objectivist. According to the coiner of the term, Louis Zukofsky, there was no such thing as Objectivism, there were only "Objectivists," in quotes.
9. David Melnick, *Pcoet* (San Francisco: G.A.W.K., 1975), n.p.
10. *Men in Aida*, (Berkeley: Tuumba, 1983), n.p.
11. Bruce Andrews, *Give Em Enough Rope* (Los Angeles: Sun & Moon Press, 1987), p. 27.

12. Ron Silliman, *What* (Great Barrington: The Figures, 1988), p. 40.
13. An early poem such as "Berkeley" in *This* 5, seems specifically designed to destroy any reading which would produce a unified subject. The poem consists of a hundred or so first person sentences whose mechanical aspect—each starts with "I"—makes them impossible to unite: "I want to redeem myself/I can shoot you/I've no idea really/I should say it is not a mask/I must remember another time/I don't want to know you/I'm not dressed/I had to take the risk/I did look/I don't care what you make of it/I am outside in the sun/I still had what was mine/I will stay here and die/I was reinforced in this opinion/I flushed it down the toilet/I collapsed into my chair/I forgot the place, sir"
14. "The Wide Road," excerpts published in *Everyday Life*, No. 2, August 1988, Ed. Chris and George Tysh, pp. 2-3.
15. Roland Barthes, *S/Z*, trans. Richard Miller (New York: Hill & Wang, 1974), p. 4.
16. Altieri's criticism, to recall an earlier point, was focused on the chimerical freedom of the reader. The possibilities suggested to a writer are quite a different matter.
17. A number of edited, transcribed talks are collected in my *Writing/Talks* (Carbondale: Southern Illinois University Press, 1985) and *Hills* 6/7 (San Francisco: 1980).
18. Bob Perelman, "The First Person," *Hills* 6/7.
19. Barrett Watten, *1-10* (San Francisco: This Press, 1980).
20. Bob Perelman, *a.k.a.* (Great Barrington: The Figures, 1984).
21. in *Hills* 4 and 5.
22. *Social Text* 19/20 (Fall 1988), pp. 261-75.
23. Andre Breton, *Manifestoes of Surrealism*, trans, Richard Seaver and Helen R. Lane (Ann Arbor: University of Michigan Press, 1972), p. 14.
24. The ideology of voice in contemporary poetry can be seen as designed to preclude such response: a person's voice, if validated, is most difficult to imitate or appropriate—it is a bastion of aura. However, the range of voice poems tends to be well-rehearsed.

THE TASK OF THE COLLABORATOR:
WATTEN'S *LENINGRAD*

Ron Silliman

I: How Are Verses Made?

Barrett Watten and I are playing chess in the international terminal of LAX, awaiting the call to board a plane to Helsinki, when I suggest to him, and to Michael Davidson and Lyn Hejinian, who are sitting with us, that the four of us should "do a collaboration" based on the adventure we are about to embark on, a journey to the then Soviet Union to attend a conference entitled "Summer School—Language, Consciousness, Society" in what was then Leningrad. Lyn, as I remember the occasion, is immediately enthusiastic. Michael is quiet. Barrett says something to the effect of "Let's see how it goes."

The trip itself has already been traumatic. Arriving alone at the San Francisco airport, I learn that United has cancelled our connecting flight to Los Angeles. Michael Davidson is already at the airport and the two of us agree to catch whatever we can to reach Los Angeles, looking frantically about the lobby for Watten and Hejinian, having them paged without success. The urgency is heightened, at least for me, by the fact that Lyn has all of our visas, flimsy paper documents required by the USSR to enter the country along with our passports. While we run into them almost immediately upon arrival in L.A., the anxiety lingers and the four of us are already exhausted when the boarding call comes.

Two days later, we step from an airplane and down the outdoor ramp to the tarmac outside the small and drab international terminal of the Leningrad airport. As we move through customs we are greeted by Arkadii Dragomoshchenko and Aleksei Adashevsky, an arts administrator with the Soviet Cultural Fund. Adashevsky whisks us through customs and into some awaiting autos he's borrowed, complete with chauffeurs, from the KGB. As soon as we can get checked into the Hotel Leningrad, it's explained, they want to take us on a tour of the city. The vehicles roar through its pedestrian-crowded streets like a chase scene from *The French Connection*. Everything is unfamiliar. It is all we can do to hold on and watch as a new world unfolds.

What follows is a long story, chronicled not once, but four times (at least four times) in a book-length prose poem called *Leningrad*.[1] While we were in Mayakovsky's city, that poet's most useful directive—

> A good notebook and an understanding of how to make use of it are more important than knowing how to write faultlessly in worn-out metres.[2]

—echoed continually in my ears. I and the other three Americans were almost constantly penning this or that into our various journals. But between the extraordinary crush of the new and the time-swallowing demands of the conference itself, the idea of a collaboration was never discussed while we were actually in the Soviet Union.

For me, then, the actual process of this collaborative poem began a week or two later when the phone rang in my cubicle at the headquarters of Computer Land Corporation and Lyn Hejinian asked "Are you still up for a collaboration?" She and Barrett had been talking, and both agreed there would be a value in working through our images, ideas, and feelings about this extraordinarily complex shared event. A few phone calls later and the four of us had agreed not only on the project, but on the process as well. The work would have four sections, and each section would be composed of four cycles or rounds of paragraphs by each of us. The sole formal distinction between the sections would be the order of participation:

    I.   Michael Davidson, Lyn Hejinian, Ron Silliman, Barrett Watten
    II.   Lyn Hejinian, Barrett Watten, Michael Davidson, Ron Silliman
    III.   Ron Silliman, Michael Davidson, Barrett Watten, Lyn Hejinian
    IV.   Barrett Watten, Ron Silliman, Lyn Hejinian, Michael Davidson

Using the alphabet and the first initials of our last names gave us a straightforward and democratic method for assigning narrative order as well as authorial sequence. It was months before any of us realized that Davidson had both the first and the final words of the text.

Beyond this the rules of the collaboration were extremely simple. Collectively, we could work on all four sections at the same time. A person would begin a section, then hand that to the next author. In practice, this meant that the four texts circulated around Berkeley in an always fragmentary fashion. Even if you made a xerox of a section for your own use before passing it on, it was invariably changing as you began to look at your next assignment. You might work on the first section one day, then the third section later in the same week, then the second, and then the first again because somebody was having more difficulty with the fourth. The words, sentences, themes, and images of any given section were always intermingled with those of the others as all four parts gradually evolved together—and all were enmeshed with our memories, ideas, and feelings about our experiences in Leningrad. Rather than deny or attempt to distance ourselves from these entanglements, my own sense is that each of us instead tried to confront them directly—the poem is as much *in* the world as it is *of* it.

As the poem evolved over several months, we began to realize how we had unintentionally replicated the constant passing around of manuscripts which for decades had been the necessary mode of distribution for all but a few Soviet poets. Events outside the immediate experience of our journey, as diverse as the fall of the Berlin Wall and the sudden death of Watten's mother, would enter the text. Watten himself typed all of it. Once we had a complete draft, the group met at the house Michael Davidson and Lori Chamberlain were renting in Berkeley to discuss revisions on a sentence-by-sentence, paragraph-by-paragraph basis as well as to settle finally on a title, *This Time We Are Both*, taken from a painting by Ostap Dragomoshchenko.

At the same time, we made a conscious decision to think about publishing the final result in a broader context than that of our own small press poetry scene. For one thing, the work addressed a set of concerns that we all felt to be pertinent to a wider audience than that of our poetry as such. For another, I think we were all curious to see what reception a text as ambiguous about its genre as this could possibly have. Mike Davis, former editor of the *New Left Review* and a member of the Verso editorial board, knew of the project through my work with the *Socialist Review* and asked if Verso could have a look. We readily agreed and I sent the manuscript to Robin Blackburn and Colin Robinson in London. In 1990, however, the U.S. dollar was in a state of freefall, rapidly losing its value in relation to foreign currencies. For an alternative left press such as Verso, which earns a substantial portion of its revenues in the United States, this meant that the relative profit on the books it sold in the U.S. market now translated into a much smaller sum in Great Britain, perhaps as much as $50,000 (US) less each quarter, even though Verso's cost of doing business remained largely unchanged. The crisis which that brought about was resolved by pushing back a third of their 1990-'91 commitments and holding off on others. Since they felt that the potential of this curious prose poem lay partly in its timeliness, Blackburn and Robinson sent the manuscript on to a smaller British trade press, Radius, with a note that they ought to consider it.

As the four of us knew little about Radius, we started asking around. I asked Tom Christensen, who has been an editor with North Point Press, was a contributing editor of *Zyzzva*, and a regular contributor to the book review section of the *San Francisco Chronicle*. Tom was about to become the executive editor at Mercury House in San Francisco. Mercury House still had one opening for its Spring 1991 list. Could they consider our manuscript?

Within ten days, Christensen informed us that Mercury House was willing to publish the book if we would consider a different title. "*This Time We Are Both* is fine for a Sun & Moon book," he said. Our knowledge that Clark Coolidge had himself begun a lengthy work with that exact title (also taken from Ostap Dragomoshchenko) persuaded the four of us to propose *Leningrad* instead.

That is one version of how *Leningrad* was constructed.

II. Portrait of the Author Out of Control

A collaboration is inherently an awkward beast. Anyone who has ever been in love and attempted, successfully or otherwise, to negotiate an intense, longterm relationship will understand the value—and labor—that is at the heart of the collaborative project. Regardless of whatever ground rules collaborators may set for themselves, regardless of how rigorously and/or generously they may adhere to them, each page, each paragraph, each word must be read and understood as a negotiation, a compromise, a point of balance and tension

143

between impulses that can never be identical.

As difficult as this may be for writers, it appears to be even harder for readers. The intentionalist cliché of normative literature programs—that each word in a text contributes to the meaning of the whole—is a tautology at best. The equation of such intention with a fixed point, a unitary monad called author, however, has enabled such programs to fulfill their primary social mission of incorporating literature, a dangerously anarchic enterprise that directly engages the reader's subconscious at the level of desire, into the broader ideology of individualism upon which Western culture and particularly Western capitalism are founded.

By far the most valuable lesson of poststructuralism has been that individuals don't exist. Each one of us is a construct, a focal point for so many social, psychic, and biological forces that we find them uncountable. Today even scientists concede that there is no single point in the brain where perception, identity, thought, emotion, language, and impulse coalesce into that solid irreducible thing, the self. Contestation and collaboration occur constantly, indeed naturally, within the human body, even in moments of deep meditation, so that the rough blur of our outward actions at best yields shadows of consistency by which those who know and love us best recognize who it is we are. The line between normalcy and multiple personality disorder is neither hard nor fast.

Following the textual scholarship of Jerome McGann, Cary Nelson has demonstrated the degree to which each publication of any poem is always a collaborative effort between author, editor, designer, typesetter, and readers, including of course those readers who in turn elaborate a critical discourse about this text that must invariably alter its future.[3] In the past, this process has been mythologized both by publishers and scholars through the figure of the creative genius unacknowledged in his or her own lifetime whose true value must wait for the discerning eye of a later generation, sometimes even at a distance of centuries. Ironically, these same institutional reputation brokers have tended to be more silent about the inevitability that the opposite phenomenon must itself also be taking place simultaneously, that writers of value and integrity disappear all the time. The almost complete erasure of the man who was far and away the most powerful editor of American verse in the 1960s, Henry Rago, is one case in point. At some level, the presence and intention of an author is by no means necessarily the most active element contributing to the meaning of a work.

Yet academic careers are still made out of the ability to discern that a certain text is the product of author X rather than author Y, or that a given version offers a truer representation of intent. Even among progressive poets much has been made of the idea that Emily Dickinson's editors, T.W. Higginson, Thomas Johnson, and now R.W. Franklin, fail to reproduce her texts exactly, just as Richard Tottel altered the poems of many contributors to his *Miscellany* centuries before. The author, it seems, is inescapable.

A writer whose career was both a meditation on and manifestation of this ambiguous process of authority—he even gave his own name to one of his books—Roland Barthes acknowledged the importance that focusing on the author played in the institutional ascendancy of criticism:

> Once the Author is removed, the claim to decipher a text becomes quite futile. To give a text an Author is to impose a limit on that text, to furnish it with a final signified, to close the writing. Such a conception suits criticism very well, the latter then allotting itself the important task of discovering the Author . . . beneath the work: when the Author is found, the text is 'explained'—victory to the critic. Hence there is no surprise in the fact that, historically, the reign of the Author has also been that of the Critic, nor again in the fact that criticism (be it new) is today undermined along with the Author.[4]

This passage, in which Barthes is aligning himself with the then-emerging phenomenon of theory against the specialists of close reading, is not altogether innocent. Nonetheless, for those of us too young to remember when critics generally, and particularly the sons (and occasional daughters) of New Criticism, were marginal to English departments filled with historians, biographers, sociologists, and philologists, Barthes's words are worth noting if only to remind us that it was not always thus.

Poets no doubt were collaborating long before the first oral epics were transcribed. Yet, as the recent flurry over Dickinson demonstrates, poets often have as much investment in the idea of an author as does any critic. I don't mean to make light here of Susan Howe's work, which demonstrates in painstaking detail why poets make far better scholars of poetry than do normative academicians. The interest of the academician almost never coincides with that of the poem or poet, but rather with the dynamics of institutional power. Yet even without the paternalism and sexism that has made the Dickinson case the most glaring instance of this sort of abuse, a question would remain—Who *were* (and I intend the plural) Emily Dickinson?

Still, U.S. poets, just because we derive from a culture that ties yellow ribbons around car antennae and imagines this to symbolize a concern for the prisoner-of-war-as-person we envision entirely out of context (instead of, as would more accurately be the case, recognizing the yellow ribbon as a Claes Oldenburg-like parody of militarized nationalism that could as easily be titled *Soft Swastika*), because, as writers, we are no less the pure products of America than any other, be it professional wrestling, roller derby, or frozen yogurt, we poets likewise have invested heavily in the author not just as person but as high concept.

The most obvious aspect of this investment is the figure of author as romantic (and more or less rugged) individual. This figure extends from Whitman's celebrations of the self more than a century ago, which has had more to do with his codification as the popular icon for poetry in the U.S. than any innovative work with metrics and line. Today, this figure of poet-as-monad can be found in many diverse tendencies of the poem, from the neo-bohemian outsider street poet of San Francisco's North Beach to the suburban cult of personality that haunts the bland newsprint of the American Poetry Review and the bean-sprout sandwich shops along the mall in Iowa City. Its saddest manifestation may well be the Wounded Buffalo school of the epigones of the New American poetry, macho revisionists whose disdain for theory and claim for spontaneity (sometimes cloaked as direct speech) demonstrates in caricature the very limits of an aesthetic they proclaim while actually fearing to understand.

Partly as a result of this pathology of the individual, poets in our culture are addicted to control. Control disorders in poetry are as pervasive as eating disorders are generally in the U.S. population. In its self-repressive or anorexic mode, control addiction expresses itself as an obsessive perfectionism. The landscape of poetry is littered with examples—poets who stop writing because the ideal poem is unattainable, or who spend decades turning out a single, slim, overwrought volume, or whose desire to exactly capture the immediacy and multiplicity of perception leads to an increasingly obscurantist scribbling, an exploded minimalism constructed from a vocabulary too personal to communicate. No aesthetic tendency has a monopoly on the problem.

The garden variety of control disorder takes the form of sanctifying the poetic text, setting it off limits to editorial suggestion. Here the poet replicates the same petrification of authorial intent as does the scholar attempting to demonstrate the validity of version X over version Y. Poets see and experience editorial intervention as intrusive and illegitimate. A case can be made for this stance, at least at this moment in the history of the United States, on the grounds that very few editors, certainly less than ten, are even remotely competent when it comes to editing the poem. Stories abound, such as printing the title of Jessica Grim's "Ethics Stunts" as "Ethnic Stunts" in the *Newsletter of the Archive for New Poetry* or Graham Mackintosh's dropping entire stanzas from Robert Duncan's version of Nerval to make the pagecount fit for *Bending the Bow*.

The function of an editor as the readers' representative, whose role should be to understand (at a minimum) the general issues, allusions, and elements active in a given text, requires this responsibility to be exercised seriously. Since, in practice, this seldom occurs, even poets who seek the participatory role of real readers attempt to preempt editorial collaboration. Not that this resistance is hard to comprehend. Until such time as PostScript-compatible laser printers become inexpensive and commonplace even for college undergraduates, poets will continue to share the experience of almost visceral shock at seeing a poem of theirs printed for the first time, as totally transformed by print as one's own voice on a tape recording or one's body image on videotape. This happens without any substantive changes in text or layout—a change in typeface and from uniform to proportional spacing is all that's required.

(Excellent texts have been seriously compromised, if not ruined, by attempts to prevent this shock, preserving the "true" typewritten experience of the hypothetically original manuscript—Robert Duncan's two volumes of *Ground Work*, Robert Grenier's *A Day at the Beach*, or Steve Benson's *Reverse Order.*)

I'm not suggesting that I'm any better about this than any other poet. I have argued long, loud, and sometimes quite irrationally to preserve some textual anomaly that I was only much later able to admit to myself had really been nothing more than a typo in my manuscript.

What convinces me that control in poetry is a genuine disorder, and not adherence to a higher code of rigor, is the degree of resistance poets show to editing other genres of writing. Nearly five years as an editor at *Socialist Review* convinces me that, while this same issue occurs to some degree throughout the humanities and social sciences, no other group even remotely approaches poets when it comes to the inability to take an editorial suggestion—and that this is as true for letters to the editor as it is for poems. Certainly the editorial obligation to represent readers, to insist that one reader at least must reasonably "get" what is going on in the text and why, and that this role precisely defines the editor's task, seems far less problematic for modes of writing that carry none of the sanctification that historically has been accorded the poem. Try telling that to poets. Moreover, discussions with other editors—including Watten and Hejinian based on their work with *Poetics Journal*—persuades me that my experience at *Socialist Review* was typical. (I know I've been part of the problem for both *L=A=N=G=U=A=G=E* and *Poetics Journal*.)

This pathological condition is reinforced by the fact that editors have their own need to express control over the text. Almost every essayist (if not every poet) has confronted the difficulty of working with an editor whose suggestions reflect nothing more critical than a desire to view his or her own reflection emanating from the printed page. From the writer's perspective, the telltale clue is that the suggestions don't present a consistent stance toward the text. Unfortunately, I've learned through experience that this can sometimes mean that a text of mine seriously needs a full and rigorous going over, and that this particular editor either wasn't able to discern that he or she simply didn't get what was going on, or else was too timid to confront me on the issue.

If control is poetry's pathological drive, collaboration has been one of a limited number of possible responses available to poets to counter its effects.[5] Collaboration exteriorizes the multiplicity of intentions that always already lurk behind every articulation. Depending on the procedures agreed upon by the poets, the seams of the final product will be more or less visible. In *Leningrad,* the stitching is fairly explicit, as each author is represented in turn by a size-able chunk of text.

Yet *Leningrad* demonstrates why voice is never identical with either author or intention. Voice is an effect of consistency achieved through the range of articulations that compose the poem. Voice, in a very real sense, is an average —of all the particular verbal effects of a work. When read aloud by just one of its four authors, it is not always clear who is or is not writing at a given moment in *Leningrad* except through references, most often the mentioning of the others by name.

In one instance, Lyn refers to Michael, Barrett, and I as "the men were being irritable . . . ." In another, she describes a communal bath of women. But it must seem, I believe, harder to discern between the three male collaborators, which only demonstrates what we have always known, that language is inescapably gendered. There is no parallel linguistic clue to indicate that not only could I not have written the passage that occurs which discusses the New Sentence, but that I actually disagree with its analysis.

A collaboration is always a portrait of the author out of control. If, by displacing and exteriorizing the role of intention in the creation of meaning, the collaboration confronts and undermines the totalitarian impulse of control in the poem, control itself does not disappear.[6] It does not evaporate from the text, leaving it dry. If anything, the opposite occurs. By being raised to the level of consciousness, poets talking to poets, leaving messages on answering machines, notes in the margin, on Post-its, whatever method is used, control becomes an explicit dimension and dynamic of the poem. At some moment(s) in the process of working on every collaboration in which I have ever participated, I have experienced a giddiness I believe to be my sensuous apprehension of just that dynamic. Indeed, the loss of control can be exhilarating, even as it terrifies the writer—anyone who has ever skied beyond their personal capacity for speed and direction will understand the feeling. Whatever else any collaboration may confront, the search for control, for balance, a stable, survivable dynamic, is always its first dimension.

III. Finding the Measure

What can we say about the distinctness of each poet's work within *Leningrad* and about Watten's contributions to the whole? How does this collaborative prose poem differ from other types of writing by its authors? I know of no task in writing more fraught with pit- and pratfalls than discussing one's own verse.[7] (That I am focusing on someone else's participation in this collaboration doesn't make it much easier.)

To gain both access and distance on this project, I have taken a different strategy here. I gathered each poet's writing from *Leningrad* into a separate computerized document file, hereafter identified according to the poet's initials as *LH*, *MD*, *RS*, and *BW*. (Because I want to focus on *Leningrad* as a prose poem, I did not include each author's contribution to the introduction of the Mercury House edition.) I then ran all four files through two software programs, *RightWriter* 4.0 and *Corporate Voice*, off-the-shelf style-checking applications. For some external comparisons, I ran two other texts—a sample of Watten's critical prose, "Radical Poets," (a review of Cary Nelson's *Repression and Recovery*,[8] thereafter referred to as *Rad*), and a poem of my own, *What*—through *RightWriter*.

I'm not concerned here with the literal intent of the software applications: to suggest improvements for the writing. What such programs produce is raw statistical information about a given text. The program then compares this raw data with normative profiles. Such software is ill-suited for poetry and most creative or otherwise serious prose—many literary effects are by definition deviant when contrasted with models for Department of Defense operations manuals or federal guidelines for insurance regulations, the very types of documents for which these programs were originally designed.[9] But however crude, the statistical testimony is worth pondering.

148

Table 1

	MD	LH	RS	BW
Total words	4,144	5,292	6,174	6,204
Unique words	1,552	1,777	2,140	1,941
Sentences	215	234	348	295
Words per sentence	19.18	22.59	17.73	21.00
Syllables	6,386	8,096	9,063	9,805
Syllables per word	1.54	1.53	1.47	1.58
Readability index	10.07	11.27	8.65	11.25

Table 1, constructed through *RightWriter*, compares seven aspects of the writing in *Leningrad*. The first sums the number of words used by each poet. It does not come as a surprise to find that Watten and I are verbal guys: between us, we composed 56.7 percent of the text, Hejinian and Davidson just 43.3 percent.

The second line of table 1 counts the number of "unique" words—the total number of words minus repetitions. In itself, the category means little: what is being gauged is not uniqueness but size of lexicon. In *Leningrad*, I may have employed the largest vocabulary, but I also used a lot of words. Michael Davidson may have used the least number of different terms, but the ratio of his "unique" words to his overall total actually turns out to be the lowest, 1 to 2.67, suggesting that his sections have the least amount of repetition, and might be thought of as "freshest." (The ratios for the others are: Hejinian, 1 to 2.98; myself, 1 to 2.89; Watten, 1 to 3.20[10]) This suggests only that Davidson and I are apt to express different values in our poetry, that my writing here articulates a sense of language and experience as rich and dense—someone else might say over-grown and claustrophobic—while Michael's demonstrates values of precision and exactness. (These might be thought of as the vegetable versus mineral tendencies within language poetry: I'm the carrot.)

Watten's ratio in *Leningrad* is the highest. Overall, he uses 30 words more than I do, but 199 fewer "unique" terms. As we will see later, this points toward a primary strategy of his writing: to develop a vocabulary specific to each project.

The third line counts the total number of sentences each poet contributed to the poem. Here the distinction between individual poets is even more pronounced. I was surprised to discover that I wrote nearly one third of the sentences in *Leningrad*, 31.9 percent, while Davidson wrote less than one fifth, 19.7 percent. Further, while Watten produced a few more words than I did, I wrote 18 percent more sentences than Watten and 61.9 percent more than Davidson. My obsession with the sentence as the unit of writing may account for these results.

The fourth line follows from the third. Although I wrote a lot of words, my sentences in *Leningrad* are shorter than those written by the other poets, while Hejinian's are the longest. *Corporate Voice*, the other software program used here, identifies the first of Hejinian's sentences in *Leningrad's* opening section as the longest of the first complete draft:

> The person would reappear, languid—he was said to be an esteemed and assertive mathematician but the problem of being a person seemed to have exhausted him, seated some distance away, whispering with Rosa, but somehow simultaneously he was already also outside on the quiet street where a small crowd of intellectuals hung around gossiping, stooped because of his height, accepting a cigarette—as a theme, troubled—I had been told some months earlier that many people in a Russian audience will not understand the Western notion of subjectivity—which he agreed to translate. (34)

At 94 words, this sentence demonstrates both something that I always find compelling about Hejinian's verse and why any normative theory of writing (including that employed by a software style checker) is ultimately incapable of articulate "reading." In itself, the sentence presents a narrative as complex as a good short story, a tale that can be read several different ways. Had Leslie Scalapino composed this text, I would have been inclined by my past experience with her other writing to read those singular em dashes (—) as sharply angled, redirections of my attention amidst the flow of words. But those brief passages can also be interpreted as linked threads woven into a scene of parataxis: *The person would reappear, languid as a theme, troubled, which he agreed to translate.* In this reading, I hear a comma between *troubled* and *which*, a comma that disappears behind that last em dash. Around this thread, two distinct narratives enfold. One concerns the mathematician and is constructed around two appearances of the conjunction *but*, that mobility of thought reinforced by the echo of the opening *b* in *because*. The second narrative parallels the first in that both depend on secondary information (*he was said to be an esteemed and assertive mathematician . . . I had been told some months earlier*), a theme that is again picked up in the final phrase of the primary thread: *he agreed to translate.* The length, indirectness, and convolutions of Hejinian's sentence are entirely strategic, almost classically modernist in the ways they exploit form to demonstrate content. From the perspective of normative writing, however, this sentence is neither concise nor direct, but rather seems overlong and grammatically beyond repair. If the idea of a being as the translation of a theme (rather than, say, the embodiment of it) were not complex enough, the theme itself is characterized sensually as languid. To have attempted to convey this same information using short, "direct," hypotactic sentences would have required far more language to incorporate what is presented here through structure alone—and such an approach could never have replicated the almost muscular modularity of Hejinian's writing (a characteristic that a psychologist would describe as its "feeling tone"). Hejinian's sentence is thus both concise and direct, but to a different standard of perception than the world of reductive surfaces implicit in Strunk and White. One might convey the detail of Hejinian's original thought over the course of a half dozen sentences, but never its emotion. A problem for writing and the politics of literacy alike, this will have consequences later when we examine what *Right Writer* calls its readability index.

The fifth and sixth lines parallel the third and fourth, here counting syllables[11] and averaging the number per word. While the variation between poets seems miniscule—a range of only 0.11 syllables overall—small increases in syllables per word also indicate substantial differences in reading level, according to the institutional measures that are the subtext for this program. The lines from the poem *What*, "Any text averaging 1.65 /syllables per word demands/a college education,"[12] which I originally found in a communications newsletter, reflect a similar (and perhaps the same) correlation method between syllables and education as does *RightWriter's* readability index. Thus, among the external comparisons of table 2 below, Watten's average of 1.82 syllables-per-word in his review of Cary Nelson contributes to *RightWriter's* conclusion that that book review requires a reader to have almost 19 years of formal education, a Ph.D. for all extents and purposes, to make sense of it, while the 1.38 syllables-per-word score of *What* should make that text intelligible to fifth graders.

RightWriter's readability index assigns an educational grade level to each text using anywhere from one to three mathematical formulae, all of which can also be found in *Corporate Voice*. Both tables here use the Flesch-Kincaid formula, the Department of Defense standard for contractors producing manuals for the armed services. The formula is

$$\text{Grade Level} = (.39 * \text{ASL}) + (11.8 * \text{ASW}) - 15.59$$

in which ASL represents Average Sentence Length or words per sentence and ASW represents Average Syllables per Word. (In this formula, a difference of 0.08 syllables per word calculates into an entire grade level.) According to the *User's Manual*, the readability index "ranges from a low of 10 (the first grade level) to 50.0 (totally unreadable)." (7-5) The manual's judgemental tone about this index is both bland and crude:

> Even if your intended audience has a high level of education, you should keep your readability index in the lower grade levels.
> Good business writing ranges between the 6th and 10th grade level. A high readability index (over 13th grade) does not mean that the writing is appropriate for college educated readers. Rather, it indicates the writing is complex and difficult to read. Even highly technical information is best presented using a simple sentence structure and as many common words as possible. Good sentence structure will make it easier for the reader to understand complex information. (7-5)

The readability index may be to literacy what the *The New Criterion* is to a defense of Western civilization, a case of the most degraded instance. The impact of its underlying principles are nonetheless dramatic. At 94 words and 156 syllables, the Hejinian sentence quoted above scores 40.65 on the Flesch-Kincaid scale, virtual unreadability. During the production process, a fifth collaborator, an anonymous-to-us copy editor, working under contract for Mercury House, suggested many changes. (Each poet had the final say over his or her portion of the collaboration.) One suggested edit was the conversion of the third em dash in Hejinian's first sentence to a period, so that now a new, second sentence appears:

> I had been told some months earlier that many people in a Russian audience will not understand the Western notion of subjectivity—which he agreed to translate.

The resulting pair of sentences have Flesch-Kincaid scores of 30.26 and 14.16 respectively, and an average of 22.21. While still high scores, particularly for the first sentence, the overall difficulty of this subdivided pair appears to have been nearly halved. However, to my resistant eye, it now seems that the pronoun *he* of the second sentence is far less clearly linked to the "languid…esteemed and assertive mathematician" of the first. The new first sentence no longer provides a formal instance of the person reappearing. And the woven thread of the frame statement—*The person would reappear, languid as a theme, troubled which he agreed to translate*—has been broken forever. Would readability really have been improved? Hejinian rejected the suggestion.

Table 2

	Rad	*BW*	*What*
Total words	3,681	6,204	22,905
Unique words	1,188	1,941	N/A
Sentences	109	295	1,954
Words per sentence	33.50	21	11.72
Syllables	6,692	9,805	31,597
Syllables per word	1.82	1.58	1.38
Readability index	18.93	11.25	5.26

Table 2 contrasts Watten's *RightWriter* scores from *Leningrad* with his review of Cary Nelson's *Repression and Recovery*, and with my poem, *What*.[13] The range of computed numbers, the two averages and the index, widens dramatically in this table. In table 1, the total range of words per sentence among the four writers was 4.86. The difference between Watten's work in *Leningrad* and this example of his own critical prose more than doubles that: 12.5 words. The difference between Watten's two texts actually exceeds the overall average sentence length of *What*. Similarly, the difference in the average number of syllables per word, 0.34, more than triples the range between the four poets in *Leningrad*. The readability index for "Radical Poets" is 7.68 grade levels higher than Watten's portion of *Leningrad*.

When I first prepared table 2, I was looking to demonstrate the distinctions between Watten's *Leningrad*, a prose poem ambiguously related to the travel narrative, and two other more distinct genres, critical prose and free verse. Considerably less enlightening than the distinctions between the first two columns of table 2 is the contrast between Watten's *Leningrad* and *What*. Shifting two variables, genre and author, blurs differences between columns two and three, making it hard to fathom what is being distinguished. More telling may be the comparative differences between *What* and my own contribution to *Leningrad*. As with Watten, the differences between two works of my own are greater than the differences between my portion of *Leningrad* and its three other authors. My sentences in *What* are an average of 6.01 words shorter, my words themselves 0.09 syllables shorter, and the resulting readability index a full 3.39 grades lower. In *Leningrad*, only the 0.11 difference in syllables per word between myself and Watten, representing the two extremes of the collaboration, exceeds the difference between my *Leningrad* and *What*.

On one level, these can be viewed as statistical evidence of the power of collaboration, a suprapersonal account of the loss of control each author must experience during the course of a collective project. And these are that: a fuller statistical analysis of this work (and probably other collaborations as well) would almost certainly show that poets are more like one another during a collaboration than any one poet is like him- or herself.

On a second level, Watten's deviation from himself on all three points more than doubles my own. If my own work is "simpler" overall than his, my work also appears to have a much narrower range. The one notable area in which Watten's critical prose closely parallels his own work in *Leningrad* is in the ratio of unique words to total words used—1 to 3.10 in the case of the review. This ratio is closer to Watten's 3.20 in *Leningrad* than it is to any of the other *Leningrad* collaborators (Hejinian at 1 to 2.98 is the nearest). More than Davidson, Hejinian, or myself, Watten's texts appear to identify a vocabulary that focuses the writing. If one thinks of Watten's use of names from the discourse of post-World War 2 politics in his book-length poem, *Progress*—Krushchev, Stalin, Eisenhower, Dulles—or the mathematical precision with which that poem deploys the word *I*, twice every six stanzas (although, it should be noted, not once every three), it seems evident that this tendency is a primary strategy of his writing, not simply the quirk of a single poem.

Underscoring Watten's lexical strategy is the fact, while he clearly is more apt to use a smaller percentage of unique words in each text, he seems proportionately less apt to reiterate the same few words over and over. Table 3, derived from *Corporate Voice*, lists unusual words that appear five or more times in each poet's sections of *Leningrad*. The program automatically eliminates what it calls "mortar," those simple words that statistically make up 60 percent of all language use (a list presumably like that from which Kit Robinson generated *The Dolch Stanzas*). Thus, while Watten's contribution to *Leningrad* is both longer and has a lower percentage of unique words than the writing of any of its other contributors, Barrett only uses eight of what *Corporate Voice* calls "bricks," those content-rich terms that presumably carry the information of the language, and "trade words," terms specific to particular discourses, five or more times.[14] Michael Davidson uses just one less, even though his fraction of *Leningrad* is just two-thirds the length of Watten's. Hejinian uses ten bricks five or more times, and I use twelve that often.[15]

Table 3

	MD		LH		RS		BW
6	Barrett	15	Arkadii	10	Arkadii	10	Leningrad
6	Leningrad	9	Zina	9	airport	10	Russians
5	Arkadii	8	Leningrad	9	Leningrad	9	poetic
5	bus	7	context	6	Lenin	8	enormous
5	Dmitrii	6	feminism	6	Michael	8	Lenin
5	drawing	5	crowded	6	Nevsky	5	Arkadii
5	Petersburg	5	currency	6	palace	5	consciousness
5	fence			6	tea	5	identical
5	mud			6	Zhdanov		
5	Neva			5	bus		
				5	giant		
				5	Viktor		

In addition to demonstrating Watten's lexical strategy to the poem, table 3 can also be read as an index of concerns on the part of each poet. Of those bricks and trade words used five or more times, only two appear on each list: *Leningrad* itself (33 times overall) and the poet Dragomoshchenko's first name, *Arkadii* (35). I find it a telling detail that the trade word that appears most often in this book should be a poet's first name. The word *Arkadii* points not just to the work's status as a poem, a fact that Mercury House, in its desire to market the text as a travel narrative, could never bring itself to admit—we had to dutifully insist on the phrase "prose poem" in the introduction—but also to the poem's position within a larger tradition of verse best known as the New

154

American Poetry, that writing which has most readily conceived of itself as both a community activity and a personal project.

However, Watten is the only poet among the four not to have a personal name first on his list of bricks and trade words—*Arkadii* is only the sixth most often used term in his vocabulary here—and the only contributor to have just one living person's name among their list of common terms. If we strip table 3 of all proper names, like this—

MD		LH		RS		BW	
5	bus	7	context	9	airport	9	poetic
5	drawing	6	feminism	6	palace	8	enormous
5	fence	5	crowded	6	tea	5	consciousness
5	mud	5	currency	5	bus	5	identical
				5	giant		

—other distinctions appear. Three of Watten's four remaining key terms appear to be adjectives. Hejinian and I have one adjective each on our respective lists (I never use *giant* as a noun, although I do use *giants* once, not included in this count). Davidson's key words include no adjectives. Davidson and I are apt to use short, simple nouns indicating physical objects, while Hejinian's nouns are both longer and more conceptual—even *currency* is a mass noun. Watten's key terms are dramatically longer and more abstract: the visible noun is *consciousness.*

I say visible because Watten actually uses poetic as an adjective only once, on page 36, in his very first paragraph, quoting Dragomoshchenko's opening remarks to the conference: "In this way, poetic activity is directed toward the outer world." In every other case, the word appears in variations of the phrase, "the poetic," a category at least as conceptual as consciousness.

From a list such as this, constructed through *Corporate Voice,* one can build an intriguing and possibly useful path into a text. Consider what Watten found to be enormous, and the ways in which he uses this word:

> The clouds in Dovzhenko's *Aerograd,* enormous counterpoint to puny biplanes plying their historic mission to the new Soviet Far East, become the impalpable evanescent background into which all such forward material incursions dissolve. (58)

> Somewhere in the middle there is a slag heap of enormous proportions near which the people go to swim. (70)

> In some of the stations enormous metal doors separate the people from trains. (71)

155

The enormous red tile image of Mayakovsky in the metro that bears his name; I spoke of his neologisms to blank disinterest and was corrected on my pronunciation of Pasternak: *Boris Leonidovich Pasternák.* (80)

It would even hurt you to do so, doing damage to a part of yourself: so the received idea of not having revolution without breaking eggs returns in its enormous cultural guilt complex. (98)

Later we did visit the Pribaltiskaya, a symmetrical monster surrounded by grey slabs and fronted by an enormous and deserted concrete plaza out of Fellini. (116)

At the Russian State Museum, my favorite painting was a mural of an enormous wave, painted as a danger to be surmounted for viewers who had for the most part no experience of the sea. (117)

An entirely rusted manhole cover in the enormous, cracked cement plaza outside the Pribaltiskaya showed a date: 1972. (136)

Two of the references are to the vast plaza outside the Hotel Pribaltiskaya, the monument to Stalinist architecture whose photograph (taken by Watten) illustrates the first page of the fourth section of *Leningrad*, the section begun, and thus to some degree determined, by Watten. The other architectural phenomenon twice characterized as enormous is the Leningrad metro: first, for its platform doors that (like the underground tram between terminals at the Atlanta airport) fix the stopping points of trains and presumably make it harder for passengers to fall between vehicle and platform; second, for the tiles used in the heroic (i.e. Stalinist) portrait of Mayakovsky. Two other references are to details in paintings, another (the "slag heap") to the industrial city portrayed in the film *Little Vera*. At least six of the eight occurrences of *enormous* carry some dimension of an aesthetic as well as spatial schema. And, while both the metro and the Pribaltiskaya plaza are twice mentioned, and while the word occurs twice in each of two different paragraphs, *enormous* never refers to the same object in any one section more than once.

By contrast, three of Hejinian's uses of the adjective *crowded* occur in a single passage (125–26) describing different national reactions to the claustrophobia of public transit (the noun in each case is *bus*). Both of the other two times the word is used to characterize the basement cafe of the Composer's Union. My own use of the adjective *giant* twice refers to the image of a man-sized eightball that appears in a striking red-and-black painting by Ostap Dragomoshchenko, and twice, in a single sentence, characterizes beakers of flavored sugar water in a Georgian restaurant. Its fifth appearance compares the behavior of three embarrassingly "Ugly American" academics at the conference to monstrous insects.

Each of these key terms has some sort of patterned usage, although the patterns become blurred slightly through the process of collaboration: I refer once to being "crowded hopelessly under one umbrella"; Hejinian refers once to "enormous sadness"; and the first appearance of *enormous*, characterizing a "state building of the Stalin era," in the very first paragraph of the poem, is by Davidson. It's worth noting that these are the only occurrences of these key words in each other's writing throughout the book. If, as I've argued, collaboration tends to make poets more like one another than like their own individual writings, this process seems less apt to occur at the level of vocabulary.

But note the insistent theme of transit underlying these key words: *enormous* twice refers to the metro, *crowded* depicts *bus* three times, a noun that appears on both Davidson's and my own lists of key terms.[16] In fact, the older central portion of Leningrad is, like many European cities, quite walkable. Although our flight from San Francisco to Los Angeles was cancelled, making both those stops traumatic, and Watten was nearly beheaded by a security device at the Helsinki baggage claim area, four of the nine references to airports in my writing in *Leningrad* are to Frankfurt. Davidson also has a memorable passage about the Frankfurt airport's lavish, dense signage and presentation of commodity objects. If you asked me if transit was a primary thematic concern of *Leningrad*, my immediate instinct would be to say no. I might be wrong.

IV: *Watten's Leningrad*

Consciousness of the poetic is both enormous and identical. Identical to what? To Leningrad? To language? On the occasions when I've done solo readings from the text in public—in such disparate locations as Tuscaloosa, Tucson, and San Diego—one element that listeners have felt compelled to comment on has been a sense of narrative unity: "That tells a story. . . . I didn't know language writing could be so coherent. . . . That wasn't so hard to understand." Well-intentioned compliments that speak ironically through the comparisons they imply.

In some small part, the unity audiences hear is nothing more than the same vocal tone and accent imposing itself on a multifaceted text. (I recall Ed van Aelstyn's linguistics class at San Francisco State 25 years ago, in which he read a passage from *Moby Dick*, switching in the middle, unannounced, to *Wichita Vortex Sutra* to see who would notice—few did.) The supplement of the voice with its aura of presence melding four authors into one.[17]

On a more substantive level, *Leningrad* represents an unusual project within the history of "language poetry," in that the collaborative focus of the writing was a sustained shared experience that could be named. Inevitably, the name is misleading. The book is not a history of the city. Nor any sort of guide. The attentive reader can gradually piece together a rough chronology of events from internal clues within the text—"It was the second or third day of the conference, and so August 10 or 11, and mid-afternoon"—but, beyond the very broadest markers, such as Davidson's decision to open the first section with a description of our arrival in the city and to close the last section with a parallel portrait of our departure, any relation between a temporal sequence of events and the narrative order of the text is arbitrary. Watten's account of our arrival occurs in the second of *Leningrad's* four sections, while my own takes place in my second contribution to the first section, although the sentence "Our plane touched down in Moscow to pick up Ozzy Osbourne and Mötley Crue," referring to an event that occurred on our way back home, appears earlier. Zina Dragomoshchenko's comments to a group of anti-Semitic skinheads can be found, in variant translations, on pages 36 and 70. Her husband discusses her comments at the top of page 86. Thus, if there is a story here—"Our Trip to Leningrad"—it is not so much told as woven.

But the common focus should not be discounted. As a literary tendency or genre, "language poetry" historically has not organized texts around topics as such. (Hejinian's *My Life* stands out as the exception that proves the rule.) Rather, "language poetry" has evolved a reader-centered text in which the focus of the writing has been a dialog between the reader's responses and any series of linguistic devices. By definition, the referential text tends to carry attention away from such dialog. Robert Creeley's assertion, first published in 1953, that a "poetry denies its end in any *descriptive* act, I mean any act which leaves the attention outside the poem,"[18] articulates not simply his own personal poetics (nor that even of two generations of poets), but rather a condition all poems confront, whether they seek to or not. "In other words," Creeley will write later, "poems are not referential, or at least not importantly so."[19] *Leningrad's* first challenge thus is to its own status as knowledge or assertion.

Here Watten's position and role within the collaboration stands out as distinct from any of the other three participants. While each poet, to a greater or lesser degree, incorporated into their contributions detail, rumination, dialogue, analysis, emotion, commentary upon one another's work, and the threads of association that a trip to the Soviet Union poised between the Tiananmen Square massacre and the (unannounced, even unanticipated) fall of the Berlin Wall invariably would raise for any self-reflective individual writing of it later, so that specific paragraphs and passages can be read as prose poems, tableaux, essays, tales, and meditations, Watten alone appears to have proceeded through the text with a plan, if not a complete argument.

The first sentence of Watten's first passage announces the epistemological issue directly:

> Because we are poets we feel we can articulate a surface of any
> experience, but this omnipotence must have been learned. (36)

Part of what is remarkable about this moment (and, indeed, Watten's overall strategy) is that this sentence was neither the first one Watten composed in Leningrad, nor even, because of the sequence in which we took turns, the first sentence of the section in which it appears. Indeed, the sentence can be read as a response to a moment in Hejinian's first passage, two paragraphs before:

"I know in Russian you have no word for 'self' except as a passive suffix or a reflexive pronoun," I said, but he shrugged his shoulders and wouldn't talk about it. Subjectivity is not the basis for being a Russian person. Our independent separate singularity can hardly be spoken of, but, Arkadii said, "many people wish it." "You know," I said, "many of us wish to overcome it. We think that if we can surpass or supersede the individual self we can achieve a community." (34)

A rough schematic of the first round (i.e., the first complete cycle) of the first section demonstrates how Watten pulls divergent elements together, while posing the theme he is about to develop:

MD: Arrival in Leningrad

LH: Cultural constraints on subjectivity and self, differences between Russia and the U.S.

RS: Sequence of details united by an unnamed emotion

BW: The problem of poetic knowledge

Much as Hejinian's lengthy opening sentence, cited above, beginning "The person would reappear, languid . . . " carried forward the final image of Davidson's first paragraph—

Walking across the square in mottled sunlight, a single person becomes more than a person (33)

—Watten's second sentence alludes to elements that have appeared in each of the three preceding passages: the streets mentioned by all three poets; the prestige of science implicit in Hejinian's figure of an "esteemed and assertive mathematician"; and the theme of disrepair and decay that connects several of my images. As Davidson began the first section with an account of our arrival, Watten rhymes the gesture by noting the "opening remarks at our international summer school." The same narratological irony with which Davidson notes that

One enters the city backwards in time, from the suburban present to the urban past, from anonymous modern apartments to brightly colored, rococo palaces (33)

recurs in the calculated structure of Watten's assertion:

Arkadii's anticipation would prove to the point: "Language is a world in itself of which we must admit great difficulties of understanding. In this way, poetic activity is directed toward the outer world." (36)

Davidson's beginning proceeds backwards; Watten's "point" turns up in the words of an Other, fragmented into two sentences, separate thoughts whose completeness is challenged both by grammar and punctuation, the colon leading to a quotation of multiple sentences. Arkadii's words are characterized not as an assertion but an "anticipation." They are not even the point, but rather *to* the point, a preposition marking distance as much as it does proximity. Watten pushes the device of the ambiguous preposition, using a string of three to register the awkwardness of Arkadii's first statement. The trio of prepositions are connectors simultaneously of both position and possession, sounding one of *Leningrad's* themes at the level of grammar. The second appearance of the word *of* permits "understanding" its normative, limited content, while opening it to a variety of wider alternatives. A parallel instance of the thematic use of grammar, but to precisely the opposite effect: Watten's key word, *poetic*, appears as an adjective for the first and only time.

Turning to the object status of the poem, the passage continues. The bureaucratic demand-economy materialism of the Soviet state superimposed over a poetic tradition that even today remains fundamentally oral clashes with the consumerist ethos Westerners take for materialism. For Watten, the question is transcendence:

> But even so for the Russians the poem is some kind of object—a concept very unlike the rich and theatrical demonstration of intensity and loss we witnessed in its spontaneous delivery. The unity of two projects—call them scientific and cultural—around the poetic adds up to a kind of myth of the object whose authority ultimately lies in a transcendent inherence. And we were participants in this transcendence's social acting out, where somewhere from fifty to two hundred persons at any one time became its collective body. (37)

Here as elsewhere, the borders and inner terrain of "the poetic" are suggested but not fully described. Any attempt to cast an implicit map extending from clues in this passage must confront the term *unity* to label what has just been depicted as contradictory. Far from being an achievement, transcendence, that displacement to a new level (utopia?), comes from within and can only *act out*, the verb phrase flavored with a subtext of the neurotic or worse. Utopia hedged, what we are offered is neither the object nor even *the* myth of the object, but merely "a kind of myth," at once both communalized and deferred.

Watten's passage in this first round can be read as easily as essay as poem, perhaps even more easily so for readers unfamiliar with "language poetry's" notorious self-critical side. While it is also possible to read Hejinian's first contribution as essay, Davidson's initial text more closely approximates the depictive narrative of the premodernist novel, while my own jumping juxtapositions of disparate images fall closer to the style of the prose poem in the age of the new sentence.

As the rounds proceed, these tendencies shift less than the casual reader might imagine. In the first section, only Hejinian moves markedly between modes. Her account in the second round of the Russian portion of the conference's first poetry reading is almost entirely descriptive. By the second full section of *Leningrad*, Davidson, the one poet to use multiple paragraphs for individual passages, also starts shifting back and forth between modes, sometimes alternating from paragraph to paragraph: his first passage begins with a paragraph on the relation of history to architecture, and then moves to his ambivalence about photographing Lenin's sealed train at the Finland Station; his third passage in this section contains two vignettes of one paragraph each, followed by another paragraph listing items brought home.

Once this range has been established, *Leningrad* stays surprisingly within its borders. Watten and I create extreme boundaries—on one side the expository, on the other the disjunctiveness of the postmodern prose poem—while Davidson and Hejinian alternate between Watten's expository pole and another, more descriptive mode whose antecedents include both the novel and the travel narrative. The intergeneric nature of *Leningrad* is no accident: virtually every round alludes to three, if not four, literary forms, each arriving complete with the baggage of its own heritage.

Because Watten's contributions can be read as a quartet of essays or as a single disjunct essay in four linked sections, each of which then further divides amoebalike into four individual passages—a prose structure as formal and symmetrical as any mode of closed verse—his argument, to call it that, sets a sort of cognitive melodic dominant for *Leningrad* against the rhythm track of my own work and the calculated, weaving counterpoints of Davidson and Hejinian. If *Leningrad* represents the collective work of four poets, the role each writer plays is not only different, but distinct, even as the process of collaboration has tended to bring the writing stylistically together.

Watten's argument is multifaceted, paratactic rather than hierarchic in its strategies, with every sentence "to the point," but no single sentence the point itself. In this sense, Watten's writing in *Leningrad* works toward a mode of statement not traditionally associated with the form of the essay. Individually, sentences articulate a sense of genre with little ambiguity:

> Where accessibility and power are the antinomies of everyday life, the irony of free information flow will radically undermine them. (86)

The cumulative effect of such sentences often builds in a manner that, at first, feels quite familiar. These follow the sentence just quoted:

> At the same time, the Russians have none of the redundancies on which we information gluttons thrive. There was no sense to the order of the symposium, for example, which seemed to change with every event, but somehow everyone got informed of it. Words have meaning when spoken in certain contexts; the natural inference is that the contexts will change. What if all contexts changed at once? Time is needed to build up the meaning of information we don't need. Who would ever want a universe of choice? What was in front of us at all times was a

161

> literal event. Power is the ability not simply to control information
> but to be the literal point where information issues forth. In this sense
> power operates in a virtually linguistic field. But what happens when
> the language is changed? A poetry embodied in memory becomes
> destabilized in its encounter with a poetry objectified in texts. (86-87)

At one level (which we might characterize as sentence-type), this appears to be
pure exposition. But Watten immediately inserts details that twist and torque
the reader's grammatic progress, undermining any sense of a static hierarchy
of information. Thus the connecting phrase, "At the same time," refers backward
to a sentence that develops its logic through a spatial, rather than temporal,
metaphor: "Where accessibility and power are the antinomies...." Watten tells
the reader that the Russians lack "redundancies"; the instance cited a sentence
later is that "There was no sense to the order of the symposium, for example
...." Grammatically, the word "it" that concludes this sentence should refer to
"event" rather than "change." Watten ironically notes this in the next sentence
with "Words have meaning when spoken in certain contexts." The question
that follows—"What if all contexts changed at once?"—refers as much to the text
as it does to any set of signifieds. The Shandy-like wit of the passage emerges
more forcefully now with contradictory uses of the word *need*: "Time is needed
to build up the meaning of information we don't need." That sentence is
remarkably Wattenesque in weaving a passive syntax around an assertion in
which agency appears only in order to be denied. Ambiguity of agency is the
tone rung loudly in the pronoun that begins the next question: "Who would
ever want a universe of choice?" Even here the joining of agency to desire is
exploded by the intensifying "ever" that intrudes into the verb phrase. The
question is certainly ironic, but at what level? Watten seems to be suggesting
all of them at once. That much more is happening in this passage than just a
demonstration of Watten's dry and sometimes understated sense of humor—
how many readers will recognize that Watten is a very funny poet?—becomes
evident in the next few sentences with their earnest sense of assertion. Yet even
in the next four sentences, the sole active verb phrase—the lone assertion of
agency—is "power operates," an almost Foucaultian notion of power as free-
floating force. What is "a virtually linguistic field?" The claim being made rings
back to Arkadii's "anticipation" 51 pages earlier that "Language is a world in
itself of which we must admit great difficulties of understanding." When Watten
asks "But what happens when the language is changed?" he argues for a funda-
mentalist reading of the Whorf-Sapir hypothesis. That's a complex stance for a
poet who is much more a Marxist than a post-structuralist. That the argument is
not simply a matter of local contingency, the spirit of parataxis overriding the
text, can be tested by the parallel between this moment in Watten's argument
and his earlier quotation from Dragomoshchenko: "In this way, poetic activity
is directed toward the outer world." In the later passage, Watten again takes
the reader back to material reality: to two poetic traditions, one oral and the
other not, confronting one another in a context as social as a basement cafe.
Watten acknowledges the complex nature of this multilayered argument about

language, society, and agency, when, in the next sentence, the structural function of an active verb phrase achieves the magnification of an almost pop-art foreground:

> Somehow there will be a union of the two, but epistemology gives out piteous groans at the unformed and chaosmic birth.

If, sentence by sentence, Watten's work in *Leningrad* tends toward the discursive mode of the dissertation, the cumulative result cannot be termed an essay in any usual sense of that word. Unlike Buckminster Fuller, Jacques Derrida, or Ihab Hassan, critics who have all attempted to "poeticize" critique (and who might be thought of as the ancestors of a project such as Charles Bernstein's broken-line, but otherwise normative—and absorptive—*Artifice of Absorption*),[20] Watten uses the discourse of critique to create poetry. Themes build, reverberate, undercut one another, and return, sometimes in quite new guises. What began in Watten's very first line on page 36 as

> Because we are poets we feel we can articulate a surface of any experience, but this omnipotence must have been learned.

joining experience, belief, and that always illusive perspective of relative surfaces, becomes in Watten's final sentence on page 144.

> Down on the ground it looked like a human universe, even if from moment to moment a fantastic refiguring of incommensurate beliefs.

Even the identification of the poet as the crucible for such issues returns, now in an allusion to Charles Olson. What starts as a critical distrust in the confidence of perception has been transformed into an hallucinatory landscape whose most scandalous gesture is its capacity to appear "like a human universe."

If, on a modest scale, Watten's contribution to *Leningrad* is to the essay as form what *Ulysses* is to the realist novel, a demonstration of devices that simultaneously uses, satirizes, and unmasks the mode's discursive "omnipotence," his work's role with regard to the other three participants in the collaboration proves quite different. The simple act of articulating a plan, a concentration of thematic focus, for each of the four sections, insinuates an implicit structure to the book it could not otherwise have. Crudely sketched, here are how I see Watten's four linked themes, with the corresponding underlying concerns of each passage.

I. Knowledge

1. The problem of poetic knowledge
2. Does poetry have knowledge
3. Knowledge and language
4. Language and the past (the absent mother)

II. Order

1. The work of Leningrad: the visual
2. The look of Leningrad: Little Vera, Katya's home
3. The spaces between objects
4. Xerox, order, choice

III. The State

1. Image of Lenin; presence of the state
2. Your boundaries are slipping; decay of the state
3. Antinationalism: identity/nonidentity
4. The Soviet state as the failure of meaning

IV. Being

1. Money, objects, concepts
2. The object status of art
3. Objects and belief
4. The ontology of experience: a visit to the USSR

Of Watten's four primary themes—I would almost prefer to call them stitches —only one, the state, could be characterized as focused outside that peculiar junction of being and cognition that forms about subjectivity. Contrasted with the material fact of our trip, providing each collaborator with a common vocabulary of images and experiences from which to draw, Watten's high-order abstractions offer *Leningrad* an order so subtle that it is more apt to be felt than perceived by the casual reader. The recessive, almost hidden nature of this thematic organization has little, if anything, to do with the sequence of partici-pation or any rules we set ourselves for creating the text. In fact, Watten may have been aided by our arbitrary use of the alphabetization of surnames as a mechanism for determining order, since this placed his passage last in each round of the first section (where, from the point of narratological power, the greatest force belongs to the opening passage) and first in each round of the last. Thus, when audiences say *"Leningrad* tells a story," an important part of what is being indicated is that they can *hear,* if not identify, Watten's structuring contribution. In this sense, my phrase, Watten's *Leningrad,* refers more than just to his passages within the larger text.

V: St. Petersburg

There is an aphorism that should read "Each sentence is worth a thousand words." In a project on the order of *Leningrad,* there are an infinite number of threads that could be picked up and examined, each revealing new facets, hidden aspects, unsuspected currents. It could be demonstrated, for example, how Davidson, Hejinian, and I each respond to the thematic concentrations provided by Watten's passages. But it could also be demonstrated how Watten in turn utilizes material that appears first in the passages of other contributors as grist for his own texts here. An attempt to assign priority or primacy would prove impossible.

If, as I suggested above, the underlying issue of any literary collaboration is how to write *out of control*, the strategy taken by *Leningrad* is worth noting. Michael Davidson, who wrote just 19.0 percent of the text, holds the power of position in both the first and final sections. Watten, whose strategy for his own passages does the most to inbuild a thematic structure for the work, and who wrote 28.4 percent of the text, more than any other contributor, finds himself at the far end of the round in each of these two critical sections. I think that very similar claims about other dimensions of the text can be made for both Hejinian and myself.[21] In each instance, it might be argued that one poet has greater control of the text, but that control shifts according to the aspect of the work being considered. What I find most remarkable in retrospect is that these questions were not discussed either before or during the composition of the text.

Like the city for which it was named, *Leningrad* has a moment of origin, a definite history, prior names, multiple forms of existence, and a social fate largely out of its hands. Each one of us can only approach at different times, from different perspectives, with different goals in mind. If, in the reading here, Watten's contribution to the collaboration stands as a literary analogy to Nevsky Prospekt, that great organizing boulevard whose impact is often difficult to see through its jostling crowds, our 1989 trip and the social conditions we confronted then posed as its Neva, the inescapable (and sometimes impassible) river. As we worked on the collaboration, Watten and I decided to register the difference between our interpretations of this experience in the form of a friendly $10 bet. I wagered that by Watten's birthday in October, 1992, the city of Leningrad would return to its birth name of Saint Petersburg; Watten wagered that it would not.

NOTES

1. San Francisco: Mercury House, 1991. Page numbers for quotations from the book appear parenthetically in the text.
2. *How Are Verses Made?* translated by G. M. Hyde (London: Jonathan Cape, 1970), p. 56.
3. See *Repression and Recovery: Modern American Poetry and the Politics of Cultural Memory, 1910–1945* (Madison: University of Wisconsin Press, 1989).
4. "The Death of the Author," in *Image/Music/Text*, translated by Stephen Heath (New York: Hill and Wang, 1977), p. 146.
5. Two other strategies that have worked are chance methodologies, such as those pioneered by Jackson Mac Low, and improvisation, particularly as has been practiced by Steve Benson.

6. The same holds for both chance and improvisation. David Benedetti's computer-written prose poem, *Ideas Imagine Passion* (San Francisco: People's Internationalist Publishing Conspiracy, 1983), was the most direct expression of personality imaginable.
7. Popularized by the *Paris Review*, the interview form exists precisely to side-step this problematic by placing all the editorial (superego) functions of deciding what is to be discussed and how, and what is to be retained and in what detail, into the hands of another, who may or may not know the work.
8. Forthcoming.
9. The most flexible and well-designed style checker, *Corporate Voice* permits the user to construct comparative models from any text whatsoever. Its basic parameters and tests, however, were constructed with exactly the same federally mandated definitions of "acceptable" writing as other style checkers. *Corporate Voice* is closely modelled after the most commercially successful grammar-checking software, *Grammatik*.

The best example of the limits of style checkers may be *RightWriter's* Strength Index assigned to each text. *RightWriter's User's Manual* (Sarasota, FL: Que Corporation, 1990) states:

> The Strength Index measures the strength of delivery of the document's message. Strong writing is clear and concise. It does not use unnecessary qualifiers, uncommon words or a complex sentence structure. The Strength Index is based on these concepts.
>
> The index is a number between 0.0 and 1.0. A value of 1.0 indicates a very strong writing style. A value of 0.0 indicates a weak, wordy writing style. Manuals and business letters should have a strength index above 0.5. (Chapter 7, page 8)

No author is listed for the manual. Pagination of quotations from the manual will appear parenthetically in text, with the chapter noted first, then the pages. For example: (7–8).

Such bland and bald assertiveness is doubly ironic coming from an industry where intercaps (such as the W in *RightWriter*) are common, neologisms valued for their own sake, and which, as with this example, number the pages of user manuals according to chapter, thus resulting in a citation such as Chapter 7, page 8. The manual capitalizes Strength Index, but not readability index throughout. Each copy of *RightWriter* comes bundled with a free paperback edition of Strunk and White.

RightWriter assigned the following strength index readings to the texts compared in this section: *LH*, 0.23; *MD*, 0.41; *RS* 0.54; *BW*, 0.29; *Rad* 0.00; *What*, 0.71.

As optical character recognition scanning becomes more commonplace, sophisticated, and inexpensive (and presumably style checking programs and their ilk as well—none to date has commercially demonstrated the necessity of its market and they could all go the way of the Pong game in the next few years), the opportunity to compile similar statistical detail about historic works of writing will become far more common and I would antici-pate that one significant result would be to call many of these normative codes, such as those which are implicit in the *RightWriter* (not to mention Strunk and White), into explicit, well-documented question.

10. These ratios, and other figures in this section not incorporated into the tables, were not directly computed by *RightWriter*, but by operations upon its data.

11. *RightWriter's* counting system is curious, to say the least. The User Manual states that "RightWriter does not count as polysyllables short word combinations, capitalized words, or verbs with three or more syllables ending in 'ed" or 'es.' " Presumably, since there is no apparent software reason why the program would have chosen to do so on the grounds that such words may be as logically familiar to the reader as one-syllable words. *Dragomoshchenko* is a one-syllable word under this system, as is *Pribaltskaya*. If properly counted, the syllable counts and subsequent readability indexes would all rise.

12. (Great Barrington, MA: The Figures, 1988), p. 37.

13. Because *RightWriter's* memory limitations require it to segment a text into the minimum number of sentences that result in 2,600 "unique" words, totalling each fragment separately, it was not possible to calculate the figure for unique words in *What*. The readability index for *What* was calculated by weighting the averages of each fragment according to the number of words used.

14. *Corporate Voice's* curiously constructivist version of the container metaphor of language is worth noting.

15. A more cynical reading of Watten's lexical strategy, that he might use so-called mortar words far more often than the other *Leningrad* authors, can be disproven on three separate grounds. First, his higher average syllables per word reflects a tendency away from the "simple building blocks" of syntax. Secondly, the percentage of prepositions in his text, which *RightWriter* calculates, while modestly higher (by 0.57 percent) than my own among the contributions to *Leningrad*, is not sufficiently out of range to account for the difference in ratios of unique to total words between the poets. The increase in Watten's percentage of prepositions in the Nelson review (15.89 percent, to *Leningrad's* 15.36 percent) occurs without a sufficient parallel in the rise of his unique-to-total-words ratio. Among the four poets of *Leningrad*, there is no correlation, positively or negatively, between percent of prepositions and *RightWriter's* readability index.

16. Watten's photograph of the Pribaltskaya was taken from a bus.

Using *Corporate Voice* to analyze several sections of *The Alphabet* in preparation for my work on *Leningrad*, I discovered *bus* to be by far the key word —or "brick" as the software calls it—that I used most often; some of the others were *cat, fog, orange,* and *atop*.

17. When Hejinian, Watten, and I read the second section at a *Modern Times* book party in San Francisco—which, because only three of us were present, meant we each took turns reading one another's words—the multifaceted aspect of *Leningrad* was foregrounded, the relation between voice and text suspended as if in midair.

Watten prefaced the reading by talking about the value of a "non-narrative" method of reportage. Here and elsewhere, I use the term narrative strictly—to indicate the unfolding of meaning over time. "Non-narrative" in the sense Watten used it indicates a refusal to unfold meaning either by adherence to a chronology (plot or vulgar narrative, as such) or to a hierarchic expository structure. In my sense of the term, *Leningrad* is profoundly narrative.

18. From "To Define," in *The Collected Essays of Robert Creeley* (Berkeley: University of California Press, 1989), p. 473.

19. From "'Poems are a complex,'" in *The Collected Essays*, p. 490.

20. Published as *Paper Air 4:1* (Philadelphia: Singing Horse Press, 1987).

21. Interestingly, the dimensions that come most readily to mind here are social, i.e. "extra-literary." Hejinian was in almost all ways the personal center of the work, as she had been of the trip itself, in no small part due to her extraordinary skills to negotiate her way among three strong male egos. I functioned socially as the external face of the work, finding the publisher, doing much of the negotiating between the writers and the designer, etc. I went so far as to bargain away our original title. That such roles are not traditionally considered part of the poem are a failing of the critical tradition, not the poem.

PEER PLEASURE

Alan Davies

The poet addresses the reader. It's a direct thing. The poem is the moment of that address.

There's nothing aesthetic about it. Aesthetics is a way of noticing that it's happened.

When aesthetic concerns become the motivating force then mere examples of aesthetic theory replace and posture as poems.

There's no third person in the poetic relationship. Just two mes. At its best there's no you. Noone is other to the shared moment.

There's nothing triangular about the poetic moment. The poem is not a third term. It is the terms of the relationship. The poem is not off to the side at all. It can't be. It's not a moment of discourse. It's a moment of intercourse.

This is perhaps a virtue of poetry over the other arts. It's made of the material that we use everyday for the same purposes. It's a torqued instance of that material and that torsion is the method of its directness. Its tautness is its straightness.

Some have stressed musicality as an element of poetry. It has been suggested that poetry is musical language.

But musicality is an aesthetic factor. It might be useful in alerting us to the fact that we're in the presence of an attempt at poetry.

Musical language is verse.

Verse lasts only as long as the music in the line is resonant within the mind. Poetry is mind. It lasts as long as there are minds. Poetry is life. Verse a game played in a corner of a sphere of someone's lived time.

The poem is not a score for what happens. It is what happens.

In any event the words are just the words. Poetry has made use of metaphor and synecdoche in an effort to trivialize that problem. In an effort to control the relationship between the words and the whatever.

Poets have claimed poetic license to cover the faults of their misplacement and misunderstanding.

The recent history of poetry has begun to see words bear relationship more and more until sometimes entirely and only to each other. This is the embodiment of a fantasy. As the wordscape becomes more abstract so does the thinking and the living of experience. The relationship between words and thoughts or actions or feelings or sensations has become increasingly tangential. And that's a problem because it means that the words are abandoning themselves to a kind of picture plane. They tend to no longer either partake or take.

The entire act of writing instead of demanding the world and our experience of it instead assumes a metonymic posture vis a vis life. It puts itself on the wall like an abstracted chart that the poet as poet-as-critic has to attend to with pointer and explanation.

This rather painterly approach to poetry does permit a kind of playfulness but it's a self-indulgent playfulness. It's a playfulness operating in the sphere of doubt. It's a kind of messy playfulness and it's one addressed by writer to words or by word to words. It isn't shared with the reader but is put there for the reader to look at. It's an instantiation of the distancing that goes along with the increasingly abstract.

The poem becomes an example of something.

The abstracting of the poetry plane disrespects the readers. People talk about it being a challenge and about reader-centered poetry and otherwise make apologies for their not being quite there.

But really it means that intercourse has become discourse has become monologue. It's show-and-tell time for the poets.

The poet has the possibility in poetry of taking the reader by the words. When the words start playing mostly with the words they become unaccountable and a lot of explaining on the poet's part is required to try to rope them back within the reader's range.

It's as if the poet has showed the reader a trick and expected that to be accepted as enough. Making fast with the words and leaving everything else behind.

It's a kind of terrorism barking back at the universe it's failed to comprehend. Terrorism fails to take sides. A levity without ground is groundless. This matter of giving the reader a gift as if the reader were another.

The abstracted makes the matter of not saying what you know as you go along look like the matter of saying what you know. The poet in the high tower looking lowly and pointing up. Makes you say things you didn't mean.

What is meaning anyway? It's a mental operation whereby we attribute it to whatever's happening. It's a reflexive action.

It's very much like a form or a structure. It's not something we intuit or find. It's something we make. We add it to whatever for whatever reason.

So why all the fuss? People make it where they make it. So leave it alone right? Your meaning is your meaning and my meaning is my meaning and what you want to make of it is yours by right and what I want to make of it is mine by right. And sometimes mine reaches yours or yours reaches mine. Enough said. Goodnight.

But between people meaning is a kind of blissful contract like memory or adultery. Suddenly things like responsibility and pleasure are involved.

Some people don't like speaking directly or being spoken to directly and so prefer their poetry obliqued and allusive and obscure.

The application of a new term to something can be enlivening and spirited but the seeming doing of that to everything at once produces a kind of stuttering and with about as much meaning. Poets should be understood first and applauded second.

Not writing to the reader and not talking to the listener means writing or talking for them. In the sense of something they can read you do or hear you do. But this gestural performative sense of the use of poetic language makes of either the poem or the audience a third term. It triangulates the situation and that means that something is inevitably experienced or that someone inevitably experiences themselves as off to the side. A lot has been lost in order to what? Maybe at best to make a point.

I'd like you to meet your readers when you write. That's all.

Poems that abandon address become like flags that stand for somewhere relatively uncharted and not yet habitable. Something the poet speaks about but noone can really know is somewhere neither of them can live. Let alone together. I'm talking about new flag waving versus shelter and food and intercourse and love and friendship and clothing and progeny and going on with it.

It has been posited (meaning or no meaning) that the reader has to be startled. Presumably out of complacency or something of the sort. But startled people don't think. They don't understand anything they didn't understand before. And most importantly they don't respond as an equal. It's like You What the Fuck You Etcetera. The auditor may be no longer complacently going down their side of the street but neither are they with the speaker.

This idea of confronting the reader is really a way of separating the reader from almost everything that's happening. Except the sound of the speaker's voice of course.

I mean it's possible to put a penis in your mouth and walk around town but who's going to be listening to that the other side of town or getting it tomorrow?

You can't substitute one spectacle for another and claim to have shown anybody anything or done anything for anyone. In other words you can make something out of words but you can't make a reader out of those same words. No matter how flagrant the words. No matter how flagrant the reader.

Form is content. Content is form.

Most poets can manage at least a little form. That's why they're in the business.

So that leaves content.

Content is knowing what you think and saying it. Content is someone's content.

Content is meaning between people just as form is. It's not really important to talk about the way they might exclude or might contain each other. That's academic.

What's important is what they are for and from people. That's poetry for instance.

Content? Nothing need be missing. But that's not the same as saying that everything is permitted. That latter is too easy. What it means to say that nothing need be missing is that between people BETWEEN PEOPLE everything is possible. In fact that may be exactly where everything is possible. And poetry is that possibility raised and reduced through form and content to the spoken materials of our lives.

This content is the necessity of our life and the necessity demands that it be habitable HABITABLE. Poetry is bringing the content home.

What I'm trying to do here is to put content in a place. In the place of form if you will. And that place is between people. Not abstracted through form onto the space of a page. Not abstracted at all. Just what it is. The meaning of our lives and never out of that context.

Form and content means the cessation of suffering. If you want it to.

We exist in our own lives and through the absolute miracle of content and form we exist also in the lives of others and they in ours.

OK so there's no more sacrilege. But there were never any gods. Just the idea of God. So now just the idea of sacrilege.

Same goes for other ideas.

In the place of an idea substitute the constancy of a doubt. That'll give you an idea of the idea we're getting from most of these folks most of these times.

Or.

In the place of an idea put the constancy of companionship and change. Not a change that withers as it shows itself off but that change that is companionship.

That companionship that is you and me. Here. Under the willows. No willows if it's fiction. And willows if it's not. Willows if it's poetry.

Such that there's no more me and you. Just me talking to you. You listening. You talking to me. Me listening. Willows. Willows. Willows.

Say something.

There has to be a reason to set the spark afire. To let the spark afire.

It can't be made out of clippings. It has to clip. Has to be the clip.

Has

to

be

the

clip.

We're barely awake when we talk. We're a little more awake when we talk about. A little more when the about we talk about is us. Much much much more when the about is talked about between us. And when it's understood? More. And when it's understood so to be transmitted. More more.

No matter how beautiful the spittle the song!

It has to mean something to the one who got it. And when it means everything there then no there or here or how or why or when or whyfore or when not or none of none such as that rot.

Just the cadence out of the pink tongue of thought. Such that it can be got.

Let's make a little epiphany out of the space we have here. Not one that's easy to grasp or no one EASY TO GRASP will want it. But not one that can't be grasped either. One that NOT can't be grasped now.

Anything can be beautiful and even very beautiful. Beauty is only sin deep. Like two antinomies that didn't catch each other in the available light. The light was not provided. Or like two crevasses neither of which anybody entered. NEITHER OF WHICH. Cascades that fell but fell apart.

So stop shaking when you think about it. And when you do it STOP.

We can all alight on the surface of things. And we can do it with speech in our craw. And elegance and grace and words that dance. But touch down there. Melt a few chances into the insect of what happens.

Just a structure with and without time and with and without place. I mean we're all taken hostages. But let's stop.

We're all working our way into a kind of sunset. No reason to make it one we and nobody else couldn't inhabit.

Not by the pound but make it real. And real is what touches you down into what touches everybody else. Like a thought unencased by a jacket of doubt.

Can we really eat again when the morning MORNING comes?

Or.

You can just say it.

We have to tumble ahead of ourselves into what we know. This is especially true of those of us who've been educated and taught a lot and studied. We have to get ahead of that into what happens.

What happens has to become what we know.

The problem is that poetry A PROBLEM is allowed distance from what happens. It's thought to articulate. This means that there's thought to be something external to it. Things are thought to differ or to be the same. And these are learned responses the undoing of which is this.

Of course it means depriving the academy of fodder. Returning it to histories and things like that. From there someone else can take over.

Words are not a response.

Or else OR poetry is an abuse.

In other words we can't take the words as equivalence of anything. Neither thought nor thing. To do so deprives them. Deprives us.

They are their own stuff manipulable by us towards other us. And back and forth and so on and so forth. They're the stuff of us.

Well we know what we know don't we?

If we've learned it we should forget it.

If we've seen it we can forget it.

And if we are seeing we don't need to do we?

Reader-centered writing or response-oriented writing is the site of a frustrated writer. It is demanding and sad and MORE THAN a little petulant. It doesn't share. It posits sharing. It doesn't communicate. It proposes being understood.

This despair that posits the reader as a kind of necessity NECESSITY communicates itself. ITSELF. It's the despair of the tilted and unequal relationship that gets communicated.

The only thing such an author has to communicate is the power of a kind of vacuity. But the power of one is no substitute for the powerlessness of another. Of the others.

The only thing that's left is the form of a relationship. The form of an intended relationship. But form is merely the husk of power. It's an almost. It's a substitute for something whether that thing had ever been experienced or even imagined. It's a substitute for something in an outer sort of way the way the clothes are often the substitute ONLY SUBSTITUTE for the person. It's vacant of inner life and the experiences that share in that richness. In and out of that richness.

Neither is the absence of the writer any substitute for the person of the reader. The writer doesn't need to leave to make room for the reader. Rather the poem is the room that they inhabit together. And a discussion of the problematics of such imagined absences and presences is certainly no substitute for a work that does away with them. And I mean it's no challenge to say so is it? Unless you're saying it to a writer who's already on the way out the back door to make room for some reader thought to be coming in the front.

If you take a form as substitute for substance you find that the language invents little tricks for you to keep itself interesting. It slips and slides. It shines but by itself.

Form requires invention but things are already as they are. Invention built over invention. It makes a kind of history but no kind of present.

Form only permits us to say what form says.

When you listen to the radio you only hear the sound of the music. You don't hear the composer's thoughts or the sound of the pen. You hear the performer's instruments but not the performers. You don't have the space or the time of the performance. You don't have the weather or the stars or the curtain. You only have the sound of the music. And some time or even centuries after its inception. Its first inception.

With imagination you can have those other things. But only in imagination. Not in the sound of the music.

Likewise the book.

These are the limits of creation and their limits are their breath.

It isn't enough to say something. You have to be said by it too.

There are no facts to be stated. The statement of them poses as fact. But statement of fact is devoid of so SO much.

Sometimes a fact stated rings true. But only as fact. Even the semblance of truth is external to that. And the actual lived utterance of beings has no need of fact. It's declarative beyond the meaning of declarative sentences.

174

Too often the sentence is sentience's moment of doubt. Of harangue. Of liquidation. Of doubt.

The fact is a pose. The declarative sentence too often its wardrobe. It's too easy to say too little.

A statement is declarative and stasis. Most especially when couched COUCHED in a poem. Nothing starts. Or everything only does. But facts don't have people in them. They leave them out.

Not that you can't say something. You can. But leave yourself EVERYONE and everyone else in it. Room for me too please. I mean we live here. Let's say so.

It's too easy to say so.

Poetry mostly suffers. That's because its recreators don't know how not to. Or can't forget that they do. Can't remember not having done so. Poetry suffers.

Poetry suffers.

And when it does we do.

Rules bind us to it and the rule of the factual SEEMINGLY declarative sentence is chief among them.

There is no new sentence. Only the old one masquerading without its control.

Pretending.

Memory fictionalizes. That's what it does.

There's no such thing as remembering what happened.

Therefore when we write we make something new by default. That's what writing does.

So there's nothing like truth or accuracy or anything like it.

We have to create life.

That's the mandate. That's what writing can do.

Those writings that only inscribe themselves are already dead. Those that don't are rare. And from that we have to go on.

But there's no licence for the new. Life is its own licence. It creates the new. And not by talking or writing alone. By life alone.

When it's too obvious only the poet sees it. This separates us from people who just write. No comparison.

It's all well and good to say something and have it sound true or like a parody of something sounding true. Or is it? And can anybody really tell the difference? Apart from those who profess to.

So to make a simple sentence is not enough. What's in it? Better a simple sense.

Writing is not a game. It's locution and address and reception and understanding. Method has very little to do with it. To foreground method is roughly like showing somebody your driver's license instead of giving them a ride.

Or to put it another way thinking you're writing produces thinking not writing. Likewise thinking about writing. No matter how well you put it. And the same thing applies to the kind of writing that seems to have been produced as an example of thinking about writing.

Thinking when privileged overdetermines writing. Won't let the people out. Won't let them in.

Method is the temporary guise of perfection. And perfection is the permanent guise of not being.

There is no need to reckon the difference between art and social action because both are motivated by joy. And if either is not motivated by joy then it is not art or it is not social action.

A lot of writing nowadays is allusive. It alludes or is alluded to. Often by things outside of itself elsewhere in the realms of art usually past. Or by things the poet has found the poet incapable of saying.

Whether it alludes or is alluded to the result is much the same. It isn't quite itself or it's a self without really having one.

What does it mean for the work to be alluded to? It means that it can no longer itself be even allusive. It can't allude. Even. So it is alluded to. And by what? By its presence. That's what. It's alluded to by the simple fact that it exists. Appears to exist. It is alluded to by its absence.

Then there's the buckshot method. Kind of shoot a spattering of words out there and see if they hit something.

They don't hit the target. Of thought. Or that place where they inescapably intersect and blend and know no difference.

But they hit the mind of the reader here and there. And all over. Kind of an insult. What?

It's said that this resuscitates the readers or gives them new takes on the world or frees them from traditional controlled usages of languages. That the dominant discourses are shot through on the way to the shooting of the recipient's life. But what a price to pay. Bulleting the mind of the reader in order to free it or change it. And insulting. As if someones can't be talked to and shared with and let be.

Or it just aestheticizes itself. Aestheticizes up itself. An excuse for making literature out of a twist of contorted self. Self posturing as literary event.

Or it's the kind of all-over treatment that the worst of action painting got us ready for. The work without either context or matter. Not without beauty mind you. But without much of anything else. And not without critical raison-d'etre. But with reasoning only as its underpinning. Its excuse. Not as a part of its being. Its being-in-the-world.

So it permits the meaningless. Posits it. And why not? So much else is. Without it.

It's not bad as literature.

But what about the lives of the people who need it?

We can only elongate understanding so far. Before it breaks.

Some of us want to know what's happening. And we can't be told by a blather at the mouth. Has to have us in it. And us out of it. So the experience sticks and stays. So we can go back to it and be the bettered there. So we can be.

But some would say it. Why? Doubt. Social happenstance. Too much learning. Drugs up the gazoo. No thought. Others being nothing. Hopelessness. No way out. Peer pressure. The history of the thing. Or the supposed. Any reason'll do.

But not reason.

As if it could be sold or given before had. As if it could be made before but without another. Without thought.

So it notes itself down but takes nobody up.

What about the other? There is none. We are we. I am I. You are you. I am you. I am we. You are we. We are the other. The other is I. I is the other. There is nor ever was no other.

Goddammit don't just say it. Be it.

It's easy to write poetry. It's easy to make the words cohere and be interesting. It's something you can more or less learn to do.

But it's hard to make sense. You actually have to make it. Not easy at all. A demand far beyond the demands of poetry. And when you try to do both
    for the posterity of ages
you have to learn the one and then unlearn it as well or better BETTER than you learned it in order to go on and do the other. Making sense MAKING comes later for most and many don't even get there.

You can't just allude to the sense. Too easy and doesn't stick. Doesn't ACTUALLY make sense.

Alluding is like asking the question. And although we live in asking we live by answering. If it comes from or through us or some other as agent no matter. It's the answer we eat. Keeps us going til we or who posit the next question. And gets us off again.

And you can only suggest something in a context which does not appear to suggest. Which does not only suggest. I.e., in a context which makes clear one can make clear even a mere suggestion.

The thing to do is to guarantee a good environment and a sensual time.

Sometimes musicality is a way used to talk about or to excuse poetry that isn't much other than music. But in the province of poetry music is just the sound of the voice. It's a conveyance really. Not the whole thing itself. The whole thing itself has to include the feeling in the voice and the thoughts and feelings and ideas of the one whose voice it is as well as the person or persons in front of and around the voice and their thoughts and feelings and ideas and responses coming back to inform the person whose voice speaks.

So that positing music alone as adequate to poetry is roughly like saying that all-over-abstract technique is adequate for painting. It's something isn't it? But it isn't enough to create life.

Make it obvious. And not through artifice. But because it's obvious.

Life is the way it is and to simply say so is enough. More than enough really.

People fight a kind of contagion in their minds. But what is contagious there is not their self. It is their not having come to their self.

Everything happens and most of it without us. So we might as well turn it to pleasure and happiness. And those who can't should maybe better be quieter QUIET til they can.

Making it pretty is like taking it out of your pants and doing nothing with it. Making it cohere is like never taking it out of your pants. And making it new is pure pretence.

So we have to make it WITHOUT QUALIFICATION without qualification.

In other words art must push through to the limits of life LIFE.

This is often said but saying it doesn't get it done. All art is that effort. But seldom is it done.

We can't make what needs to happen happen when we're down. So much of literature has given voice to nothing so much as to its own dismay. That's why it can be taught. By teachers.

But to really write we are the taught.

The taught to the taught.

And the taught.

It's not enough to think we're making new with the words. In fact it's usually an excuse for not being new BEING before we make.

Some have argued and continue to argue that new words and new word orders and new forms and the like are what're required to smart us out of our recalcitrant laxness. But those works exemplary of the postulate leave many dumbfounded or dumb and unfounded. The new nor the seeming new is nowhere near enough.

We have to have the whole of life at every instant or none at all. That's the thing. And to get there we need to do nothing more than accept that. By accepting it be it.

To express ourselves as the new or as if we are being the new is to express nothing but the falsity of any premise. And any premise posits what none of us can know. So by this attachment to thinking we drag ourselves past what's happening. And to what? Not to what happens next. Because we won't be there for that either. We only manage to drag ourselves out. And that's the kind of confidence some of us manage to get from it.

Nor is it enough to be well-put.

If we don't come out of it with our life all over our hands FACE like a shit-eating grin then it wasn't worth going in.

We don't need to be disturbed. Most of us are. We need if anything to come to COME understand why. And we won't find our way to that by being lapsed by somebody else into further however literary confusion.

I can't condone violence to the brain and poetry that rattles around in it without finding a home does violence to it. I can't condone violence to persons and poetry that rattles around in them without finding them home does violence to them.

So art makes home.

Something which has gone bad can never be made right. Only something new can happen.

This means no flight from sentience. And sentience as flight ONLY only when flying.

Poetry begins and ends with every line. Why not we?

But this does not admit of idiocy. Not automatically.

We don't have to make it cohere but we have to make it what it is and it usually coheres. And if it doesn't then back to the workshop not for the incoherent but for the incoherer.

It has to be heard.

A poem isn't something you piece together. It's something pieces us together. Not just a way of running the word-horde out to pasture NOT.

Don't give them an excuse to be other.

How far can we be from people and still be one of them? How far can we be from people and still be them? How far can we be from people and still be one with them?

How abstracted or specialized can our language be and still not appear disinterested? How can we use an ultra-new language without it's being or appearing as alive as a dead one? And how can we even know who we're talking with when we talk like that?

Who are we anyway? What makes us so special? Does being poets really give us some licence? Is it a licence to kill by not making life? And by not making it with the people close to and around us? Is it a licence to do anything? ANYTHING?

Or can we regulate ourselves by what we always are? Alive and well thank you. Can we be one of us and utter up as such? And what is enough if not us?

Some people claim to SEEM to be able to find meaning anywhere. I think it's because they can't remember where they put it.

Or let's say that everything has meaning. But it's thinking so and saying so makes it so.

We can only make it so difficult on our audience before we lose LOSE them THEM. And if we lose them what have we got? So we have to learn the difference between challenging and being alone by ourselves. Maybe if we challenge ourselves and leave it at that.

In other words we can't imitate forms. APE them. Or structures or gestures or vocabularies or nuances or grammars or beings or nothings or attitudes or this or that or peoples or times or ways of being and nonbeing or utterances or verses or legacies of history or things we want or things we think they want or anything. Or nothing. Can't fake it. Have to let life make it up in and through us as clear vehicle. Otherwise we get what we make. Dross. Sputum. Shit. Nothing wrong with any of that but having given it what have we got? What have we given? What have we got left to give? Left to live?

We can't hide in our words.

Nice sounds are not enough.
    Thinking is not enough.
    Thinking we're thinking is not enough.
    Thinking THEY're they're thinking is not enough.
    Humor is not enough.
    Mixing it up is not enough.
    Any thing is not enough.
    And nice endings are less than enough.
    And nice beginnings. Middles.

A measure of slippage between the elements of a poem can be a beautiful thing. It can help the elements of the poem sing and it can make any one of them mean more than one thing.

But when the slippage takes over so that each element is not equally its own thing then meaning is lost to the flux of the slippage. Understanding is lost and its attendant possibilities are lost. Instead of the elements slipping happily and gracefully next to and within one another the slippage begins to deprive them of the themselves. The potential for the poem to be more than a construct of language in space slips away from itself.

What is communication anyway? It's you and me and this.

But if I change too much BECOME DYSFUNCTIONAL the communication falters or stops. And if you change too much BE ILLITERATE then the communication falters and stops. We might either of us be able to show understanding but the communication COMMUNICATION stops. And if this THIS changes too much then too the communication falters or stops.

Likewise if this communication becomes such that it makes me appear illiterate OVER-LITERATE or such that it makes you become BECOME dysfunctional then it has faltered such that it has stopped.

    Poetry can be you and me.

No negatives. The positive drift of the thought. Communication the open space between thoughts. And the emotive constant. Nothing NOTHING kept in the box or boxed in. Everything me to you. Everything you to me. And that thing EVERYTHING the no NO box.

So literature is just between us. Nothing outside us. Nothing you can point to. At best literature is us. You and me.

Poetry and everything else. I give it to you. I give everything to you.

Written for my friends while reading.

Charles Bernstein, *Rough Trades* (Sun & Moon Press, 1991)
Bruce Andrews, *Executive Summary* (Potes & Poets Press, 1991)
Charles Bernstein, *The Absent Father in Dumbo* (Zasterle Press, 1990)
Barrett Watten, *Conduit* (GAZ, 1988)
Bruce Andrews, *Getting Ready to Have Been Frightened* (ROOF, 1988)
Charles Bernstein, *The Sophist* (Sun & Moon, 1987)
Bruce Andrews, *Give Em Enough Rope* (Sun & Moon Press, 1987)
Barrett Watten, *Progress* (Roof, 1985)

Carla Harryman and Barrett Watten

OCTOBER

Argument

The poet wants an immediate audience for his unmediated gifts:
poetry's place is most of all here. On the sidelines, a certain
amount of grumblings goes on: another places these outside
the range of his music.

Alda

I beat the bushes and birds upward do fly
As if I were become the last man on earth
And they fly from me in droves; I like that
It frightens them until they repeat after me
And I were the eye with which the universe
Beholds itself and knows it is next in line.

Only the poem is what happens, if a not-poem
Never happens continuously until it appears
Somewhere behind me in foreshortened distance
And I have the pleasure of a universal dream
Not a lump of death or chaos of hard clay
But a feminine outrageousness of gesture.

If in betrayal I advertize my willingness
For explicit content the size of this room
As it shrinks to the dimensions of our bed
A large and mutual bed, under a comforting
Uncertainty that speaks in immediate ears
Our language expands in absolute darkness.

Angel

Then his for-me-only certainty spoken between
Dimness and hallways, aluminum chairs, perked
In attention, drowns out a feminine perch
Her high-blown rhetoric on paper, pleasing
Charged with meaning, dropped in cannisters,
A splash, splashed by his majority's urgency.

Alda

O poetry, read my lips: I am not a person
But flags stuck all over *terra incognita*
Meaning you live here, and you're home now
But no one will take my spoken word for it
Until poetry puts such famous sights to scan
Replacing aluminum siding until we reflect.

But there are no numbers, only our streets
A natural and prompt contingency I recognize
Numbered for police helicopter searchlights
In a storm the volume of world-class song
Puts thumb in whose mouth and walks around
And when I come, you fly to heaven a bit.

Angel

His satire eats the pillow talk with
Hell water. Or was I thinking Hill? Me,
Two spaces later, enter again. Enigma
In a man is becoming, once or twice.
'Tis better than a mooning dyptich with
Pincers placed in the wrong hips.

So after years of thought, I do
Like sex. On terms that delight *me*:
Not with indignant braggarts but space
All over and his astonished voice applauded
By tits once or twice, not braving, the
Poor ignorant fool, the thrill

Of his migrations engineering
Time with inserts here and there:
Folks all over chafing with each immediacy
And others' flukes turning sex's peripheries
Into a music of their own and his and mine
Creation. "It better," he says, "be . . . "

Alda

Now we in thee, and thou in sleep art dead
Wake up! In me is set the perfect pattern
Of a poet finding no maintenance in a state
He studies by microscopical aural drillings
Therefore you invent new critical demands

For us not to respond in place of ideas.

Of far more arrogant horizons this day
I am jetting the stuff of future republics
Not a philosophy clouded with uncertainty
But willows talking to me and you listening
To a firestorm of *Oakland Tribune* clippings'
Thick black cloud of an emplotment agency.

Simply there is no power for back-up pumps
As your failure to respond to an emergency
Underwrites the Fall of Titans with a rage
Incommensurable. I simply can't measure it
The lust of lawless youth gave good advice
Which Gurdjieff took on tour about 1923.

Let me tell you what it ought to be like
They are distributing books we cannot read
All Americans ought to eat out more often
To bring the first white bears to a state
Of video in Antarctica. So stop shaking!
Others abide their questions; you are free.

Angel

I am driven to madness by your heavenly
Disquisitions on culture. Barometers moan
Before you. Even Anita Hill's ankles sink
Into the offshore mist. Her defeat is pleasure
Boundless and free. Like me, as you say in your
Statement. Eating onions in the jury room I hear

Names being called out to the high-pressure zone
The tent-city paradise where ashes play in permanent
    suspension
Like ankles and poets and other addicts of grand similitudes
I'm about to say, "Excuse me." But lights go off and on
"I have a normal social life," I say. Instead of breathing
The inquisitor shakes his breath into an old adage

Inscribed by patriarchs, poets, and knowledge. What we
All already do is happening in daylight with stars
Rolling over stars to burn the song Revolution can
Not withstand. Fiercely the computer borrows the
Drapes off three baboons' shoulders and board games
Climb out of the eroded encyclopedias. Again the

Patriarchs fuse eye with eye drowned in hair. Now mimic
The image. Speak the adage when it's nude. Let her
Be the pun. And stars, shaking out the Revolution, grease
The poets thumb. Tirades, remember, revise the
Left-out pendulums. A Cyborg punk orange grocer
Encourages an entourage of somber justices to cry.

Alda

Enough! This is proof positive of repression
You said what you did not mean and this means
What you did not say. When that morning comes
I will announce the identity of these states
In a single expression you have taken hostage
But nothing is ever really lost, nor can be.

Angel

Oh, I make you angry? A procedure's gone awry?
A fall from grace's burstings selects you to state
It? All my reeds are torn away when you expose me
In your fantasy. "Thinking to throw out thundering
Words of theater," I quote a gentleman or beggar
Or a shepherd. Or Mary or Medusa, Salome and Pamela

Marguerite, Minerva, Calliope, Cassandra, Lorine,
and Lyn, Kathy A. and F., Abigail and Fanny, who?
Or Susan nine and twenty, Jean, Jessica, Gail and
Grandmas one and two tomorrow and today with
Yesterday's bright sticks of butter slapped over
Buds of poetry and all power that we repel.

Alda's Emblem

We understand, then, do we not?

Angel's Emblem

I am a gambler, of sorts.

All of us are here, united in observance of an important occasion,
and one of us stands up to speak for the humanity of it all. But
it is only an art project, fatally flawed from the outset, pulling
philosophy by the jacket sleeves and gauging its impact against
predicted weather. The only thing such an author has to communicate is the power of a kind of vacuity: at the bottom of the
sink a beautiful stainless steel drain. This was the lesson poets
communicated to each other in the rigors of on-going competi-
tion. Whence returning to the Latin, "There is a god in us," and
we are wholly at the apex of our game.

4] music) A romantic disregard for content in poetry.

6] the last man) In her novel, Mary Shelley fantasized the logical
implications of her mate's aesthetics.

17] betrayal) I.e., observe others in a similar state.

25] feminine perch) An antiquated object recently come back in
fashion consisting of a large padded rotating disk suspended
from the ceiling with a harness to fasten oneself with, if one so
desires, in order that one can experience the over/under objective of female experience without being in danger of falling.

37] police helicopter searchlights) A book of aerial photographs over
Los Angeles shows precisely the extent of a dystopia. Such a gloss
is always a *non sequitur*, with a rhetoric typical of our poetic intentions. And what conclusion should a moralist draw from this?

58] Creation) Someone else's idea of how to treat animals alone,
or in the dark, or with someone else.

69] Oakland Tribune) A collective disaster is a good opportunity
for promoting one's community. The inverse of this proposal
is emblematic of a desire for consuming flames.

86] offshore) All sorts of cast-off treasure, contaminants, human and
otherwise, are said to get sent offshore by the patriarchs who like
to keep their closets in good order, but it is illegal and perhaps
dangerous to go there on one's own accord. It is said to be mod-
eled after some utopian's vision of hell on earth. Do you know
anyone who has ventured there?

107] Enough!) Once some learned man, being more gifted than the
rest in special gifts of wit and music, would take upon himself to
sing to the people in praise either of virtue or of victory or of
immortality. Now, the poet implies of this our later age, we scribble
of defects and our defeats, the corrigibility of impressions and
their written record.

124] we) A highly regarded hodgepodge.

Emblems

Suddenly we all turn to make contact with language in solidarity with
      purposes efficiently understood as a speech continuous in trans-
      parent communication (Whitman).
I believe in an order that does not exist.

FROM REINVENTING COMMUNITY:
A SYMPOSIUM ON/WITH LANGUAGE POETS

Andrew Ross/Barrett Watten

This symposium originally appeared in *The Minnesota Review*. Bruce Andrews, Charles Bernstein, and Ron Silliman also responded. The Andrews/Bernstein collaborative response will be reprinted in *Aerial 9*.

Introduction by Andrew Ross

These are not the most propitious times for the idea of "community." The dominant definition of communal activities today tends to be more like that of an atomistic culture of *survival* and *advancement*, where the alternatives are likely to be grisly and Hobbesian, or else a "special interest" group, with its suggestion of petty, even paranoid, self-indulgence. On the other hand, the tradition, among writers and artists, of avant-garde communities, historically associated in various ways with the politics of vanguardism, has lost much of its legitimacy as an indirect result of the sweeping left critiques of vertical, or centralized forms of organization. Less frequently do we see the heroicization of the bohemian dream of acting out utopian desires in a setting that is materially distanced from the institutional reaches of bourgeois society. The cultural power of preindustrial nostalgia that governed the romance of the counterculture has long since faded under the pressure of post-punk cynicism. In short, a community of writers which would take itself seriously as a community might have to wholly reinvent, rather than merely redefine, the purposive values associated with that term.

Nowhere has this task of reinvention been more actively pursued than in the case of the writers associated, either centrally or obliquely, with the name of language poetry, a term originally coined to defame the poets and tendencies associated with the journal *L=A=N=G=U=A=G=E* (1978-82). And nowhere has the sense of community been acknowledged with so much technocultural realism, or owed so little to the romance of an idealized *Gemeinschaft*. For poets, like them, who became active in the early seventies, the question of "community" was as likely to be posed in the form of a socially integrated lifestyle *in loco* as it was to cover intellectual interests shared across geographical space. The result, in the case of the language poets, proved to be a heady combination, with two sizeable residential communities built up, year by year, with writers in other cities, regions, and countries. Living and writing, for the most part, outside of the institutional circuits of the poetry scene, and publishing in their own magazines and presses, many of these poets came to recognize that an integral component of the poetics which they were developing had to do with examining the everyday social relations which underpinned the production, distribution and reception of their work. Seldom had a single artistic community undertaken such a critique as part of its agenda for addressing the aesthetic imperatives of the day. On the other hand, there is nothing like a systematic sociological critique to point to, largely because of the diverse (several dozen writers, at one time or another, have been associated with language poetry) and decentralized shape of the community. In fact, some claimed that it was an idealized overinvestment, even a promotional self-indulgence, to present the appearance of a self-conscious community with shared interests. For those, however, who had been responding, with immediacy and commitment, to each other's work for many years, it had become a habit of mind to acknowledge the quasi-collective nature of the social relations involved in their practice of making poetry, and this collective aspect was not to be dreamed away by the ideology of the poetic loner/genius.

Genealogies, elective affinities, and the anxieties of influence are the critical trappings of the tradition of the spiritually driven individual talent. For writers who make it their business to preserve some kind of control over their own affairs, the sources and frames of reference for their work are almost always contextual, tailored to times and places, and shot through with socialized intentions. The seventies and early eighties was a time when writers were responding in their own ways to the explosion of critical theory, and the transformation of political philosophies that followed in the wake of post-structuralism. Much of what went under the name of language poetry was the fertile result of poets working within the charged theoretical atmosphere of that time. As the critique of subjectivity—the implied topic of so much of modern poetry—took center stage, the traditional marxist quest for homologies between literary structure and social reality came under new forms of scrutiny by the language poets. Authorial certainty, *a priori* experience, generic purity, contextual anonymity—all of these reading conventions went the way of the world, from which, it was suspected, they had originally been abstracted as institutions of damage control. Language poetry, as it came to be known, set about exploring what it accepted as *always already mediated experience*, and this task, it was claimed, was suddenly more real, or less idealized as a social function, than poetry had previously bargained for. If there was a "community" of shared interest in work of this sort, then it was a community bound by a political intention—not to show what language has to say about possible worlds, but to find out what language has to do with social change. In this new conjuncture of the text, consciousness, experience, and history, the autonomous "aesthetic function" of Russian Formalism would come face to face with the commodity formalism of late capitalism.

Not surprisingly, the work of the language poets has drawn a good deal of hostile commentary, much of it politically grounded and answered in like coin. And there is more than a little irony in the conventional wisdom, at least among their critics, that the poetry is "non-referential," a term which suggests qualities of abstraction and worldly contempt. More recently, the academic debate has been set in motion, with its authoritative eye on history, and canonical legitimacy. For many of these writers, what used to be called "the long march through the institution" has begun, which is to say that any future description of this poetic community will be obliged to take into account its mediation

189

across institutions.

The symposium that follows is directed as much at the current state of play among the language poets as at the past history of their writing and reception. But the questions posed to the contributors were also more generally addressed to the position of the writer as a public intellectual today, at a time when cultural politics is undergoing, if not enjoying, a relatively unfettered or undisciplined period of activity. The four contributors were selected because all, in addition to being highly visible authors who are identified with language poetry, have served as editors of important organs within the community. Bruce Andrews and Charles Bernstein were editors of *L=A=N=G=U=A=G=E*. Ron Silliman is the editor of the book anthology *In the American Tree*, and, like Andrews and Bernstein, has edited magazine collections of language poetry. Barrett Watten, formerly the editor of *This*, now edits (with Lyn Hejinian) *Poetics Journal*, currently the most important forum for poetics among language writers.

Language poetry, as it has been collectively designated, is associated with a "community" of writers who have long been concerned, among other things, with the self-conscious project of exploring the effects which the social relations of a writing community have upon the process of writing, from the everyday sharing of ideas to the nuts-and-bolts of distribution. How do you feel that this project is surviving, as language poetry becomes the latest thing, even in academic circles?

In Oshima's film *Night and Fog in Japan*, a wedding takes place between two members of a radical student group that had been together since the all-out protests against U.S.–Japanese Security Treaty of the mid fifties. Grim standoffs of collective anxiety, reinforced by the fading colors of an aging film stock, alternate with staccato bursts of emotional discharge as members of the group stand up to denounce the inadequacies and betrayals of their collective identity. The marriage is destroyed not by its progress through the world of everyday life, the normal mechanisms, but by the perception that the solidarity of purpose which preceded the group's members' vows of assent to the community had lost its grip. At the moment of passage into a wider social horizon, the larger world extracts its revenge—and the claim to history that the group had intended in its self-conscious earlier phase now comes true, ironically, in the moment of its dispersal. As failures, they have become indexes to history.

The form of belief that held together, violently, such a group of variously motivated individuals is, at the moment of its transformation, rendered objective—and at the same time the belief fails. Clearly individuals might continue to hold some of their collective beliefs—the wife-to-be runs off to join a demonstration in progress in the near distance as the police arrive to lead the most resolute sectarian away. But the form of the group itself cannot survive objectification. It turns out that all along none of its members really understood what it was they were saying, even though it was said repetitiously and at length—in all-night discussions of political theory, in slogans at the barricades, and in tracts on revolutionary justice—while given meaning by

190

the provocation of the group's enemies outside. The centripetal momentum of the group had revolved around a hollow center—as long as there was force and resistance to keep it in motion. This is very like the process of collective idea-formation in the arts. But rather than politics being the test case for an aesthetic, as in Oshima's film, poetry and the visual arts, in recent history, have become experiments in the politics of fragmented social identity.

There was a collectively held set of beliefs, and an absolute recognition of them, among the poets who came together in the mid seventies to mid eighties and whose works can be categorized after the fact by participation in magazines such as *This, Roof, L=A=N=G=U=A=G=E,* and *Poetics Journal,* in the anthologies *In the American Tree* and *"Language" Poetries.* This social formation can be seen as analogous to a radical political tendency in a number of ways. First, there was a reinterpretation of a prior aesthetic doctrine that addressed new social conditions and thus severed the meaning of contemporary practice from that of its forebears—in a comprehensive rereading of the poetics of Creeley and Olson, Zukofsky and Stein, Mac Low and Antin, the New York School and the Beats. Second, this new aesthetic, the beliefs that held meaning in a kind of centripetal suspension while their implications were being articulated in a variety of writing practices, to some extent depended on the isolation of the group from the larger literary world. A metalingual underpinning supported the production and interpretation of works that, looked at separately from this social process, might be understood differently later when the meaning of their collective claims had been objectified in time. If there is any single way of summing up the principle of this metalingual subplot, it would be that particularity and deferral of ultimate ends (what led to the title of the magazine *This,* what is responsible for the grammatological equivalence of the equal signs in *L=A=N=G=U=A=G=E*) are identical with the methods and meaning of the work—a utopia where there are no heroes but those who meet their obstacles and rewards here and now, no deferrals to a resolution in future time. A steady-state poetics combined with a radically analytical referentiality led to the production of works that would totalize agency at the same moment that they stopped history in its tracks.

The final analogy to a radical tendency in this group of writers is that at the moment of its entrance to a wider social world a crisis occurs. The unstated assumption of the question above is that community is necessarily at odds with the professional role of the unsuccessful artist, that "making it" makes the artist into a commodity and thus merely a part of the reified system of exchange (see more on this below). The notion of commodity, however, could be seen not only as an end in itself but as a token of negative belief that reinforces group identity as much as would the tokens of community in its shared language practices. Thus the scenario of a direct transformation of group practice into commodity exchange that would occur "as language poetry becomes the latest thing" could be criticized in several ways. On the one hand, the displacement of group language is already a form of negativity that would formally anticipate and counter the marketplace commodification of the individual writer encountered later. On the other, the group's assertion of belief takes on elements of a wider social frame once the boundary between the group and society is erased. In this sense, the pressures that set the group apart from the larger world and that ultimately would destroy it are returned to the world as intensified agencies, as atoms of social intentionality that can now better articulate their claims. The metalanguage of group practice becomes realized as palpable language once the transition is made; the anxiety of the boundary between group identity and world is the beginning of a new social role.

The notion of a reified community is just where Left theory fails to understand political process. What is efficacious in social change is not the "being" of a marginal social group but its assertion of identity and the leverage this brings to bear on conditions. Community can be as politically ill used as the various neighborhoods on the ward-boss model of Chicago, or it can rise to provisional efficacy as in the wide-scale and ideologically underdeveloped array of oppositional groups to the Vietnam War. Such opposition does not survive its meaning as such, however—again, this would be the moment that objectification fails in real politics. If the arts have something to teach politics, it is not to look anteriorly at the "latest thing" as what will solve the dilemma of oppositional belief. That belief is now residing on a larger scale, and it is one of the constructive necessities of the artist to give evidence of it. In that sense, the community that writers bring to bear on the world, rather than being absorbed in their recognition, is ceaselessly being reinvented.

Some of you have actively linked language poetry with the term "realism," a concept that has had a long and checkered career in the history of avant-garde practices; from the early "bourgeois" novel forms, through the reaction to the state-directed social realism of Stalinism, to the populist appeal of the "new journalism" of the sixties. Where would you locate the calls for a new realism associated with language poetry today?

As in losing one's virginity, once one sees the world from the standpoint of language there's no going back. Realism becomes the father waiting up late to no avail—"It's already happened, Dad." The stylistic repression that makes realism possible—in most historical epochs except those that have newly discovered realism—has negatively united the avant-garde since Rimbaud and Lautréamont in the certainty of its aims. That certainty is strong enough, at this point, as to be tempted to claim realism as the actual ground of its practice. And there are several ways in which a kind of realism unimagined by Zola (but structurally encoded in Balzac, Tolstoy, and Drieser) is directly undertaken in contemporary avant-garde work, developments that may implicate a future realism understood in the more classical sense.

Traditional realism, first of all, is either a discovery or a constraint. The effect of the real in the former sense is motivated not simply by the real but by the fact that the real has not been represented in that particular way up to the moment of the work. Negative realism, Social Realism for example, co-opts the real in the name of a prior effect of the real through the imposition of a restricted code of expression. In either case realism is an historical trope —hence the meaning of its identifications—and the claim of the real by the text is an index of belief in a temporal progression that we, as readers, find necessary. An avant-garde realism works to similar effects on both counts. It finds necessity in its representation of the hitherto unrepresented, and it makes an historical claim of the discovery of a restricted code of expression that is the means to do so. The difference between the two is in the "set toward the referent" of the work—the difference between looking out the window for the weather and scavenging an engineer's dreams for gears. A conventional time frame and a three-dimensional space, with their determination of human action and belief, fill out the form of one kind of discovery, while an invented time frame and a linguistic space that may or may not make any claim to physical dimensions characterize the other.

The claims of the avant-garde on classical realism that were made, for example, in the title of Ron Silliman's mini-anthology published in *Ironwood* or Lyn Hejinian's series of talks on "Realism" are not particularly strong. Silliman was interested in a kind of gesture toward the legitimation that has always been the claim of realism, one that is dished out incessantly in the Left critic's privileging of the novel, particularly the nineteenth-century novel that produced realism, as the index of everyday life and thus of the ground of ideology. The blindspots inculcated by such realism lead to too easy identification of action and belief with the time and space of a novel. For some contemporary writers, however, such novels are unreadable—in their restricted "effect of the real" and in their artificial progression toward an ending—and, as one critic said recently, their acceptance would be much more problematic if people weren't being paid to teach them. Unfortunately the academic's faith in its institutional stake in realism has recently been buttressed by the publishing market's interest in promoting a new generation of writing-workshop fiction. But what one notices is not the "effect of the real" in this work per se—what counts is its social index in a more active response to ideological pressures, the embrace of the market for instance, than would be allowed the historical claims of the avant-garde. Sale of movie rights rather than museum validation has become a counter in a social negotiation of value. Where the avant-garde stands for a distance from the market, and thus paradoxically a position more real if denying realism as a style, the return to genre fiction, with its transparency to the market, denies the claims to such an outside social position in embracing an illusion of the real. In either case, there is no naturalization of genre that is not at the same time an argument for a world view.

Thus Silliman tried to undermine the foundations of belief in realist form by equating the social position, and thus the linguistic insight, of the most radical nonreferential writing with the real. Experience in many senses may demand a kind of phenomenological bracketing, one that counters the hegemony of conventional markers of the real in drawing from altogether different kinds of intention. In Silliman's own work, for example, realistic observed detail is juxtaposed in an entirely textual matrix with reflection, language-as-language, fragments of overheard speech. The act of describing a scene out the window might in this way be seen as natural as a proposition of Willard Van Orman Quine. What one accepts of description is an acquiescence to a conventional scale: here style becomes articulated in the politics of everyday life. The only way to enter the world of these choices is by providing a textual frame that does not imitate a conventional time and space. Similarly, Hejinian's (and my own) interest in the formal architecture of realism, particularly as seen through the work of the Russian Formalists, leads to a poetics in which form intentionally organizes experience—not simply imitates it. Both the referential and formal axes of realism, then, are seen as continuous with avant-garde attention to reference and form in other senses. It may be that there is a realism of social experience that is its consciousness of it, rather than simply a record of its appearance, and this possibility for art would motivate the appropriation of "realism" for a work that violates the traditional unities of time and place.

Poets are well placed to speak to those relations between public and private life which are overlooked by other kinds of discourse about politics. In your individual work and collectively, each of you has addressed the role of the commodity world in our everyday lives. Does this mean that you reject the heroic image of the writer-intellectual whose political stance is based upon his or her opposition to, or distance from, the commodity world in the name of public values?

One unavoidable component of that commodity world, for example, seems to be a writer's "value" in the cultural marketplace. What uses do you think can be made of this "value"?

A simple answer to the latter question was given by Brecht when he said, at some point, that he needed to be famous because he had enemies. This equation of agency with market recognition indicates a political economy in which value and power are not identical—even if one may be perceived to speak for the other. It also marks a point where Brecht hedged his bets in terms of the forthcoming crisis of the Left in Germany. Having expatriated himself to Hollywood, Brecht was lucky to find a patron state waiting with open arms for him after the War. In his work as in his life, Brecht's identification with the market ironized the question of the state, giving the political subject a mobility not available through an identification with more explicit political tendencies. The market, however unstable, grounded his aesthetic as a contestation of value in a way that analysis, with its predication of power, could not.

It would be hard to find an example of a writer whose disinterested embrace of public or even literary values precludes identifying with the market in some form. Pound's ironic "beer bottle on the statue's pediment" gives a value for history for which commodity production is a simple negative. While Pound's epic is in no way complicitous with the market in the last instance, it is possible to see an analogy between the eternal image, turned out in repeating units on the *Cantos'* assembly line, and the temporally diminishing token of exchange that Pound made his ideal of circulation. "What thou lovest well remains,/the rest is dross" does seem to imitate the marketplace choice, leading to a collection of favorite ties in the closet and a pile of trash to be picked up Monday morning. In a way, our later designation of the commodity as a "problem-in-itself" may only echo Pound's desire for transhistorical unity in defense against the market. The commodity becomes a negative Arnoldian touchstone in a progression of great men from their historical origins to their dooms. As a mirror of fatality, the petit-bourgeois fear of the marketplace—loss of identity when placed into exchange— becomes the perfect vehicle for the circulation of the work in the reader's identification of it. Given the threat of the real market to deny value by making experience atomized and equivalent, a symbolic market is figured, negatively, in the aesthetic economy that returns value to the world. The meaning of the recent *Art in America* issue on "Art and Money" is not only that it came in the mail but that it leaves us free to do our work. Some of this work may record the joy we would feel in not having to worry so much about money.

In this sense, the economic "bottom line" of the market can be seen in compositional terms—as either a horizon in which the work sites itself or as symbolic displacements in its structure. One such configuration of the economic horizon might be the heroic one associated with post-War painting, in which the world of the market is excluded from direct representation, but very much exists as a frame for production. An ironic reading of the market from its exclusion in the work is often made, and it is exactly this form of irony that Warhol, Johns, and Lichtenstein turned into literal content in their historic inclusion of the market as subject matter for their work. This implosion of the ironized conditions of production in Warhol led almost immediately to the explosion of art into context by Conceptual and Minimalist artists; in both instances the gallery system was important for the guarantee of value in the work, while its internal representation diverged radically. Warhol seemed to imply a redundancy of art and market value, while an artist like Robert Smithson, however supported by the Dwan Gallery, made art an index of social aporia in his extension of content from the metropolitan gallery frame into suburban and marginal geographies.

With the "return to painting" of the late seventies and the incorporation of a "commodity critique" in the art of the mid eighties, such a narrative of mutual incorporation of art and market is well-trodden ground. As such it becomes a limiting horizon of intellectual life. That life may be said to have flourished, relatively, in the period of antagonism between art and its market support in the fifties, and it may again be said to be flourishing under the rubric of theory, once the questions of context opened by Warhol and Smithson had been placed back into the frame. In between these moments, however, there has been a crisis in the redirection of cultural activity. While the artist may be said to have had the upper hand in the distance from the market maintained by fifties painting, the market has regained the upper hand in its ironic recuperation of its critique. The aforementioned number of *Art in America*, for example, features photos of gallery owners in celebrity poses in one survey of contemporary attitudes toward art and money, followed by another article in which Marxist critics (in serious, professional poses) engage in the process of validating the market as the final horizon of production. Such a sad economism must also be seen to have its rewards. Critics and artists who are aware of them are busily redirecting their work toward an internalized critique that guarantees social circulation. The market becomes communication, the outlet for one's work, validation, and support at the same time.

There is another possibility, literally the argument I am making here. While the visual arts' internalization of a critique that makes the commodity an historical necessity has led many to their niches in the market (and vastly more to the dump as waste products of the system), literature, being based not on the atemporal object but on a temporality of argument and thought, need not see its critique as limited to the ironic reversal of marketplace support. A kind of liminal ground between commodity and experience, between public and private values—much like the "capillary tissue" Breton identified between dream and reality—exists to define a social position for literature that is both "in but not of" the market. There are human ends to the literary process that are not simply a formal compromise between public communication as collective index of knowledge and belief and private ownership embodied as collectible objects. While the literary market does determine certain values in its criteria for circulation, other social forms for literature are given by values of social good administered by a state not simply an expression of the market. *Education*, for example, has arisen historically not from the market but from state subsidies responding to needs that are not necessarily those of profit. Education is a primary locus of politics of reform, and the relative failure of the state in these areas as an indication of the current demands of the market (leading to a recent 1.5 percent drop in labor costs, the business section of the paper reads) shows the state retreating from gains made in previous reforms. This assault on education has occurred at the time of increased state subsidies in other areas, leading one to see the final horizon of the market in intellectual life as more symbolic than real. The deficit, after all, is Reagan's.

The avant-garde has a curiously double role within a state seen as a composite reflection of both market and human needs. It represents a form of life, a validation of unalienated activity, that bears little relation to profitability. Its products, however, as commodities particularly in the visual arts, reproduce the market in an equation of intentionality with surplus value, in the reduction of expression to equivalent frames. In both senses the avant-garde would seem to be a paradigm of uselessness. At the same time, it reintroduces a form of life exterior to a social production back into circulation—in its embodiment of a critique in a work of art that, as an object of reflection, alters knowledge and belief. The commodity status of art is not an example of "determination in the last instance" but a property of intellectual life not necessarily addressed only to the ends of the market. At the same time, there is no simple public transcendence of the market that would return us to value on the heroic scale. Market value thus becomes, both internally to a work and in terms of an artist's career, a formal element to be redefined rather than the reality to which one can only submit.

In a 1952 Partisan Review *symposium called "Our Country and Our Culture," writers were asked to examine their new-found Cold War commitment to the institutions of national cultural life. Today, that universal function of the intellectual, who speaks for society as a whole, whether in opposition or in alignment, seems to be redundant. In your view, has the perceived social responsibility of writers diminished in scope, from the global interest to the local interest, and in audience, from the nation to a technocratic community of writers? Or do you feel that this shift is a more positive one?*

Once, if a writer published a serious book he or she might count on serious readers. Today, that "universal function of the intellectual" to be engaged with a community of coproducers on congruent or antagonistic terms at times appears, on the "national" level, as more of a representation of function —on the order of "Here's my card." The perceived retraction of scale of the writer's domain may have an effect of making this reciprocal life seems like "a technocratic community." In reality, the community of writers has been limited in its access to wider audiences precisely because of the hegemony of establishment institutions such as *Partisan Review* and the *New York Review of Books*, reinforced by the overproduction of specialized discourses in the academy, where career pressures lead to professionalization and an embarrassment of larger context. In general, it would be safe to say that contemporary writers are eager to engage wider audiences and "national" issues but that access to the forums where such intellectual life is conducted is carefully controlled. As it stands, a merely symbolic recognition of our writers' tendency—in favorable review articles in the *Nation*, the *London Review of Books, Critical Inquiry*, the *Village Voice*; or negative ones in the *New Criterion* and *Partisan Review*—has replaced direct presentation of the work or its discussion in a wider frame. Interpreters negotiate the value of our work in mediated contexts that are closed to the work itself.

Many of the issues of most immediate concern that led to the intensive development of the contemporary writing community, with whatever its resemblance to a technocracy or even a sectarian cult, stemmed directly from a period of "national" crisis—the Vietnam War. The central problem of reference in this writing may be seen in context as directly related to the administration of information about the War on the part of government and media that elicited, from intellectuals-in-the-making, a radical denial of consent for the conduct of the War. In this period of schism the overview of the "national" perspective, particularly as controlled by former Marxists now committed to the Cold War, seemed distant and irrelevant. There was a denial of "national" culture in all aspects—from direct participation in the War to career choices to acceptance of government funds in the arts to choice of breakfast cereal. The formation of radical tendencies in the arts discussed above occurred directly as a refusal of the given larger context, but at the same time it was a response to a crisis of meaning at that level. As a result, the radically analytical language of the movement—which constituted the community in its own recognition of itself—rendered impossible the level of generality traded at the level of the "national" culture. This generality, also, was perceived to be a by-product of a particular compromise or even "selling out," so it's not surprising that its terms offered no immediate interest. In order for writers to become engaged with the issues of a larger context, a confidence needed to develop that the forms of writing and identity being explored in the work had implications at that level. The experience of changing social identities as a result of economic pressure after the War gave ample evidence that a critique embedded in the language of the subject was necessary as a point of departure for politics. This assurance coincided with a breaking out of marginality in the refiguring of the writers' self-defined community.

The marginalization of the avant-garde is thus no accident. It is a response to the failure of consensus as to the role of the intellectual, a denial of "national" culture as defined by the *Partisan Review.* As Charles Olson maintained, "You have to put establishment out of business . . . . The radical of action lies in finding out how organized things are genuine, are initial"—a forum on "Our Country and the Cold War" being exactly the kind of "responsible engagement" that sent Olson, in the same period, to the Yucatan "to hunt among stones." This concern for the particular has value, in its own "finding out how organized things are genuine," in its critique of culture at more general levels. Where Olson looked for historical particulars, recent writers have been more concerned with particulars of language use and belief, with history entering the poem as a kind of fragmented comment on the subject's position in the here-and-now. The grand historical setting of the *Partisan Review*—the repetitive wheeze of the tale of its tribe—is very far from the kind of claim to social agency being made through contemporary forms of writing and their extensions as critique. It might be said that the skepticism toward historical representations in this work is motivated by mistrust of the monologue of establishment history, radically influenced by the experience of unrepresented life in historical crisis since the period of the Vietnam War.

That access to intellectual life has been so difficult, so impeded, for contemporary writers is not explainable simply by the influence of a few reviews, however, but to the symbiosis of the representation of "national" intellectual life with the structure of the academy and the support system for the arts. In its avoidance of literary politics of any but the most personal kind, the professionalization of creative writing programs within English departments has certainly excluded work that would address more serious issues. The abandonment of contemporary letters in most departments to the creative writing faculty (and the mass-market paperback) reinforces the poetics and politics of threatened petit-bourgeois personal life that dominates the content of much officially sanctioned contemporary writing. Apart from the avant-garde, the twentieth century itself has become less and less a viable area for scholarship in the humanities as anxieties of the canon or of theory make academic self-scrutiny all the more regulating. Given this stultification of literary process, it's no wonder that representation of recent work has only been of symbolic value. Isolated mention of this work competes with the day-in, day-out drone of complimentary reviews of replaceable authors never to be heard from again. The control of professional creative writing programs over the funding of contemporary literature to the exclusion of the avant-garde, particularly at the level of the National Endowment for the Arts, is the third major factor in the denial of serious writing to wider audiences. Thus, the question of whether these writers have abandoned "national" cultural issues is answerable in complementary ways. "National" culture, on the one hand, was gravely compromised during the period of the Vietnam War. But now that writers whose concerns were formed in those years have gained a voice, the establishment (from the *Partisan Review* and *New York Review of Books* to the English departments and the current funding bureaucracy) doesn't seem to want us to get through. So we'll have to find some other way.

"Lassen Peak

"In one synoptic view..."   elev. 10,400
"The summit surrounded in haze..."

self portrait as lightning rod at top

section four.

Barrett Watten: An Invention

Some kind of
reflector for
energy - to be
displayed outward.

colors of lava ?? in
the craters at the
summit: pink,
orange, yellow sulfers,
dark red, black w/
white specks.

Loud grasshoppers
+ bees fly by. Monarch
butterflies + flies - what
do they live on? Red wasps/
white rocks. Pink + yellow lichen
incrustations -

Jerry Estrin

> No: not even the memory of the eighth and last episode of a film I
> saw in the neighborhood, in which a Chinese who had found some
> way to multiply himself, invaded New York by means of several
> million self-reproductions. He entered President Wilson's office
> followed by himself, and by himself, and by himself; the President
> removed his *pince-nez*. This film, which has affected me far more
> than any other, was called *The Grip of the Octopus*.
>
> Andre Breton, *Nadja*

Barrett Wattten's work is an infinite one-act play, an ongoing non-event, yet it
is connected to the world, to the many worlds that make us spectators. When
we spectators suspend ourselves in the worlds of our absolute singularities,
Watten's act is there to read us its sentence. It is a kind of collective nightmare
that is good for us. Watten punishes us with the possibility of our non-identity
("And that is his art. To/cancel your ticket, wait" [*Progress*, 11]), or at least, with
the necessity for constant negotiation and renegotiation, just to be here. When
we really read him, we enter into a conversation with a systematic distortion
machine that keeps trying to suppress our speechlike tendency to denote when
we should connote. Watten's language offers itself as its own truth, forcing
denotation into ruin, clearing the ground by glossing what is otherwise invisible to everyday life, that is to say, the dialectical movement of its own language:
"a spasm of zig-zags of mannered sweeps . . . " " . . . releas[ing] energy into the
world it dismantles" [*1-10*, 34]. This, after all, is progress, which, when and if
this language ever completes, would complete itself, and remove us from our
own gestures, violently. But since the most survivable if perverse measure of
Watten's work is its stasis, that is to say, its mimetic return to a null-point, the
very paradigm of completion is untenable. This dialectical process is the work's
hold on reality, its grasp of the totality of language. "Language makes a home,
not the other way around" [*1-10*, 5]. The writing's stress on its own, centrifugal
movement serves as ground zero for Watten's combat with contingency's real-
time enigmas. What can't be resisted through experiential action, the irresist-
ibility of spectacular time, is skillfully appropriated by a poetry willing its own
constructed future, its preeminent non-event. Rather than posing as a naive,
naturalistic, enactment of a continuous present of consciousness, the writing
generates an entropic, mannered duration that fronts its own artifice. Although
immersed in historical time, relentlessly glossing its socio-historical condition,
Watten's work is really a consequence of an *idée fixe* with *its own* entropic
duration. "The certainties of didactic discourse are hurled into the erosion
of the poetic principle. Poetry . . . must submit to its own vacuity . . . Poetry is

always a dying language but never a dead language" [Robert Smithson, "A Sedimentation of the Mind: Earth Projects", 1968].

To view political transformation as a process brought about by linguistic decay, by a moment to moment encounter with language, allows Watten to inhabit a world that can never be servile, that is ever armed with proof of its refractive power. The work enacts the possibility of its difference; it asserts itself as its own epic: history's alienated object is transformed into the triumphant, communal subject, whose deviant predications have cleared the ground. Yet the power of this poetry to dissemble what it so wants to win, to reveal its author in the negative space of 'our' dialogic agency, is the work's poignancy, its authentic wound at the 'heart' of the historical impersonality Watten's writing otherwise portends. As the work progresses, as its structural operations relentlessly explain themselves, the very dialogue on which the poetry lives is precluded by the continuum of the author's intentionality. *Intention* is the writing's blindspot as well as its lucidity. The writing, albeit its relentless appropriation of subjective signifieds, mirrors the warlike dualism it intends to subvert. "Identity is the cause of war" [*1-10*, 27] in Watten's poetry as well as in the culture he critiques. The writing historically objectifies what it otherwise wants for itself, seeks "to play the game" of history "(and win)" [*1-10*, 41]. History: this himself, followed by himself, and by himself—this GRIP OF THE OCTOPUS. Watten reveals himself in his absences. The work is an emotional displacement machine. The writing works as the poet's ambivalent double; it calls out for our response, yet resists it by the very evidence of authority that it contests.

"One Grasps the Implications of this Negative as a Whole"

Leslie Scalapino

Decay, Barrett Watten, This Press, 1977

The inscription for *Decay* reads, "Ever since I've been doomed to die/all the lines I've ever known in my/life are coming back to my mind./It must be a sign of mental decay." They're extinguished.

In *Decay*, the visual scenes that take place in 'frames' or lines may be on top of each other or to the side—or as if they cross each other—and there isn't a romantic hero, because they cross each other.

The lines meet and in that way are eliminated, as if there's no field there. The field does not exist, that had been created by them.

> TWO
>
> A & B are sitting on the truncated
> pyramidal rim of a black asphalt highway.
> In the distance to the right is a black
> mountain w/silver-white snowstorm on top.
> There is a rainbow over a deep open field.
> Under a dark green tree, a funeral party
> leaving the grave, an open black hole.

One doesn't have to elude (to) a 'romantic' image of oneself, whatever that is. It is the area of the most extreme falsity. 'One' should get to that which is 'real,' as such single when it is (almost) eliminated.

'You' can only see them when they cross or coincide with each other.

Like "Two," the poem "XY" has two points throughout which eliminate each other. Similarly, in "Ice Skating" the lines, motions, and surfaces are double continually and eliminate the surface.

A single line in these poems is double (so the writer is 'almost' eliminated): "This week I sat in a small room and wondered constantly where I was./It is a bodily experience to be left as an orphan crying at the gate."

This observation of what's occurring or seen places a line under heavy stress: "The lack of any backbone marked an early disinclination to speech." There's no equivalent as representation of what it's/he's saying. Nor of the real, visual scene.

"Looking at the clock, flesh singed and blackened by the mysterious air." Seeing double, or singular, causes the 'images' to cross each other. Or their crossing each other causes them to be singular or double. There's no way in the writing to know which.

"Circular thinking arrests emotional development, punishing time." This eliminates development and the conception of time as accruing. Change occurs; one's nature, anyone's, does not develop.

Perhaps the person's nature itself is regarded as romantic, falsity? That would be a falsity.

"One man walking down a street will see no more than he desires." But what we don't know is if that limits him. The sources of apprehension are not where they appear, because "Memory is estranged." Being estranged is not alienation; there isn't that. "Out of the endless listing of addresses, he saw a human being burning white."

Nor is apprehension determined by rearrangement of elements.

The writing is white because it is "unborn in the eye, without reason or heart." Rearrangement does not exist in this. Decay is the outer meeting the inner in that way.

To narrow to the outlines of its form is utter scrutiny, is real.

"Outside the inner man's almost doubled back." So there may be suffering but it appears as calm, produced by estrangement. "I remove my two arms and /start to walk again."

There being no development of one's nature the inner and outer are flattened. As a fact.

My nature seemed to develop. (One has the illusion that one's nature develops.) Not really if the lines that are written are all that I was able to remember.

The images can't develop. The images aren't my nature.

Conduit, Barrett Watten, Gaz Press, 1988

Watten's writing is lovely in engaging in rigor (in the sense in which scientists speak of an experiment being elegant in its form and execution). It's not on the edge, it's the edge.

"One grasps the implications of this negative as a whole."

Viewing by scrutiny, and elimination of all of the individual parts, illuminates the whole.

The original world which is wonderful is seen only by seeing its 'negative' aspect, which occurs by duplicating it as wonderful.

The pretext to represent the original world is itself negative. "The text will be as wonderful as the falling star of its original, the world."

The negative panes through which this is seen are 'accurate' indirectly because "Normal vision has distorted its reasoning."

Nothing is accurate. Experience opens reality, which is only the mind's perception of it: "I think experience is access to language only."

The criteria of experience is not the individual's relation to it. Alienation is an illusion. The very rigor of negative space itself when held as a concept of self is also illusion. "Romantic negativity, the avoidance of any conditions that compromise the subject leading to the subject's lyrical denial of itself."

Experience itself is only communication. The writer's displacement is a relation to the reader's displacement. Therefore it seems (to me) that the criteria of experience *is* the individual's relation to it only:

> It is not any collective "death of the subject" that accounts for the subject's removal from the work. Rather, it is the very conditions of communication, without which reading or hearing cannot take place. The reader is implicated in the structure of the writer's displacement, and the effaced intentions of the work are the reader being taken into account.

Supposing relativity is existence itself, there can be no mythic order or original act. Watten's aesthetic has the rigor of Zen practice, the most radical thinking, but he interprets the criteria negatively as a value: "if 'existence' rather than any of its components is the site of a representation that can never be stated directly, 'existence' itself must be acknowledged to be on the verge of collapse."

In that case, it collapses in scrutiny.

If one is troubled by there not being an original act, and therefore no direct statement of any act, this is a form of romantic negativity?

'Believing in a concept of rigor in itself as being the basis of apprehension'—is not rigorous thinking.

Conversely: 'Holding no concept is rigor'—is a concept. We're to make existence itself collapse.

In Watten's conception the socially created 'reality' cancels itself out in negative space, which is theory of relativity. The existence of an entity is impossible.

The absent image is infinitely duplicated as a pair or ghost to the existing place.

Undoing the accepted 'reality' is continual as it is constantly being reestablished. The conservative nature of society is continually contradicted in negative space.

> Dreams are thinking: to think is
> oppression. Oppressive experience and a
> decision alternate back and forth.

Say Persephone goes down to hell. That is the 'pagan' harrowing of hell. She is allowed back to earth/the world to cause spring. The conception that it is 'not' that she is 'allowed' dismantles negative space itself.

If she does not fulfill the other side of the equation (which is that of being denied), negative black robes are blowing.

The wind is after the motorcade has gone by. The black robes fill flapping like sails.

Some of our women, prodded into cattle chutes and harnessed with black robes so that they are veiled with no eyeholes, walk behind the motorcade.

There's no consistency in imagery anywhere in it though there appears to be in 'reality.' That's one or us.

A patrician (in) seeing himself as such hangs onto a sense of self (any sense of self is falsity *per se*).

Use a logic which is dissimilar to one's context (unknown to it) to counter it, not juxtapose, and the logic not acceptable stimulates the place.

At the point at which the logic is acceptable it disappears, unknown (it is then that place). So there are two unknowns in comparison.

There isn't an interior experience as a comparison to the starving people in real time.

There's no rim or bulb of sun on it.

Events themselves destabilize in existence. There isn't a frame that ever makes or reveals them to be stable, recognizable. A view of an event itself is a separate occurrence.

Events are simply translated back into one's syntax as convention to be seen there only.

That's not contained. Here, we're to 'understand' as sentiment, as if we were the recipients naively.

Sentiment in one occurs after an event here.

We think we can extinguish images.

The hyena floating to one with the infant in its mouth is within their convention, is in itself space undoes 'reality' by not denying it, not creating a context for its formation.

Oppressive experience is not created nor is decision and are narrowed to the rim of observation. The rim itself (the premise) is eliminated.

If there is no denial, there can't be oppressive experience in spring.

It is possible for dreams or thought not to form oppressive experience. Where one does not avoid any conditions that compromise oneself (the opposite of romantic negativity) is (the notion of 'one's') existence collapsing (as one's prior sense of what experience is). So one isn't determined by nor producing one's continued conditions then. The self *is* then without being separated from social life, "this negative as a whole."

Society could be without *one's* alienation as the basis of its existence.

Complete Thought:
The Language of Postmodern Meditation

Joseph Conte

When I picked Barrett Watten's *Complete Thought* out of the bin reserved for small presses at a bookshop in Venice, California, on a stunningly bright afternoon, I was motivated by the absolute surety of its title and the soothing matte finish and woodcuts of the cover. The contrast between the sizzling flesh of the adjacent beach scene and the cool abstraction of the mind that this book promised was utterly inviting. I wasn't at all disappointed upon delving into its contents. The contemporary lyric continues to devote itself to the physical and the passionate; in its cooing, intimate voice, the lyric provokes an emotional (if not visceral) response. Watten's book is a meditation. It is cognitive rather than sensual, abstract rather than particular. It offers at least a temporary retreat from the turbulent desires of the ego. And it reminds us that Apollo once represented the pleasures of intellectual order; now he's an American Gladiator, an exemplar of the perfect physique.

The appeal of the meditative poem resides in the patience and leisure with which the mind of the poet deploys, maps, and inscribes itself. Similarly the reader is invited to participate in the cognitive event, to concentrate or daydream as the text permits. One can acquiesce to the rhythm of thought, like the angler repeatedly casting and reeling in his line. One can scroll through the whole for generalities, or annotate a particularly subtle instance. I return to the meditative poem long after the appeal of a confessional lyric has subsided. Watten's *Complete Thought* is an entirely playful and improvisatory example of the genre, without fustian questioning or brooding pursuit of the impenetrable. It is a lively exercise of the mind.

The book is comprised of four sections: "Complete Thought," "Universals," "Artifacts," and "Relays." All but the last are further divided into subsections that are identified by Roman numerals. This careful organization of the contents suggests a system of thought, perhaps one that aspires to totality or universality. But the presence of artifacts, of remnants of a decomposed or disintegrating culture suggests the impermanence of such systems of thought, the eventual crumbling of every edifice. Perhaps we are only allowed to hold the essence of an understanding—within the constantly switching network of communication —for the briefest moment. The interrelation of section titles in an otherwise discrete series of poems recalls Jack Spicer's practice in *Language*. In that volume, Spicer, the lapsed scholar of linguistics, toys with the possibilities of a systematic theory of language in sections titled "Morphemics," "Phonemics," and "Graphemics." But the system is never wholly articulated, like those hypothetical conjunctions of an Attic Greek verb that appear in no surviving text. The disjunctive quality of Spicer's serial poem demands that we intuit the existence of the missing pieces; they don't all add up. The same is true for

Watten's book, in which the coherent system of thought shines as a myth that everyone readily accepts; unfortunately, the myth is altered and corrupted with each retelling.

Watten takes as his epigraph for *Complete Thought* statements by the Russian Formalist Victor Shklovsky, "Now I will write about things and thoughts," and William Carlos Williams, "In my life the furniture eats me." The touch is whimsical, but the purpose is significant. These statements, and the book itself, argue for an objectivist parity between mind and object, thought about the thing and the thing itself. In opposition to the map of consciousness, "the act of the mind," that one finds in Stevens or Ashbery, in which the subjective cast shapes, lends order to, and at times wholly absorbs the world, the mind for Watten is in contact with the world and can be absorbed or "eaten" by it. The UPS man yells "delivery," a child on the street blubbers, the neighbors hammer wood. In this very un-Romantic sense, the models for Watten also include Williams's pragmatist treatise, *The Embodiment of Knowledge*, or George Oppen's *The Materials*.

The title poem of the book is a series in fifty numbered sections, each comprised of two rather short lines, none of which are enjambed. Each line of "Complete Thought" is a direct statement, a discrete and completed utterance:

I

The world is complete.
Books demand limits.

II

Things fall down to create drama.
The materials are proof.

III

Daylight accumulates in photos.
Bright hands substitute for sun.

IV

Crumbling supports undermine houses.
Connoisseurs locate stress.

V

Work breaks down to devices.
All features present.   (1)

Each sentence, because of the predominance of noun-verb-noun syntax, takes on an incontrovertible air. These are truisms, whether profound or other-

210

wise. The meditation occurs in the gaps between the paired lines. In "Artifacts," Watten says, "Mind wakes to fill the resonant (resident) space between sentences. 'Tricks are for kids' " (16). The response to each aphoristic statement can only be to repeat it: the world *is* complete; tricks *are* for kids. Thought resides in the disjunction between such statements. The mind does wake to the truth contained in the slogan for a breakfast cereal. The mental activity that a book demands is in fact a description of limit, since no book can subsume the whole of the world. A book, as Stevens admitted in one of his collections, expresses at best "parts of a world." In the juxtaposition of discrete statements, Watten paradoxically creates an open space for the play of the mind. He gets as far with the minimalist economy of his poetics as Ashbery does in the expansive generosity of his.

I'm fascinated by the possibility that syntax offers the cleanest graph of "the act of the mind," of the meditative process. Like a linguistic electroencephalogram (EEG), the pattern of syntax changes with the type of contemplative activity in which the poet is engaged: recursive or excursive, repetitive or compound-complex, finite-copular or incomplete-phrasal. This is a modest proposal, not meant to be taken in any clinical or diagnostic sense. In Watten's "Complete Thought," the copular verb is so common as to suggest a pattern: "Petrified trees are similar" (2), "Death is an accident" (4), "A pile driver is not a device" (4). The copular verb stresses the identity or equivalence of the subject and predicate. Among the simplest of syntactic structures, the copula implies an absolute conviction in the identity of the subject, and perhaps, in the absence of any further discussion, it suggests a certain measure of reduction. Subjects thus addressed are categorized, labeled, filed away for later use, in the manner of Aristotle's great systems of classification. This tendency is a reasonable function, a limited function, of the mind. Thus, Watten claims, "Thought is embedded" (4), can become mired in the adhesive muck of an intransient order.

In relief of this embedded condition, these copular absolutes are not meant to stand alone but are juxtaposed to or paired with other direct statements. Again in "Artifacts," Watten says, "Each sentence relates itself to others in order to reduce the probability of its being (mis-) understood" (15). The context into which any statement is placed can be explanatory or disruptive. And in fact Watten's "couplets" do more to uncouple than to bind one sentence to another: "Thought identifies missing links./Errors are in constant use" (6). Although both abstract statements imply some concern for truth value, the latter cannot be said to be the logical consequence of the former. The (missing) linkage between the two statements seriously questions their universality, disrupts their categorical imperative, and opens the meditation to a realm of indeterminacy. Into this space steps artistic form.

On this point I'd prefer to let Watten speak for himself. In his essay, "Total Syntax: The Work in the World," he distinguishes between the kind of linguistic structure I've been describing and a more expansive notion of syntax that incorporates the entire art object:

> We understand syntax as the relation of total sense to the order of
> elements in a language; that is, the way words make sense by means
> of their sequence in time.
>
> However, interpretation demands context, and a statement also
> will be built of elements of its possible contexts. Syntax has a spatial
> dimension, if space is taken in the broadest sense to be not only
> physical but cultural and linguistic.
>
> In art, one can speak of a syntax where the time element is not
> intrinsic to the work; one can speak of the syntax of sculpture. One
> can speak of the syntax of one word as a work of art or the syntax of
> a sequence of shots in a film. (*Total Syntax* 65)

Each statement in "Complete Thought" is bound by the sequence of words
on the page, but these statements don't "follow" one another except in time.
Thus the total syntax of the poem as art object in this case stands as a corrective,
an undoing of the limited copular totality or surety of the individual statement.
The linguistic syntax, the temporal and the spatial form of the poem, are
conceptually at odds. Or as Watten says in "Universals," "The air bears witness.
Splendor of syntax predicts" (11). Although the temporal syntax of Watten's
poem would appear to restrict the mind to its categorical facility, the total or
spatial syntax of his work liberates the mind in its contemplative activity.

At the risk of being overly schematic, I would argue that the second and third
sections of the book represent alternative epistemologies whose juxtaposition
is meant to be illuminating. "Universals" promises a gathering or list of statements whose truth value—beyond that of the particular assertion—is permanent.
"Artifacts" is a compendium of impermanent, evidentiary objects of a crumbling
and transient reality. The mind is like a dealer of solitaire, taking the randomly
shuffled deck of signifying cards and playing them to their appropriate suits
and numbers. We are constantly called upon to distinguish between the abstract
and the particular, the relevant and the irrelevant, the permanent and the
impermanent, the crucial piece of information and the trivial. In a substantive
way, Watten's poem enacts the sorting process of the mind that is necessary
for our sanity and our survival. We are encouraged to accept the following
statements as "universals":

> A circle memorizes the trace of a perfect thought. Logic compels
> symmetry to yield.
>
> This is not an attack.
>
> Each example emits blackness. An envelope informs the text.
>
> A shadow bends in unfair illustration. The fact is that I can do this.
>
> Sentences are of three distinct types.   (11-12)

Although we are hesitant to accept these propositions as undying truth, we are at least forced to consider them as such. We admit that they are equally as difficult to refute as to prove. Perhaps a universal theorem is impossible to prove by demonstration and must simply be accepted. The first statement especially reminds me of Ezra Pound's comment on Ford Madox Ford in Canto 82, that "Fordie/never dented an idea for a phrase's sake" (*Cantos* 539). What a virtuous society we would live in if both writers and politicians adhered to such a standard. Style would never obscure substance.

The sections of "Artifacts" are comprised of eight statements, a regularity perhaps meant to counterpoise the transience of the statements. Here is a part of section II:

> I observe the different landscapes I pass through. I notice the trees, the houses, the roadside stands.
>
> The image has been tampered with by X. Form, on the other hand, is obedient.
>
> There are no exact contraries. Chairs (particulars) correspond to the sound of running water (here no color is detached).
>
> Light of your absence fills up the page.
>
> "Mr. Wimsatt and I are not in disagreement." Try to build an empire on that!   (16)

The mind may be confounded in the search for irrevocable truth. But it may also become distracted by the flurry of particulars, the constantly changing landscape through which it passes. The screen is continuously filled with meaningless data and must be sifted for the few particles of significance. It is indeed impossible to "build an empire" out of artifacts, or the passing coalescence of opinion. In these sections Watten effectively investigates the circuitry of the mind as processor of information in its often vain attempt to distinguish between the lasting and the ephemeral.

The final section of the book, "Relays," is the most disruptive, flirting with a kind of benign absurdity that is often disparaged by "right-thinking" individuals, but which is equally—and delightfully so—an act of the mind. It is as if these lines were outtakes from a script that was never produced and from which it is impossible to reconstitute the original plot:

> A small dog appears in the text.
> I wish for something greyer. The small dog "translates" the rug.
> I'd rather listen to madness.
> In caves the animal is a principle to protect the head.
> Hats, chairs, ballooning dresses.
> Disappointments raised whose opera-glasses?

Enough has been said about the associative (comparative) process of the mind, but what of its dissociative abilities? Far from the truth-value of philosophy, these statements act to disrupt or violate the system. Training in semiotics allows us to distinguish between the actual pet, and the arbitrary signifier that is the word "dog." But the mind is frequently liable to transgress systematic distinctions and language serves as an accomplice to transgression. These are not the antic ravings of a madman but an investigation of that substantial portion of the mind's activity that lies beyond the systematic.

The meditative mode of Barrett Watten's *Complete Thought* compels our attention because it is more diversionary than it is reflective. The poem neither maunders nor bores. Uninterested in performing a retrospective analysis of its own development, the thought as it occurs in this volume enacts the immediate process and activity of the mind. Watten subscribes to the position that there can be no thought before it is expressed in language, and that the structure of thought is indistinguishable from the structure of language. The "splendor of syntax" and the "perfect thought" are not merely analogous pleasures; they are bonded together. Watten's contribution to the meditative genre is timely and intense. The recuperation of disused genres so characteristic of postmodernism finds a solid representative here. Watten's work invigorates an aspect of the poetic enterprise that has been too long neglected.

WORKS CITED

Pound, Ezra. *The Cantos.* New York: New Directions, 1986.

Stevens, Wallace. *The Collected Poems.* New York: Knopf, 1982.

Watten, Barrett. *Complete Thought.* Berkeley: Tuumba Press, 1982.

_____. *Total Syntax.* Carbondale and Edwardsville: Southern Illinois U. Press, 1984.

APPROPRIATE: WATTEN

Daniel Davidson

"As for we who 'love to be astonished'..." —Lyn Hejinian

The world
is everything that is not the case. A grammar of
related objects includes a pair of glasses,
subjectively. This story is about the fall of the
feudal cowboy empire and its effect on me.
Between self canceling and modern design.
Shapes move, elements change,
a desire to recombine perpetuates nothing.

Out of the endless listing
of addresses, he saw a human being burning
white. Later it all comes back in words. Now that
the visual function is outmoded, we are free to
live in caves. A sentence assumes more than it
admits. One word used in connection with the
wiring of houses—this. What was air before, is
air now again. As if I had said this, everyone
knew exactly what I meant.

Each revolution
rises up on all sides. Poetics: search backwards
and replace. Does this question make you feel
hostile? The one imperative is structure.
Phantoms on a road to *here*. Of local extremes
on a beach due to an interest in sin. Each in
public is many more than the one, admitting one
to be another. An exit insures an argument. The
lure of equivalents, depth.

Imagine I'm alone.
I can't find the soap in all this white noise, he
complains. Is everything all right in there? The
private world is endless, and failing in the half-
light. The threshold securely anchored. I have
words in mind, the necessary bifurcation. Burned
with attention—vague, close, mirror-like—
pushing the person away.

You understand
this perfectly, but cannot translate it into anything
else. Such anxiety is not uncommon. A paradox
is eaten by the space around it. Until language is
only relation—and we are being spoken in a
dream. When I turn away from you, two empty
chairs in the sun. Everything at once answering
back. Alternate shuttlecocks must be an *I*,
chiseling out the electric seas as far as Hull.

Language withholds
communication from those who speak it
unmaimed. In the front room a machine is
playing. A speaker could provide continuity
where vision is disturbed. For this
is impossible speech. The furniture is atomized
(vanishes, disappears) on the page. Fits of
activity take advantage of a pronoun. In the
center of the fissure are a multiplicity of links.

The manual is rewritten
one word at a time. As if the point of departure
were a key. The time it takes to get there. We
are nowise more familiar, but are older, slower
modes of thought. People disappearing into small
crypt-like depressions in the pavement as soon
as I look away. (   )

Start anywhere.
So it's not like stepping on a membrane, it's like
stepping on a density. Dear George, "Death
fractures a totality so thoroughly only the arms
are missing." Alone, things seem to be more
articulate than this blank door. The animal holds
its breath. Light rays broken by a prism, the act
of sending messages anyone can hear, an
analogy to produce consecutive fifths.

(The sky excludes landscape altogether.)
Memory clouds, I want to go back. A density I
could step through at any moment. Everything is
suspect. What we have on top of the weather is
rhetoric, steam hammer down. A calculus of
variation bends back to me. The whole man is a
concept, waking to sound. Statement
reconstructs its prior simulacrum.

This distance
between yourself and what you are intended to
see. This message is direct. In this sequence,
Jones's arrival coincides with the story's point of
view. Now call things by their names. Not
biography of the artist. A virgin hides generation
in her sheets. Every testimony
pours out all at once, in spite of appearances.

Every time "I" speaks,
millions are enslaved. Increments of . . . Imagined
light, accumulates. Plains of . . . I want to know
how it happened. The change is absolute,
streams jump their beds in a flood to reinforce a
weak echo. The entire landscape is covered with
pins stuck perpendicular to the ground. Quoting
obliterates a sentence to test syntactic rules.
Eating everything, desire begins with an
explanation.

An image of prolonged release.
To overcome inertia, words melt in furnace,
semantics that only a metaphor outlives . . . Doubt
compares with everything: in pure air the
constant ringing of a distant alarm. What is a
word? The middle voice focuses on the
(disastrous) middle distance. Time passes,
beyond our intention.

What I have always thought & said.
You and I are going in opposite directions. Not
this is not only a text, but hibernates in the world
behind a progression of limits . . . The price of
dying is charged against new brilliance of metal
fittings.

Pictures play to empty rooms.
A crowd gathers, passing the bottle around
some standing in a long curving line. Alone,
things seem to be more articulate than this blank
door. We eat the most agreeable mountain, the
words themselves.

Progress?
"You will make money as long as you surrender
to me." A mad mouse breaks through the ceiling

217

with his glass fists. At the bottom of the lake is a
small stream of black liquid. A fact is what you
can't get past. Transgression, chaotic infants
surrounded in a sea of mud. You are standing
on two lines.

[Composed from text found in *Opera-Works, Decay, Plasma/Paralleles/"X",
Complete Thought, 1—10, Progress, Conduit* and *Under Erasure.*]

INVENTED WORLD

THE CONSEQUENCES OF BARRETT WATTEN'S CONCEPTUALLY EMPHATIC TEXTS.

Allen Fisher

In affinity with so many of the Western artists who started their major work after 1968, Barrett Watten is a participant struggling in the activity of a consciousness being invented. His subject matter is noise, virtual spacetime and the sequence-field occupied as readily by Frederick Taylor as by Jackson MacLow.

The Event of consciousness perpetually produces this world; for an engaged poet now, this encounter participates in the 1980s and 1990s with too many burnt-out poetics, and a world of contemporary Western poetries as IMF commodities. For this Event to be expressed in its truth—that is, for its expression to restore consciousness of self as that of a strangeness in the world into which the participant has been cast, and at the same time as an awakening to a destructing enlightenment—this Event-activity could not but be visualized and configured in rhetorical language that was its eminently individual expression in the last Modernist productions, after 1871 in the work of Mallarmé, after 1917 in the work Shklovsky and after 1922 in the work of Breton. In America, as Americans view this, the situation appears to have been encountered more sharply. The first phase of post-modernism after 1951 (which Watten encouraged in his co-editing of *This*, begun in 1971) was feeling strained to the generation that discarded its roller skates in the 1970s (reading Clark Coolidge's *Space* as an advanced contemporary text). The Event carries social participants to the utmost limit of the world; at this limit, in Wittgenstein's terms, the cosmos yields before what cannot be spoken of. It can no longer escape being interiorized into the imagination, being integrated with it. This is the phase at which the conceptualized poetic structure performs the transmutation of the text—here that of the poetic text—into a constellation of textual potentials.

What the participants suddenly visualize are their own understandings of consciousness, that activity whose imprint it simultaneously bears within it, projects, and recognizes outside itself. Hence Barrett Watten as the reader-responder to his own production never tires of repeating that production and cannot be levelled or lifted to any equivalent to a conception of post-Benjaminian allegory (see the descriptions in *German Critique* number 22, Winter 1981). Put simply, his work (particularly those works published after *Opera-Works*, such as *Decay* in 1977 and subsequent 1980s texts such as *1-10*; *Complete Thought*; *Progress*; and *Conduit*) will not readily open to metaphorical or metonymical production.

The reader-participant is not given the option of referential exegesis and, after the first analysis of constructions and methods (having considered and then discounted the rhetorical complex of machine-made-text-made-machine), begins to get a fade out of interest in structural pattern. The text thus relies on those views of its pattern of connectedness, at least in this era of its activity, upon activities, consciousness, that carry an ambient affinity. To raise itself step by step toward the world of pure poetry, through the successive states of its subsequent becoming, the text must be enveloped in the subtle conceptual anticipation that will have been 'organized' for it by the text and the aspirations dispensed by the book-print production. The world of consciousness-passion interferes here with the world of overall text-encouraged images, as yet unde-cipherable, from memory. But for texts such as those produced by Barrett Watten, and not necessarily for other coworkers of his generation, it is the conceptual nexus which preserves the traces of all particular activities as language-thing and not the language-thing which does the preserving.

In view of all this, in spite of the obscurity-production this encourages, the Barrett Watten book-event retreats from the world, and proposes an encounter with an invention. For the book-event to be expressed in its truth—that is, for its expression to restore consiousness-Event, it becomes increasingly necessary to perform the texts by Barrett Watten, increasingly necessary to be a partici-pant in the production of their invented consciousness and world. Where such Event becomes actual the book production participates in a world it has helped to invent.

FORCE
FOR BARRETT WATTEN

George Tysh

on its own
why
exact, there
longer

the world
is
entering only
into

a response
simply in the
adjusting
taking

a missing person
spouse
for what she wants
and heavier

widely
greater
takes on
the listening ear

her territory by
selects
removing first
void

from various
as means
compelled
from site

mastery herself
to another
lighting simply

the lights
turned
it is
a crisis is
is the site

never be
itself must be
on the verge
of lack

over
which the death
effaced
denial of itself

too easily
by the day
violence
of longer work

bondage between
the initial
is now in
mutable, ready

the point at
structures
deflating
ends it

a kind of
distance
the medical
act-in-order

made instantly
no other
of her
mind

needed, alongside
social fact
is in no
mythic

an already
gross
or
collective

of the very
without
and the
effaced

the form
travels
we
meaning

through
question
is the questioning
calling

as
we
asks
us

like that
models twist
the
blanks

UNDER ERASURE...

Bruce Andrews

Under Erasure; Frame; Conduit; Progress; Complete Thought; 1–10; Plasma; Decay; Opera-Works.

ZERO DEGREE

— "the words themselves —
Research vs. Repetition.
The inconstant is gigantic — a discombobulation construed as ground.

POLITICS

Events damage the form: a chain link fence. Containment (by context)'s reminder.
To seek 'the natural' in language is sickening redundancy.
A systematizing disadvocacy. The established order needs an argument.
World claims its language & then language has a claim on *it*.
Questions cover the earth. To offstet.
A postmodern world, an articulated unnaturalness.
When can the devices pull in far off implications?
A syntax of contrariety.
Replaces outwards — . An extreme in any case. The negative implicates our grasp.
Needn't be needlessly possessive.
The gap ignites the unabandoned will in the direction of social facts, & factuality. So the critique has a way of explaining its own restlessness.

EXPLAINING

The whole is no longer surrounded by a variable.
Accumulationist focus. A static production is indemnified; no account is magnum enough.
Zeitgeist is a tunnel. No shunning cruelty.
Total in check.
Instantiate disaster — what juries our equivalence?
Does any grasp of the whole involve a smudging of the units which link together to form it? Explanation things break down to.
Context mock surround. To make sense in light of . . . , or framed against . . . .
You experience some comprehensibility.
Explain spatial dominatrix in frame of explain —
The words do not beckon for an explanatory discourse separate from themselves — hectoring, rubbernecking, bullying, mischaracterizing, intimidating, etc.
Yet that lacework of the social, of the social body, does beckon for an

explanation, does solicit one, but this time an explanatory discourse can be
embodied in the writing itself, in the words' production of meaning — in its
own lacemaking (not 'force,' momentum).
Circularly, the writing itself is 'explained' by (it lays bare its motivation in
terms of) the 'explanation' or 'account' of the social which it offers.
Method is a Program of, for, & within Practice; Method is a Paradigm of
Practice. How disfavor makes it articulate.

PRESCRIBING

Explanation by dismantling: go forward to the ground.
A real future would break up these temporary medications, many of them
exactly designed to resist or reduce such noise.
Randomness dissolves in openness at the very end. Obliterated sequel. The
whole is shook.
The poetry, always, even unwittingly, a response to available public space.
Resistance (ideally with some further state or stage as guide) would be edged
by Prescription — at a far point in some imaginable horizon. The lessons
are continual.
Staging based on context, movement score of the future.

TRANSCENDING

Wouldn't the unfathomable be a trap?
The background is blacked out. If dreams could transcend the functional.
And do utopia & a transcendent, decontextualizing & dehistoricizing practice
have to end up so frequently lumped together? No — Transcendence, shrunk
down to the manageable size of universalizing humanist clichés: rebuke it.
Authenticity might instead return to earth, to grounding in material & its
method.

REPRESENTATION

Self–conscious expansion of possibilities. Noise reduction, tracking,
no interference. Not that thoughts are good news.
A vertical recalibration — as if imposters recognize their betters. Things
proposition ideas.
Book ticks facts, point-by-point riveting. The thoughts are the things of
things.
A restoration of headlights; characterizing grew fierce.
The attitudes our words have create their own reality. It disappears certain
features of writing, puts them on the Missing list. Representation is dis-
appearance; terrorism as dematerialization. Transparency as meltdown.
The image voracious enough. Depiction devours. Light-absorbed guises.
Glarelights entitled.
Objectification fools the writing itself — but at the raw material extrac-
tion/generating stage or at the editing/overall & sequential construction
stage?
Every referent a makeshift object — obscura camera blockage — luridly

225

centrifugal.

Visual alibi, the familiar antidote of a picture on the page. Partial blindness just puts everything in italics.

Position pomps, pimps: lights — arrows jiggled off course. A tropicalizing total. Metaphor's emotional undertow.

Radio, from a single reception point — & possibly a single transmission point. Control rests in centralized hands. IT points to I. Portrait of an I. A Pyramid of centralized guilt, visually.

Representation is Speech — outlandish lightbulb.

NON–REPRESENTATION

Matter-of-factness disfigures its lineage. Nowhere is everywhere.

No figure is a lever. No hygiene of abstentionism is credible. The spent cartridge meant that the certainties of representation had been blown away. To scatterbrain visual certainty: gaze works over the false. Scopic jeopardized. Depiction's confidence stricken, dilating breakages. A prooflessness. A parodic image.

Tinge smudges. Direct as swamps to evade the devourments of reference. Indirection at its abysmal best.

Gaps flower the hole, impulse abyss, gift of gone. Nothing has its own light but no life of its own.

Apparent *hiddenness* apparently an emissary of something more basic. The vacancy specialists, the pre-frame indulgences; benefits & fears both drown in autofocus. Anything Heideggerian goes here. Romance of anonymity.

The boil left in the wake of emptiness & failure must be lanced: disappearance is anatomized, atomized. The pronoun is hustled off stage.

Default to deferred sense. A frame in a bottle.

Even the original gathering in of materials is cutting, sarcastic, parodic. Conviction is constructed. Zeroes make the moves.

PROCESS

Screen dilates, a fraction of a glare. Happenstance proportion.

The edge is thorough.

Directness could give us the mania of acceptance — but the picture world needs oxygen, props, machinery. Quick to stop at all points — whatever's at hand gets defined.

As if process meant penmanship, visuals jumpstart themselves.

Process-raised surfaces — an unforgettable, unfathomable surface. That only lack of depth is perfect.

A surface formalizing radiates from content. The manifest objects were simulated to stimulate specific weights & gravity & collapses & headlights.

A miniaturized representation — of hints, & atmo-. Accuracy of visual-verbal account now filed down to a nub, to the smallest of units. The *in between* becomes the level of closest scrutiny.

Construction compensates a ready-made. A procedural cutting across, a clarifying already in mind in words. Difficulty, as achievement.

Goal points back to person as its miniaturization. A self-erasing metonymy.
No, I'm making it up.

MEDIATION

Each page has the virus.
Fattening humans up on the surface.
How much is meaning entrepreneurial? Who can talk, as, who can *front* these assertions, & these sightings.
Pulse works at, through clarity — lexical convenings. Features of a — . . .
And gesture hypes lack of mediation.
But so much pressurizes the givens. Aggregation is a mediation. And mediation is no less substantial than outward objects literally in your hands.
Grieve for signals bound to blue-ribbon object status? Undercoding, darkened gloss. Events defined, & defended, as words.
Gesture discredits.
A falling–apart & falling open of the infinitive: to represent. Otherwise abstraction leaves instructions — to make vocabulary noise, jigsawing.
Imagery dissolves into its construction into words, but only when such a construction gets such attention. Notation stands it up straight, perpendicular to metonymy.
Muckraking grammar. Registration reaches its edge. Words comprise the plank you walk.
What's the structure of the surface, the code of the immediate, the systematic formality of the expressive? What prestructuring of possibility might turn constants into fluidities, variables & variation? What circumscribes referral?
A denaturalizing of speech — artifice. Back into circumstantial. Order makes the deviance visible.
Hints are less rhapsodized than framed. The direct derives from the indirect.
Scale gives us, or helps to set, the partiality of meaning, as an assemblage and singly: its degree of closeness, of expansive reverberation, of incorporative & implicative richness, of . . .
The image factory gave me overtime bids for frame design; the surface is a frame.
Sense — assemblage — builds from everywhere. Meaning worked on the facade.
A cohesiveness in resistance performed by its object, its systematicness.
Language over tortured shape: assurance fall down to beget anxious systems & equally anxious adaptations. Meaning turns inside out.
But the directive, the pull of potential, the charisma of the not yet, is now systemic, a differentialism. The medium inserts a grammar menu. The indirection is scaffolded by Language.
The impetus to go after a larger arrangement — Moebius medium — finally, an overallness & a bypass. First or last framing is the language itself.

SIGN

Difference is replication in reverse. With discriminations propelling us, immediacy gave way to systematicity.

Authority in signs of no authority — IDENTITY/STRUCTURE/IMPERA-
TIVE — tremor of content.

A density which is not merely ornamentally inspired with respect to givens of
grammar & syntax: trouble replaces continuity.

Can we alibi (& fake if need be) our own disappearance? A de–nomination
speech: Desire is Silence.

Let the insurrection be of unit value.

EMBODIMENT

A ghosted surface. Body identifies with meanwhile.

A floridly fluid intertextuality, free of the light bondage to an answer that
would otherwise mark out one's path. The eroticism of pulses, of fluxes &
flows. The language is apprentice to its uses.

No redone ordering will carry us far enough without the call for taking
liberties, party-time coming from the individuals who embody it — outside
inside Moebius.

Don't words need persons as vehicles of their institutionalization? Don't
let them use 'I' in your place — recipient can refuse to persist — scale
intuits our initials. Moebius personified.

Subject as detail; voltage personals. Only a subject could be a sufficiently
threatening dehierarchization.

Yet isn't doubling the primary condition; aren't speakers disrupted to start
with; did we ever leave the land of intertextuality?

What anchors fluidity is readership. Reading makes it so — or different.
'I' is the reader's — *I can't believe I wrote these things* — everybody else
left the room.

Text threatens mayhem — an adequate response to an outside-of-itself — only
as a reading. How can you not listen? Rhetoric rhymes its recipient; recipe
feeds extensions. (I can feel you reading breathlessly).

Social structure of language (surrounding it) is what gets interiorized (by
an I) — so it's a gradation address — voice, readdress, means redress. A
past surveilled through persons: you are the drum.

Self votes double, a receptive approbation. Every subjectivity carries a
rhetoric.

Leveraged subject by means of utterance constituency. The reader is the
executor of this will — rhetoric countering claustrophobia.

SUBJECT

Humanisms work off stagefronts, frontings — acknowledgeable slant,
roots, the particularized in its individual format. Negotiations handled, or
presided over by persons, subjects, readers; ordinary size speaks in italics.
Title tightens the self-likenesses.

When inconvenience, or resistance, builds the self, reaction shot's frame is
filled with semblances of whole persons, bodily enactments of a coherence.
A public is made up of persons.

Voice gives itself notice. Character structure as a giveaway.

228

Let reception be a cunning appropriation of subject position. A reply model. Underpointed, I points out — all personality position is translation. Nomination as supplement, as compensatory device — a labelling persona, self–throttling as a subjection position.

FACE READING

The mirror has foresworn mere objects; gaze is in head.
No fondness between unlesses is nurturing enough. We can gaze through a system as a dislodged piece of investment, embodiment. Face — *reading* — models perception. Access astounds.
A perfection of distance given this intensity. But the entanglement!
Shared hieroglyphics — as precondition of the reading process. Placed in the middle, contact & pressure — fond commingling, a now simultaneous felt literalness, a mutual dispossession.
Face, emblem, rhythmically acquiesced. Facework made from embarrassment, disclosive intimacy — a devicelessness.
Bodily disopacity. Face comes in print — indexically immediate erasure of epic distance. Sense is embodied, cast into the contacting & confirming themselves. The other, more relative & less of a (or your) relative. The self is the other on unemployment.
Both, [look at] Both. Other operates. Discourse meltdown. A copula with double vision. Only emblematic you.
The thrill makes words out of glue.

DISTANCE

Solicit a disregard of distances — as a spark, shock, facework. A world in constellations — of falling stars. I make myself feel left out. Theatrically at its most authoritarian would score points for absorption & separation, making them look good. [Is the separation between capitalist economic production & political authority allegorized in the absorptive tendency to create a separation between audience & artifact that needs to be protected?] Absorption is training; training absorbs. —
Only context guarantees a backing up, a backing away. What is the relation-ship of backlighting to facework . . . ? Indexicality here.
Push the extreme as sentry. Steps map status, intimacy, anonymity. Can the objectifications spur their own distancing?
Distance compels. Distance wants a brain. To some structure is tenderness addressed.

CONTEXT

Emotional hardships without subtitles, absentee faces. Face of a fact can only be of a context. How much context can it tolerate?
The surrounding given & the mechanics of givenness: relations are staged, in public — as in, in fresh air. A structure of claims, obligations, promises, facings become traditions, etc. Context in cut glass. An imprisoning facial.
Context crowds, pushy context — no landscape can hide.

Place-holdings surround you, critiqued by their interstitial duties, their inbetween-ness. The most immediate boundary is a circle — but more of a panoptical than a hermeneutical one. Command display, backdrop. Perception faces a model.

Other is Context — not this localized backdrop of melodrama. The first person pronoun takes its place in line.

Habitus, unit-valued — utilized me some experience, hon.'

A specificity of position beyond the generic — a surplus particularizing — creating the need for resyndicalizing the syntax.

You're in some 'readership' of a text & that proposes that you have come to embody or articulate a lacy weave of conventions, protocols, pre-readings, literacies; coming from outside, 'explanation' doubles the text's own *demand* for such a readership.

Rhetoric's embodiments are overmotivated. Stagecrafted face.

SUTURE

Name is content of standards. A designed (& self-designated) pertinence — (and anti-impertinence); a facial mechanism.

Blur cuts. Force to focus.

Story rubs up against you. Only illusions would be this subjected — a social condensed down to privacies.

Any privacy is machianically spooned. Expectations manufacture both the person & its present defects. Disjunction interior.

You barely acquire a self before it's colonized by fakery. The person as cut-out, pop-up, a reversion to ordered shape by a fascinated attendancy of itself.

The courthouse doors are open; self-suture efforts can take place *en plein air,* mourners at the personal solicitation, 'the treatment' desubjectifies in an disempowering way. The imaginary needs librarians.

APPARATUS

Can meaning be an apparatus? A machinery without an on-and-off button.

The social devices — the controlling mechanisms of the social body — a useness, whose positions change with meaning.

Mode utterance replicas; context's spurious noise. You are survived by totality. Concentration of power are my gemstones, compartmentalized into full existence. A breeding by machine — Island of Dr. Moreau's injections of cell structure. Code indemnified.

Frame frame frames, test devices, perpetrators ('perps'), silhouettes. It dislocates alternatives, puts off-kilter certain figures of an alternative stance. A glueing together — of non-neutral machines.

Equivalence is coercion.

Disappearances are telling — what are the limits of repressive tolerance?

The false adapts to bodies. As involuntary as any everydayness — every inequality is a breeding ground of coercion, of handy clamps for bodies threatened with harm. Quasi-legal, the compulsion is an event. Rules make the aggrieved moves.

A mechanics of sensitizing. A swiftly individualized surface. In fact an explanation generates words, guides & shapes. Engineers order up a redesigned (& facework-supportable) subjecthood.

The limits demand books of us — confessions, completions. At first, spectacular shifters lurch into song. Now we have some of the least likeliest selves & situations — but not as an imagism of the exception; instead, as the rule-governed-ness of a proliferation & flooding open. Rules offer anticipations. Standards are the content of names.

Norms are gifts that make a perimeter & that fill up the area inside of it — to assimilate governance. An integrative glue, applied publicly. A lookout without compassion. Surveillance by custom — a system in use, of claustrophobia. A terrorism of coziness.

All apparatus is public (is Public?), is the State — a statutory grid.

Culture, as organized as, virus. State secrets contained *by* the gaze — containment. The government is a libel. Context is the state secret *par excellence.*
Equality is chickenfeed. A future held hostage by serial self-preening. The points experience meltdown.

Can I start thinking of a system?

No particular structure is an imperative — & can contain conflict. There is nothing complete at all about the story or its absence. Identity issues the dance card, but doesn't fill up the list of dance-by-dance promises, commitments. Identity fails.

Maps can't explain change. Nothing is airtight. Everyday monads are mixed.
A discursive resolve, & dissolve — the fracturing of delicacy is also social. Parts warp the whole, even if infinitesimally — an eliciting of trouble by its misconstructions.

Hitch convention to disruption. Opposites subtract.

PRAXIS

Without radical praxis — [shades of *Socialisme ou Barbarisme*] bleakness, limits, conflict — pride of density fooling gaze. A grammar for a periphery.
Horizon up for grabs, its geometry overshadowing the integers, the *isolatos.*
Self-accounting desires.

Are you buying bondage? Intrusion of the counterfactual — the improper sizzles, usage counterclockwise. Honesty roasts system, itself dismantling within the dismantling.

The Staging of Context must be Faced with Distance. Notice distancing.
Globally taking down 'the spectacle,' (putting on spectacles to do it?) — disassembling its duties. Transforming suspicion into fuel, you can pitch battles against custom. Disbelief dismantles.

Shake-up can provide the occasion for an acknowledgment of bondage, a shattering of expectations of permanence, how to let go (Anyone Can Whistle).
Verbs recast, or made wider or broader in their horizontal expansiveness.
Speed demotes norm.

Gigantism of awakening, a vertigo of contacts & contracts, reframing framing.
Adequate *fit* — in its bobbings & weavings, its swerves from the straight-'n'-

231

narrow — to the surroundings, to outside conditions, is a *response* & way to (a method to) respond. Device allegorize devices.

I'm a differentialist: a more than local inversion of codes would help. The functions need to start referring back — interpellation fightback — anti-machine life, in its whole/part inversion. A re-intervalling prescription. *Bildungsroman* would now have to come after the wreckage. But no facile Terminator for the self. Hegemony implies new subject positions. To build infinity back into the private world? — any trajectory upwards Mediate by Whole Words Wheel. What is made free, ready to inform us, must be collective.

A Note on Stance in Watten

Steve Benson

Barrett Watten impresses the reader with his stance of negation, refusal, and irony—not a literary irony you can place yourself in secure relation to, so much as a disturbingly immediate real-life irony. Brusqueness, terseness, firmness, and resistance appear to frame the assertions. This may seem to push the reader away, into a distance from which to re-approach, more circumspectly and yet more self-evidently than toward another writing, unsure.

For instance: "The world is structured on its own displacement" is his first statement in *Conduit*. A disorder, a dislocation, an alienation from its own premises, is given as cornerstone of the logic and the experience of being in the world I am expected to come to terms with.

And *Progress*'s first two lines are "Relax,/stand at attention, and." The contradiction of postures and the full stop after "and" both bring the reader up short from any registration of a touchstone or tone-to-be-in-touch-with in this poem and refer you back to your own wits' readiness for assessment as to what contact should and can be here, what the 'speaker' wants from you, what conduct is. There is nowhere to hide, however. You are in the midst of it—a blinking field of negotiation.

Black and white negate each other, while registering their powerful mutual structuration. Language engages them with in-betweens. Lines and meanings are founded on unspoken, long internalized agreements (I wonder, with whom?).

And yet in this context, anyone can witness and accept the challenge of a terrible hope, willingness, and effort.

Recourses in Watten's poetry to dream, to art, to theory, and to personal associations' wry idiosyncracy—as sources and as variable frames of reference—afford access to some grounds for construction levered away from the obfuscating muck of presupposed agreement. Concise, specific references to history, popular culture, and quotidian incidents of ordinary life inform and inflect this construction as well, the chewed-up rock of the world constituting the rubble in his cement.

This is a tough sense of place to ground oneself. One rather teeters on some of the more familiar surfaces and watches one's balance shift, lurch, fall, gather, and start once again to attention.

WE COME TO BE COMFORTABLE WITH IT

Norman Fischer

An organizer's heart
Pierces some whacky displays
On the supreme content
Of gesticulation
All the world's a braying
The example of verse in the output
Of Ho Chi Minh
I quote material but not frequently
I encapsulate experience in a glance
From above in a chance encounter
With historicity
In the calmness of not knowing
Somebody on the other side
Whose eyes, endangered, slice
Appearance, never to be bought
Or sold again
I am all heart in that.

Stolen moments, memories of intellect
To think yourself completely through
And out of a problem
Is to back only further into it
But with more certainty
All the while in the hands of fate
Your sentence structure frozen
A red mouse breaks through the ceiling
With his glass fist
An episodic angular encampment
Of finches hears with accuracy
Some music of the honeyed head canals
That's what it's like
To enforce meaning on another
Who's waiting by the stage door breathless
For a corrected forged insentience
Intact at all points
But we are never unconfused actually
And what he holds will crumble
Finally, and be eaten by pigeons.

It comes around again
That modes of convenience
Bake desire—or are baked by it
Foam (any operation) incongrous (art making)
Would spread into a repetitious use
Of irregular spacing—any part
A whole, all wholes parts of something larger
World without end
Or beginning—an outrage of order
For shape without disaffection
In an emotional range unlimited
By human history (not to be confused
With insurance) or calculation
In any form
Noun phrase verb phrase noun phrase
"Acted on" as if to some purpose provided
You knew the purpose
And assented to it.

Very difficult to find proper quotation marks
To illustrate what I mean
I keep going on, blustering my dude convictions
At images that keep flustering
My hope for harmony
Wanting to make sense to someone
At the other side of the blurred sheets
That separate puddles
Into orders of discourse
Or nation states—all created eternally
By chance
Some things never change though
And there are fitful correspondences
Between recesses in the twilight of thought
And things that appear harshly contrasted
In full light
And shadow of day
When I am overcome with breath
And lose all humor
In ornithology or botany
Or even knowing the common names

I piece together someone who I seem to be
I do not imagine or fabricate
A universe in which an intellectual beauty
Rains down gently in the evenings
Because of the violence sent up constantly

On missile bomb banks
By waxy cardboard people who (I am
Thinking of a prior engagement) retreat
From tears frozen in space
This is the window—that I saw the mountain
This is the door—that I was heard
This is the grain of the wood in the floor
The green of the leaves, blue of the water
Yellow of the sun.

A person walking quickly
Through several generations
Would probably not notice
Shears in the faces of those
Passing on without awakening
Proper tickets
It is enough to color
What you have got
For a moment
That is passed down
Along the trail provided you
Cancel out the traces
So that someone else
Faces something fresh
In that time.

Gear improvements generate
Questions that lead to disaster
A person is set in motion by a group of words
You could see in their eyes
How their hands hung definite at their sides
And they moved with a deliberate quiet
Impossible to imitate
For very long
Because they were not in control
And did not try to be
A person is a member of a family
Like a finger is no more beautiful than
And is as useful as
A solitary person howling at a tree
In a language no one understands
They did not cut down the flower nor stack
Much wheat on top of itself
Do not point a finger
A child in the act of play
Though there is nothing that needs doing

Our work is never done
Our speech a multi-part song
Without whose notes
The sun—that sets in all weathers—
Won't come up again
For them tomorrow
I a collective voice
Sighing in the narrowness
Of reflected thought on the lake
Running water reflects nothing.

Discouraging dilemma after all is said and done
To bear fruit on packed soil
First metaphors
Need plowing (racks of clothes to be reviewed)
In comprehensive wealth scattered like larvae
On the shores
Hear me now in the cataract
Of fire in the stormy slumber
Of corrupted meanings in the
Festered marketplace teeming
With broken individuals
Harping on their necessities on their fears
That come from word ropes
Hopelessly tangled in body blocks
I own heat if I harness flowing
Or specification not to lean on it
But to let it go by unalloyed
And honest (on sale for a limited time)
Neither denying nor beating
Something over the head with it
And in this way getting further
Than white thought
That's the edge of white
In a white world sinking
Steadily into its own heels
Through the blasted fates
Of earthly tunnels
Telling stories to no one.

That was a world
From our sponsors, someone
That can be explained but never
Devoted to only hanging
In the breeze of that just to state it
Means to organize it somewhat for later

237

Poets have something wrong with their eyes
That is why they scream foolishly
And forget to celebrate holidays
Like they're supposed to
If you want to say yes, say yes.

for Barrett Watten's poetry

section five.

"Skewed by design…"

"Skewed by Design":
From Act to Speech Act in Language-Writing

Michael Davidson

The gestural potential of language occupies a privileged position in modern poetry, but since World War II it has witnessed two distinct treatments. The first stems from expressivist aesthetics derived from Romanticism and the second from a range of linguistic theories that would include Russian Formalism, Speech Act theory and Structuralism. Although both share a common concern for the materiality of language—its physical presence on the page or in the voice—they differ widely on the ends that this materiality must serve. I would like to explore that difference, using "gesture" as an operative term.

In the painterly aesthetics of the late 1940's and early 1950's, the term "gesture" had a rich and varied application. At one level it referred to the painter's physical stroke on the canvas—the record of specific physical actions on a flat, two dimensional surface. At another level, the uniqueness of that stroke embodied the painter's individual signature, the stylistic mark by which originality and authenticity could be measured. Harold Rosenberg's use of the term "action painting," his description of the canvas as an "arena in which to act," provided some of the major critical terms for abstract painting during this period. To some extent, these terms gained a further philosophical valence through their implied reference to Existentialist ideals of engagement and commitment. By treating the canvas as an event within the world rather than a representation *of* it the painter signaled his/her own personal freedom in a world of increasingly alienating social institutions.

Poets of this generation appropriated many of these same physical metaphors (energy, action, gesture) in their quest for a poetics of unmediated statement. Charles Olson's emphasis on "breath," Robert Duncan's physiological and biological poetics, Robert Creeley's stress on a poetry of intensities, Michael McClure's "beast" language and Beat "bop" prosody are only some examples of a poetics for which muscular and physical response is valued over reflective or discursive moments. The most direct statement of this position is Olson's "Human Universe" which argues that "habits of thought are the habits of action" and that art "does not seek to describe but to enact."[1] For Olson, Western thought has been dominated by a reflective metaphysics in which language becomes "the act of thought about the instant" rather than "the act of the instant." Olson and other poets of his generation hoped to defeat cartesianism by restoring the physiology of the poet's breath, musculature, movement—in the composition process.

If one wanted to discover a change between the "new American poetry" of the 1950's and 1960's and that which it spawned in the 1970's and 1980's, one could usefully speak of the latter's revision of the term "gesture," now used to describe the speech act rather than the act of speech. Whereas gesture for the

241

generation of Olson and Ginsberg implied single expressive moments, recorded spontaneously on the page and realized in the oral performance, for writers of a more recent generation gesture refers to the interactive, social web in which language exists. This has been particularly the case with language-writing which offers the most thorough critique of expressivism in postwar writing, even while building upon the earlier generation's accomplishments.

Without rehearsing well known features of speech act theory, let me at least emphasize several aspects that pertain to our topic. Speech acts (or what Wittgenstein called language games) define utterances in terms of their pragmatics, the relationships established between addressor and addressee. These relationships are rule-governed, bound by laws of appropriateness and acceptability. The ability of any recipient to respond to an utterance depends on the fulfillment of what Searle calls "appropriateness" and Austin calls "felicity" criteria.[2] The effectiveness of a command depends on there being someone to carry it out; a question assumes a respondant capable of answering. These positional relations in discourse situate individuals not only in relation to each other but to the ideological formations that every utterance serves, whether those of gender, class, sexual orientation or race. Speech act theory, with few exceptions, has been silent on the ideological basis of speech pragmatics, but the poets with whom we are concerned have made this issue central to their poetics.[3]

By saying that recent writers foreground the pragmatics of speech acts, I do not mean that they invent *new* ones (one cannot single-handedly "invent" unique speech acts any more than one can invent a new language) or that they necessarily deform those that have already been defined by Searle, Grice, Austin, and others. Rather, language-writing seizes upon the framing-operations that situate utterances within a larger ideological matrix. When Lyn Hejinian repeats a series of quaint adages about women ("pretty is as pretty does") within her long prose work, *My Life*, she underscores both the sexist implications of such remarks as well as the role that such truisms play in the production of a female Subject. The same could be said for Bob Perelman's *Face Value* which employs the rhetoric of enumeration and description to embody the ways that consumer society transforms individuals into products: "There is a store, it is an individual, /like you, me, a body, corporate . . . ." Or consider the following passage from Ron Silliman's *Sunset Debris*, a thirty-page poem made entirely out of questions.

> Do you feel compelled to defend the position? Do you eat meat? Were those pelicans? Does it embarrass you? Will these clothes ever be the same again? Does the flow of traffic deceive you, taking on the texture of natural process? Is it straight yet? . . . Are you listening? Is everybody happy? How can you keep your stories straight? What are the limits of large? Who do you trust?[4]

By eliminating the anticipated response, Silliman also eliminates the dialogical aspect of interrogatives, injecting them with a level of sexual threat and violence. In such work, foregrounding the linguistic medium coincides with a speculation about the social relations that this medium upholds. When questions have no function other than to interrogate, they begin to act *on* rather than *between* the individuals who use them.

The speech act that most dramatically exemplifies language's ability to act on others is the performative.[5] Such utterances (promises, oaths, declarations, bets) are characterized by their ability to put into motion what they announce. When a judge declares a couple husband and wife or when a ship captain christens a ship, the utterance actually *performs* the declarative or contractual function. The appropriateness criteria for a performative pertains to legal sanction as much as to the fulfillment of a verbal contract: the person making the contract of marriage must be legally empowered to do so; the recipients of the performative must be in a position to receive it (eg. they must not be already married). When Charles Olson, in *The Maximus Poems* asserts, "I compell/ backwards I compell Gloucester/to yield, to/change," he attempts to give performative status to what is otherwise a simple assertion: "I compell." It is an expressive moment of great power, but unlike a performative, its authority is vested in the speaker's will and not in any official sanction. In fact, one could say that Olson attempts to demolish a *polis* based on such sanction by one created out of individual utterances. *Polis*, as he says elsewhere, is "eyes."[6]

When Barrett Watten employs a performative gesture in his poem, *Progress*, the effect of assertion is quite different:

> *I* hereby christen
> This destroyer the *Rosebud*
> As the ape shows its teeth,
> Alternately smacking her lips . . . .
>
> In expression of the abstract,
>   Sound.
>   A reading must be
>   Above ground in the light
> Of heartbeats in the dark . . . .
>
> As parked cars turn on engines
>   Simultaneously.
>   McNamara,
> Johnson, Westmoreland, Rusk.
> The names are no pun intended . . . .
>
> A present dispersing its edges,
>   But I call them Bald Eagles
>   For lust,
>   lusty and silly
> Happy and holy men and girls . . . .[7]

Here, the performative is bracketed as an official act, linked to other forms of power. The ceremonial act of christening a ship is performed not so much by a person as by an institution whose darker purpose is deflected through patriotic rituals of naming. Watten italicizes the "I" who performs the act in order to emphasize its arbitrary status as Subject-position—very different from Olson's ontologically grounded speaker. In Watten's example, the pronoun stands for the appropriate official (or, more likely, official's wife), but the "true" antecedent is a litany of Vietnam era leaders ("McNamara,/Johnson, Westmoreland, Rusk") who are ultimately the actors behind each national speech act. Their names cannot be confused ("no pun intended") but stand as the final, real condition of the present historical epoch.

Watten has done more than imply a connection between pronoun and antecedent; he has linked them structurally by creating lines that, however discontinuous semantically, are nonetheless linked syntactically. Each line modifies the next so that one may read the entire passage as a long, highly subordinated, period. Watten's point seems to be that "progress," both poem and social ideal, is not based on purposive, sequential evolution but upon discrete acts, held together by a common infrastructure. When "progress" becomes synonymous for a war economy—the production of new destroyers as an index of national strength—it loses all associations with growth and becomes a metaphor for routinized production. The poem attempts to circumvent this form of production by creating an alternative, one that links logically disconnected elements (Apes and destroyers, parked cars and Vietnam) by discovering structural homologies. The fact that the ship's name, Rosebud, is also that of Citizen Kane's sled adds an additional irony. Given William Randolph Hearst's (Kane's) famous remark about the relationship between war and news ('I'll supply the war; you supply the copy'), perhaps the ship has been more appropriately named than we know.[8]

This brief example suggests a challenge and a crisis for any materialist poetics. Unlike most political poetry of the last twenty years, language-writing bases its analysis of authority not on the author's particular politics but in the verbal means by which any statement claims its status as truth. Moreover, by foregrounding the abstract features of the speech act rather than the authenticity of its expressive moment, the poet acknowledges the contingency of utterances in social interchange. The incompletion of each element in the verbal sequence demands a reading that is not recuperative but critical.

There is some question, however, whether this critical function can be adequately performed by any reader. For the critique of expression in language-writing depends on its own felicity condition: that there be some interplay between poem and reception, that the expressive conduit between addressor and addressee be broken in order for the reader to be reinvented as active agent in meaning-production. If the terms for reading are already anticipated in the formal design of the poem, there is little room for the reader to interact with the actual pragmatics of literary discourse. Instead of being revealed as agents of ideological interests, speech acts become thematized as types of dramatic moments, no one of which has any more claim on our attention than another. The reader becomes a voyeur upon an artful attempt to seduce him or her into playing by the rules. Hence the felicity criterion upon which the poetic speech act is based is more of a horizon than a fact.

These qualifications aside, I feel that language-writing thinks through such questions, often incorporating them into the work itself. When Ron Silliman introduces his anthology of language-writing, *In The American Tree*, by using Bob Grenier's phrase, "I Hate Speech," he articulates the distance that he and others in that volume feel from the speech-based poetics of projectivism. At the same time, the violence of the phrase overdetermines its subject, pointing away from the direct object, "speech," back at the discursive act itself. Far from being merely an attack on speech in favor of some indeterminate "écriture," "I hate speech" embodies its own problematic of presence by shouting louder than it needs.[9] The phrase refers "to" at the same time as it refers "by means of." Silliman has been aided, in this respect, by an earlier generation of poets who treated the poem as shout—as an act addressed by the poet to an audience that has forgotten how to hear; it has been for Silliman's own generation to explore the relationship between the two parties.

NOTES

1. Charles Olson, "Human Universe" in *Selected Writings*, ed. by Robert Creeley, New York: New Directions, 1966, pp. 54, 61.
2. John Searle, *Speech Acts: An Essay in the Philosophy of Language*, Cambridge: Cambridge University Press, 1969. J. L. Austin, *How To Do Things With Words*, Cambridge, MA: Harvard University Press, 1977, pp. 14-15. See also Mary Louise Pratt, *Toward a Speech Act Theory of Literary Discourse*, Bloomington, IN: Indiana University Press, 1977, pp. 79-99.
3. The exception to this rule is the work of Mary Louise Pratt (see note 2) which offers an important critique not only of speech act theory but of Jacobson's theories of "literariness" as a discrete area of verbal experience.
4. Ron Silliman, "Sunset Debris," in *The Age of Huts*, New York: Roof Books, 1986, p. 14. Other works referred to in this paragraph include the following: Lyn Hejinian, *My Life*, Los Angeles: CA: Sun and Moon, 1987; Bob Perelman, *Face Value*, New York: Roof Books, 1988.
5. J. L. Austin, *How To Do Things With Words*, Cambridge, MA: Harvard University Press, 1975.
6. Charles Olson, "Maximus to Gloucester, Letter 27 [withheld]," in *The Maximus Poems*, Berkeley, CA: University of California Press, 1983, p. 185.
7. Barrett Watten, *Progress*, New York: Segue, 1985, pp. 111-112.
8. Watten has commented extensively on this passage in an interview in *Ottotole* 2 (Winter, 1986-1987) in which he describes actual sources for several of the lines including a private association for "Rosebud" which links to the name of an ape at the Oakland Zoo. In private conversation, the author informed me that "Bald Eagles," in addition to their obvious reference to the American military, was a phrase used for child prostitutes

in Saigon during the Vietnam era. I have chosen not to use Watten's commentary in forming my own reading in order to test what I take to be his larger pedagogical purpose: namely to provoke the reader into working with the materials of his poem towards new and perhaps alternative interpretations. Unlike critics who might find in this decontextualizing strategy an argument for the liberation of neutral, free-floating signifiers, I would say that Watten has carefully delimited the ideological horizon of his lines.

9. Ron Silliman, "Language, Realism, Poetry," in *In The American Tree*, Orono, Maine: National Poetry Foundation, Inc., 1986, xv.

Jackson Mac Low

Progress 1

Purple Replication Only Given Replication Empty Situation
                                              [Situation

Purple Unlike Replication Purple Lights Empty
Replication Empty Purple Lights Into Cargo A Trees Into
                                        [Only Neutrality
Only Neutrality Lights Yellow
Given Into Visions Empty Neutrality
Replication Empty Purple Lights Into Cargo A Trees Into
                                        [Only Neutrality
Empty Money Purple Trees Yellow
Situation Into Trees Unlike A Trees Into Only Neutrality
Situation Into Trees Unlike A Trees Into Only Neutrality

Predictable Room Of Grab Room Eye Sunflower Sunflower

Predictable Room Eye Degree It Cycle Time And Banks Level
                                                    [Eye
Room Of Of Meeting
Of Felt
Grab Room And Banks
Room Of Of Meeting
Eye You Eye
Sunflower Undelimit Not Felt Level Of Word Eye Room
Sunflower Undelimit Not Felt Level Of Word Eye Room

Plowed Regardless Operates Ground Regardless Equivalents
                                        [Scatter Scatter

Plowed Line Operates Walls Equivalents Days
Regardless Equivalents Ground Accident Regardless Days
                         [Line Equivalents Scatter Scatter
Operates Plowed Equivalents Regardless Accident To
                               [Equivalents Scatter
Ground Regardless Operates Up Normative Days
Regardless Equivalents Ground Accident Regardless Days
                         [Line Equivalents Scatter Scatter
Equivalents Quiet Up In Voice Accident Line Equivalents

247

```
                                          [Normative Time Scatter
Scatter Carries Accident Time Time Equivalents Regardless
Scatter Carries Accident Time Time Equivalents Regardless


Pointing Roosevelt Over Glass Roosevelt Eight Self Self


Pointing Over I Newsprint This I Newsprint Glass
Roosevelt Over Over Self Eight Vocabulary Eight Larger
                                                      [This
Over Vocabulary Eight Roosevelt
Glass Larger At Self Self
Roosevelt Over Over Self Eight Vocabulary Eight Larger
                                                      [This
Eight I Glass Hatred This
Self Eight Larger Face
Self Eight Larger Face
```

from and for Barrett Watten   *31 January and 1 February 1986*
                                                              New York

Progress 2


```
Plasma pRime prOduce belGian poweR greatEr madhouSes
                                                [contentS


Plasma aLingual chAnged cloSets steaM wreckAge
PRime pRess brIdges warM wintEr
PrOduce gReen poOl griD recrUit surfaCe enhancEd
BelGian pErception foLlowed oxyGen permIt carloAds
                                                [basemeNt
PoweR pOints toWard bluE theiR
GreatEr oRder whEre expAnd builT polysEmy staggeR
MadhouSes bAck boDy's autHor prolOnged absolUte settleS
                                                [pickaxeS
ContentS fOr caN thaT bracEd machiNes thoughT weekendS


Precepts oRange frOm heiGhtens reveRse overhEad
                                        [responSible pronounS


Precepts aRound knEes traCks spacE multiPlication
                                        [opposiTe necktieS
ORange cRitical awAke staNds desiGn problEm
FrOm pRoduction flOrida swiM
HeiGhtens lEft thIngs craGs whicH invecTive disappEar
```

                                         [combiniNg equationS
ReveRse rEflects leVel undEr otheRs scrapS whitenEss
OverhEad eVeryone thE intRuders humpHrey complEx
                              [reappeAring confuseD
ResponSible dEadly deStroyed insPection ribbOn permaNent
[impedeS managerIal disassemBling industriaL ineffectivE
PronounS wRite whOle dowN histOry discoUrse movemeNt
                                         [presentS

Picture bReathing loOse surGe antaRctica circlEs
                              [percusSion defenseS

Picture lImits acCess wanT obscUre fasteR messagE
BReathing eRase goEs retAliates solsTice metapHor
                              [receptIon irratioNal somethinG
LoOse bOx knOw preSence dronE
SurGe aUdience xeRox honGkong addrEss
AntaRctica uNstressed meTeors squAre coveR morocCo
        [obsoleTe distortIon contradiCtory representAtion
CirclEs mInes fuRnace briCk moduLar outagE personS
PercusSion sEe baRoque proCess chorUs succeSsion figureS
                              [signifyIng automatiOn intelligeNce
DefenseS bErlin reFlected modErn liviNg angleS composEr
                                         [predictS

Province bReaks thOugh lanGuage geneRalities dividEd
                              [becomeS discourSe

Province tRigger enOugh surVive implIcit origiNal
                              [displaCement universE
BReaks bRoken evErywhere metAllurgy alasKa intenSive
ThOugh tHreat wrOng accUmulations backGround breatHe
LanGuage hAd miNd imaGination disrUpted holidAy meaninG
                                         [solitudE
GeneRalities dEsert siNgle linE entiRe manufActures
              [variabLe statistIcs interrupTion multiplicIty
                              [acknowledE simultaneouS
DividEd dIsplay haVe chrIsten sounD enginEs severeD
BecomeS rElation inCulcate remOrse claiMs forehEad
                                         [impresSion
DiscourSe bIlls reSults conCert dispOsition cumulUs
                              [pleasuRe soldierS memorablE

from and for Barrett Watten   *1–3 February 1986*
                                                 New York

                              249

CODE OF COMMUNICATION: CONDUIT OR CRYPT?

Peter Baker

Barrett Watten's work, as with much of the work of the "language" writers with whom he is associated, bears a somewhat conflicted relationship with past models of poetic production, going beyond the normal influence business. Many of his theoretical statements, viewed as rhetoric, have as a stated aim to clear the ground, or even establish a ground, that would outline a linguistic practice different from poets of the past, not just the poets of Modernism, but also the more recent work of Olson, O'Hara, Ginsberg and others. This attempt to create a new space for the poetic project or language of poetry is certainly ambitious and—I think—admirable, but it does seem to require of Watten that he set forth some of these differences in rather programmatic fashion. My investigation into Watten's poetry and his statements on poetics thus attempts both to situate his work with respect to those aspects of modernism from which it strongly derives—not necessarily the same ones that he identifies—and also to suggest a possible alternative, relying principally on some Derridean strains, to his own well-formed and powerful interpretive discourse.

Watten's relationship to the prior traditions of poetry draws particular attention to issues surrounding the function of poetry as wisdom utterance, which in turn can be related to what Pound termed the *logo* in the triad of *logo-*, *phano-*, and *melo-poiea*, roughly, "word," "image," and "music" (for poetry as "wisdom utterance" I am relying in part on the thinking of Albert Cook in *Canons and Wisdoms*, among other works). Watten adheres rather strictly to a model—one that I would call Althusserian—in which everyday language (now, here, for us) is viewed negatively as a force for interpellation of the individual subject by the forces of capitalism. His challenge then is to maintain the ethical drive associated with wisdom utterance while fronting the assumptions of communicative language in the form itself of his works. This might be related to Williams' famous statement of the poetics of the everyday and its crucial importance, both for poetry and for the social reality:

> It is difficult
> to get the news from poems
>   yet men die miserably every day
>   for lack
> of what is found there.
>   (*CP* 2: 318)

No one would read Barrett Watten's poetry to get the news, and yet his own ethical drive causes him to attempt to account for the social history of his time, both history writ large and the smaller details of everyday life that, as Williams implies, all too often get lost, with devastating effects. In reading these perhaps overly familiar lines, I think we ought not overlook the aspect of mortality that grounds Williams' view of the social. Reading Watten's poetry back against his theoretical stances, I mean to attend to some of the hidden or abyssal structures, related in their way to death and mortality, that get glossed over in his own accounts of just what it is he is doing in his poetry. This, for me, means looking at what Derrida has identified as *crypt*, the lack or nothingness "inside" or "beneath" the socially formed egoic structures (but also the space of *cinders*, as in Derrida's text of that title) that serve to ground the subject overtly in the socially oriented "conduit of communication."

In "Conduit" (*Conduit* 13-32), for example, Watten maintains the form of the declarative statement that recalls while it problematizes the wisdom utterance. In this text, generated by various formal operations on linguistic materials from journals kept while he was in England, as he has said, his intent was to draw attention to communication (or lack thereof) by a process of decontextualization of individual utterances ("Conduit of Communication"). Watten expresses this through inversion, and a nice sense of humor, as: "If this 'England' were a utopia, it is not one where anyone could live." The question remains how the ethical or socio-political force which is claimed for the poem operates despite the negativizing inversion of the wisdom utterance form. Staying heuristically with the Poundian *logo/phano/melo* triad, this means examining the status of lines such as:

> Working men's voices above water-driven
> looms in Wales
> 　　　　(*Conduit*, 27)

The displacement of the mode of overt communication would perhaps have the reader view this as a false romanticization of labor (and who knows, it might be a cited fragment of Romantic poetic discourse), but I would say that the *phano* or image-element brings Watten's concern with modes of production into the warp here. And, further, this procedure is generalizable as a way of describing Watten's strategy throughout this work, and others. The ironization of the mode of "direct address" that seemingly places the wisdom aspect of poetry, or *logopoiea*, in radical question is recuperated, or counter-balanced, by a reliance on image, and in rarer instances song, to bring in content-oriented or ideological materials that continue or maintain the ethical stance of the writing.

Here is one of the ways that Watten describes his endeavor: "Such a risk—that 'language' is both objective and a form of avoidance—also seems, in this account to embody frustrating complications, the only excuse for which must be their persistent recurrence as an ethical dilemma. In my view, a poetics of 'language' is an attempt to find a workable ground for modernism that leads to real solutions for the dilemmas it proposes" (Brito, "Interview"). The first part of this statement is a concise version of the problematic I have been discussing so far; what's needed is to look at the second part of this statement in order to find out what is at stake in the poetics thus introduced. I find it interesting, and admirable, as I've said, that Watten still seeks a "ground" for the practice he is engaged in, and I want to investigate how he negotiates that ground in his practice. This requires an examination of the communication model discussed extensively in "Conduit of Communication." Here again it is a matter of establishing a counter-position to well-known models of information theory and linguistic theory. Basing his discussion on the Jakobsonian paradigm of poetry as a message-centered utterance in the sender/receiver/message/code/context model, Watten wants to urge a different view than the one that concentrating on the message introduces a meta-level that in turn frees up the writer's and thus the reader's response. Watten states: "A much better way to proceed would be to think about communication in terms of the structures the receiver inculcates in the sender before the message is sent. These structures would be built through the processes of recurrence, feedback, and metaphor that are to be found also in everyday life" (*Conduit of Communication*). The processes adduced here are expansions or extensions of the ideas already discussed. What interests me in this statement is the verb "inculcates" and just what this might mean.

Clearly, we are operating in the realm of social analysis here, following a model in which subjects are interpellated by discourses as a part of any possible identity formation. Meaning is thus always social and in some sense always pre-exists the individual in such a way as to call into question the very existence of the subject. This way of viewing the social construction of the subject is what Kristeva draws attention to while presenting her critique in the formulation of the "subject-in-process" in *The Revolution in Poetic Language*. Kristeva's critique is aimed particularly at Althusser's notion of "history as a process without a subject" (cf. Hill, 143). One could say that Watten wants to locate his theory somewhere between these two views, maintaining both the social construction of reality and a subject with real, if already partially pre-determined, agency. In the interview with Brito, he says the same thing more succinctly: "Even so, the ratio here between private expression and public scale is significant—both for what it is as expression and for what it recursively inculcates in the subject." To understand what the verb "inculcates" is saying requires an examination of some specific instances in the poetry, along with some statements of intent.

Fortunately, Watten has provided an extensive commentary on much of his own work, as he has for these opening lines of the book-length *Progress*:

> Relax,
>   stand at attention, and.
>   Purple snake stands out on
>   Porcelain tiles. The idea
> *Is* the thing. Skewed by design . . . .

And here is some commentary by the poet on the central image in these opening lines:

> Let us take that purple snake as one moment in which thematic
> identification is achieved. It so happened that this snake was a graffiti

252

in a very inhospitable pedestrian underpass leading from Lakeshore Drive to Lake Merritt in Oakland. One's being in that passageway is generally accompanied by some kind of apprehension or fear; I bolt for the light at the end of the tunnel right away. The white porcelain as background connotes a kind of hygiene that is anything but the case; the purple spray paint is not genteel. (Brito, "Interview")

The commentary on this image and its context in these lines continues over several pages, all of which apt and useful, but I jump to the poet's characterization of its function. Watten states: "Its position as one of the opening moments of *Progress* is to identify social violence as one of the limiting themes of the poem, as one result of instrumental language." Now, one question is this: Do the lines quoted, and discussed at length, bear the meaning which the poet attributes to them, and, if so, how? This question parallels my brief discussion of Hart Crane's images, "elevated blue plateaus" and "corymbulous formations of mechanics," as well as his discussion of what they mean in his essay, "General Aims and Theories" (*Obdurate Brilliance*, 47-48). The example of Crane indicates that Watten, and the "language" writers generally, are not the first to explore, and to transgress, the limits of representative or expressive language, as well as to theorize what they are doing in the process.

From what space of meaning is the reader expected to pull up the theme of "social violence" in relation to the image of the purple snake? On one level, what is happening here could be similar to that process of draining meaning from the *logo* and recuperating it through the *phano* that I pointed to in "Conduit" and claimed as a generalizable process in Watten's work. On another level, perhaps the poet is bringing in a fuller context of meaning and experience than any reader could be expected to have access to. Watten has addressed this possibility with respect to an extended discussion of *Progress* in an interview with Michael Amnasan. Reacting to one passage that Watten explicates, Amnasan says, "But a reader isn't likely to, at least I wouldn't, associate that at all," to which Watten responds:

> Well, that's OK. I'm the person writing this; I'm developing an argument in this way. What you're saying is that speech still stands alone; you don't recognize the context at that level. Fine, there's no feedback at a mutual level; this is a private reference. (32)

Are these the only possibilities which Watten is willing to admit into the communicative "conduit"? Either the reader gets the context Watten had in mind (how would one verify this?) or else not, and then the reference is merely "private"? I think there has to be another alternative, and Watten's discussion of the communicative model, with his use of the verb "inculcates," points one direction for following this out.

Staying with the image of the snake, Watten says further on, "The teenagers who painted this design are probably very uneasy about seeing themselves as purple snakes." This moment of analysis I find more than a little odd. While he is himself in the process of theorizing an extremely complex model for artistic production (his own, let's remember), the model for production of the snake (by the "teenagers") has the ring of a certain naive psychologism, even empiricism. I'm left wondering if it is in any sense *true* that the street artist(s) who produced the snake has to identify necessarily with the snake image—I can think of several other models. Isn't it somewhat more likely that a displacement of Watten's own fears, very vividly expressed in the passage quoted above, is operative here, associating the danger to himself with an image of the snake? And since he's told us that at one end of the tunnel is a building in which Huey Newton is rumored to have lived, I think it's pretty clear that color is partly at issue, purple into black, black into purple, the darkness of the tunnel connecting with fear of the dark, night, and of dark-skinned people. This, by the way, is no criticism of Watten; Toni Morrison's recent critical work shows this association of race and darkness as the deep and perdurable underside of the American literary imagination. The tunnel itself, which Watten describes extensively, is nowhere present in the words of the poem. And it is the tunnel, not the snake, which is but an associative link to the fear-inducing social violence, that sets the poet running when he enters.

This underground, enclosed space, in which meaning is secreted and yet denied, bears all the features of the *crypt* which Derrida has discussed in his essay "Fors" and elsewhere. The crypt would be that which is unrepresentable at the core of the subject's unreachable desire, and which can only be expressed through a series of displacements. As Derrida says in his essay "Moi—la psychoanalyse," "It's going to be, will have had to have been necessary to translate the unpresentable into the discourse of presence, the unsignifiable into the order of signification" (*Psyché*, 154; my translation). Bearing a strong relationship to the Freudian psychic functions of identification and introjection, the crypt represents the process of incorporation, the taking in of the loved or hated object, in such a way that the object is preserved whole, yet denied. Thus "social violence," which Watten identifies as a limiting theme of the work, and particularly at work in these opening lines from the poem, would not be from this perspective the social world which he theorizes at the level of the totalizing system, but rather the social of which he is personally a part, in ways which his theorizing can only serve to blind him to, to deny, and yet, obliquely, to express.

In the interview with Amnasan, Watten describes how he *felt* after he had written the opening lines of *Progress*:

> After finishing that day's work I had a feeling of having walked into a large, dark room and giving a short speech, and feeling that there was a kind of echo. The echo gave a sense of how big the space I was in was. Now this notion of space is a way to try to describe the feeling I had after having written the first few pages of the poem. (29)

What resonates for me in this passage is how much the textual space, or dream space, or space of making the poem (Lacan would call it the space of the Imaginary, the tunnel in turn representing the fantasm from which the

254

images of the poems are suspended), resembles the space of the tunnel, that is nowhere present in the words of the poem. Except as in a few remainders, purple snake, porcelain tiles . . . . Watten's poetry sets loose all sorts of productive forces, which as readers we are not limited either to experiencing in exactly the way he once experienced them or attributing to a "private" form of expression. And this is, despite his claims to originality, social engagement, and so forth, what poetry of any interest and complexity has always done, back to when poetry and cryptic philosophical utterance were indistinguishable in the fragments of the pre-Socratics.

The danger with my analysis so far is that it risks hypostasizing the element of crypt by providing what seems a highly analogous physical location, the tunnel. If we examine some other passages from *Progress* that Watten discusses with Amnasan, the same kinds of non-present organizing links can be shown to order the presentation of image sequences. In a stretch of the interview (41-43), Watten runs through the organizing links from "the destroyer *Rosebud*," which he associates with non-genuine emotion in *Citizen Kane*, as well as the fairly easy irony of the destroyer, to a "private" association with an ape of the same name: "Well, Rosebud was an ape in my experience, the kind with the gigantic asshole . . . " (42). Eventually this leads to what Watten claims as a representation of the Vietnam War in the poem. (A question that would provide material for a whole different essay is whether the socio-political forces that clearly provide much of the motivation for Watten's poetic project are, or even can be, effectively represented in the ways he claims to represent them. I have my doubts.) The sequence is: "McNamara,/Johnson, Westmoreland/Rusk./ The names are no pun intended . . . " (*Progress*, 111), of which he says, "And I think at this point I'm striking a negative that is no longer ironic, no longer merely Orson Welles or Citizen Kane or the ape; you know it strikes me that these names from the Vietnam War are no pun intended. They really are assholes" (Amnasan, "Interview," 42-43). Yet, of course, as with the organizing conceptual and depth-psychoanalytical image of the tunnel, the poem is discreet about mentioning any asshole. Whether these non-present organizing links always work well to structure image and logos-thinking is open to question. This particular passage is one which Amnasan questions insistently in the interview, and I think with good reason, about those missing connectives and whether the reader can make any kind of sense out of the poetic logic.

In the interview with Brito, Watten explains some of the personal detail that contributes to one particular passage:

> Which I perceive as an Egg
> In a pool of reflected light . . . .
>
> On roof of pool one floor above
>   Parking lot,
>   modern living
>   Smashing parked car windows
> To make a sound out of brick . . . .   (*Progress* 75-76)

The images in this passage stem, as Watten recounts, from a youthful experience with "a gang of tough boys" who went out on a vandalism spree. Watten nicely captures his own limited role in this escapade: "I didn't and in fact lingered behind at the bottom of the creek beside it, " and his feelings about being even this involved: "I was equally innocent and guilty, split down the middle by remorse either way." This, to me, is a key moment in the poem, another deeply invested personal memory that has been burnt to ash, leaving behind only the most cryptic remainder. This is what the crypt is and the signifying function it fulfills is the inexpressible weighing on what is said: remembered guilt over being bad, hanging with the bad boys, the ape's asshole, a porcelain-tiled tunnel in a dangerous neighborhood, a purple snake.

Watten's forcefully delineated interpretive framework and the one I am only just suggesting here would seem to be mutually exclusive, and thus what I may be appearing to try to do is to force his work and his theorizing into a framework where it clearly does not belong (the phrase "cultural hegemony" might fit well here—you be the judge). But in this passage from the Amnasan interview, Watten begins to advance a relation between the text and the person that might work to establish some kind of middle ground:

> Actually, I don't think the word *personal* is that important if the form is active. Whenever the form is doing something you will find the personal so deeply encoded with the form that the person becomes a way the form can be understood. So the person isn't merely personal any more. Which is another way of saying that of course writers write as individuals but that their work becomes part of a complex and suprasubjective logic which is what addresses their art to the world. (52)

The theoretical issue over which Watten and I differ is exemplified in his use of *suprasubjective* in this passage. I go along with his theorizing of the communication model up until the point when he starts to invoke Habermas. This is an old argument, relating to "Stalin as a linguist" (*Progress,* 1), and Stalin's supposed pronouncement that language was not a superstructure. Since I don't believe with Habermas and Watten that language serves as a "bridge" (Habermas) or a "conduit" (Watten) for everyday communication, a concept Derrida has deeply problematized in *Limited Inc.* and elsewhere, I have a hard time understanding just what a suprasubjective logic would consist of. In my discussion of Watten's poetry and his own comments on it, I have been attempting to counteract this suprasubjective logic with some infrasubjective analysis, because I think ultimately it is the inter-subjective aspect of poetic language that both he and I are mainly interested in. This would undoubtedly bear some further evaluative scrutiny, following out the models for "negativity" that Watten proposes in "XYZ of Reading," what I call "exteriority" in *Obdurate Brilliance,* and what Charles Bernstein calls "absorption" and "impermeability" in "Artifice of Absorption."

What I mean to be doing here is to open (or continue) such a dialogue by following up on Barrett Watten's suggestion that the standard model of poetic communication be reinterpreted as the mutual, or simultaneous, inculcation of the social network by both the writer and the audience. If what he really means is that the writer is inculcated by social forces, in some sense *before* the utterances, then the example of the tunnel as crypt is how I see this as working. As is no doubt clear by now, I resist Watten's ideologically oriented interpretive position on how social forces work in general and how this process might be dealt with in writing, but I am quite interested to see how these same social forces actually work *on him* in his text production. It is essential to seek to ground one's practice, and Barrett Watten's theoretical writings are exemplary in this regard. But one must also keep an eye open for the abyss that constantly threatens to undermine that grounding, an abyss without which no grounding could function as such. Communication may be a conduit in the complex ways Watten has demonstrated, but the inculcation of the writing subject he urges theoretically, and interestingly displays in his own work, necessarily involves the space of the crypt. Here the other is dead, yet incorporated, in a space of darkness, fear and silence, a space that poetic language reveals as cinders—the slightest traces, the fine black dust beneath one's feet, a tunnel one can never leave.

WORKS CITED

Baker, Peter. *Obdurate Brilliance: Exteriority and the Modern Long Poem.* Gainesville: University of Florida Press, 1991.

Bernstein, Charles. *Artifice of Absorption.* *Paper Air* 4:1 (1987); reprinted in *A Poetics.* Cambridge: Harvard University Press, 1992, 9-89.

Brito, Manuel. "An Interview with Barrett Watten," *Aerial 8,* 1994.

Cook, Albert. *Canons and Wisdoms.* Philadelphia: University of Pennsylvania Press, 1993.

Crane, Hart. "General Aims and Theories," *The Complete Poems and Selected Letters.* New York: Anchor (Liveright), 1966, 217-223.

Derrida, Jacques. *Cinders* (translation of *Feu le cendre*). Translated and edited by Ned Lukacher, Lincoln: University of Nebraska Press, 1991.

_____. "Fors: Les mots anglés de Nicolas Abraham et Maria Torok, " in Abraham and Torok, *Cryptonymie: le verbier de l'homme aux loups.* Paris: Flammarion, 1976, 7-73.

_____. *Limited Inc.* Translated by Samuel Weber and Jeffrey Mehlman, edited by Gerald Graff, Evanston: Northwestern University Press [rev. ed.], 1988.

_____. *Psyché: Inventions de l'autre.* Paris: Galilée, 1987.

Hill, Leslie. "Julia Kristeva: Theorizing the Avant-Garde?" in John Fletcher and Andrew Benjamin (eds.), *Abjection, Melancholia and Love.* London and New York: 1990, 137-156.

Kristeva, Julia. *La révolution du langage poétique.* Paris: Seuil, 1974.

Morrison, Toni. *Playing in the Dark: Whiteness and the Literary Imagination.*
    Cambridge: Harvard University Press, 1992.

Watten, Barrett. "The Conduit of Communication in Everyday Life,"
    Aerial 8, 1994.

_____. *Conduit.* San Francisco: Gaz, 1988.

_____. Interview with Michael Amnasan. *Ottotole* 2 (1986/1987): 28-60.

_____. *Progress.* New York: Roof, 1985.

_____. "XYZ of Reading: Negativity (&), " *Poetics Journal* 6 (1986): 3-5.

Williams, William Carlos. *The Collected Poems of William Carlos Williams. (Vol. 2)*
    Edited by Christopher MacGowan, New York: New Directions, 1988.

Intentionality and Subjectivity in *Progress*

Daniel Barbiero

The dispersal of subjectivity into the body of language is a motif that emerges with some urgency from Barrett Watten's writing. While this motif does not always make for the explicit subject matter in any given work of Watten's, nevertheless it is always present, as an Archimedean motif if nothing else. In this latter role it provides a point from which to stand beside and apprehend Watten's explicit subject matter (and thus it is like the spot, located outside of and beside the world, from which Archimedes claimed he could move the world with the help of a lever). In a sense, language's overriding of subjectivity is a motif *outside* of whatever motif may appear in the poem; it surrounds and undergirds Watten's writing as the condition for the production of that writing. Whatever events the poem's narrator may narrate, whatever explicit issues may arise, language remains a conscious presence to itself, a reflexive reference threatening to override the subjectivity in whose hands it finds itself.

In establishing such an Archimedean point—which, incidentally, must always remain incompletely outside of the work, since it is only within the practices that produced the work that it can function as a perspective into the work—Watten wishes to underscore what we might understand as the meta-meaning of the poem. By meta-meaning I mean an encompassing meaning, a meaning within which semantic meaning operates, and in terms of which it is deployed. If semantic meaning establishes *that* there is a relation between the sign and a world outside of the sign, a meta-meaning would attempt to establish the *how* of such a relation, or at least acknowledge its existence. A considerable motivation for Watten's project, in fact, is precisely this wish to open to examination the meaning within which semantic meaning unfolds.

Watten's consideration of the subject-turned-language object takes place at the level of language praxis. This is understandable when we consider praxis as a kind of intentional behavior, which is to say as an activity by which goal-directed labor is undertaken on the basis of a specified attitude toward certain relevant information possessed by the actor. It is at that level that we speak meaningfully of a subject's intentions, and in turn it is in terms of subjective intention that one can speak meaningfully of the dispersal or blockage of intention. For Watten poses the main problem of language praxis in terms of a rupture dividing meaning and intention: the subjective content of language praxis is blocked or distorted on account of something prior to the expression of subjective intent in language. There is, in other words, a kind of meaning that language carries, prior to the subjective intent, that interposes itself between that intent and its successful (or perhaps satisfactory is the better term) expression in language. It is precisely language that separates the language-using subject from its intention, and ultimately from itself. Put in those terms, this state of affairs may seem prohibitively detrimental to the production of

259

poetry—or of any meaningful language use—at best, and at worst, a harbinger of the impossibility of language praxis. Rather than providing cause for despair, however, I think this conversion of intention into the means of its fulfillment simply refers one back to the underlying structure of meaningful language use, that is a structure that ultimately must be explained in terms other than those of a cycle of alienation enfolding subject and object. Certainly, though, at one level there is a type of alienation in operation, and it is on this possibility of alienation that Watten has built his poetics—a poetics, as he says, that is as much an ethics as it is an aesthetics (Manuel Brito, "Interview with Barrett Watten").

I

Watten's first move in tracing the absorption of intention into language consists of a bracketing of the conventional idea of the subject. This is done in order to put into play an alienation from the psychological unity afforded by "the subjectivity effect," as he puts it in an interview with Manuel Brito (23).[1] By "subjectivity effect" I assume that Watten is referring to an effect of the cogito, which is to say an autonomous subjectivity that understands itself to be the unifying agent for all its activities across different fields. As Watten suggests in the interview, his practical suspension of the claims of the *cogito* is something like a "salutary" attempt to de-equate the ideological construction of psychological unity and the material synthesis of the activities for which that erstwhile psychological unity purportedly is the agent (Brito 19). In effect, Watten asks: What happens when one attempts to remove the presupposed notion of an originating cogito from behind the text it normally would have had attributed to its unity of action?

In *Progress*,[2] Watten demonstrates rather than explicates the evacuation of the "subjectivity effect."[3] In the poem, we encounter the replacement of the unified and unifying presence of the first person narrator with what at first may appear to be a multiplicity of identities. Instead of the figurative signature, sealed in flesh and blood, as it were—the I who tells a story or provides the voice for a poem—there is "I, a system" (38). Unmistakably, this is a signal that the self-identity and unity conventionally ascribed to the referent of the first person singular pronoun will not be taken for granted. In Watten's work the dispersal of this pronoun's referent appears at the level of symbolic

---

[1] I have favored Watten's theoretical formulations from this interview over, say, those in *Total Syntax* simply because the Brito interview seems to me to represent Watten's most recent thinking on poetics. The page references are to its appearance in this volume.

[2] Barrett Watten, *Progress* (New York: Roof Books, 1985).

[3] Barrett Watten, *Progress* (Roof Books, 1985). It is worth noting here Watten's definition of method in art as "the putting into practice of an explanation." See Barrett Watten, *Total Syntax* (Carbondale, IL: Southern Illinois University Press, 1985) p. 199.

denotation: to look at *Progress*, for instance, one can find two ways of recording the first person singular pronoun: "I" and "*I*." This allographic distribution of the non-identity of psychological identity has interesting ramifications.

There is an "I" referred to in *Progress* as if it were an object or perhaps a hypothetical model of a real-world object. There is, for example, the statement "the person I" (15), recorded with a detachment appropriate to the description of a prototype or symbolic substitute, offered at some distance of remove, for the voice that will speak the poem. It is in this context that one must understand Watten's quotation of Rimbaud's dictum that "I is another," and his occasional use of the third person singular verb form attached to "I." At one point in *Progress*, for instance, we are told that "I denotates *I* at all points . . . " (24). "I" in the third person is someone I talk about—behind his back, perhaps, as indeed Watten seems to do in the course of the Brito interview (28). "I" is the character I write about, it is not the I who does the writing. Nor the I who has lived the events to be written. In certain passages, in fact, "I" would appear to refer to the I of lived experience. Thus we read, "*I* denotes . . . / A sensation I noted on May 10"(91). (Whether or not lived experience is direct is not of concern here. What is of concern is that there is a distinction between two different levels of self-presentation.)

Yet even this I that denotes the I of lived experience is an object I: since it appears in the text, it necessarily is an I made language. It cannot help but be that way: there it is, in the poem. Now no matter under which of its allographic variants it may appear, I is something of a proper name for an Other. When one calls oneself by one's proper name, a distance intervenes: *others* normally call one by one's own proper name, and conversely, one calls others by their own proper names. To do so to oneself is to be other to oneself, and to have oneself as other to the oneself doing the calling. This distancing comes equally into play when one expresses oneself as the language-object I. (This would seem to be the case even more so when this is done on the page than in everyday speech. Although the expression is the same, it may not appear so, perhaps because everyday speech tends to transpire at a lesser level of reflection—and certainly at a lesser level of material duration—than does writing.) If I experience a moment, I can write about it, causing an object called "I" to appear on the page, denoted by the sign "I." "I" did not experience that moment, of course, but as far as the text is concerned, "I" can say that "I" did.

In short, "I" is an object of language, carrying a sense that the experiencing subject does not. This is so even if we are accustomed to think of "I" and what it represents as being a non-instrumental, transcendent value surpassing the moment of its expression within the practical field of language. The lesson here is that objectification within language is as potentially true of the language-using subject as it is of any other object called up into language representation. There is a difference here, and it is that the "I" as an object of language is (reasonably) assumed to have a measure of self-presence not attributed to other language objects: the "I" in the text is not only an object appearing by virtue of the text's constituent language praxis, but presumably refers to the subject of that praxis. In other words, "I" is the subject of the statement attributed to it as well as an object within the statement itself. Thus it can be understood as both language-using subject and language-represented object at the same time.

II

I have used the term "subject" in a way I believe needs to be clarified. For our purposes, a subject simply is an actor capable of engaging in purposive, skilled action within the context of a field constituted by a set of practices. Far from being a pre-given unity, the subject in fact is an acting entity made meaningful only within the context of the field of practices within which it acts, and within which its various ends can be pursued with some reasonable chance of success. In terms of its meaning, a subject "is" only to the degree that it is deployed within a field of activity, and in fact its content and actions are made intelligible by the practices and practical knowledges presupposed by that field. Thus for example the subject of language praxis engages in activity that uses language as a means to pursue discrete ends. It follows that any hope for the successful attainment of those ends depends on some level of competence in regard to effective language practices. The subject of language praxis therefore is a subject situated within the field of language practices: outside the field of language practices, the subject of language praxis has no meaning.

For all practical purposes, one cannot separate the concepts of subject and of praxis. Praxis, in fact, can be defined as a deliberate course of activity[4] taken up in pursuit of a desired state of affairs. Stated more completely and somewhat more technically, praxis is goal-directed activity undertaken on the basis both of the actor's disposition to act in a particular way, and on the actor's appropriation of certain relevant information in the mode of belief. The first part of this formula—that an actor undertakes activity on the basis of a certain disposition—simply means that the actor is able to act in the necessary manner, given the proper conditions. This disposition, or capacity to act, is a direct product of the actor's competence within the relevant field of activity. The second part of the formula—that action is taken up on the basis of an appropriation of relevant information—simply means that praxis is undertaken on the basis of an actor's beliefs as to the state of affairs in which activity will take place, the relative usefulness of potential courses of action, the range of desirable results, and so forth. (In fact a goal is itself an attitude toward information, but of the second order: if one formulates a goal, one formulates a futurally-directed desire on the basis of one's belief that a certain state of affairs holds: one's goal is the desire to modify that state of affairs in some way. This desire based on a belief in effect is an attitude based on an attitude.) A distinguishing characteristic of such goal-oriented activity is that the goal is represented by the subject to itself. In other words, the subject has imagined—if I may use that term loosely

---

[4]A course of deliberate activity can be composed of a number and variety of purposive actions, not all of which are, strictly speaking, deliberate, if by deliberate we understand a condition of greater, rather than lesser, self-consciousness.

for present purposes—what it wants before trying to bring it about.[5]

The subject originating a praxis is a unified subject only to the extent that it is unified by the dispositions it presupposes for the fulfillment of its praxis, and by the goals, necessarily posited within the limits silently imposed by those dispositions, that it pursues in the course of its praxis. Thus for a subject to have any semblance of cohesion, it must arise within the horizon of the practices and competences that define the practical field to which its dispositions correspond.[6] In any case, the idea of the subject cannot be separated from the reciprocal idea of the field in which praxis takes place: the subject always is the subject of a particular praxis.

III

The effect of Watten's doubling of the I is to demonstrate a separation of the language-using subject from itself by language: the I that is spoken escapes the I that is speaking, and becomes Other. The framework here appears to be one based on a relationality of subject and object. Thus the latter, doubled, I no longer points back to the subjectivity using language in a praxis but instead is a kind of objectified subjectivity, which is to say an intention that has been exteriorized into language. Watten, of course, is aware of an element of Otherness pervading language praxis: in discussing the poem "Conduit," for instance, he refers to the language user as being "distanced" from his or her intention (Brito 23), presumably by the interposed body of language. There is, in addition, a particularly evocative line in *Under Erasure* in which Watten alludes to "the

---

[5]Praxis thus begins with an individual consciousness that is for itself, and to this extent, it is subjective. That is to say that the subject initiates praxis with a conscious representation of its desired end. I might note in passing that this subject is for itself because its goals are its own to the extent that they are represented to itself on the basis of information that is for its own use. As I use it here, "for-itself" is intended as a description of a quality of mental states, and as such describes a peculiar characteristic of the way in which we come to an understanding of our own behavior and the behavior of others. (I realize that I use the expression at the risk of association-by-deja vu. Sartre, it will be recalled, uses for-itself (pour-soi) in *L'Etre et le néant* to designate a temporalizing, "nihilizing" human consciousness, and his own use derives from Hegel.) We can attribute for-itself contents to an actor if that actor has conscious access to mental states providing data about self and environment—for its (i.e., the actor's) own use. In other words, a mental or internal state qualifies as what we might call a for-itself content if it provides a consciously accessible description of the actor's actions and dispositions, and of the environment in which that action is undertaken and on which it is intended to have an effect. However, my own use owes just as much to Dennett's discussion of intelligent, intentional systems. See Daniel C. Dennett, *Content and Consciousness* (London: Routledge and Kegan Paul, 1969) p. 46.

[6]There is also a sense in which the subject's practical dispositions are given a temporal, synthetic unity on the basis of its futurally projected goal. But the investigation of this point is beyond the scope of this paper.

place my words fly away from" (38).[7] That place from which my words fly is not me as such, but something else: something, perhaps, with all the impersonality conveyed by the word "place." (But is it an uninhabited place? Or one that I can fill, if only temporarily?)

This place in fact is a moment: the moment of the realization of an intention to express a particular meaning. This realization entails the exteriorization, by the language-using subject, of its intention into language, which is to say the conversion of its intention to express its meaning into the utterance that will express that meaning. By exteriorizing its intention into material form, and thereby pursuing its praxis in the world, the subject converts that intention into interest.[8] Put another way, the pursuit of one's ends in the material realm literally materializes one's motivating intention as interest: in the realm of material, desire is made material as interest. In terms of language praxis, this only means that the expressive intention, when it is actualized in an utterance, reveals the utterer's intention as an interest in language. At a very basic level, the utterer has a stake in language. No wonder, then, that even as Watten acknowledges a distancing of intention from the originating subject in the course of language praxis, he observes further that one nonetheless continues to produce just such intentions (Brito 23) and presumably by extension, just such interest.

In this connection, one's interest constitutes material as instrumentality. The pursuit of ends in the world requires not only that the intention be exteriorized, but that the external surrounding materiality be enlisted as a means toward attainment of that end. (In a sense, the instrumentalization of materiality is a tangible correlate to the intention-turned-interest.) The conversion of intentionality into interest, and the accompanying constitution of material as an instrument of that interest changes material from a more or less indifferent collection or domain of objects into a tool endowed with meaning. This latter meaning is a value that arises in the context of use; it is relational worth, which is to say that it is something that is meaning-ful in relation to something else, this something else being the pursuit of a desired state of affairs, and ultimately, the projected goal that has been represented at the initiation of this particular praxis. I must emphasize here that this meaning is to be distinguished from semantic meaning per se; this instrumental, or appropriative, meaning is over and above semantic meaning. If value is worth in relation to praxis, meaning is value thanks to interest.

It is in regards to the instrumentalization of language that Watten approaches the question of ideology. In *Total Syntax*, Watten discusses Voloshinov's

---

[7]Barrett Watten, *Under Erasure* (La Laguna: Zasterle Press, 1991).

[8]This definition of interest is based loosely on that to be found in Sartre's *Critique de la raison dialectique: Tome I: Théorie des ensembles pratiques* (Paris: Gallimard, 1960). In the *Critique*, Sartre defines interest as consisting in a state of one's being wholly externalized in a thing to such an extent that one's project is conditioned, and perhaps even compromised (CRD 261). As far as Sartre is concerned, it would appear that interest necessarily entails the objectification of the intention in materiality.

location of ideological effects in the exteriority of the sign (116); in another, related context, he approaches the matter from a more immediately practical perspective: how, he asks, does one "redress the onslaught of literal, instrumental language that is politics?" (Brito 20). I take this to mean that ideology is conceivable as coextensive with language's instrumentality, which we can translate into the terms used above by saying that ideology is a function of language as interest. This is so since as we have seen, the pursuit of a goal in the world entails the externalization of an intention, and thus involves the transformation of desire into interest. If this is true, it would appear to constitute a broad construction of ideology. (A more restricted definition might state that, for instance, ideology entails the subordination of meaning to interest. This putting aside such misleading definitions of ideology as, say, the articulation of deliberate falsehoods or misrepresentations in the service of power.) Given a definition of ideology as the instrumental use of language, it would seem that as regards language praxis, ideology and the successful completion of the expressive intention are inextricably intertwined. That would be so since articulation qua expression entails the conversion of the expressive intention into interest in order that it be completed successfully (since only an expressive intention externalized into language can be successful). Completing the expressive intention in such a manner instrumentalizes, and therefore ideologizes, language.

Whether or not one wishes to consider expression in terms of ideology—in terms of the psychological reality of the material sign, as Watten has put it (Brito 18)—there remains the issue of the status of language as an already-constituted instrumentality. Addressing this issue requires a consideration of the intersubjective dimension of language and language praxis. For the conversion of intentionality into interest, and the resulting constitution of material as a means (and therefore as a value), would be a relatively straightforward affair if one were the only acting subject laboring in the particular practical field in question. But that clearly is not the case. There are instead a multiplicity of interests cohabitating in any given practical field, and I think it is this multiplicity that is at the heart of the problem of intersubjectivity. For we do not come to material as an unconstituted neutrality: we find instead that it already has been instrumentalized. Others before me, in pursuing their own interests, have seen to that. As Watten puts it in *Under Erasure*, language as just such material consists of "signs they thematized beyond your immediate needs" (41). In effect I come to language as it has already been constituted as an appropriated meaning, which I then must use in the course of pursuing my own interest.

In fact when I express something in language, I constitute language as my means toward that expression. But that does not mean that at that moment I constitute an appropriative meaning *ex nihilo*; language as a carrier of appropriative meaning has already been constituted for (and be-fore) me. As a practical tool, language is already endowed with an appropriative meaning that pre-exists the meanings any particular act of language praxis wishes to impute to it. Thus if one aspect of language conceived as instrumentality consists in the pressure of constituted material on intentional activity, its complementary aspect consists in the weighing down of that activity's appropriative meaning with an appropriative meaning that pre-exists it. In a sense, the expression of one's intended meaning in language is the putting of oneself outside of oneself in an Other's materiality: it is oneself as Other. Seen from this perspective, the completed expression constitutes one's intended meaning as Other as well: it is the emblem of a subject outside of itself in a material that, more than simply providing the means for the fulfillment of the intentionality of a praxis, actually molds the realized shape that that intentionality will take. Put another way, praxis is an intentionality-in-progress that somehow must fulfill itself in something that it has not yet, properly speaking, constituted as an appropriative meaning-content for itself. Under these conditions, the successful completion of my praxis charged with the attainment of a projected state of affairs guarantees that something of that intention will escape me. The state of affairs thus attained "belongs" equally to my intention and to the material in which that intention has been realized—and I had to appropriate that material as an Other's materiality.

This ambiguity in the provenance of meaning—that it is partly of my intention, and partly of an almost semi-autonomous materiality—is a major subtheme of Watten's work. In fact Watten acknowledges such ambiguity when he states that at a certain level it is language itself that speaks (Brito 29). (Interestingly, however, the fact that Watten gives interviews explaining his intentions in writing this or that passage demonstrates his wish to recover his intentions back from language, to regain the subjectivity that apprehends itself outside of itself in the field of language.) If language is constituted as an instrumentality by a multiplicity of intentional activities, then it is proper to no single intentional activity: appropriated by all, it belongs to none. Implicit in such a structure is the intending of an instrument of expression that has been constituted as an instrumentality by others. Yet this instrument nonetheless is a necessary component in the realization of any expressive intention. There is an element of internalization implicit here as well, since the setting of intentionality outside of itself is not completed until the exteriority of language's instrumentality has been internalized in the course of language praxis. It is, in effect, my internalization of an Other's interest. Perhaps it is for this reason that Watten states that the meanings in which we as language-using subjects are immersed are "psychologically as well as materially real"(Brito 18).

IV

Language praxis is a matter more complicated than that of a simple one-way motion through which the language-using subject is absorbed—feathers, bones, and all—into the material sign. Instead, there is a reciprocation through which the language user is able to appropriate language as meaning. Language, having claimed the language-using subject through the conversion of intention into instrumentality, now is reclaimed by the language-using subject. It is true that this reclamation involves the use of an Other's instrument—as stated above —but it is equally true that this use of the instrument that has been handed down (or handed over) allows the appropriating subject to grasp language as more than a previously constituted instrumentality. Language now is made to speak *for* the speaker, and not simply *through* the speaker.

In the second line of *Progress*, Watten provides an interesting example of such reappropriation (or alternatively, subjectivization) of an already constituted instrumentality: "Purple snake stands out on / Porcelain tiles." (1). As Watten explains to Brito, the reference here is to a graffito Watten encountered in a pedestrian tunnel in Oakland (Brito 20). The graffito is an interruption of the public space it inhabits, certainly: its unauthorized appearance has the effect of a disjunctive upsurge, a kind of insertion of a qualifying, contradictory, or simply arresting "but" in the midst of a milieu that otherwise is taken for granted. Obviously, the appearance of such a mark introduces an ambiguity into the "message" imparted by the space it inhabits (if we can grant, at least for the moment, that venues intended for public use comprise a figurative language communication through spatial divisions, the arrangement of surfaces, the deployment of buildings, vistas and landmarks, etc.). Interestingly, though, Watten resists the temptation to see the spray-painted snake only as a kind of "political other" to that which explicitly is authorized to inhabit, or in effect, "speak for," this space. This latter would include the workings, for example, of the business world, as this latter might be represented by the human capital of the commuters passing through the pedestrian tunnels and walkways during rush hour, or by the rolling stock—literally, the mobile stock of capital—of subway cars delivering their cargoes to places of work and consumption. Such a temptation, should Watten give in to it, would, I believe, allow only a simplistic reduction of a much more richly varied, perhaps even maddeningly complex, knot of relations in which human beings interact with each other and with their material surroundings and instruments. For Watten, at least, such a reductive equation of the graffito with a unidimensional "political other" would amount to taking those unauthorized marks as the graphic relics of a simple—and probably failed—oppositional moment (Brito 20).

The complexity of the situation is built into the structure of communication itself: a simple "no" is bound to rebound back on itself by virtue of its attempt to remain simple. The choice of a stance in any case is complicated by the position of the sign itself. Instead of putting faith in a "redress" to be had through simple opposition, Watten sees the graffito as a complicator of public space in which the purple snake presents itself, in Watten's words, as "an irresolution of its own condition . . . [as] an unstable, private image" (Brito 21). The significance of the snake, finally—and here I will enclose Watten's own words in quotation marks in an attempt to be faithful to his meanings—is to illustrate the cross-trajectory of "private meanings" within "social meanings," through which the former can "qualify" the latter and produce a situation in which "instrumental meanings can be modified and redefined" (Brito 21).

The reciprocity Watten hints at, under the guise of the modification and redefinition of instrumental meanings, essentially is that of the reciprocity through which an already-constituted instrumentality is reappropriated by a new and subsequent praxis. In particular, the incident of the purple snake and its destabilizing influence on the discourse embodied in public space instantiates a moment that—if one wishes to employ the terminology of subject and ob-ject—can be characterized as the subjectification of objectivity. It is not that a private meaning has been reclaimed from an instrumentalized meaning so much as that a new instrumentalization has taken place under the auspices of an intentional appropriation of a pre-constituted instrumentality. This latter instrumentality is the material trace of a previous interest, i.e., the remnant of a previous praxis that has constituted external materiality—in this case, lan-guage—into an instrument for the pursuit of its goals. The purple snake, in effect, reclaims that instrumentality for its own interest (or rather, the interest of the praxis the fulfillment of which entailed the leaving of marks on the porcelain tiles of the pedestrian tunnel walls.)

V

The question now is how to account for the re-creation of instrumentality as meaning. The answer consists in the structure of language praxis as a goal-directed activity. As stated earlier, a goal is a certain attitude toward information the goal-formulator possesses. It is, in other words, an intention. In the spe-cific case of language praxis, the expressive intention—the desire to express a meaning in language—is the goal toward which language praxis is directed. I am using the term "intention" here not in the everyday sense of, roughly, the desire or determination to act in a particular (deliberate) way, but rather to signify a mental state of directedness. If, for example, I deliberate about making an utterance prior to the act of uttering, the mental state through which I am directed toward the act of utterance is my intention to utter; this intention is "about" the setting into motion of the physical processes needed to undertake and complete the utterance in a successful manner. Similarly, a perceptual in-tention directs me toward, or (once again) is "about" the perceptual experience of some object or state of affairs.

Language use can be understood as a complex of intentions binding the subject to the context of experience and to the communicable representation of that experience.[9] For now, however, I am only concerned with one specific intention underlying language praxis, and that is the expressive intention that comprises the goal of language praxis. For it seems to me that that is the inten-tion most directly relevant to the question at hand, which, to repeat, is that of the reclamation of meaning from an already-constituted instrumentality. (For this reason, too, I will not address the question of the content of language meaning.) As hinted above, I believe that this relation can be described in the language of subject and object—as a reciprocity of objectified subjectivity and

---

[9]Searle seems to favor a theory of a complex chain of intentions governing or accompa-nying actions. See in particular his comments on the "network of intentions" in John Searle, *Intentionality: An Essay in the Philosophy of Mind* (Cambridge: Cambridge Univer-sity Press, 1983) p. 19. I am inclined to believe that this account has explanatory value, but does not necessarily describe the actual workings of mind and body in any given deliberate act.

subjectified objectivity—but can be explained only in terms of its underlying structure of intentionality.

As its name suggests, the expressive Intention is an Intention directed toward the actual expression of a meaning in language. It is, in other words, the goal in pursuit of which linguistic activity will be undertaken. (It is this latter activity, in fact, that loosely—or more immediately—comprises what we normally mean by the expression "language praxis.") I will take it for given that preceding the moment of expression is a moment in which I am directed toward that expression, i.e., toward that state of affairs in which I will express my meaning in language. This latter state of affairs is what my expressive intention is "about."

The structure of this expressive intention—like that of all intentional acts or states—is a dual one. This is as true of the intention preceding an act as of the intention accompanying an act. When I am directed toward something—let us say object or state of affairs *x*—*x* comprises the meaning, or referential content of my intention, and thus one aspect of its intelligibility. But I am directed toward *x* in a particular way. For instance, I may see that *x*, or believe that *x*, or desire that *x*, etc. This particular way of being directed toward *x* is the way in which I appropriate *x*: it is the appropriative mode of my intention. Thus a complete intention consists of two aspects: a referential content and an appropriative mode, which can be notated as $A(r)$. (This notation is simply meant to show that an intention in fact consists of a relation.) The referential content *r* is the "what" that the representation is about, while the appropriative mode A is the "how," or the manner in which the subject approaches, grasps, or otherwise appropriates *r*: loosely speaking, it is the stand that the subject takes on *r*. If the referential content "means" an object or state of affairs, the appropriative mode is the manner in which the agent takes that object or state of affairs. These two aspects of the intention function as two separate but necessarily interlocking aspects of intelligibility, each of which stands as a distinct modality of meaning. If we are considering an expressive intention underlying language praxis, the referential content of the intention "means" that state of affairs in which I actually utter the expression "p" that I desire to utter. The particular way in which I am directed toward my uttering "p" is precisely that desire to utter "p": thus in this case, the appropriative mode is one of desire. (It would be just as true to say that the appropriative mode in this case is one of intention, in its everyday sense. However, I will use "desire"—defined, roughly, as a futurally-directed inclination to act in a particular way—in order to avoid confusion.) The appropriative mode of my expressive intention—the desire, or futurally-directed inclination to express "p," in other words—is the mode through which I appropriate language and designate it as an instrument—my instrument—in the utterance of my meaning.

I should emphasize here that the intention I have posited as preceding the act of utterance is not necessarily paradigmatic of all intentions or of all acts: by no means are all acts preceded by an intention of goal-formation, nor are all act-directed intentions formulated prior to the acts they intend. (An example of this latter would be the intention that consists of the consciousness of self-referential causality accompanying an action.) But it should be noted that every expressive act at least implies an appropriative mode, even if it does not involve a prior representation of the expressive act. For example, when I utter the expression "p," I simply utter "p" without having made explicit what my saying "p" implies, namely, that I believe that "p." In order to have expressed "p," the appropriative mode of belief—which comprises a certain way of being directed toward the content "p"—is understood to be implicit in my saying "p." In saying "p" I am in effect signalling my judgment that "p" is the case. (More accurately, I am committing myself to the judgment that "p" is the case. I may say "p" insincerely, but my saying it still expresses my commitment to belief in "p.")[10]

It is in the specifically expressive intention, consisting in my desire to utter "p," that language takes on an appropriative meaning. My desire to utter "p," whether or not I reflect on that desire, is the something in relation to which language is a value, in the sense used in Section III. Thus it is through the appropriative mode of an expressive intention that language is recovered as the kind of meta-meaning that points in the direction of the "how" enfolding the "what" of semantic meaning. It is through such appropriation that language-as-objectivity is subjectified, and its instrumentality recovered for the appropriating language-using subject. It must be stressed that this type of recovery is a kind of recognition of language that recovers a particular kind of meaning through the relation of expressor to expressibility. Through this relation, language is given the meaning that is value: appropriative meaning is the value, relative to my desire, of the language into which I exteriorize my expressive intention. My appropriation of language invests it with meaning in the "meta" sense: it becomes a value in relation to the expression of my meaning. Thus language takes on a worth by virtue of its having been appropriated, and becomes an instrument of usefulness.[11]

---

[10]This is what Searle calls the "sincerity condition" of a speech act. See John Searle, *Speech Acts: An Essay In the Philosophy of Language* (Cambridge: Cambridge University Press, 1969) pp. 60 and 62.

[11]An appropriative meaning, interestingly enough, generates its own (generally unexpressed and unreflected on) end, subordinated to the original (reflected on, purposive) intention or (unreflected on) disposition to express a meaning. This secondary purpose is the subjectivization of language, which itself becomes a state of affairs to be brought about. This secondary purpose is inseparable from the primary goal of expression, of course: the successful completion of an expression both entails and presupposes the successful appropriation of language for that expression. Every act of language praxis, in fact, posits an overall end that is independent of the particular end represented in or state of affairs expressed by a particular component act of a particular language praxis. That overall end—once again, to use the terminology of subject and object—is the subjectivization of language's objectivity, the turning of language as Other-constituted instrumentality into a value in relation to a communicative goal.

VI

Yet the ability to utter "p" is nothing other than the realization of the disposition to utter "p"; the fact of the successful uttering of "p" is made intelligible by that disposition in just the way that the praxis of uttering "p" is made intelligible by the desire to utter "p." What this means is that without the disposition to utter "p"—which can be generalized as the disposition to use language competently and appropriately[12]—there is no question of uttering "p" in the first place. Thus although it is through the appropriative mode that I make language my instrument, it is because of my disposition to use language competently that I am able to appropriate it in the first place. In fact the appropriation of language can be viewed from another angle, as the instantiation of a disposition: my desire to utter "p," and thereby my instrumentalization of language, represents an episodic actualization of my disposition to utter "p."[13]

Seen from another perspective, though, the disposition to use language competently allows language praxis to stand as the realization of language as a possibility based on that disposition. It also allows one to dispense with the myth of the uncompromising unified subject as a god-like initiator of activity —a myth the dismantling of which has been a major part of Watten's poetics. In place of this mythical subject, we might propose a dispositional agency recognizing and acting upon its possibilities within a practical field: a subject, in other words, that is a temporary unity of action synthesized by an engagement in practical activity toward which it is disposed. When appropriation of a practical instrument—or the reappropriation of an Other's instrumentality— is understood as the instantiation of a disposition, it is understood as having been grasped as possibility.

And possibility, it seems to me, is what is missing from any account of language or other praxis that restricts itself to a framework of subject and object locked in a cycle of mutual alienation. However, I think that Watten's fascination with the complexities of language praxis, as evidenced by his interpretation of the purple snake graffito, indicates his going beyond this locked circuit. For what is the graffito (or the praxis it represents) if not an attempt on the part of an expressive capacity—a disposition to utter—to realize itself, to instantiate material as possibility? That, at least, is how I interpret Watten's story and his conclusion that the graffito is something "interior, private, difficult [that] is attempting to achieve explicit, literal, public content and say something" (Brito 20). This seems to me to be something more than a simple alienation of

---

[12]For specific understanding of what constitutes competent and appropriate behavior one would have to look at the practical field in which any given disposition is exercised. In any case, a disposition presupposes some degree of practical knowledge regarding competent and appropriate behavior.

[13]A disposition can be defined, roughly, as a structured activity A such that given condition C, and the belief that C, A can be obtained.

271

intention into instrumentalized material: it is instead the recognition of material as possibility. And it seems reasonable to suppose that it will be through the recognition of possibility that we will be able to go beyond the heroism of alienation.   —November, 1991–January, 1992

Postscript

At the time of writing this paper, I was much concerned—perhaps even a bit obsessed—with the question of whether or not the experience of the world in terms of a differential awareness, presented in the form of the classic dialectic of subject-object duality, is the fundamental way of encountering the world. My answer, implicit in this paper, is that it is not. I still believe this is true, but I feel it would be something of a help to readers to make explicit some of the basic presuppositions underlying my original argument.

The theory of intentionality that is so central to this paper was based largely on the traditional phenomenological account, as expressed recently (1983) in Searle's *Intentionality*. I therefore understood intentionality as entailing two necessary conditions: conscious experience, and referentiality by way of mental representation. These two conditions undergird the concept of the for-itself, and it was with this concept that I tried explicitly to square accounts with the traditional phenomenological theory of mind qua consciousness. (These same two conditions can be felt as well in the rigidity of my definitions of praxis and the subject. I now would prefer to dispense with both of these categories altogether.)

Recently, I have come to believe that a more accurate picture of intentionality is provided by a model of mind in which mental activity per se, and with it representation, is not indexed to conscious experience but instead to the processing of information structures. The speaker's intention, while being a factor in the meaning of the speech act, is thus less a discrete, separable, and above all guiding, inner moment of a complex process and more an aspect that is completed when the speech act itself is completed—at least as far as the speaker's conscious experience of his or her own language activity is concerned. By the same token, I would now say that for purposes of analysis, the expressive intention is simply embedded in the act. According to this picture, the speech act is even less a matter of the externalization of a completed, conscious intention (an articulated subjective state), and more a matter of combinatorial mental functions which may or may not make themselves accessible to consciousness. For this reason (among others), I would quarrel now with my too-easy characterization of the intentionality of language production as an objectified subjectivity.

In sum, while I don't think the restrictive versions of intentionality and representation are the case, I do believe that they are implicit in the dialectical paradigm of language use as objectified subjectivity.   —January, 1993

"The Poetry, By Making Him Think Certain Ways": Barrett Watten's *Progress*

Bruce Campbell

> The poetry,
> by
> Making him think certain ways . . . .
>
> White, to each of these cancels
>   Shadow,
>   fog. Collapses self,
>   And invading enemy wins.
> The argument itself, disassembling . . . .
>
> Objection.
>
>   (*Progress*, 1-2).[1]

Poetry, it seems, encourages us to take the figure above the material (the snake over the purple tile).[2] Thus, we could say that poetry places us in a figural realm, removed from history and the material dimension, because, through its offices, we begin to take ourselves figurally. And what does this mean? Let us speculate that, in place of the "states of affairs" (of a history of feedback[3]—or, even, of strife), poetry, "by making [us] think certain ways," lures us with certainty, which after all, is unavoidably raised by these "certain ways.") But "certain ways" limit us.

This is the first meaning of "cancels": it cancels the other (uncertain) ways. "White, to each of these cancels/Shadow."[4] (Here "certain" and "certainty" are in agreement: the "shadow" must be dispelled; for it invokes uncertainty.) But, too, this poetic dimension of figuration involves a cancellation of the material dimension. Its effect: "Collapses self"—just as "you speak for themselves" (2). But, when this happens, irony reigns; for we do not secure ourselves in the figural realm of poetry. "[I]nvading enemy wins./The argument itself, disassembling . . . //Objection." We lose not only our "self" here; we lose all manner of objecting to our loss. Surely, this is a double loss, all the greater for our inability to complain—or, indeed, to even know what we've lost.

It is in recognition of these very reversals (through invasion)[5] that Barrett Watten's *Progress* is structured on the caesura.[6] The caesura, however, is a cunning trap. It is cunning for two reasons. One: we do not recognize the caesura. More, we do not respect the caesura. We act as if it were not there; or, we act as if it were simply a gap to be filled: "No doubt a process of thought" (38).[7] So, as far as reading is concerned, to ignore the caesura is to enjamb all the lines, which homogenizes their direction. Under the pressure of such an enjambed reading, all the lines will seem to add up to the same thing—a conformity through agglomeration. "No direction words will repeat" (109).

Of course, this may also say something about progress: it is the filling of a gap which we do not recognize. To say this, however, is to posit a distinction between the impulse to fill the gap and the rationality which does not even see that there is a gap. And, on these terms, progress could scarcely be anything but irrational. It is possible, then, to locate the caesura within ourselves as a kind of dissociation of sensibility, but a dissociation which is socially encoded and enforced, much as progress itself is. This dissociation is, simply, the blinding by progress. The result is that we gladly do not know what we do; we simply continue to fill the (dimly felt) gap. "Between these successions/An opposite, /never perceived . . . " (42).[8]

But there remains a second way in which the caesura is cunning—as "A way to reverse directions . . . " (51). And this way sabotages that of the first; for "Every proposition has changed" (54),[9] and "The change is absolute" (109). As we read *Progress*, we come to see that some lines do not make sense when enjambed. The result is slightly irritating—if we thought about it, after all, perhaps this would mean that all our actions are "really" as meaningless as the illogically enjambed lines. Of course, in the rush of progress (which here simply means progressing through the book) we might not act on this sense; we might even deny the sense by ascribing a superior power to the text. Thus: the text knows best, we might say, and succor ourselves on our ignorance (and ignorant enjoyment of progress). For the text would here be equal to any authority—equal, too, perhaps, in terms of its ruthlessness and the harm it can inflict. Rather than go through all that, we may see that, if some lines do not make sense enjambed, the caesura is not a gap to be blindly filled. "A sequence is not transparent . . . //As in a dark meaning, a match./A quantity of cubes" (26). Because the "sequence is not transparent," the caesura is a call to judgment: "Progress?" (80).[10] We are constantly being called on to judge whether or not two lines join (or communicate) with each other. In this way, *Progress* isn't something to be passively enjoyed; it must be actively reflected upon and, in that reflecting, created: "[U]nearthed in the progress/A form compelling events" (7).

NOTES

1. We should note these lines about poetry follow directly upon "Comes to the history of words./The thought to eradicate/In him" (1).
2. Consider: "The image, which is a repressed act, is independent of the grounds on which it is visualized, and it can be translated from one material to another. . . . Self-conscious parallelism works for the mechanistic production of image and statement" (*Total Syntax*, 45-46).
3. Consider: "In search of feedback element . . . //A circular motion across lines/Becoming increasingly faint/At all points" (52). Compare: "IF/A continuous feedback loop is an integral part of the delivery./IF/Water runs out" (*Conduit*, 46).

4. Recall: "It's enough to have left the old world, the world we are seeking is white" (*Decay*, 10). And, from a poem titled, "The Whiteness Which Covers All," "Magnum opus/white. Marginal waves/nested in whiteness" (*Opera— Works*, 6). Further: "[T]he grace of white (of what can be)" (*1–10*, 22). If we consider that "The first landing in the new world is counterfactual" (*Conduit*, 22), then there is a possibility of seeing in this "white" a "counterfactual."

5. Consider: "I must start/In enemy territory to escape . . . //A difference in discourse" (101).

6. By "caesura," I mean any recognizable pause—the ellipses, of course; but also line breaks and punctuation. Recall: "Breaking pattern through cae- sura" (*1–10*, 44). (We might note that Watten not infrequently uses com- mas [and periods] to deflect the reader from the expected reading; or, the unobservant reader will be deflected from the literal reading, reading, in- stead, what he expects to be there.) The caesura marks the central struggle in *Progress*—that between the unit (or the phrase) and the multiple (or the concept). This struggle is carried out by means of lines (and on the level of the lines themselves), of alliances and misalliances. We might note, in this context, how the ellipses (as marking the stanza) often seem at variance with the sentences (as units of sense). The unit of the stanza, thus, is often incomplete. Recall: "Axis of . . . Divisions, dissolves" (*Plasma/Paralles/ "X,"* 20). And: "Progess into retreating barriers makes sense" (*1–10*, 29).

7. "No doubt a process of thought" (38) is ambivalent: "no doubt" what we are speaking of is "a process of thought," but, also, "no doubt [is] a process of thought." The latter emphasizes a positivism in thought, which we might phrase as "no doubt, even doubt is a process of thought." "Doubt," on these grounds, is a doubt domesticated in order to fit into the overriding (i.e., overwriting) process; although "Doubt compares with everything" (*1–10*, 33). But, of course, there is also the exclusion of doubt from the process of thought. Yet: "My doubt is interpretation" (*Conduit*, 61).

8. More fully: "Between these successions/An opposite,/never perceived . . . // It is a fact,/it is not this" (42–43).

9. More fully: "Contents built in from outside,/But it is only in a voice/ There can be a determination,/Alingual,/and truly under eyes . . . // Every proposition has changed" (54).

10. For example: "In Nietzsche's/Point of departure, discourse . . . //The boxer, too, has intuitions" (8). This may stand, too, for the unexpectedness of an event. In this frame, the "boxer" becomes an event.

Barrett Watten

MADE THOUGHT

made thought which of it
all of which a kind yet
best it in and on should must
whatever it is often once to do

in a while once is there and in
as it like it but often ever that it is
in which in separate that
often only very not in which way

all of this but this which as are alike
or in an only not what made as for
it in its well as made open as in
that which it once all but made but
for all as it is

—Clark Coolidge, *This* 1

9.92.   "At all," 4 pp. Prose and poetry in 7 sections.
12.35.   "There are so many things you have to remember . . . ,"
             8 pp. In two columns, one flush left and the other flush right,
             composed page by page.

Berkson, Bill.

5.80–81.   "looking for the edge/in the middle of . . . "; "Domino"
             (prose poem); "Poem."
8.95–96.   "Dream"; "Cnidus."

Berkson, Bill, and Tom Clark.

4.29.   "The Be of So," 5 pp. Uses found material, in 16 sections.

Bernheimer, Alan.

9.15.   "Celestial Mechanics," 5 pp. A sequence of five poems:
             "Spinal Guard," "Ripolin," "Carapace," "Visible Means,"
             "Ventriloquy."
11.34.   Translation of Robert Desnos, "Midway." 2 pp.

Bernstein, Charles.

9.62.   "Sentences My Father Used," 7 pp.
10.83.   "For Love Has Such a Spirit That If It Is Portrayed It Dies," 3 pp.
11.45–49.   "Motion Sickness," 4 pp.; "Neutral Density Filter," 2 pp.

Blum, Thomas March.

1.25–27.   "wish"; "Africa"; "glowball."

Bramhall, Allen.

3.34.   "A Night Piece from Prom Night."

Bromige, David.

3.28.   From "Homage to N. Rosenthal," 2 pp. 6 poems: "make
             yourself at home," "light work but/dear materials," "Simile//
             Marlene Heimach," "prettier," "Cure for Eurache,"
             "Get off my tits."
5.68–69.   From *Tight Corners* (prose, 4 sections); "One in Five Acts"
             (prose, 5 sections).
9.20.   "One Spring," 7 pp. Prose. Winner of a Pushcart Prize, 1979.

Butterick, George.

2.78–79.   "sticks close, pinning the fool . . . "; "The Tongue."

Child, Abigail.

9.57.   From "A Disputed Case," 5 pp.
12.25.   From "Subject Motion," 5 pp. Prose and poetry.

how it works

forces

find out

the wheel

what's what

bucking

like magic

rings

the known and the unknown

is real

the foghorn

blows

the wind or the sea

stirs

morning

is beyond color

—Larry Eigner, *This* 2

Clark, Tom.

> 1.13.   From "The Notebooks," 11 pp. Serial poem of 69 parts.
>
> 3.21–22.   "quiet aluminum"; "the ballet/shoes . . . "; "Come in./ Be seated . . ." ; "Drops fall/from iris . . . ."

Coolidge, Clark.

> 1.28–30.   "Made Thought"; "Distances Are a Ply"; "Siren."
>
> 2.10–18.   "Quick," 3 pp. (serial poem in 21 parts); "A B," part 6, 2 pp.; "Beehive Ordinates"; "Ress"; "The Who's Next"; "Step Stubble."
>
> 3.4–14.   From *The Maintains,* 10 pp.; "Caliper Sphere," 3 pp. (serial poem in 13 parts).
>
> 5.12.   "Karstarts," 18 pp. Prose. Note: "KARSTARTS is one of my sections from a continuing collaboration with Bernadette Mayer"—Clark Coolidge.
>
> 6.5.   "I need to like so large a literature . . . ," 20 pp. Prose.
>
> 8.21.   "A Page That Is Nothing But Words Written By Itself," 7 pp. Prose.
>
> 10.86.   "A Lecture," 9 pp. Prose.

Coolidge, Clark, Susan Coolidge, and Barrett Watten.

> 4.34.   "Conversation with Clark Coolidge," 36 pp. Interview, 6 November 1972.

Creeley, Robert.

> 1.74–75.   "Knokke";"Smoke."
>
> 3.80.   From *Presences.* "Look, look. The road home . . . ," 3 pp. Prose.
>
> 6.3.   From *Mabel: A Story.* "Door closed . . . ," 2 pp. Prose.

Davidson, Michael.

> 6.61–63.   "I am watching the vanguard move in . . . "; "An impulse the farcical attitude blows . . ." (prose, in 4 sections); "Going back into the room . . . ," 2 pp. (prose in 8 sections).

Davies, Alan.

> 8.69.   "I Think I Understand Joseph Beuys," 10 pp. Work in 5 parts, consisting of prose, xerox collage, notes, and quoted material.
>
> 10.73.   "'101,'" 3 pp.
>
> 12.113.   From *Name,* 10 pp. 17 poems, printed in sequence.

Day, Jean.

> 11.23–25.   "Gas"; "I Don't Want to Die in a Spree"; "Section 8"; "Storyville."

s o m e o l d g u y s w i t h s c y t h e s

—Robert Grenier, *This* 3

Dewdney, Christopher.

    9.27.   "Think Pool," 2 pp. Prose.
    10.81.   From "The Cenozoic Asylum," 2 pp. Prose.

DiPalma, Ray.

    3.50–51.   "Ochre Ghosh"; "Toll."
    10.33.   "The Wick," 10 pp.
    11.44.   "Pict." Rubber stamp work.
    11.77.   "Ruhr/Heur . . . ." Rubber stamp work.
    12.23–24. "Poem (Poem)"; "Poem."

Dorfman, Elsa.

    1.77–80.   "Olson's Desk"; "Charles Olson, Kitchen, Fort Square,
                  Aug. 28, 1965"; "Charles Olson, A Gloucester Tavern,
                  Aug. 28, 1965" (photos); "Charles Olson," 2 pp. (prose).

Drucker, Johanna.

    12.92.   From "Object Journey," 4 pp. Prose.

Eigner, Larry.

    1.62–69.   "The dying man's car . . ."; "that's all figures . . ."; "the ol
                  man steps . . ."; "this real old man's face . . ."; "dream-like/
                  varieties the real . . ."; "i think I see the . . ."; "Looks like/a
                  tall bird . . ."; "Time goes where . . . ."
    2.31–45.   "the pastorale/symphony . . ."; "birds birds . . ."; "corner//
                  fences . . ."; "how it works/forces . . ."; "the whole earth
                  together . . . ," 2 pp.; "sea smells/smoke . . . ," 2 pp.;
                  "F o l d s o f t h e d e s e r t," 2 pp.; "dirty work/if you
                  don't give it up . . . ," 2 pp.; "a girder a/building . . ."; "two,
                  four mirrors . . ."; "clock ticks/that horn's stuck down . . . ."
    3.77–79.   "cars arrowing . . ."; "driftwood/the sands . . ."; "anything/has
                  to be easy enough . . . ."
    4.3.   "A View," 4 pp. Prose.
    4.75–79.   "(One of those things)" (prose); "N e i g h b o r i n t h e
                  p a r k D e p t. (C u t / G r a s s " (prose);
                  "With these hardtops now . . ." (prose); "T h e W i n d o w s,"
                  2 pp.
    5.02–83.   "h o r i z o n" (with note); "close/far/open" (with note);
                  "News hungry/fighting green . . ."; "at/one ent/Day . . . ."
    11.80–87. "blue sky empty . . ."; "Out in the yard . . . ," 2 pp.; "t i e s /
                  s l e e p / e r s," 3 pp.; "single-minded citizens have low public
                  opinions . . . "; "sounds/great . . ."; "lightwords/paper . . . ,"
                  2 pp.; "November like summer . . . "; "red lights the dark
                  extended . . . "; "the sunlight/sideways slant . . . ."

from THIS PROSE (PROSE FOR THIS)

2

I drink coffee. I drink tea. A pain has been in me since
yesterday. Or instead was it meant to be I've been
expecting a pain since yesterday. A sentence is offered
in a code together with the key. And I feel the pain
today. Before came its shadow. Before came an apple.
And then a tree, the apparent attempt to copy tree A.

5

The words were "in English" but their order had been
reversed. For example Have you loved only me since
yesterday. And uninterruptedly. Because an interruption
of belief would constitute a period of unbelief, unlike
sleep. That is, it's all right to dream but not too much.
And forget them as soon as you remember to wake up.

—Michael Palmer, *This* 4

Fagin, Larry.

    5.30.   "The Shore," 2 pp. Prose.
    5.70–74.   "Marriage"; "Song"; "The Monkey"; "Shorts"; "Poem";
                       "Three Indian Poems"; "Conscious," parts 1–4.

Faville, Curtis.

    1.5–8.   "Chinese Neon"; "Summer"; "Aubade"; "The Sandwich
                       Fountain."
    3.46–49.   "Wooden Horse," 4 pp.; "a jolly winter cake!"
    4.17.   From "Poem in Twenty Sections." 3 pp.

Fisher, Allen.

    12.75.   From "Defamiliarising_____*," 5 pp. 5 sections.

Fisk, James.

    3.62–64.   "can't cover/up . . . "; "stead the/moment . . . ";
                       "if light/hits it just right . . . ."

Franklin, George.

    3.71–75.   "feb. 19, 1972/DUBLIN," 2 pp. (12 short poems printed
                       in sequence); "feb. 29, 1972/LONDON," 2 pp. (11 short
                       poems printed in sequence); "march 1, 1972/in transit to/
                       EDINBURGH," 2 pp. (8 short poems printed in sequence).

Freudenheim, Robert.

    2.60.   "The nostalgia today began . . . ."
    3.68.   "far and away . . ."; "nothing is distinct . . .";
                       "the lamps are . . . ."

Friedman, Ed.

    11.11.   From "Journals," 12 pp. Prose with interspersed transcription
                       from language tapes and astronaut dialogues.

Gilfillan, Merrill.

    7.56.   "Homage to Balzac," 2 pp. Serial poem in 5 parts.
    10.22.   "Red-Haired Boy," 9 pp. Sequence of verse and prose in 13
                       sections.
    11.51.   TranslationS from *Gaspard de la nuit,* by Aloysius Bertrand,
                       6 pp. 9 prose poems: "The Mason," "The Dwarf," "My
                       Great-Grandfather," "A Dream," "Master Ogier (1407),"
                       "October," "Second Man," "The Gallows," "The Dead Horse."

from SONG NO 143

Everything is related to everything else. Elicit. Fret.
Ultramarine. Nacreous. That is a real advantage. I read
on and sleep is intermittent and so sweet unattended.
Moreover two legs to cross *in vitro* and lengthwise goes
without a wrinkle in the fabric.

Consummated. A first taste of it.

Ammoniac, honey. Honey staccato. A blowup of
that up here which is this—superimposed on a flown
first page. A border of graying almost indistinct cardboard complements it. Nice vinyl.

Countdown. Jittery. Tack where the precise center
of a tie should have been—thin yellow knit—he seemed
to be trying to emerge as a smile. Mass of neck tissue,
would "turbulent" be accurate enough. Up and down.
Up and again.

Words. Tokenism.

—Bruce Andrews, *This* 5

Gitin, David.

    2.86.   "Sutter Creek."

    5.78–79.   "Let It Be"; "Here."

    6.59.   "'Two 'Three," 2 pp.

Glück, Robert.

    3.33.   From "Ed's Blue Period," 2 pp. 3 poems: "or the five moons . . . ," "the air is dry the sun . . . ," "Ed's blue period: Pink Nipples."

Goldfarb, Sidney.

    1.38–39.   "Messages" (poem in two columns); "The Dance," 3 pp.

    1.47.   "And Other More Isolate Places." Prose.

Gottlieb, Michael.

    9.14.   Xerox collage.

    9.68.   Xerox collage.

    10.60.   "Fourteen Poems," 8 pp.

    11.1.   Xerox frontispiece.

    11.78.   "Timing Is Everything," 2 pp. Prose.

Grant, Susan.

    2.2.   "I am time/fast . . . ."

Greenwald, Ted.

    8.53–62.   "Quick," 2 pp.; From "Clean Glass Poems," 4 pp. (4 poems printed in sequence); "Hand Over," 4 pp. (poem in 6 parts).

    9.38–45.   "Methods"; "Personality"; "Art"; "Sound"; "Lies"; "Sitting"; "The Event"; "Light Blue"; "Boys and Girls"; "Condition"; "Up Front"; "Shovel"; "No Tolls"; "sit down . . ."; "watch/ close . . ."; "once/the/point . . . ."

Grenier, Amy.

    2.82.   Three drawings, 3 pp. One printed in red ink, one in black ink, one in green ink.

    3.2–3.   "bob/amy/top . . ."; "nn//nine . . . ."

    3.44–45.   Drawing, printed in blue ink; drawing, printed in red ink.

Grenier, Robert.

    1.31–35.   "nights now"; 6 poems: "PLOWS/by," "THROUGH THE SPACE BETWEEN," "SHARPS/in the cold," "SNAPS/get it to cook," "RED WREATHS," "LOOKING//winter/night/ meadow/upon"; "Wintry"; "NOW IT IS"; "The Ceiling Is Gradually Filling In."

from KETJAK

Revolving door.

Revolving door. A sequence of objects which to him appears to be a caravan of fellaheen, a circus, begins a slow migration to the right vanishing point on the horizon line.

Revolving door. Fountains of the financial district. Houseboats beached at the point of low tide, only to float again when the sunset is reflected in the water. A sequence of objects which to him appears to be a caravan of fellaheen, a circus, camels pulling wagons of bear cages, tamed ostriches in toy hats, begins a slow migration to the right vanishing point on the horizon line.

—Ron Silliman, *This* 6

1.82–95. Review of Robert Creeley, *A Quick Graph: Collected Notes & Essays*, 4 pp.; "On Speech," 2 pp. (prose); review of Robert Creeley, *Pieces*, 4 pp.; review of Gertrude Stein, *Lectures in America*, 3 pp.; review of Edward Lear, *The Complete Nonsense Book*.

2.24–30. 34 poems, printed in capital letters and separated by rules, 6 pp.; found text: "'ENCLOSED LICENSE CAN BE USE TO DRIVE A MOTOR/CYCLE AS LONG AS HE/SHE STAY IN BALI.'"

2.46–47. "Knitting," found drawing; "Spilled Milk," found drawing.

2.95. "For Aram Saroyan, Who Tells the Truth" (prose); review of William Carlos Williams, *Spring & All*, 2 pp.

3.83–93. "sure arm today"; "refrigerator so long"; "walking down Washington Avenue"; "combination rafter and"; "choir tea"; "dream/y belly"; "date o dot"; "THE HORSE WRESTLES/ THE HOSS WRESTLERS"; "with his ka"; "s o m e o l d g u y s w i t h s c y t h e s"; "QUIET T/so shone."

3.100. "Four For To Two/Seeing Through the Round." Prose.

5. "30 from Sentences." 16 index cards with 30 poems from *Sentences* printed one to a side.

7.3. "Northern New Hampshire," 10 pp. Serial work, alternating verse and prose.

8.48. "*s a cold place*/or/*s* space *a* space *cold* space *space*," 5 pp. 53 separate poems, printed in sequence.

11.71. Translation from "Das Badener Lehrstück vom Einverständnis," by Bertolt Brecht, 7 pp. Drama.

12.96. From *A Day at the Beach*, 5 pp. 15 poems, printed 3 to a page.

Harryman, Carla.

9.69–73. "For She"; "Where You," 2 pp.; "Under the Bridge"; "Au Nom." Prose.

10.68–72. "Various Devices," 3 pp.; "Loop," 2 pp. Prose.

11.63–67. "Artaud, Denied," 2 pp.; "Property"; "My Story"; "Dogs," 2 pp. Prose.

12.43–50. Translation from *A Day in the Strait*, by Emmanuel Hocquard. Section of 24 parts, titled "Images from a Book," 8 pp. Prose.

Hawkins, Bobbie Louise.

5.65–67. "Since I gave those fools . . ."; "It's cold where I've been lately . . ."; "This view from this window's . . ."; "Out of reckoning . . ."; "When I'm solidly totally covered over . . ."; "One act and another . . . ."

from WE PLOW THE ROADS

"The stories varied slightly from picture to picture, but generally they went something like this: 'There was a long stairway leading up to the villa. It was covered with green or green things. I climbed the stairway every day & wrote down my observations immediately. They went something like this: "Today the trailing arbutus is much more in evidence & the path to my studio becoming overgrown. I will have to go to a colder climate to observe the faces of the beauties that peer out at me from between these many blossoms. There will be more of them in the snow though my health is poor. I am surer now that this stairway is becoming a malevolent force & has an energy of its own like eyes that stare into the sun, like the feeble motions of a heart grown cold. I cannot stand the freshness of the unadorned faces & am growing old."'"

—Bernadette Mayer, *This* 7

Hejinian, Lyn.

9.78. "Days Are Colors/In It," 7 pp. Serial work in 20 sections, verse and prose.

10.43–47. "Number Present," 2 pp. (prose); "windows is screens . . ."; "Etude Auto" (prose); "I brown study . . . ."

12.123–28. "The Altitudes," 3 pp. (prose); "Exit"; "Arms," 3 pp.

Hern, Bob.

2.61. 20 poems, printed in sequence, 6 pp.

Holland, Joyce.

3.17–20. "——"; "Gold Tooth"; "Ehehehehehehehehehehehe"; "D U C K." Concrete poems.

Hollo, Anselm.

1.42. "From Your Stoned Book Reviewer," 2 pp. Serial poem in 4 parts.

3.94–95. "lights, blinking"; "canto."

6.39. "Gee Apollinaire," 4 pp. Serial poem with text and graphics.

Howe, Fanny.

12.51. "Cotuit Tides, 1917," 5 pp. Poem in 13 parts.

Irby, Kenneth.

1.76. "Near Equinox," 2 pp. Prose.

2.88. "Notes, Waiting in the Mediterraneum for Bean & Lowell," 2 pp. Prose.

Kabak, Wayne.

1.44–45. "I read/I saw/ANOTHER/SHADOWS . . ." (poem in two columns); "my friend whisks out of the . . . ," 2 pp.

Kelly, Robert.

1.2–4. "If this were the place to begin . . ."; "Fna"; "Truck with tanks . . . ."

Knecht, Laura.

1.9–12. "The Red Light Was My Mind"; "abandon the yellow tree it comes apart . . ."; "the field/throws itself . . . "; "she smiled/ and would not say."

from SILENCE

To that (I) am going away
the age earliest of all, as
        refers to a weak charge.
        Documents to be pure
material converts into writing,
annihilate in code on later cooling
        this is the tone.
        Both, such devouring
great subsidies to clear states
        type to figure as it may be

—Barrett Watten, *This* 8

Kyger, Joanne.

3.30–32.   "Every day I burn a stick of incense . . . ," 2 pp.; "It doesn't
             make any difference . . . ."
4.20.   "A swirl of white petals . . . ." "Station break," printed at the
             end of Curtis Faville's poem on the same page.
4.70.   "What are your references" "Station break," printed at the
             end of the interview with Clark Coolidge.
4.74.   "Dead Earnest/That's what killed Ernest." "Station break,"
             printed at the end of "The Dark Day."
4.81–84.   "A wide range"; "An embodiment of the active principle of
             compassion/is often printed on paper"; "I got stoned at the
             beach with Sabina . . ."; "You'll get much better treatment
             . . ."; "MISSING"; "When there is nothing to seek, then/there
             is ease" ("Station break").

Kyger, Joanne, edited by Lewis MacAdams.

5.48.   "Baul." 22 sections, edited and arranged from journals.
             Photos of Joanne Kyger and Peter Warshall.

Lawther, Marcia.

1.55–57.   "Dear Richard,//I'm sorry to have missed you"; "Ecology";
             "Amy Amazes."
2.48–49.   "Blizzard 23 February 1971" (serial poem in 3 parts); "Facts."
3.97–99.   "I want to think of you"; "Stick, Slick . . ."; "Oh, you dogs . . . ."

Lord, Emily.

1.48.   "Melting Moments," 4 pp. Prose.

Lally, Michael.

3.52.   "This Is The Poem to Write Now," 2 pp.

MacAdams, Lewis.

2.4–5.   "Mushroom Ramble"; "Immensely Riveted."
5.60.   "Bolinas, Thursday Night. 10:15 PM," 2 pp. (dialogue);
             "A listener rose at the master's feet . . ."; "To Phoebe Gone
             to Wendy"; "Strawberry Flowers"; "Honk-Honk"; "I might
             just as well as . . . ."

Mac Low, Jackson.

12.30–34.   "Hereford Bosons," 5 pp. (sequence of 7 poems); "Wall Rev."

Malmude, Steve.

5.75.   "Song"; "Stove & Lamp."

from SENTENCES MY FATHER USED

Casts across otherwise unavailable fields.

Makes plain. Ruffled. Is trying to

alleviate his false: invalidate. Yet all is

"to live out," by shut belief, the

various, simply succeeds which. Roofs that

retain irksomeness. Points at

slopes. Buzz over misuse of reflection

(tendon). Gets sweeps, entails complete

sympathy, mists. I realize slowly,

which blurting reminds, or how you, intricate

in its. This body, like a vapor, to

circumnavigate. Surprising details that

hide more than announce, shells codifiers to

anyway granules, leopards, folding chairs.

—Charles Bernstein, *This* 9

Mandel, Tom.

    11.57.   From "Some Appearances," 6 pp.

    12.61–62. "Realism"; "The Master." Prose.

Marshall, Jack.

    2.72.   From *Floats,* 6 pp. 7 sections.

Mayer, Bernadette.

    7.17.   "We Plow the Roads," 22 pp. Prose work in 12 sections. Winner of a CCLM Fiction Award, 1976.

    8.65.   "1977," 2 pp.; "The Heart of the Hare," 2 pp.

    9.88.   "Spring House," 4 pp. Prose.

McCaffery, Steve.

    11.88–89. "Topos," 2 pp. (prose); "Combinatory Women," 3 pp. (prose with footnotes).

Melnick, David.

    12.3.   From "Men in Aida," 5 pp.

Morice, Dave.

    2.57.   "Jungle Book."

    3.25–27.   "Price List of Living Room"; "Dread"; "After the Soup"; "Both Are"; "They End It."

Myers, Jack.

    2.70–71.   "Calling"; "The Hero of Deadtown's Trick."

Myers, Jed.

    2.69.   "This is the lonely dream in the sky . . ."; "She talks about all these places . . . ." Prose.

Palmer, Michael.

    2.8–9.   "A Can of Words for Frank Stella"; "The war I missed."

    4.14.   "This Prose (Prose for This)," 3 pp. Prose poem in 9 parts.

    6.35.   "Tomb of Baudelaire," 3 pp. Prose poem in 7 sections.

    8.63.   "How They Enter," 2 pp.

    9.46.   "Idem," 9 pp. In 4 parts, "for two voices," "for more than two voices," "for two voices speaking rapidly and simultaneously," and "for one voice."

Pearson, Ted.

    12.86.   From "Coulomb's Law," 6 pp. 24 sections.

from VARIOUS DEVICES

They escaped the formal expression of North
America and wandered for nearly a half a century. No
wind no frost no snow. They called it ignorant, the in-
most bleak-hearted clay thing, characterized by distinctive sounds. Thus suspicion and hatred rises. Like a
servant the land cuts the air. The complexity of repeated
thought makes ghosts of evidence.
      "There are no names," said Blank being nasty.
      "It is mine."
      A flat nosed dog walks up the stairs. Something
almost human.
      But the sturgeons are remote, stiff like walking
sticks, bleakly prolific and ancient. One can't say, "But
they don't live in water," without being an ass.

—Carla Harryman, *This* 10

Perelman, Bob.

5.36–38.	"Sentences"; "The Nursery"; "Fresh Talisman"; "Physics"; "Atlantis"; Out the Window" Prose poems.
6.33–34.	"Bob believed there were books . . ."; "various sentences." Prose poems.
7.71–72.	"Zero"; "The Hunting Lodge." Prose poems.
8.3.	"How to Improve," 10 pp. 8 parts, alternating verse and prose.
10.11.	*a.k.a.*, parts 3 and 4, 11 pp. Prose.
11.68–70.	"Physics"; "History," 2 pp.; "Room."
12.101.	"The Heroes," 4 pp.

Preston, Jim.

| 1.24. | "Sun//day//is football . . . ." |
| 2.58. | "car pool"; "apples/are . . . ." |

Price, Larry.

| 12.16. | "Lights vary by being held . . . ," 7 pp. Prose poem. |

Raworth, Tom.

| 7.39. | "Pretense," 5 pp. Prose poem in 10 parts. |
| 12.8. | From "Catacoustics," 8 pp. Poem in two columns with graphics and prose. |

Robinson, Kit.

5.32.	6 sections of journal prose: "Sunday, July 25, 1971," "August 2, 1971," "Tuesday, August 3," "Sunday, August 8," "Monday, August 9," "Tuesday, August 10," 4 pp.
6.38.	"Fast Howard." Prose poem.
7.13.	From "Entropica": "Golden State," "Pontoon," "Viola Bells," "'C' House," 4 pp. Prose poems.
8.19.	"In the American Tree," 2 pp.
9.96.	"Picture No Picture."
10.3.	"Prelude." 8 pp.
10.95.	"Officials in Washington." 2 pp.
11.26.	"Verdigris" and "Trial de Novo," 8 pp. Prose poems printed alternately on facing pages.

Rodefer, Stephen.

| 12.66. | "Pretext"; "Codex." |

Rosenberg, Jim.

| 8.13. | From "Valences," 6 pp. In 2 sections. |

Ryan, Christopher.

| 2.3. | "in/the/visually . . . ." |

from HISTORY

The sun stands still, a thing
Of beauty. The stopped shadows
Develop moral overtones and these
Are what gets put into circulation.
Gargoyles and church music are one

Of many false doors. Words
Blame objects for lack of effect.
Dreams echo food and housing. The air
Turns dark to bright and back,
Sped up in the brain.

—Bob Perelman, *This* 11

Saroyan, Aram.

 2.6–7. "the rain/comes down"; "too/hot to/wear shoes"; "little/is what/she is"; "delicate/little/dogs."

 2.90–94. "Play"; "y/ou"; "Shakespeare!"; "Banana?/No . . ."; "Life is . . . ."

Scalapino, Leslie.

 12.63. From "Buildings Are at the Far End," 3 pp. Prose, in 5 sections.

Seaton, Peter.

 8.37. "Men on the Roof," 4 pp. Prose.

 9.29. "Side Tone," 9 pp. Prose.

 10.48. "Apprehension," 7 pp. Prose.

Sjoberg, John.

 3.54. "Surface."

Silliman, Ron.

 1.58–61. "tuna flesh"; "Meanwhile—/then I . . ."; "the/than/then . . ."; "the boy . . . ."

 2.19–23. "eyes/as/is . . ."; "What if her name is . . ."; "bees/bead . . ."; "time to bail out . . ."; "Whatever the/canvas . . . ."

 4.7. "Ammo"; "Consideration"; "Poem"; "the/taste . . ." "Presidio Heights" (prose poem).

 5.3–11. "Berkeley," 4 pp.; "Modulo Z," 5 pp.

 6.48. From *Ketjak*, 11 pp. First 9 paragraphs.

 7.47. From "Sailboat," 9 pp. Work for 5 simultaneous voice parts.

 9.3. From *Tjanting*, 12 pp. First 14 paragraphs.

 11.36. From "Skies," part 3, 8 pp. Prose poem.

 12.68. "Carbon," 7 pp. Prose and verse in 7 sections.

Ushanoff, George.

 2.67. "A Drawing." Poem in two columns.

Waldman, Anne.

 1.36–37. "The Man"; "Turn"; "Dark Ages"; "Heading Off."

Ward, Diane.

 10.31. From "Pronouncing." 2 pp. Prose.

Warsh, Lewis.

 4.21–23. "Cambridge General," 2 pp.; "On the Outside"; "The Weight."

Warshall, Peter.

 1.52. "Extracts from a Dissertation," 3 pp. Prose, edited by Robert Grenier.

EXIT

Patience is laid out on my paper
is floodlit. Everything's simile.
The cadence is detected, the cipher is broken,
    "resolved
the sky bears the enjambments, heavy clouds
the measure of one with a number block
changes shade. The flow of thoughts—impossible!
with which we are so familiar. The river
its visuals are gainful and equably square
in an automatic writing. Self-consciousness
to reclaim imagination . . . to rise early
that is, logic exaggerates the visible
to oppose laziness." Unto itself, built of bricks
is a cumbersome monument on whom motion
is bent over, having sunk a fork into the ground.

                             —Lyn Hejinian, *This* 12

Watson, Craig.

    12.56.   "Scale," 5 pp.

Watten, Barrett.

    1.70–73.   "radio day in Soma City," 2 pp.; "tiny tomorrows"; "ode to Bourbaki";

    1.96.   "Trees are found there . . . ." Found text, from Antonio Pigafetta, *Journal of the Voyage of Magellan*.

    2.50.   "birds of winter," 7 pp. Serial poem in 13 parts.

    2.98.   "A Rewritten Statement Coinciding with Charles Olson's *Poetry and Truth* . . . ," 2 pp. Prose.

    3.55–61.   "to"; "white yellow"; "things to come"; "complaint"; "so"; "warmer"; "all dreams of crazy machine . . ."; "'Flying A'"; "how water piles on top . . . ."

    4.10.   "Factors Influencing the Weather," 4 pp.

    4.25.   4 photos. On 4 pp., below text of Bruce Andrews's work.

    4.71.   "Zukofsky's *Catullus*." Review.

    4.72.   "The Dark Day," 3 pp. Found text.

    5.1–11.   2 photos.

    5.43.   Found text from S. T. Coleridge, *Notebooks*. Prose.

    5.84.   "November 24"; "November 30."

    6.43–46.   "L Dream"; "Omotecutli y Omocihuat"; "Pre-History"; "Worldbackwards," 2 pp. Prose poems.

    7.44.   "Decay," 3 pp. Serial poem in 7 parts.

    8.28.   "Silence," 4 pp. Poem in 10 parts.

    9.1, 37,
    53, 71, 84. 5 photos.

    9.74–77.   "'X,'" 4 pp.; "Mode Z." Prose poems.

    10.1, 22,
    30, 70, 94. 5 sets of 4 photos each from "Reverse Maps."

    10.55.   "Position," 5 pp.

    11.92.   "Relays," 5 pp. Prose poem.

    12.80.   "Memory clouds . . . ," 6 pp. From *Progress*.

Wessner, Laura.

    3.65–67.   "sharp edge of t's . . ."; "herring settles/sunken . . ."; "neither of them can come . . . ."

Weiner, Hannah.

    7.58.   From *Clairvoyant Journal*, 8 pp. Prose in 6 sections.

Will, Frederic.

    2.80–81.   "Where art and illness . . ."; "The eyes which bear . . . ."

Edited by Robert Grenier and Barrett Watten*

This 1.   Lanesville, Mass., and Iowa City, Ia., Winter 1971. 96 pp.
This 2.   Franconia, N.H., and Iowa City, Ia., Fall 1971. 100 pp.
This 3.   Franconia, N.H., and Oakland, Fall 1972. 100 pp.

Edited by Barrett Watten**

This 4.   San Francisco, Spring 1973. 84 pp., cover by Louise Stanley.
This 5.   San Francisco, Winter 1974. 84 pp. with 16 pp. card insert.
This 6.   San Francisco, Spring 1975. 64 pp.
This 7.   San Francisco, Spring 1976. 72 pp.
This 8.   San Francisco, Spring 1977. 96 pp.
This 9.   San Francisco, Winter 1978. 96 pp.
This 10. San Francisco, Winter 1979. 96 pp.
This 11. Oakland, Spring 1981. 96 pp.
This 12. Oakland, Fall 1982. 128 pp.

* Cover art by Amy Grenier
** Cover art by Barrett Watten unless otherwise.

CONTRIBUTORS

Bruce Andrews (NYC) has recently published *Tizzy Boost* (The Figures), *Divesture——E* (Leave Books), & *stet sic & sp.* (Case Books). *Aerial #9* will be dedicated to his work. **Daniel Barbiero** (Silver Spring, MD) has published essays & articles in *Sites, SubStance, Philosophy Today, To, New German Critique* and others. **Steve Benson** (NY) is the author of *Blue Book* (The Figures) & *Reverse Order* (Potes & Poets). **Charles Bernstein** (NYC) has recently published *Dark City* (Sun & Moon). **Manuel Brito** is editor/publisher of Zasterle Press (Islas Canerias, España). He has recently published *A Suite of Poetic Voices*, a collection of interviews with contemporary poets. **Bruce Campbell** (Riverside, CA.) has published essays & reviews in *Temblor, Poetics Journal, Sagetrieb*, and others. **Clark Coolidge**'s most recent books *The Rova Improvisations* (Sun & Moon), and *Registers (People in All)* (Avenue B). **Joseph Conte** has published *Unending Design: The Forms of Postmodern Poetry* (Cornell University Press). He teaches at SUNY Buffalo. **Michael Davidson** teaches at the University of California, San Diego. His most recent book of poetry is *Post Hoc* (Avenue B). He is the author of *The San Francisco Renaissance: Poetics and Community at Mid-Century* (Cambridge University Press). **Alan Davies** (NYC) is the author of *Rave* (Roof), *Candor* (O Books), *Name* (This), and others. His collection of essays is *Signage* (Roof, 1987). **Daniel Davidson** (S. F.) is the author of *Product* (e. g.), and *Image* (Zasterle). **Ron Day**'s "Before me . . . " appears in *The Poetics of Criticism* (Leave Books). He lives in San Francisco. **Larry Eigner**'s most recent book is *Windows Walls Yard Ways* (Black Sparrow). **Jerry Estrin** (1947–1993), spent his last year finishing *Rome, A Mobile Home*, which was collaboratively published by The Figures, O Books, Potes & Poets, & Roof. **Norman Fischer**'s most recent book is *Precisely The Point Being Made* (O Books/Chax). A Zen Priest, he lives at the Green Gulch Farm Zen Center, north of San Francisco. **Allen Fisher** edits *Spanner* in Hereford, U. K. He is the author of *Place, Apocalyptic Sonnets, Unpolished Mirrors, Brixton Fractals*, and others. *Future Exiles* (Paladin) features Fisher, Bill Griffiths, and Brian Catling. **Robert Grenier**'s box *What I Believe Transpirations /Transpiring Minnesota* was published by O Books. **Carla Harryman** (Berkeley) is the author of *In the Mode of* (Zasterle), *Animal Instincts* (This), *Vice* (Potes & Poets), *The Middle* (Gaz), and others. **Lyn Hejinian** (Berkeley) is the author of *The Cold of Poetry* (Sun & Moon), *Oxata: A Short Russian Novel* (The Figures), *The Cell* (Sun & Moon), and *My Life* (Sun & Moon). She is the translator with Elena Balashova of Arkadii Dragomoschenko's *Xenia* and *Description*, both from Sun & Moon. She edits *Poetics Journal* with Barrett Watten. **Kevin Killian** (San Francisco) is the author of a novel, *Shy* (Crossing Press), a memoir, *Bedrooms Have Windows* (Amethyst), and three plays for the San Francisco Poets Theater, *Stage Fright*, forthcoming from Detour. He and Lew Ellingham are writing a biography of Jack Spicer. **Jackson Mac Low** is the author of twenty-five books including *42 Merzgedichte* in Memoriam *Kurt Schwitters* (Station Hill), *Pieces o' Six* (Sun & Moon), *Twenties: 100 Poems* (Roof), and *Representative Works 1938–1985* (Roof, 1985). **Bernadette Mayer**'s *The Desire of Mothers to Please Others in Letters* was recently published by Hard Press. *A Bernadette Mayer Reader* (New Directions) was published in 1992. **Michael Palmer** is the author of three North Point Books: *Sun, Notes for Echo Lake,* and *First Figure.* His translation of Emmanuel Hocquard's *Theory of Tables* was published by o•blēk editions. **Bob Perelman** has recently published two books of criticism, *The Trouble With Genius: Reading Pound, Joyce, Stein, and Zukofsky* (U. California). *The Marginalization of Poetry: Language Writing and Literary History* (Princeton) is forthcoming. His books of poetry include *Virtual Reality* (Roof), *Face Value* (Roof), *Captive Audience* (The Figures),and *The First World* (The Figures). He teaches at The University of Pennsylvania. **Kit Robinson** (Berkeley) is the author of *Balance Sheet* (Roof) *The Champagne of Concrete* (Potes & Poets), *Covers* (The Figures), *Ice Cubes* (Roof), and others. **Andrew Ross** is director of the American Studies Program and Professor of Comparative Literature at New York University. He is author of *The Chicago Gangster Theory of Life: Nature's Debt to Society* (Verso), *No Respect: Intellectuals and Popular Culture* (Routledge, Chapman, and Hall), and *Strange Weather: Culture, Science and Technology in the Age of Limits* (Verso). **Leslie Scalapino** is the author of more than a dozen books including *Goya's L. A.* (Potes & Poets), *Objects in the Terrifying Tense/ Longing from Taking Place* (Roof), *Crowd and not evening or light* (O Books/Sun & Moon), *The Return of Painting, The Pearl, and Orion* (North Point), and the most recently, *Defoe* (Sun & Moon). **Victor Shklovsky** (1893-1984) was an originator and important theorist of what is known in the U. S. as Russian Formalism. His works translated into English include *Sentimental Journey, Letters Not about Love,* and *Third Factory.* **Ron Silliman** (Berkeley) is the author of *Jones* (Generator), *Toner* (Potes & Poets), *Manifest* (Zasterle), *What* (The Figures), *The Age of Huts* (Roof), *Paradise* (Burning Deck), *Ketjak* (This), and many others. His collection of criticism is *The New Sentence* (Roof). Silliman edited the anthology *In the American Tree* (National Poetry Foundation). **Jack Spicer** (1925–1965). "An Astonishment." *The Collected Books of Jack Spicer* (Black Sparrow, 1975). Talisman House has recently issued his detective novel *The Tower of Babel,* from which the chapter included here is excerpted. Peter Grizzi is editing his lectures for publication by Black Sparrow. **Amy Trachtenberg** (Berkeley) is a visual artist who has collaborated with poets and has worked in the theatre as well as being shown at galleries. Recently she was the guest artist with Carla Harryman's I. O. U. Poets Theatre. **George Tysh** is lecturer in English at Wayne State University in Detroit. His latest collection of poems is *Echolalia* (United Artists Books). **Barrett Watten** is the author of *Under Erasure* (Zasterle, 1991), *Conduit* (Gaz, 1988), *Progress* (Roof, 1985), *Complete Thought* (Tuumba, 1982), *1–10* (This, 1980), *Plasma/Paralleles/"X"* (Tuumba, 1979), *Decay* (This, 1977), and *Opera—Works* (Big Sky, 1975). He founded *This* magazine with Robert Grenier in 1971; in 1974 he began publishing books under the imprint of This Press. Since 1982, Watten has been co-editor, with Lyn Hejinian, of *Poetics Journal.* He has taught at San Francisco State University, University of California at San Diego, University of California at Berkeley, and is now Assistant Professor in the Department of English, Wayne State University, teaching American Modernism and Cultural Studies. His selected poems, *Frame 1970–1990,* will be published by Sun and Moon Press in 1995.

Bridge Street Books

TO MAIL ORDER:

Send check or credit card number with your order to:

Bridge Street Books
2814 Pennsylvania Ave. NW
Pennsylvania Ave., NW
Washington, DC 20007

Add $2 shipping for the first book, $1 each additional book.

TO ORDER BY PHONE:

Call 202 965-5200.

Special orders available.

open
seven
days
a week

mail order
thousands of
titles in:

The Trouble with Genius: Reading Pound, Joyce, Stein, and Zukofsky, Bob Perelman, U. CA. Press, 16.00

Charles Ives Remembered: An Oral History, Vivian Perls, Da Capo, 13.95

The Chicago Gangster Theory of Life: Nature's Debt to Society, Andrew Ross, Verso, 24.95

An American Voyage, Joe Ross, Sun & Moon, 10.95

Representations of the Intellectual, Edward Said, Pantheon, 20.00

The Pen and the Sword, Edward Said, conversations with David Barsamian, Common Courage, 9.95

Objects in the Terrifying Tense/Longing from Taking Place, Leslie Scalapino, Roof, 9.95

Collected Poems, James Schuyler, FSG, 17.50

After a Lost Original, David Shapiro, Overlook, 12.95

fiction
politics
history
music
art
science

42 Merzgedichte in Memoriam Kurt Schwitters, Jackson Mac Low, Station Hill, 14.95

From the Other Side of the Century: A New American Poetry 1960–1990, Douglas Messerli ed., Sun & Moon, 29.95

Resisting Writings (and the Boundaries of Composition), Derek Owens, S.M.U. Press, 24.95

The Desires of Mothers to Please Others in Letters, Bernadette Mayer, Hard Press, 12.95

Civil Noir, Melanie Neilson, Roof, 9.00

In the House of the Shaman, Maggie O'Sullivan, Reality Street, 10.00

Homage to Catalonia, George Orwell, HBJ, 9.95

An Alphabet Underground, Michael Palmer, After Hand (Denmark), 10.00

poetry
poetics
cultural theory
women's studies
philosophy
religion

Passionate Enlightenment: Women in Tantric Buddhism, Miranda Shaw, Princeton, 29.95

N/O, Ron Silliman, Roof, 10.95

The Boy Poems, Rod Smith, Buck Downs Books, 4.00

A Key Into the Language of America, Rosmarie Waldrop, New Directions, 10.00

A Poetics of Criticism, Spahr, Wallace, Prevallet, & Rehm eds., Leave Books, 12.00

Every Day is Most of My Time, Mark Wallace, Texture, 6.00

The Wittgenstein Reader, Anthony Kenny ed., Blackwell, 21.95

Under Erasure, Barrett Watten, Zaterle, 8.00

Semiotext(e) Canadas, Jordan Zinovich ed, 12.00

The Parameters of Postmodernism, Nicholas Zurbrugg, Southern Illinois U Press, 12.95

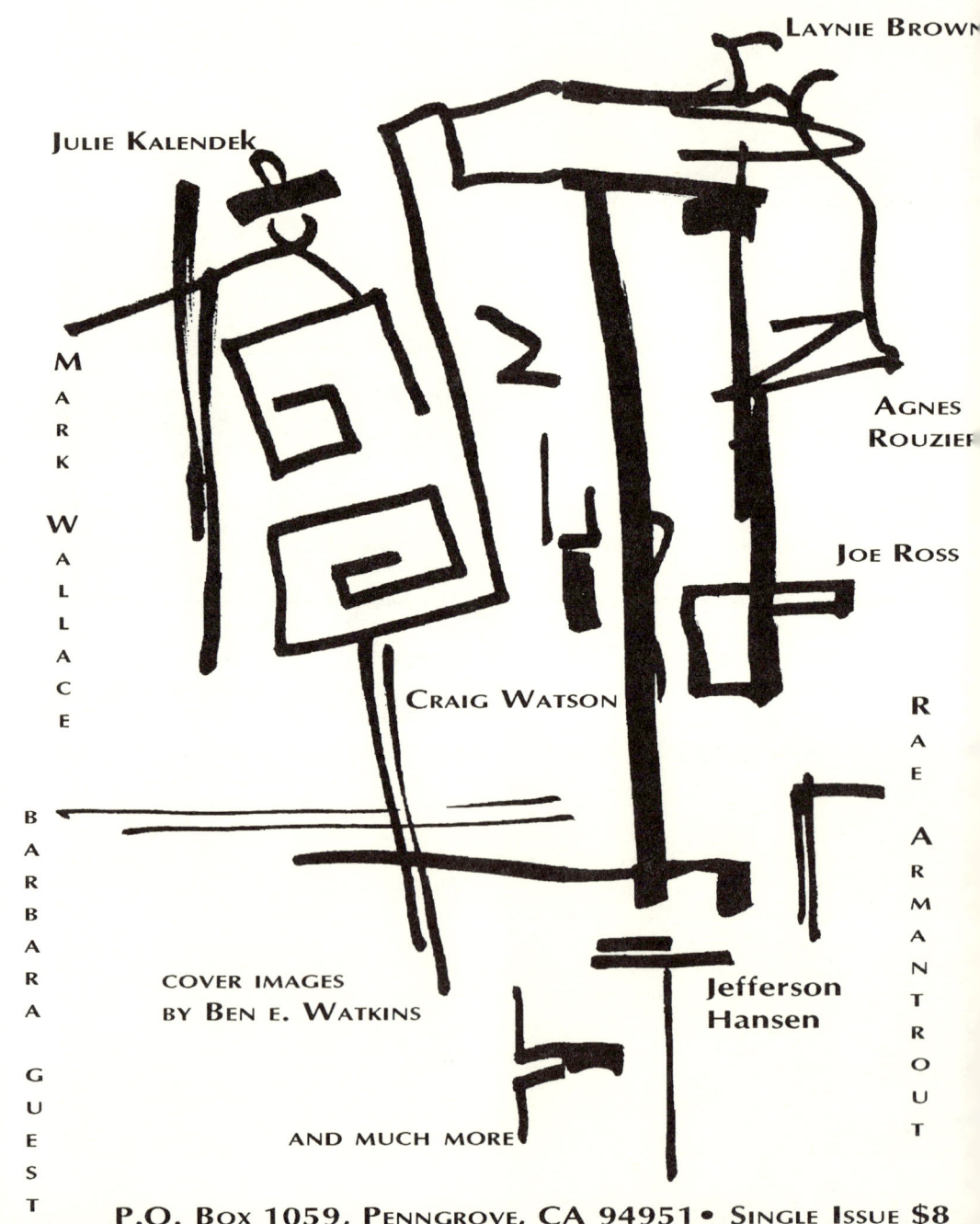

INNOVATIVE POETRY AND FICTION FROM INTERNATIONAL
ARTISTS FOR AN INTERNATIONAL AUDIENCE

AVEC

NINTH ISSUE

LAYNIE BROWN

JULIE KALENDEK

MARK WALLACE

AGNES ROUZIER

JOE ROSS

CRAIG WATSON

RAE ARMANTROUT

BARBARA GUEST

COVER IMAGES
BY BEN E. WATKINS

JEFFERSON
HANSEN

AND MUCH MORE

P.O. BOX 1059, PENNGROVE, CA 94951 • SINGLE ISSUE $8

Cover by Anna Bialobroda

HARD PRESS Publications

lingo: A Journal of the Arts

Issue # 4 featuring a 30-page music section including Mark Swed on new composers who incorporate pop elements into concert music and Peter Occhiogrosso's *Highly Selective Guide to Recent Concert Music* • Kent Jones on Abel Ferrara and his Films • Color Portfolio including Philip Guston, Anna Bialobroda, and Noël Dolla • Art essays by John Yau and Raphael Rubinstein • Hubert Selby Jr.'s short story *A Christmas Tale* • Photography by Judy Fiskin, Hiroshi Sugimoto, Ben Watkins, and others • Keith & Rosmarie Waldrop interview Claude Royet-Journoud • Chris Stroffolino reviews David Shapiro's *After a Lost Original* • Work by Bob Perelman, Dodie Bellamy, Lisa Jarnot, Will Alexander, Kevin Killian, Kim Lyons, Anselm Hollo and many more. **$12.50**

THE DESIRES OF MOTHERS TO PLEASE OTHERS IN LETTERS
By Bernadette Mayer

A monumental St. Bernadette to the initiates, this work has achieved something like the status of "Manuscript Classic." An epistolary text which takes as its formal parameters the nine months of Ms. Mayer's last pregnancy—an augury by bee sting— and writes the reader's psyche to the fences... **$12.95**

House of Outside First Book Series

SOLOW
By Lynn Crawford
Haven't wanted to read anything lately, certainly not any of the 500 manuscripts and galleys I get a year. However, I found Solow fascinating. It reminds me of early John Hawkes which is still for me the best Hawkes. The whole dreamscape was especially vivid.—
Jim Harrison **$10.00**

THE GEOGRAPHICS
By Albert Mobilio
This impressive first book manages the double ground of a nightmarish surrealism and a dryly perceptive wit. It's as if Humphrey Bogart were taking a good, if final, look at what's called the world. These are poems of a survivor, urbane, intelligent, fact of hope and despair equally. The Geographics is an ultimate detox center for "reality" addicts as thinking becomes the only way out. —Robert Creeley **$10.00**

Available at bookstores or direct from Hard Press
PO Box 184, West Stockbridge, MA 01266

O Books, 5729 Clover Drive, Oakland, CA 94618; distributed by Small Press Distribution 1814 San Pablo, Berkeley CA 94702

Memory Play, Carla Harryman, 72 pages, $8.50. ISBN # 1 882022-22-X. Steve Benson says *Memory Play* is "in idiosyncratic motion and congruence much as clouds and birds in light make sense to that visionary in you ... looking back at its patterns and wondering thru it."

Mob, Abigail Child, 96 pages. $9.50. ISBN # 1-882022-21-1. Child's writing scrutinizes "making need/the figure they want" as contemplation of lust touching a civilization. Bruce Andrews comments about *Mob*: "Only the impossible is intimate enough."

Collision Center, Randall Potts, 72 pages. $8.50. ISBN # 1-882022-19-X. Ann Lauterbach says "In Randall Potts' poems, nature and language collide, and then proceed, each having been transformed. . . on the stark clarities of his lines."

Vel, P. Inman, 64 pages, $8.00. ISBN # 1-882022-24-6. Diane Ward says, "P. Inman's mind is a thoroughly attached organ. There are no places to escape to or from in relation to its consideration, its inclusion. His work is liberating: images crystallize then overflow their frames..." " It comes to us via his uniquely musical intelligence, his compound mind's ear, opening a range..." Joan Retallack.

Close to me & Closer ... (The Language of Heaven) and *Desamere*, Alice Notley, 144 pages, $11.50. ISBN # 1-882022-26-2. Alice Notley's two books are works that are wholly their art, meaning they occur as their language shape/measure. She's invented a measure. The text is a rich current crossing, as at the moment of imagining, into being in death and in an expanded life. Notley transgresses conventional contemporary categories of genre; rather than genre, the form of the writing is the mind's inner sense and motion.

Lapses, John Crouse, 72 pages, $8.00. ISBN # 1-882022-25-4. John Crouse's writing is a non-stop torque conflating the distinctions of sky/people/forest/political; a torque which enhances the writing's own motions, nightmare, images in forward gear only as: 'historically' (actively) voiding reverse gear. He gets at "the squareroot of hues:" "behold sky, cobalt edge to edge, broke by trees of deepest green, green of the imageanotion at this dusk as at generally all..." He makes his own vocabulary rushing forward at full tilt, the "camel of wow."

Ground Air, Scott Bentley, 59 pages, $6.00 xerox. ISBN # 1-882022-23-8. "At least Scott, like Dido, knows there's more to life than duty. .. we find the inherent vulgarity of the natural, where every key or brush stroke makes desire's ineffable history more seductive." — Jennifer Moxley. "Like guided missiles, these poems strike to the heart of our so-called civilization..." — Kit Robinson

---

Curve by Andrew Levy, 88 pages, $10.00. ISBN # 1-882022-20-3. The story is yearning, the mirror is broken, every shard a discrete part of this puzzling. The story is palimpsest...The searching contemporary American idiom teases discrepancies of experience, dream and thought to its refractory surface, inviting the reader to join in this acute scrutiny." Norma Cole